Books by Alan Paton

SOUTH AFRICAN TRAGEDY

TALES FROM A TROUBLED LAND

SOUTH AFRICA IN TRANSITION

TOO LATE THE PHALAROPE

CRY, THE BELOVED COUNTRY

South African Tragedy

The Life and Times of Jan Hofmeyr

ALAN PATON

South African Tragedy

THE LIFE AND TIMES

OF

JAN HOFMEYR

Abridgement by Dudley C. Lunt

CHARLES SCRIBNER'S SONS

NEW YORK

PRINTED IN THE UNITED STATES OF AMERICA

LIBRARY OF CONGRESS CATALOG CARD NUMBER 65-25406

ILLUSTRATION ACKNOWLEDGMENTS

Cape Times, 1, 6, 8, 15; Department of Information, Pretoria, Republic of South
Africa, 9; *Die Burger,* 7; Albert King, 4; R. O. Pearse, 2; Photo-Hausmann C.T.,
S. A., 5; *Pretoria News:* 13, 14, 16; Rand Sport and Press, 10, 11; Herbert Secretan,
3; *The Times,* London, 12

Prefatory Note

A RUDIMENTARY knowledge of the origins and development of the four dominant racial groups in South Africa is essential to an appreciative understanding of the biography of Jan Hendrik Hofmeyr.

For all practical purposes the franchise in South Africa is limited to the whites, or Europeans as they are known. This first racial group comprises slightly in excess of three million persons and all political power is concentrated in their hands. Broadly speaking they are divided into two groups. On the one hand there are the descendants of the early Dutch, German and French Huguenot settlers, who, known today as Afrikaners, are said to comprise sixty percent of the white population. Then there are the other Europeans who are for the most part of English extraction including Jews who, though insignificant in numbers, are potent in influence.

In the mainstream of South African history, there flows the rivalry and accommodation between the Dutch and the English. The Dutch came first—in 1652 in consequence of the setting up of a victualing station by the Dutch East India Company. Comparable to the Dutch seats in New Amsterdam and on the Delaware River, there was little immigration and the growth was slow. As a matter of fact South Africa has never experienced the ameliorating influence inherent in successive immigrations such as those into the North American continent. At the end of a century and a half there were only about 33,000 people in the Cape Province. Significantly, a little over half of these were slaves, the consequence of importations from East Africa, Madagascar, Ceylon, India and Malaya. Miscegenation at the outset involving both white people and the local Hottentots with the slaves set in train the development of a mixed race, the members of which are variously known today as the "Coloured" or the "Cape Coloureds." They number about a million and a half, are concentrated for the most part in the Cape Province and constitute one of the racial groups that are the major concern of the public policy of South Africa.

Significant also in this first century and a half, was the existence and expansion of the northern frontier. Two facets of this deserve notice. The first was the pushing upward into the interior by the *voortrekkers* (pioneers) on the treks that have exercised so vast a formative influence in the development of the character of the modern Afrikaner. Psychologically the traditions of the treks are akin to those that stem from the sweep across the continent of the American frontier.

Secondly, in the course of this early expansion, the trekkers came into contact with the native tribes that were pushing down out of the interior vastness of the dark continent. And in conflict as violent as any that characterized the American struggles with the Indians, they encountered and overcame the largest of the four racial groups within the confines of present-day South Africa. These are the natives, the Africans, who are known officially today as the Bantu, and who number nearly eleven million people.

The Napoleonic Wars marked a turning point in the history of South Africa for in their train came the establishment of the British, temporarily in 1795, permanently in 1806, and reinforced in 1820 by the emigration from England of 5,000 settlers. Then commenced what General Smuts called the Century of Wrong. The points of conflict between British colonial rule and the Boers were many and often violent. The year 1836 saw the commencement of the Great Trek. This migratory movement up into the interior was the attempt by the Boers, fortified by the authoritarian strength of their Calvinist religion, to remove themselves from British rule and to isolate themselves from British influence. Its consequence was the establishment of the two Boer Republics—the Transvaal and the Orange Free State. Prominent among the causes of the Great Trek was the freeing of the slaves in 1834 and the sharp conflict of views in the area of race and colour.

The fourth group complicating the area of race relations, which is the major concern of South African politics, comprises the so-called "Asians." These people derive from the policy initiated in 1860 by the early sugar planters in the east coast colony of Natal of importing indentured labour from India. These Indians, or Asians, today number approximately half a million persons, who are still largely resident in Natal.

Until well into the last half of the nineteenth century, the economy of South Africa was pastoral and agricultural. Then the discoveries first of diamonds in Kimberly in 1870 and later in 1886 of gold on the Witwatersrand (Ridge of White Waters) set in train the course of events that has lead to the modern industrial development of the country. More immediately there was ushered in the era of Rhodes and Milner, and this high tide of British imperialism lead ultimately to the Boer War (1899–1902).

The modern consequences of these economic and social changes in the structure of South African society are of particular significance in relation to the largest population and racial group—the 11,000,000 Bantu. The natives traditionally had been located on what are known as Reserves. These are areas that have been set apart for them and they are not unlike the reservations of the American Indians. But there is a significant difference. The Bantu are the source of the large force of unskilled labor that is needed on the farms, in domestic service, and in the mines and industries of the South African economy. The inevitable consequence is that a very considerable proportion of the blacks—over a third according to the 1960 census—are at all times located outside the Reserves in urban and semi-urban areas. Moreover, the successive census figures show that this proportion is increasing.

In the decade that followed the Boer War with the accession to power of the Liberal Party in England, self-government was restored to the two Boer Republics, and in 1910 the four provinces—the Transvaal, the Orange Free State, Natal, and the Cape Province—formed the Union of South Africa within the then British Empire. In the Act of Union were two significant provisions that were, in South African constitutional terminology, "entrenched." This means that they could only be altered by a two thirds majority of both houses of the South African parliament in a joint session. One of these so-called entrenched clauses guaranteed the dual existence of the two languages—Dutch, now called Afrikääns and English; the other protected the limited franchise which had existed in the Cape Province in favor of the Coloureds. Another clause provided for what might be called a legalized gerrymander in that the votes cast in rural and urban constituencies should be weighted to the extent of fifteen percent in favor of the rural vote, and this was destined to have far-reaching effects on the outcomes of future elections.

Thereafter there followed the successive premierships of the Boer generals, Louis Botha and Jan Christian Smuts. The opposition was lead by another general, J. B. M. Hertzog, whose policy stemmed from a speech in 1912 in which he argued that the two groups in white South African society—Afrikaans and English-speaking—should each enjoy a separate development until each achieved full stature. This so-called "two-stream" concept is the modern political premise from which the present day Afrikaner Nationalism has derived and developed.

General Hertzog came to power in 1924 and this coincided with the start of the political career of Jan Hendrik Hofmeyr, the subject of Alan Paton's biography.

Dudley C. Lunt

Contents

xi

CONTENTS

South African Tragedy

The Life and Times of Jan Hofmeyr

Chapter 1

The Early Years

His mother was ill, and lay in her bed in her small room in the small house in Rheede Street. From this street, as from so many others in this city, one looked up at the great mountain. Indeed one could not help doing so, for it loomed like a presence over the city. Life might take one later to the highveld of the Transvaal, or to the thousand hills and valleys of Natal, but there was nothing like the Cape, which Drake had called the fairest in the whole circumference of the earth, the Cape, with mountains falling everywhere into the sea, and some age and grace not known to the harsh hinterland, with its bitter problems of history and race.

While Deborah Hofmeyr was ill, she was visited by Nelly Morgan, a young girl. Nelly always remembered the Sunday morning when the small 6-year-old boy with the heavy spectacles brought the two boxes into the room. She would have spoken to him, but his mother said, 'Take no notice of him.' He set up the two boxes to make a pulpit and put his books on it. Then he conducted the service, reading from the books, and preaching that morning on the words, 'Little children, keep yourselves from idols.'

He spoke earnestly, using the English language. His mother watched him openly, for after all he had come to preach to her because she was ill and could not go to church. Nelly watched him covertly, knowing it was more than a spectacle.

He was christened Jan Frederick Hendrik Hofmeyr, but his name Frederick dropped out of use. His names Jan Hendrik were family names, borne by many Hofmeyrs throughout South Africa, of whom the most illustrious was his father's cousin, the venerable statesman 'Onze Jan', member of the Cape Parliament, a founder of the Afrikander Bond. The Hofmeyrs had been in South Africa for a century and a half, and had produced many illustrious men. The small boy's father, Andries Brink Hofmeyr, was not one of the illustrious ones. He was a quiet and unassuming man. He had been married before, and had four daughters by his first wife. In 1888, he married again, Deborah Beyers, who was known for her forthrightness and outspoken judgements. She was not highly educated, but was shrewd and practical, and one soon became aware of her imperious and indomitable will. She was 25 years old when she married, which was a late age for those days. Men were not drawn to her, for she was too fierce for a woman. Her judgements were sharp and cutting, though spoken deliberately, and this deliberateness was heightened by a stammer. It was a surprise to all when she decided to marry the gentle Andries Brink Hofmeyr, with four daughters of his own.

It was not a happy marriage. Whatever it may have been at the beginning, it was embittered by her difficulties with her stepdaughters. There were four, but she always said there were three. That was because the eldest, when she had qualified as a teacher, ran away. The other three knew that imperious will, that could brook no opposition. But she did not get her own way easily, especially with the two older girls. She made them obey, but she could not make them love her. She was to say years later, 'But now they know that what I did was for the best. It was I who c-conquered in the end.'

In the year following her marriage she gave birth to a son, Andries Beyers ['A.B.'] Hofmeyr, but he did not unlock the doors of her heart. He too had a will, and perhaps it was this that prevented the growth of any deep bond between them. It was more than five years afterwards, on 20 March 1894, that she bore her second son, Jan Frederick Hendrik. He was born healthy, with a great head. He soon showed a quiet and gentle nature, and was from his early years docile and obedient, and strongly attached to his mother.

This relationship was made yet stronger when at 2 years of age he fell seriously ill. She nursed him with the greatest devotion, and his recovery set the seal on their relationship. She had always regarded him as a gift, but now she regarded him as doubly so, for in a sense God had given him twice. He was a reparation to her for her troubles with her stepdaughters.

His illness caused a crisis in the family. They were poor, and how were they to pay these heavy expenses? The minister in charge of the Groote Kerk, the Mother Church of the Dutch Reformed people of South Africa, failed to do what Mrs Hofmeyr thought the church should have done. It was the Rev. Ernest Baker, the minister of the Baptist Church in Wale Street, who came forward to offer help. He was a stern moralist and an inflexible fundamentalist, believing that the Bible was literally the Word of God. He was also a man of big and generous heart, and his action turned Deborah into a devoted admirer; she became a regular worshipper at the Wale Street Baptist Church, and she took the small boy with her. Her husband did not approve of her action, and continued to take his daughters and eldest son to the Groote Kerk. But she, having made up her mind, went her own way with implacable will. This had one great consequence for the small boy: he learned his religion in an English-speaking church amongst English-speaking people.

When he was nearly 3 years old, his father died. He left the family poor. Onze Jan was a great help to her at this time. Though he spoke vigorously on the public platform against Afrikaners who deserted their forefathers' religion, her defection made no difference to him. She was always glad of his advice, but otherwise she was fiercely independent, and although the future looked bleak, she would take no money.

Her love for her second son continued to increase. He was never out of her sight, and she watched over his food and his health. Her step-daughters and her eldest son knew that this love was a thing apart, and while they did not like her any better for it, they did not like the small boy any less. They continued to worship at the Groote Kerk, but the friends of the family were largely drawn from the Wale Street congregation, and were mostly English-speaking. She herself and her family were true children of the Cape, as confidently at home in English as in Afrikaans. Her husband had made it a rule that both languages were to be spoken in the home, and the children could move from one to the other without a thought.

Meanwhile something like a miracle was happening at the Wale Street Church. His mother was astonished to discover, when the small boy was five, that he could read, not only in the language of Wale Street but also in the Dutch language of his grandmother's church in Stellenbosch. She realised then that this was no ordinary child. The news of his genius spread through the neighbourhood.

The year the small boy turned five was an anxious one for South Africa. The threat of war between Great Britain and the Transvaal republic hung over the country. Lord Milner was determined to secure control of the Transvaal, and President Kruger was determined to resist him. If any two men could have averted war, these were not the two. The greatest anxiety of all was felt by the Afrikaners of the Cape Province, who were bound by blood and language to the Transvaalers, and yet had been British subjects for nearly a century. Onze Jan, proud of his ancestry yet loyal to the Queen, strove to prevent the coming calamity, but his earnestness and goodness were unavailing. On 11 October 1899, war broke out, and was at its height when the small boy celebrated his sixth birthday.

He was the model child of those days, quiet until spoken to, but when spoken to, strangely calm and self-possessed. He was the pride of the Wale Street Sunday School, forgetting nothing that he was taught, reading faster and better than many an older child already at school. A regular attendant at the church was one day astonished by the small boy's powers of memory. Walking back up the Avenue with mother and son on a Sunday morning, he had asked the small boy what the sermon had been about, and was overwhelmed when he heard Mr Baker's sermon repeated, word for word it seemed.

From his mother he learned also a fondness for cats. His own cat was white and small, and her name was Floss. She was his constant companion, for he used to carry her about with him inside the blouse of his sailor suit. The story was told that one of the cats had kittens, and there was no room for more cats in the house. So the small boy took the kittens to the shopkeeper at the corner of the road. When the shopkeeper, who knew the family well, protested that he too wanted no more cats, the small boy said to him, 'But you ought to take them, because your cat is their father.'

His religious upbringing was strict. His mother was a praying and worshipping woman, and a daily reader of the Bible. Family prayers was the custom of the house. She was also a stern moralist. She was honest in money matters to the extreme degree; there was no talk in her house about taking bus rides without paying the fare, nor about keeping quiet when shop-girls gave back too much change. In matters of sexual morality she was inflexible. Her whole life long she frowned on divorce, and would dismiss some person with the words, 'Of course he was divorced.' It is almost certain that she never fully realised her own woman's nature, and that sexual expression, unthinkable as a purely physical pleasure, unrealised as a pleasure of the whole personality, was to her a duty allotted by God to married women. Her own experience gave a bitter quality to her character and tongue, so that she enjoyed any story of the sexual and marital deviations of others. Yet no one could call her a hypocrite; she was too proud, too fierce, for that. She was scrupulous in those outward observances that in her opinion showed the world that one is faithful, in church-going, Sunday observance, and in the leading of a moral life. This morality was concerned mainly with sex, marriage, work, money, liquor, dancing, gambling, duty towards children, duty towards elders, obedience to the laws and to those in authority. She exalted one virtue at least to the level of a morality, and that was punctuality. Those who were late for a meal or an appointment often felt the edge of her tongue. She did not shout or rage; in anger she showed rather the nature of a basilisk.

It was under this rule of love and law that the small boy grew up, in a confusion of greater and lesser moralities. Yet though there was this confusion, the greater moralities were great enough. From her he learned that God was no respecter of persons, that rich and poor, white and coloured and black, were all alike to Him. From her he learned no angry pride of race and blood. From her he learned that though a Christian child should honour his mother and the magistrates, it was to God alone that he owed the ultimate obedience.

So it was not strange that when he heard the bells he would be all eager to go to church. They were proud of him there, the 6-year-old boy, spectacled and grave, who, though he had never been to school, could read and speak like a sage.

It was the same in Stellenbosch, too. His grandmother was a strict disciplinarian, and after family prayers, she would question the children about what she had read, and keep them behind for a re-reading if they answered badly. But not the small boy. If she questioned him it was only for the pleasure of showing that he remembered all. Katrina Beyers's home was the centre of the neighbourhood. She was sweet and tender, and people were in and out of her house the whole day long. Her kitchen was a place to remember, with its shining pots and pans, and so was her pantry, with those long rows of jars, the white pears, the yellow peaches, the pink guavas, the red plums and the jams and konfyts. It had a smell to remember.

One of Katrina's sons had a farm at Caledon, and the small boy would go there too. Sometimes the pigs were let out of the sties, and allowed to root about the farm. Then the small boy from Cape Town was given the job of keeping them out of the vegetable garden. So he was able to say in later life, with an irony sharp but not bitter, 'Smuts looked after the sheep, but I looked after the pigs.'

He was almost 8 before he went to the South African College School [SACS], on 24 January 1902. The school taught in English, but had a strong non-political tradition, and was proud of educating English-speaking, Afrikaans-speaking, and Jewish boys in harmony together. According to the historian Eric Walker, the school 'had blown neither hot nor cold' during the Anglo-Boer War, and because of that, it was regarded with suspicion by both the ultra-British and the ultra-Afrikaner elements at the Cape.

When the small boy first went to the school he could read both English and Nederlands, and could write in the first. He was physically not a beautiful child. He was below average height, and wore thick glasses that concealed his eyes. His arms and legs were short and thick. So were his fingers, but unlike those of many children, they did not change in later years. They remained short and thick, of a piece with his short and stocky body. His most striking physical characteristics were his head and brow, which matched the massive gifts that he had already shown.

The education of a wonder child presents many problems. The solution of 1902 was simple and devastating. Such a child went forward as fast as the authorities would let him go. His growth in breadth and depth was left to the gods. In the classroom he stood alone because he could do everything. On the playing-fields he was even more alone because he could do nothing. He wandered through the grounds in his sailor suit, even when he was high up in the school, and his classmates were walking like lords in their football blazers and cricket flannels. He was in his way the most notable boy in the school, but he was not a member of its community. Big boys said to him, 'Hennie, I wish I had your brains,' and put the thought out of their minds, where it had no place amongst the thoughts of cricket and football and girls. How sincere their envy of him was, who can say? But his of them was sincere, because of his passion for cricket.

Although the problem of the gifted child is still a real one, the schools of today offer music and art, they have rooms for hobbies, they teach you to make tables and chairs and cupboards. The small Hofmeyr boy had none of that. Music and art remained closed to him his whole life long. Of the birds and flowers and trees of his country he knew almost nothing. He never made a table or a chair. Of great areas of life lying to right and left of him, he knew nothing, because he was allowed to go forward at fantastic speed.

No one was prouder of him than Onze Jan. He was now a kind of unofficial guardian to the child. There was not only a strong facial resemblance between them, but also a strong attachment. Once Onze Jan's wife said to him, 'If I didn't know better, I'd have said it was your son.'

His own part in politics had been a strange one. He had made the Afrikander Bond into a powerful weapon, but he always used it to influence government, not to capture it. Between Rhodes and Kruger, and later between Milner and Kruger, he was the voice of reason and moderation lost in the thunder of the storm. He lacked the quality that he found in the small boy's mother, the same quality that there was in Rhodes and Kruger, later to be seen again in Smuts, a supreme confidence in oneself and one's mission. Nor had he that quality of personality that impresses itself at once on the beholder, nor had he the gift of making himself immediately known, of entering immediately into a bond with some other person, who would then always remember him. When the Afrikander Bond, after years of knowing him, suddenly decided to call him Onze Jan, (Our Jan) he was deeply moved. It was not the result of the flame and fire of personality, but the reward of devotion and integrity, and a recognition of goodness and gentleness too. Perhaps it was this same gentleness that he saw in the small boy, so that he was filled with fatherly feeling for one whom life could not help but wound. He himself had written in 1894, 'I am dead tired of the whole business,' and in 1895 he had resigned from Parliament.

Therefore he watched the small boy enter the world of school with feelings of pride and responsibility, and felt no constraint in counselling and encouraging him as a good father would have done.

The small boy's progress was quite astonishing. From 1902–1903 Hofmeyr did the equivalent of five years of school and although the authorities wished to keep him in one class for a whole year in 1904, by the end of 1905 he was four classes further on. In 1906 he entered Form D, the Matriculation class. He was not quite twelve years old, and for the first time was to spend a full year in a class. His school reports over these five years were always excellent, except in respect of his writing, which declined from very fair to fair, then to untidy, which it remained for the rest of his life, except when he made a special effort.

When in his third year the small boy shot up into the Upper School, his mother said to him, 'You mustn't think too much of yourself, because you can do things better than other boys.' He replied, 'I know, it's a gift of God, and could be taken away.'

Ah, she was proud of him! She watched over him incessantly, especially over his food. She held the theory that a great brain required a great deal of strengthening food. She hardly needed to coerce him, he was always quick to obey; and if she had to rebuke him, he would obey too. It became understood between them that in the matter of food, her word was law. But it was love as well as law. Her love was poured out over him, enveloping and possessing him. Her love and his genius isolated him from the world.

The small boy's genius was not troubled or tormented or sublime or dazzling. It was a sober and industrious and polite genius. Though he did well with such ease, he read and studied much. He played marbles and impromptu cricket, but it was no hardship to return to his books; not just school books, any kind of books. When he was eleven his mother was unwell and in bed, and Dr Julius Petersen walked with his wife to Rheede Street. While the doctor went upstairs, she said to the small boy with his Latin book, 'What a pity to be doing lessons when everyone is out playing.' He smiled at her politely. 'I've finished my lessons,' he said, 'now I'm amusing myself.' As she and her husband walked home, she said to him, 'He was amusing himself, translating from one language to another.' Her husband said to her, 'Don't you realise you've been talking to a future Prime Minister?'

So at the age of eleven he passed into the highest class of the school. Now he worked as hard as ever. Dr and Mrs Petersen went off to Europe, and left their two sons in Mrs Hofmeyr's charge in Rheede Street, where his intense industry appalled them. When the Petersens returned, they took the small Hofmeyr boy and their two sons to Onrust, one of the coastal resorts under the southern mountains. They bathed in the lagoon because the sea was dangerous, and did not think to ask if their small guest could swim. It was Mrs Petersen who saw him rising and sinking in the water; he was doing so with a nonchalance so foreign to him that she drew her husband's attention to it. 'The boy's drowning,' he cried, and they pulled him out and had to give him artificial respiration. For the rest of his life he had a fear of being under the surface of water.

By this time Mrs Hofmeyr had her two sons alone at home. A.B. was eighteen years old, taking articles with the legal firm of van Zyl & Buissinne. He was a man, and to a great extent went his own way, so that Mrs Hofmeyr and Jan Hendrik had the house a great deal of the time to themselves. Now that Jan Hendrik was going to the College, she asked Onze Jan to give the boy a fatherly talk, which he did, on the theme that character was more important than intellectual achievement. The talk made a deep impression on the 12-year-old boy. Its theme he was to repeat on many occasions, in conversation, in talks to boys at camps and prize-givings. What was more, he accepted it with heart and soul for himself.

So he set out to conquer yet another world, a world not of boys, but of young men. In his short trousers he set out to conquer it.

While he was at school he had always gone to bed at nine o'clock, but now he told his mother, 'The work is getting harder, and I must stay up a bit longer.' Professor Ritchie, head of the department of Classics, came to Rheede Street and urged Mrs Hofmeyr to put the boy into long trousers, but she replied, 'I'm keeping him simple as a child; just take no notice of him.' There was one matter on which the College authorities stood firm. They would not allow him to take the B.A. in less than three years. He had to choose between the B.A. in Languages and the B.A. in Science, and he chose the first.

He did not plunge into the community life of the College. At his age it was hardly possible. It was probably in his second year that he joined the Debating Society and the Students' Christian Association. The older students were busy with their own affairs, and he was not observed as a person, though of course everyone knew of him as a phenomenon. References to 'chasing' were frequent in the College Magazine; 'but,' said his mother, 'while his fellow students were thinking of young ladies, he was playing marbles'. He attended the welcome to new students, which was more or less obligatory, but he did not stay to the end. Some wag terrified him by telling him that he would have to speak on behalf of the new-comers, and he stole away into the night. He apologised for this some years later, when he himself was making the speech of welcome.

At home a pattern of life was being set which was to last throughout his life. He would go out to his work, and when he came home she would be waiting for him. He would call 'Ma, Ma' at the door, and she would answer him. Something would be ready for him to eat, and while he ate it they would discuss the affairs of the day. If he went out at night by himself, it would always be for some good and proper cause, a meeting, or a special lecture, and when he came in she would be waiting for him to make him a cup of cocoa.

If it was good to go out in the morning, it was just as good to come home, to the security of her companionship and the pleasure of her conversation, with its pungent judgements on the looseness and carelessness of men and women. It was a comforting routine, safe, orderly, punctual, and righteous; it fully satisfied both mother and son. She had no need to watch over his work; at the age of twelve he watched over it himself. But she watched jealously over his health, his sleep, and his food. Perhaps it was at this time that she devised the breakfast that he ate without variation all his life whenever he was at home. It consisted of fruit, porridge, and a plate of three slices of bread on which had been poured gravy made from a pound of beef, with an egg, fried on both sides, on top of the bread. So fortified, he went off to his lectures.

His first year was brilliant. In his second year he won the medals in all five of his classes, in Latin and Classical Philology, Greek, English, Philosophy, and Dutch.

It was during this year of 1908 that Alfred Hoernlé arrived at the College as Professor of Philosophy, at the age of 27. He was a remarkable man, cheerful, sociable, humorous, and yet outspoken. He had one of the clearest of minds, succinct in statement, powerful in argument. It was impossible to know him without admiring his unswerving loyalty to the greater moral principles, and the courage with which he expressed his views on social questions, in an English with a marked and attractive German accent.

The young Hofmeyr conceived a great admiration for this vigorous teacher. The boy was however attracted by the man rather than by his subject, for although he was an excellent student, he was not much interested in philosophy. His views of life, morality, duty, destiny, he had learned from his mother and the Baptist Church, and they satisfied him. Hoernlé, on the other hand, while a respecter of religion, had no orthodoxy and belonged to no church. Yet even then, as throughout his life, he was to be esteemed by men and women of no religion and all religions, as a champion of the right, especially in the new field of race relations. Another student who admired Hoernlé was Winifred Tucker, who later married him, and with him made notable contributions in this field. She and her husband were to play their part in Hofmeyr's life, but in 1908 she knew the boy only by his tremendous reputation, for she left the College the year before he arrived.

Yet another two persons in Cape Town who were also to play their parts in Hofmeyr's life, and in this same field of race relations, were J. D. Rheinallt Jones and his wife Edith. They first met the young student because of their common interest in the work of the Students' Christian Association, and both predicted a brilliant future for him.

The young Hofmeyr was distinguishing himself in the debating forum as well as in the lecture room. At the age of 14, still in short trousers, he strongly opposed women's suffrage. His speech was written out in his terrible handwriting, and after the debate he sent it to Onze Jan. In a later debate on the same subject he made use of the 'Native question' to strengthen his case on women's suffrage, using arguments that later in life he would think to be shocking. He said, 'No one can doubt that there is impending a struggle, or at least a keen rivalry, between the white and black races of South Africa. To face this position it is necessary that the whites should present a united front, that there should be no falterers, no disunion in our ranks as we meet the common foe.'

Despite his debating prowess, it is clear that he was regarded as a child. Of friends at the College, he had almost none. An exception was Peter Clouts, an old scholar of SACS, who came up in 1908, but though he was a year behind Hofmeyr, he still looked upon him as a child. Hofmeyr's closest friend was still at SACS, Theo Haarhoff, another brilliant pupil, was always in and out of the house in Rheede Street. The two boys had much in common. They were equally at home in English or Dutch, they had both been brought up frugally and simply in strict and religious homes, they were both outstanding scholars in Latin and Greek, and they both had a deep love for the English game of cricket, though neither was a good performer. Both were the obedient and gentle sons of loving mothers, who, though proud of their children's brilliance, would rather have seen them good than clever.

Mrs Hofmeyr approved of the Haarhoff boy as a friend for her son. He was industrious, with none of the carelessness of the rising generation, and he submitted himself to her authority. If they made some plan, they would wait for her approval. She might say, in her brief incisive way, 'Yes,' or she might, thrusting forward her lower lip a little, say equally briefly, 'No.' If they continued to look at her questioningly, or if she sensed their disappointment, she would say, her voice rising, sometimes a little, sometimes more, 'Of c-course not, of course not, how could such a thing be?' And one could see at once, of course not, of course not, such a thing could not be.

For all that, the young Haarhoff rebelled against it; inwardly, because who rebelled against her openly? It could have been done of course; but if it had been done, the person who did it would from that moment have ceased to be. If it had been done, it must be done by one who would not care whether he ceased to be or not. Therefore he did not rebel.

The two boys had the same politics too, very much the same as those of Onze Jan. They were both Dutch-speaking, or to use the new word, they were Afrikaners, yet they used English as if it were their own tongue. They both looked forward to a Union of South Africa embracing the Cape Colony, the Transvaal, the Orange Free State, and Natal, a State with an independent government, entrenching equal rights for English- and Afrikaans-speaking people, and for their languages. Although they were both so proficient in English, and had been at an English-language school, and although one was already at an English-language college and the other soon would be, yet they wanted the full recognition of the second language, whether it be Nederlands or Afrikaans. They were both proud of Onze Jan, who in March 1905, delivered at Stellenbosch that remarkable speech 'Is het ons Ernst?', which means, 'Are we in earnest about it?' It was a fighting speech, and Onze Jan told Afrikaners that they should cherish what was their own, their language, their customs, their religion.

But these three, the old man and the two boys, were Nationalists of a gentle kind. There was another and much fiercer Nationalism, which was the creation of what Smuts had called 'The Century of Wrong'. This Nationalism had been humiliated in the Anglo-Boer War, robbed of its two republics, brought back under the Union Jack.

It was true that in 1906 the British Prime Minister Campbell-Bannerman had restored self-government to the defeated republics and that the defeated leader of the Transvaal, Louis Botha, had become its first Prime Minister. It was true that there was in some measure a healing of wounds. But to the Nationalists that was justice, not generosity. One did not have to kiss the enemy's hand because he took his foot off your neck. Botha invited the Afrikaner to 'forgive and forget', and the Nationalists replied, 'Forgive but never forget.' For to forget would be to be swallowed up with language and custom and future and selfhood. The restoration of self-government and of the franchise had one magnificent implication, that, when all Afrikaners became Nationalists, they would rule again, not only the two republics, but the whole of South Africa.

To do this they must separate themselves, keep themselves apart. Therefore with implacable will they addressed themselves to their task, establishing their cultural societies, their economic Bonds, their separate schools, their own youth organisations. God had a purpose for them in Africa, else why had He put them there? In such a programme, Botha with his determination to reconcile Boer and Briton, Smuts with his eyes on the world, Onze Jan with his moderation, had no place. And the young Hofmeyr and the young Haarhoff, with their English education and their gentle natures, merely flirted with so fierce a lover.

Afrikaner Nationalism was hardly an actor on the stage of that time. The National Convention was meeting, first in Durban, then Cape Town, and finally in May 1909 at Bloemfontein, to draw up the constitution of the new Union of South Africa. 'Conciliation' and 'reconciliation' were the words in the air. Wedding bells were ringing, and Englishmen and Afrikaners drank one another's healths. Afrikaner Nationalism was like a disapproving relative at the feast, dark and angry, contemptuous of the fine speeches and the fine clothes, uncomfortable to see, therefore not seen.

One of the problems of the Convention was the Cape franchise, which was open to any white man, coloured man, black man, who could qualify for it. On the contrary in the former republics, and enshrined in the constitution of one of them, the inflexible rule was 'no equality in Church or State'. Onze Jan was one of those at the Convention who maintained that there could be no Union unless the Cape Colony retained its own franchise. He was not the only Afrikaner to maintain this, for he was supported by the great majority of the members of his Bond.

The Cape franchise and the equality of the English and Dutch languages were especially entrenched in two clauses in the constitution, which clauses could not be altered except by a two-thirds majority of the two Houses of the Union Parliament in joint session. The draft constitution was presented to the British Parliament by a delegation of which Onze Jan was one. Deborah and her son went down to the docks to see him off, and he gave the boy his blessing and said to him, 'Send for my eiderdown tomorrow, it is now yours.' The young Hofmeyr used it all his life, though it was once re-covered. His mother used to say, half in jest and half in rue, 'That's where the politics came out from.'

On 13 October 1909, Onze Jan returned to England after taking the cure at Bad-Nauheim, and three days later he was dead, at the age of 64. His death was a grief to many, to none more than to the mother and son in Rheede Street.

Two months after Onze Jan's death, the young Hofmeyr scored another great triumph. At the age of fifteen he graduated B.A. with first-class Honours, taking first place in the examination and the University Gold Medal for Literature. For this achievement, and for all his achievements, he was awarded the coveted Rhodes Scholarship.

It was now wisely decided to halt the boy in his headlong course. Although he won the Scholarship at the end of 1909, it was decided that he would not go to Oxford till 1912, when he would be eighteen years of age. In fact he did not go until 1913. He was also made the honorary holder of two other valuable scholarships.

So again the white light of publicity beat upon him, and this time more brightly than before. *De Goede Hoop* published a full-page photograph of him, in a Norfolk suit with long-short trousers, and a cat on his shoulder. He himself must have been given an access of self-confidence by so much recognition. In faraway Japan the *Osaka Manuchi Shimbun* had a paragraph about him, entitled 'A Rare Genius'. He must—there is no possibility he could not—have given thought to that word *leadership* which was so much spoken about in connection with the Scholarship. It meant two things for him—responsibility and recognition. His willingness to accept the first he would have acknowledged openly; it was part of his deep religion. But his pleasure in the second he concealed, remaining as modest as before.

He was now an important figure in the Students' Christian Association and in the Debating Society. His passion for cricket was as strong as ever. One of his friends remembers him patiently standing at the Third Eleven nets, hoping that he would be asked to play. There was never a sign that he was embarrassed by his lack of skill, and this was remarkable in a boy who excelled in most things that he attempted. Often when he was dismissed after scoring nothing or very little, there would be a burst of ironic clapping, and this would provoke him to a kind of snort. But it would not deter him from playing again. In fielding he chose, with his thick spectacles and bad sight, the most dangerous of all positions, wicketkeeping, where he displayed courage, vigour, and a lack of co-ordination. If he was not batting or fielding he liked nothing better than to score. The very purity of his passion wore down all opposition, and of all those who were to develop a deep affection for him, none were so faithful as his friends of the cricket field.

Young Hofmeyr was not a rugby player. He had now reached his full height of 5 feet 7 inches, and his body was strong and stocky, but his sight made football impossible. Without his thick glasses he was almost blind, and he almost never took them off, one of the exceptions being when he went to bed. He went so far as to organise with his friend Peter Clouts a meeting in the Engineering laboratory in favour of starting the gentler game of association football at the College. It was a game he could have played with glasses. It was a bold move in a College which worshipped rugby and rugby players, and regarded association football, or soccer as it was called, as a game to be played by the socially and physically inferior. The move came to nothing, and the College Magazine was contemptuous of the whole proposal. It announced a Grand Pageant in which Mr P. Clouts was to be 'Champion of the Oppressed', 'who moves at a meeting that *a soccer club be formed* with an amendment that the Ambulance Class be retained for special duty at matches, in case of shocks from over-exertion, or in event of the knees giving way'.

This was 'nonsense and beneath contempt', said Hofmeyr to Clouts; if people wanted soccer, they should be able to have it.

Although a graduate student, he was still wearing short trousers. Whether he ever raised the question with his mother, no one is likely to know. He was extremely untidy in his dress, even grubby. He wore his hair very short, and made little attempt to part it. Whether this carelessness about his appearance was a genuine indifference, or in some way affected, would be hard to establish, but some of it was undoubtedly due to a kind of ignorance or innocence, and a lack of sensitiveness to the opinions of his fellows and the requirements of society.

After he had taken his second degree in 1910 at the age of sixteen, Hofmeyr resumed his classical studies, and prepared to take his M.A. in the Classics. He became treasurer of the College Magazine, of which Haarhoff was now joint editor. He was still one of the important members of the Debating Society, but his most vigorous contribution was to the Students' Christian Association, under the guidance of Oswin Bull. Bull was an attractive personality, tall and well built, with a fine face and head, a strong voice, and a compelling presence. He was an Anglican but his understanding of the nonconformist churches was deep and real, and his claim for a personal relationship with Christ was readily understood by them.

He had an eye for key men, and it soon fell on the young Hofmeyr. He had no difficulty in attracting him, because his own religion was very like that of the young man—it steered a middle road between Baptist warmth and Anglican propriety. Though the young Hofmeyr had been brought up in a Baptist world, he had also entered another, the more austere world of *pietas, gravitas, aequanimitas, virtus*, where he and the young Haarhoff felt so much at home. He was slowly moving away, not deliberately or knowingly, from the world of Ernest Baker. But from the dedication of the will he did not move at all. There was less talk of sin, blood, and salvation, and more talk of service and dedication. Yet words are empty after all. It was really young Galahad with the shining armour and the shining sword, seeking the shining Grail. Only the face did not shine, it was impassive; and the eyes, if they are the gate of the soul, were barred by the heavy glass. He moved solitary, made so by gifts and love.

Bull stirred the Association into new life. He started his students' camps, opening in the morning with prayers and coffee and a cold bath, after breakfast a hike over the mountains, camp sports, and a rowdy sing-song in the evening followed by an evangelistic talk and prayers. Some of the students he recruited as officers, and began to organise the same sort of camp for boys. Under his encouragement some of the students became street preachers and helped a Presbyterian missionary in the coloured slums. Seaside services were held for children on the sands of Somerset Strand and Kalk Bay. Bull and his helpers would build a pulpit of sand, which with its banner attracted the children. They would organise games, and after the games, one of them would mount the pulpit and preach a children's sermon. Children's hymns were sung, and the message of sermon and hymns was constant, that even the young could enrol themselves as soldiers in a great army, which led by Christ could save and redeem the world.

In all these ventures the young Hofmeyr became one of Bull's right-hand men. The boy turned to the man as he turned to few in his life, and the mother approved and encouraged the relationship, for Bull was carrying forward a father's work.

Mrs Hofmeyr could be grateful that her son was in such safe hands. She could be grateful too that the man was clearly no rival for the boy's affection. And a mercy it is to know that your son is in such hands, that his feet are constant on the road that you wanted him to go, that he is chaste, honourable, industrious, clever, thoughtful, and, even at this age, obedient. A mercy it is to know that when he calls for you in the house, it is no deception, that he knows what you have done for him, and are doing, and that he is thankful, that he shows no signs of discontent, of wanting more than you have given him. Outside it may be godless and careless, but here it is constant and secure. And if a time must come when he must go out and fend for himself, then it must come, for a weaning time must come, though not just yet. But you hope he will choose neither newspapers nor politics, for they are hard lives, and seem to fill a man with care.

The year closed with another triumph for Hofmeyr, a first-class in the M.A. examination. He still had eighteen months to go before he could begin his studies at Oxford, so it was decided that he would still remain a student of the College, and that Professor Ritchie would keep an eye on his reading and study.

Then an exciting task was found for him. A strong committee was formed in Cape Town under the chairmanship of the Hon. F. S. Malan, to arrange for the writing of the life of Onze Jan. It was hoped that Malan would write it, but he would not, and the committee then offered the task to the 17-year-old Hofmeyr, at a remuneration of £10 a month while he was writing it. Modestly he accepted.

This was the first money he had earned in his life, and he handed it over *in toto* to his mother, who gave him the first allowance of his life. He was no doubt the last of his group to have money of his own to spend.

Young Hofmeyr was to write the book, but ex-President Reitz undertook 'to collaborate in the production'. In the end it was clearly the young man's book. Reitz was content to record his objections to this and that in the text.

Mrs Hofmeyr certainly never regarded the *Life* as owing anything to any person but her son. Her pride in it was immense. She could not see how a mere child could tackle such a task. Of the worth of the book as a book, she had no idea whatsoever. To her it was not a book, but a monumental piece of industry performed in a snatch of time. She was proud not because of its truth or insight or power, but because it took only one year, and was then translated into Nederlands by the author before he sailed for England six months later. Professor Arndt, in his memorial tribute written thirty-six years later, wrote that 'meanwhile the short-trousered boy also still found time to coach privately for their examinations several grown-up men'.

It was the young Hofmeyr's new task that brought him the first letter that he ever received from the great General J. C. Smuts, then Minister of Mines, Interior, and Defence in the first Cabinet of the new Union of South Africa. Smuts was distantly related to the young man by marriage, for his wife Isie was related to Deborah Hofmeyr through their common descent from the Retief family which had produced the great Voortrekker hero, Piet Retief.

Smuts wrote to the young Hofmeyr from the Treasury, Pretoria, on 6 September 1913, in a form of Nederlands already showing concessions to the new language Afrikaans.

Dear Mr Hofmeyr,

Forgive my delay in answering your letter of 15/7/13. I have not had time to go through my old correspondence, but find that my wife destroyed all important letters during the English occupation of Pretoria because the house was repeatedly searched for compromising material. Thus I have nothing that throws light on the important period you are dealing with.

With best wishes for good progress in your important work.

t.t. [*totus tuus*]

J. C. Smuts

It was to be expected that young Hofmeyr would produce a competent and painstaking biography. It dealt meticulously with every event in which Onze Jan took part, but of the man it said nothing, except that he was wise, conservative, honourable, and almost without fault. Young Hofmeyr had no interest in, and at that age certainly no gift for, psychological observation. He refers twice to 'pessimism so characteristic' of Onze Jan, but it certainly does not characterize the life as it is related.

The dramatic relationship between Onze Jan and Cecil Rhodes does not emerge in any dramatic form. The Jameson Raid destroyed it, and Onze Jan would have nothing further to do with Rhodes. When Rhodes was dying in Cape Town, Onze Jan cabled from Naples, GOD BE WITH YOU—JAN HOFMEYR. The young biographer wrote: 'It was a graceful action, the pity is, that Rhodes was already unconscious, when the message arrived.' The language of the book was undistinguished, and in parts bad.

Hofmeyr was later to be acknowledged by many as the finest speaker of English in South Africa, but his mastery was distinctly utilitarian, a fact disguised by his oratorical skill. He was no poet, not even in prose. This too was often disguised by his love of quoting verse, but this he did—with rare exceptions—to drive home some moral lesson, or to encourage his audience to greater moral effort. For him the sound of a 'woman wailing for her demon lover' came from an incomprehensible world. He was more at home with Newbolt's 'Vitaï Lampada':

> *And it's not for the sake of a ribboned coat,*
> *Or the selfish hope of a season's fame,*
> *But his Captain's hand on his shoulder smote—*
> *'Play up! play up! and play the game!'*

The young Hofmeyr made it clear that he strongly approved of Onze Jan's tolerance in matters of race. He did not however call it liberalism, which in those days meant the religious liberalism which was challenging the orthodoxy of the day. Onze Jan's racial tolerance was a remarkable one, full of inconsistencies not apparent to the young biographer. Commenting favourably on the treatment of servants in the home of Onze Jan's childhood, young Hofmeyr wrote: '. . . it is to the spirit of the better sort of masters of the old slave days—the spirit of firmness tempered with kindness—that one must today go back for a solution of the native problem.'

Onze Jan spoke out openly against a proposal 'to exclude natives' from the Gill College at Somerset East. In 1882 when the Farmers' Protection Association amalgamated with the Afrikander Bond, he spoke against an amendment to limit membership to white persons, and won his argument by 47 votes to 12. In that same year he declared in the Cape House, that if 'the number of those who speak some native language is strong enough to return two-thirds of the House', he would be willing to give them the right to use their language. In 1891 however he proposed to raise the qualifications of the Cape franchise in order to limit the number of non-white voters, and young Hofmeyr wrote that the 'native franchise', excellent in itself, became a danger when it threatened to produce a contest between civilisation and barbarism.

Young Hofmeyr said that Onze Jan's policy had two sides, which were friendly treatment and a recognition of racial differences. He told two anecdotes to illustrate them. The first was that Onze Jan stooped to pick up the hat blown off the head of a black man on a passing cart and restored it to him; when a friend remarked on the unusualness of such an action, Onze Jan replied, 'Why, he would have done the same for me.'

The other anecdote illustrated the second side of Onze Jan's policy. A deputation of coloured voters asked whether they might join the Bond which had no colour bar.

'Mr Hofmeyr made no reply; instead he invited the deputation to dine at his house. The men saw the point; they felt it was impossible for them to accept such an invitation, neither therefore, could they expect to be treated as the white man's equals.'

Nothing could show more clearly the strange nature of Onze Jan's tolerance, of a Bond which had no colour bar but wanted no coloured members, of a courtesy that would allow one to pick up a black man's hat but not allow one to have him to dinner. The young Hofmeyr was certainly not questioning this world at the age of 18. The conflict between Christian principles and racial policy was not yet a fierce one. As in the early stages of a total eclipse of the sun, the shadow was there, bringing a faint chill to the air, imperceptible to most, and leaving ample light to see by, so that few knew that there was a darkness growing over the land.

Of such a darkness, the young Hofmeyr knew as yet little. In his own world the doors of opportunity opened to him before he had even knocked. He was so full of activity, so conscious of achievement, he had such a mother to guide him, that he had nothing but hope for the future.

There has persisted a legend about him. According to the legend, young Hofmeyr did fall in love with, or was attracted by, a shy gentle girl who was a member of the SCA. The young man being what he was, heavy of body and gesture, with eyes hidden by the heavy glasses, this attraction would have gone unnoticed by many. But one person would have noticed it at once, and that was his mother, for their symbiotic relationship was such that each would have sensed at once any variation in the behaviour of the other. The legend says that she spoke strongly to him about both the folly and the unfairness of entering into such a relationship, when so many years of absence and hard work lay ahead of him, that she reminded him of her devotion and of her task not yet completed. Whatever the incipient relationship may have been, it came to an end.

It is all speculation, but it is speculation about the possible. One thing is certain, that whether this legend be true or not, whether some other similar thing happened or not, young Hofmeyr learned that the price of his mother's devotion was his own devotion. If he was to break with her, then was the time. Boys have been known to wean themselves from possessive mothers, but men seldom. For a moment young Hofmeyr was able to thrust his head out of the symbiotic shell, and see what was happening there within, to himself and his mother. He was able to realise that, although years of absence and hard work lay ahead, they were not her deepest reasons. He was able to realise that if ever he wanted to be free, it would create such a crisis of recriminations, claims, self-pityings, and other ugliness, that he could not have borne it. So he came to heel.

Many years later Judge Leslie Blackwell, a man forthright to a point some thought rudeness, asked her, 'Why didn't you let the boy marry?' To which she replied, 'I never tried to stop him marrying. If the right girl had come along, I'd never have stood in his way.' The judge said to her sceptically, 'You knew the right girl would never come along, so long as you were alive.'

Mrs Hofmeyr laughed at him, but if it had been someone else, she would have been unspeakably angry. If someone else had said deferentially to her, 'Why didn't your son marry?', she would have answered, 'He's like that, he has no interest in women.' If she felt it necessary to stress the point, her voice would rise, and she would say, with that slight stammer that gave such distinction to her sayings, 'D-Don't think I haven't t-told him, but he won't listen to me.' It was magnificent play-acting, but the rising voice was a warning that she did not want to talk about it any more.

Maternal possessiveness delays the sexual development of a boy, and in young Hofmeyr's case this was so. At no time in his later life was the attraction of a woman strong enough to make him defy his mother, or take the step that would involve them both in ugliness and pain. If he had spent some time away from her, it might have happened. While he lived with her, any relationship with a woman was impossible.

Some insinuated that he was a practising homosexual, and his interest in boys and boys' camps, which lasted throughout his life, was adduced as proof. To anyone who knew him, the insinuation was absurd. Something quite different was true, namely that he was sexually normal but pretended to be asexual, and joked about his bachelordom because he could hardly have joked about his mother's possessiveness. All through his life he was attracted by women, and made infinitesimal sallies towards them; all through his life his mother knew when such a sally was being made. She was instantly aware of the slightest deviation from the pattern, and he knew at once that she knew.

Was his sexual temperature, so to speak, low? It was, I think, but not inherently. It was low because of the symbiotic shell in which he lived, and if he could have broken out of it, his temperature would have risen to normal. Why did he never break out of it? Was it too comfortable? Or was he merely used to it? Or was he unwilling to face the emotional upheaval that he would cause by breaking out of it? One thing is certain: he never, in the language of the Bible, knew a woman, and one could hazard the guess that he never, except in the most decorous fashion, kissed one either. Another thing is certain, that, aided no doubt by the lowness of the temperature, he lived a chaste and disciplined life.

Hofmeyr's last SCA function was the biennial conference at Beaufort West. There were addresses on 'The Moslem Peril', 'The Native Question', and 'The Poor-White Question'. One of his last debates was on 'South African Native Policy', and he championed the tradition of Cape liberalism, which aimed at a tolerant society, in whose government non-white citizens, if they possessed the necessary qualifications, could participate. He said:

'There are in general two broad Native policies possible with no via media. The first is the policy of segregation, the policy of repression, the policy of the Dark Ages. The other is the enlightened policy which we put forth this evening, the policy inspired not by prejudice but by political wisdom, the policy of justice, expediency, and necessity.'

He warned against the attempt to stave off the inevitable:

'. . . the French revolution was caused by not giving the vote to eligible men . . . the day may yet come when inspired by the sense of unjust wrongs they may sweep the whites of South Africa into the sea, and South Africa may come to be a black man's country again . . . you may build a wall over the roots of a tree, it will spring up all the same. You may refuse to educate the native but educated he would be.'

Here we have to deal with a young man whose religion, having concerned itself with personal conduct, was now beginning to concern itself with politics. He was beginning to concern himself with the profound problems of love and justice and power, and the profound difficulties of reconciling their claims in the life of the State. His leader in this venture was not Plato or Mill or Marx, but Jesus of Nazareth, and from that loyalty he did not deviate his whole life long. Gradually but inexorably it was to lead him to question, and if necessary to challenge, the beliefs and customs of his people and his day. A gentle and obedient child could hardly have chosen a harder way.

On 20 September 1913, on the Royal Mail Steamer *Saxon*, he and his mother set sail for England, Oxford, and Balliol College. He was now wearing long trousers.

Chapter 2

Balliol and Oxford

HOFMEYR's three years at Oxford, although the First World War was to empty the colleges after his first twelve months, must be reckoned as three of the happiest years of his life. Though he was accustomed to conceal emotion, he never attempted to hide his love of Oxford. About no other period of his life did he ever speak with such affection; it came as near to longing as anything he ever felt or allowed himself to feel. One might say that those heavily protected eyes, which seldom shone, came as near to shining as they ever would when he remembered Oxford. Hofmeyr's emotions were in general very like his body, substantial and stolid; however, in this emotion there was a strong element of the tender.

But it did not happen all at once, in fact some of it did not happen there at all. It was a love that seemed to grow with the years.

It was at Balliol that Hofmeyr first met the young men from the English public schools, and he did not like them at all. He thought that they were arrogant, supercilious, and extraordinarily self-satisfied. It was not only understandable, it was also not uncommon. It was the dislike of the 'colonial' for a self-assurance that made him feel uncouth, for an etiquette that would catch him out taking a roll from a plate that had just been in fact proffered to his neighbour.

And with Hofmeyr there was something else; it was the Nonconformist uneasiness in the presence of the Anglican, distrusting its formality but impressed by its beauty, these ancient chapels, this ancient liturgy . . .

'. . . grant, O most merciful Father . . . That we may hereafter live a godly, righteous, and sober life, To the glory of Thy holy Name. Amen.'

That surely must be religion, even if a queer one; but this young man, who was thought by many to be insensitive and cold, used these very adjectives to describe the practice of religion in the Anglican communion. Hofmeyr practised prayer, but it was ritual that he could not understand. I think that he considered that one worshipped with the will, by the dedication of the will, and that to say too much about it, and chant about it, and kneel, and genuflect, and cross oneself, and communicate weekly, sometimes daily, and for ministers of religion to dress up in quite fantastic costumes, actually served to distract one from the central necessity of the dedication of the will. He was puritanical and intolerant at that age, but he was later to become a champion of the public-school tradition, and to be an honoured and willing guest in any Anglican institution. It is true that he was later to say to Bishop Karney of Johannesburg, 'I am the complete Nonconformist'; but he was a great man then, and could have had any public-schoolboy in South Africa eating out of his hand, so he spoke no more intolerantly.

Hofmeyr was intensely critical of the Student Christian Union at Oxford. Once when he went to a meeting, five seniors were standing round the fire. 'We were coldly welcomed and left to wait in a corner, while they discoursed for about fifteen minutes on politics, dogs, and such like.'

At this first Sunday meeting, he met another freshman at the foot of the stairs, and they introduced themselves. The other young man was John Macmurray, later to become a British philosopher of repute. Macmurray had been an enthusiastic member of the Student Christian Movement in Glasgow, and he and Hofmeyr left their first meeting in Balliol disgusted. They decided that the SCU needed revitalising, and they decided to do it. They got permission from the committee, and began to organise work on the SCA lines known so well to them both.

Hofmeyr and Macmurray had much in common. They were both in a sense 'colonials', they both found the public-schoolboy a trial, they were both non-Anglicans. Another member of the Balliol group was C. K. J. Underhill, who maintained a correspondence with Hofmeyr until his death. Macmurray was a Presbyterian, and Hofmeyr and his mother had already attached themselves to the Presbyterian congregation. In this turning to the Presbyterian Church, the Hofmeyrs were in fact turning away from the Baptists, and retracing their steps to that type of Christianity known as the Reformed. Such a step was not surprising in a young man who believed so profoundly in freedom with order, who had become an admirer of the great Augustus, and who was not inclined to self-revelation. Yet though he was retracing his steps in a direction more in accordance with his temperament, he remained strongly evangelical.

Hofmeyr was shocked, after having come from the fairly cloistered college life of Cape Town, to find how relatively much was drunk at Oxford; and he was shocked by something else too, the absence of the colour bar.

'I was rather shocked when I got there that just next to me was an Indian named S—, even more so when another Indian asked me to breakfast with him, and I had to go. It is rather hard getting used to different ideas about colour just at first. Still one has to take things philosophically. Last Saturday two or three of the Indians collected in S—'s rooms and went and got drunk. There was a regular Indian mutiny. It was all very pleasant. However these are the mere details of Oxford life. On Saturday nights it is quite the ordinary thing to get tight, and as my windows overlook Trinity, I had them on three sides last time—our own people in the quad, Trinity people in theirs, and the Indian mutiny next door.'

It is quite probable that at that time Hofmeyr would have considered the noise of conviviality to be a sure sign of drunkenness. When he described these events as being 'the mere details of Oxford life', it seems that he had already seen the reality behind the appearances. One thing is certain: his pride in Balliol, and his pride in being at Balliol, were evident from the beginning.

He knew the names of all the distinguished sons of Balliol, and used to say, avoiding any appearance of pride in himself, that it was the hardest college to get into. 'At Balliol one gets the Balliol manner—in other words one comes to imagine oneself a superior unapproachable person. So you must not be surprised if you find that I, too, have become infected with the deadly poison.'

Balliol certainly did not improve his dressing habits. He wore ready-made clothes, which fitted very badly his short, stocky body. He was indifferent to dress, and his indifference resulted not in a Bohemian care-lessness, but in something approaching grubbiness. His indifference may have been to some extent aggressive, but it was mostly insensitive. There can be no doubt that he regarded character as the supreme essential, and the manner in which a man was clothed as unimportant. This carelessness persisted, even when he had become the Principal of a University, then the Administrator of a Province, then a Minister of the Crown. It was in what one may call the years of his gravity, when, strangely enough, he had done with the pomp of the world, that he began to pay more atten-tion to his clothes, and to dress in dark well-made suits. He was a Cabinet Minister before he gave up wearing boots, and while he wore them, one could always see the tops of them below his trouser-ends; he wore soft shirts, and his collars and cuffs were always limp and sometimes dirty.

Was he so insensitive to public approval? In a way he was, but this insensitivity was an armour that he had made for himself. Some thought, when they looked at his heavy body, with its thick legs and short fingers, with its immobile face, which, except for the blinking of the eyes that was so characteristic, would not change in expression when he was under the bitterest attack or receiving the highest praise, that he was as solid as his body. Soon after his arrival in England he went up to London to attend a South African dinner, and met E—, a SACS man, in the street. 'I almost burst out laughing. It was awfully funny. I was just dressed in ordinary togs with the same old hat which I had when I left home. We were both going to the same affair, and in the course of the evening he succeeded in taking rather more wine than was good for him.' Nevertheless he had a dress-suit made for himself, and recorded that he cordially detested having to wear it.

There can be no doubt of his happiness at Oxford. In his reserved way he developed a great love for England the physical land; especially did he like the clear streams and rivers flowing through the flat countryside, the towpaths and bridges, the green quietness, so unlike anything at the Cape. He and Macmurray, Byth from Australia, and Miles from New Zealand, used to go cycling along the green roads, and play billiards at a pub in Bicester. Macmurray liked talking to Hofmeyr; he liked the quality of his mind, and found that they could discuss the problems of the day in the 'most fundamental terms'. But Macmurray found it difficult to be intimate with him; he never walked arm-in-arm with Hofmeyr in the quad, as he did with his other friends, and it was not until a year had passed that he learned that Mrs Hofmeyr was living in the town.

Although Hofmeyr was active in the religious field, it was not in this activity that he found his greatest self-realisation, but in an institution known as the Balliol Boys' Club. This club was to be found in what was then a squalid part of Oxford called St Ebbe's, in a disused sweet-factory in Littlegate Street, where the Balliol 'toffs' ran a club for the boys of the slums of the university city.

Hubert Secretan, who was to become Hofmeyr's lifelong friend, was a member. Secretan was not a member of the Christian Union, but was a member—'a pretty poor one', so he said—of the Anglican Society. If praying and worshipping were to be done in public, then they should be done with dignity and decorum, as they were done for example in the Church of England. Secretan would never have described himself as an evangelical; on the contrary he disliked any display of fervour. But behind the reserved exterior lay a complete dedication, an extreme sense of duty that never showed itself otherwise than moderately, of richer to poorer, privileged to less privileged, Oxford man to Oxford boy, but fundamentally of man to man. He had private means, and performance of this duty was in fact to be his life.

The other Hofmeyr, the private, the solitary, the admirer of Augustus, what one might call the non-evangelical, was strongly attracted by this reserved but active follower of Christ; and as time was to prove, it was rather to this kind of religion than to any other that he was temperamentally suited. Their friendship lasted till Hofmeyr's death, a deep and outwardly unemotional attachment, each of them cherishing in his own strange, apparently passionless way, a passionate love for the Balliol Boys' Club.

Secretan and Underhill were both devoted sons, and never married; they and Hofmeyr would in later years make dry jokes amongst themselves about bachelordom, but one might say, using a term without defining it, that Secretan and Underhill were 'true bachelors', bachelors by choice, whereas Hofmeyr was a bachelor by consent.

Many of the club officers had come from the hated public schools. Secretan later found it hard to believe that Hofmeyr had any prejudice against the products of the public schools, but he came to hold the opinion that the club had helped greatly to modify the prejudice, not only against the public schools, but also against the English themselves. In fact Hofmeyr later became a generous admirer of all that was good in the British character, and while he was to keep all his life a republican coldness towards royalty, he was to range himself on the side of Smuts as a stout supporter of what was later to be called the Commonwealth. We shall learn, however, that these prejudices were by no means instantly overcome.

A gay crowd it was, for the Balliol Boys' Club was a Balliol Men's Club too, and the officers used the club log book and the club magazine as vehicles for their wit. At least 250 of the members and ex-members of the club went away to the war, and were kept in touch by the publication of the little magazine *The Club at War*, to almost every number of which Hofmeyr contributed a letter. Many of these boys wrote to Hofmeyr for several years; one wrote to him until his death. This was Albert E. King, who, nicknamed Babu, was born in 1897, at the age of eleven was doing a milk-round before school, at fourteen was working full-time in a shoe-shop, then became a grocer's boy, and in 1912 joined the Balliol Boys' Club. He tells how a friend described his first encounter with Hofmeyr.

'We was in the old bashing room,' said Slatter, 'with a football when that South African toff, what was his name, Hofmeyr, wasn't it, poked his head round the door and the ball hit him straight in the bloody clock. He went off, took off his coat and specs and came back saying, "Now if you want a rough house, you can have it." Then the fun started.'

Hofmeyr was a terror to ordinary men in any kind of a rough house, to any man who had only ordinarily strong bones. His body seemed to be of superhuman density, making amongst men what the white dwarfs are amongst stars. He was short but his body was tremendous, and it had a concrete-like quality. He would stand in the middle of the mêlée, all but blind, and would giggle and snort as lesser men bumped him from all sides. He expected no quarter and gave none. When some opponent bit the ground, or when he himself received some more than ordinary shock, his laughter would sometimes become uncontrollable, which was rare indeed with him. He never laughed like that except on two sorts of occasions, the one when he was engaged in this kind of a contest, the other when someone (a friend though, not an enemy) read a lampoon of which he himself was the subject. Whatever psychologists may make of this behaviour, it endeared him to boys, though it was only one of the things they liked about him.

It was not long before Babu King decided to challenge him to wrestle. To attempt to tackle him from above was a failure, so he tried to pull him off his feet from below, with no more success. The memory of this contest, and challenges to future struggles, were to be amongst the themes of their correspondence for years to come, and they gave way to others only when age began to find them no longer appropriate. The friendship was real, although it was not based on any intellectual community; but Hofmeyr's friendships seldom were—they were based on the simplicities.

It was with King as much as with anyone that Hofmeyr enjoyed the greenness and peacefulness of rural England. They and others camped at Wytham, which was to become almost a holy place, and they cycled up to Shotover. When King joined the army, Hofmeyr cycled over to Bicester to see him and took him to tea. Hofmeyr taught him to play chess, and how to pronounce *physiology* and *psychology*, and gave him some idea of the content of these two sciences. The boy in his turn teased his mentor untiringly, and attacked him on the grounds of his weight, his corpulency, his inability to look at himself in a mirror without experiencing great shock, his devastating effect on any camera used to photograph him, his physical inferiority to King in any contest of strength and skill, in fact all the jokes which boys use to conceal their affection for men.

King and Hofmeyr met again three more times during their lives, in 1921, 1929, and 1945. After King left the army, he became an engine-cleaner and then a fireman on the Great Western Railways, and after 21 years he was promoted to driver. His father had died when he was three, his mother when he was thirty-eight. After her death he went to live with his sister and was very attached to her children. In the middle thirties he started the Federation of Enginemen's Mutual Improvement Classes, which grew to have 137 branches and over 10,000 members. In 1938 he founded the Oxford Folk Art Society, took classes in etching, and taught himself pottery. In 1947 he became porter at the Acland Home, a private hospital, but left in 1948 to become studio assistant at the Oxford School of Art, and in 1950 took up the playing of the guitar; still later, he began the study of astronomy in a simple way. Such was Hofmeyr's friend.

King did not keep many of Hofmeyr's letters but Hofmeyr kept all of King's, 126 of them, written over 32 years, letters characterised by peren-nial jokes, by nostalgia for the past, and pieces of homespun philosophy, telling us not only about the simple man who wrote them, but also about the far from simple man to whom they were written.

Hofmeyr, because of his South African degrees, was entitled to qualify as a senior student, which meant that he could take the Honour Moderations in two terms instead of five, and could complete Greats, the classics course, in three years instead of four. This he decided to do, and he wrote to a friend in South Africa that everybody at Oxford held up his hands in horror at the idea. Nonetheless he succeeded in what he once uncharacter-istically described to a friend as a 'hopeless task'. Cyril Bailey was one of his examiners, and speaks of his sound knowledge of the prepared books, most of which he had already read in South Africa, and had to offer again because of the shortness of time. Bailey also regarded his translations and compositions as competent, but lacking in distinction and elegance. He said of Hofmeyr's mind that it was sound and sure.

'He had a clear and synoptic grasp of what came before him, assimi-lated it thoroughly and formed a reliable judgement on it. A wide-embrac-ing and retentive memory enabled him to cover much ground and to recall his conclusions for future use. I shall not say that his mind worked quickly—certainly not hastily—or that it was imaginative or inventive. Rather it was a most trustworthy critic of what was presented to it.'

Just what kind of genius did Hofmeyr possess? Bailey came near the mark. Hofmeyr had a prodigious ability to make order of any material presented to him, to comprehend it, to analyse it and to put it together again, to remember both it and his own conclusions for future use.

Bailey was wrong about the quickness of his mind, but for a good reason. Hofmeyr was never a lover and a comprehender of the classics. He sucked the juice out of literature as one sucks it out of an orange, but he could not distil from the whole fruit an essence. What is more, he knew he could not do so, and he knew it was desirable and advantageous to do so, therefore he approached literature with caution. Bailey contended that Hofmeyr was much more at home later, with Ancient History, and there can be no doubt that it was so. History he understood, and the actions of rulers; most of all he understood noble actions, and gave to them his whole approval. History which told of the deeds of good men was to him the best of all literature, just as verse which dealt with good deeds and noble sentiments was the best of poetry. If he had had to study the works of T. S. Eliot for an examination, he would have had no choice but to memorise the criticisms of others. He would have been a brilliant student of the law, and a judge without peer.

His magnificent gift of ordering and comprehending material was the subject of countless stories, many of them told by persons who did not unreservedly admire him. One of the most difficult things to do is to master the contents and significance of correspondence containing statements, contradictions, amendments, and reaffirmations, that suffers from deaths of participants, changes of governments and policies, and besides all this, deals with a technical and intricate subject. Persons who presented such material to him were staggered by his ability to master the contents, and sometimes failed thereafter to argue their cases adequately; some of them blamed him for their discomfiture and said he made them feel like schoolboys. Certainly he did not suffer gladly any person who presented an unprepared case.

Bailey, in his mention of Hofmeyr's analytic and synoptic gift, remarked also on his powers of memory. One does not know in how far these are related gifts, but in any event his powers of memory were so great as to constitute a quality of his genius worthy of independent mention. The stories of these powers are also countless. Hofmeyr would say, if asked, that he could *see* the printed text when he was answering an examination question. He used the briefest of notes when speaking, but on one important occasion, he was reported to have held a sheaf of papers behind his back, and without looking at them, to have peeled them off one by one as he reached the bottom of each of them.

He had yet another outstanding gift which is also no doubt closely related to the others, and which was to show itself soon after he left Oxford. He was an administrator of superlative ability. He knew every part of his machine, sometimes better than his departmental heads, a gift which did not always endear him to them. He was also able to look after the machines of others, and when he was a Minister, was sometimes in charge of five portfolios besides his own.

Therefore this gift of ordering, comprehending, and remembering material was by no means solely academic, but was put to use in public affairs. But was it limited to a mastery of whatever machinery existed already, however complex? Why were people to say that he was not creative? One of those who said so, but privately, was himself, and he was speaking then about his political life. Yet one might well ask whether his creative gift was limited by South Africa itself, a country whose parliamentary politics have for many years been devoted to a preservation of white supremacy and of the status quo, a strengthening of racial barriers and a raising of new barriers like them; one might well ask what creativity was possible under such circumstances.

He was as keen as ever on debating, and was a member of Balliol's own undergraduate society, the Arnold. But of course it was the famous Oxford Union, where were gathered the wits of all the colleges, that attracted his attention. Just at this time there was considerable labour unrest in South Africa, and the South African Federation of Trades had declared a general strike throughout the country. The Government declared martial law, called up 60,000 white men on duty, and arrested the leaders. Fighting broke out in the Fordsburg area, and Smuts, who was Minister of Defence, rushed up from Cape Town to Johannesburg. A famous story is told of his arrival at the scene of fighting. As he left his car, an angry striker came up to him with his rifle at the ready, but Smuts, holding up an impatient hand, walked past him saying, 'Man, I'm in a hurry, I've no time for that now.' Smuts soon had the situation under control, deported nine syndicalists to England that very day, and went back to Cape Town and secured the passage of the Riotous Assemblies Act and the Criminal Law Amendment Act, measures which were highly authoritarian.

These events aroused anger in Labour and Socialist circles in Britain, and 5 February saw the Union debating the proposition 'that Parliamentary action is discredited as a solution for labour disputes', the affirmative being taken by that formidable pair, Laski and Joad. Hofmeyr must have arrived late, for he wrote to Cruse: 'When I got there I heard some people slanging our Government with the most complete ignorance of the true facts. So though I was not prepared—or partially so—I got up and let them have it.'

This may have been the debate when a future Prime Minister of Great Britain passed him a note which read, 'May I venture—or would you think it terribly impertinent of me—to congratulate you on one of the most interesting, lucid, and moving speeches I've ever heard? Yours, Harold Macmillan.'

In any event, his first year as a debater in the Union was promising. Both *Isis* and *Oxford Magazine* recommended that he should be heard earlier on in future debates.

A few months after these events, Britain went to war, and though the Union debates continued, the great ones came to an end, so that Oxford, which was later to honour Hofmeyr the statesman and administrator, never really heard Hofmeyr the orator.

The Michaelmas term ends in mid-December, and the Hilary or Lent term begins in mid-January. Mrs Hofmeyr and her son spent Christmas as paying-guests on the farm Ashtead, near Godalming in Surrey.

After the holiday at Godalming they travelled up to Swanwick in the Midlands to attend the Student Movement Bible Training School from 2 to 7 January. Hofmeyr was extremely critical of the training school, and looked at it from a Baptist and fundamentalist point of view. He wrote to Bull that 'everybody who was there swallowed everything that was said with the greatest gullibility and without the least sense of discrimination and affected a most superior scorn of the old-fashioned people who still cling to the old ideas'.

Swanwick disappointed him by its search for 'the truth in modern terms', and he said that he came away from it rather a believer in Verbal Inspiration—'always of course bearing in mind the conditions of the times and the character of the writer'.

Yet in fact he was only writing words; already and unknown to him, his fundamentalism was breaking down. *Pietas, gravitas, virtus*—law, order, truth—justice, mercy, love—these were the stars by which he was beginning to set his course. But the faith remained the same, in a God who was the Maker, the Judge, the Ruler, and the Father of men, to whom men owed a humble and filial duty. There is surely no task more difficult and dangerous than to imprison in words one's deepest beliefs about God and man; some evade it by expressing their religion almost entirely in worship, others in action, in living according to the loftiest ideals. Hofmeyr was undergoing an apprenticeship to this last class, but it was only begun and was not to be easy. At this time his interpretation of the great universals was strongly puritanical; and that of course was largely the influence of his mother.

Mrs Hofmeyr was meanwhile living in her lodgings in Wellington Square. During that first year of her son's time at Oxford she certainly did not obtrude herself. Macmurray, as we have seen, learned only at the end of the fourth term that she was there. She encouraged, as she had always done, her son's fullest participation in college activities, the debating society, the boys' club, and the various outings. Cyril Bailey, that gentlest of critics, thought that she kept away from her son as much as possible in order to show how baseless was the belief that she would not let him out of her sight. Even an informed person like Bailey thought that Mrs Hofmeyr was the first mother to accompany a Rhodes Scholar to Oxford, but he was wrong. Sir Frances Wylie, the Oxford secretary of the Rhodes Trust, could remember at least four cases; his own view was that it was undesirable, and Mrs Hofmeyr knew that he thought so. Accustomed to quail before none, she tackled Wylie at a Rhodes Scholars' function, and said, 'I hear you don't ap-p-prove of me.' She then went to Lady Wylie, and expressed her belief that she had been very necessary in Oxford, because her son had been able to come to her to relax in a way that he could not do in his own rooms. Lady Wylie was very courteous, and did not explain to Mrs Hofmeyr that her husband opposed the mother's presence on quite other grounds, namely that her presence at Oxford was preventing her son from preparing himself for an independent life, the life of leadership that Cecil Rhodes had had in mind. Another mother might thereafter have felt constraint with the Wylies, but not Mrs Hofmeyr; she had a massive self-containedness, and if there were constraint in her presence, it was invariably others who felt it.

Of the South Africans who were at Oxford with Hofmeyr many feared not only Mrs Hofmeyr's cutting tongue, but the ugly feelings that it aroused. It is a shock to see suddenly, in matron and mother, the stark and naked will. Some never saw it; they saw only the most devoted mother in history, and were angry with those who saw otherwise. It was one of the strange things about her, that some saw in her only courage and devotion, while others disliked, even hated her. One might be tempted to say that the first enjoyed only a formal relationship with her, but that would not have been accurate, and would not have accounted for the warmth of their defence of her. It would be truer to say that for some reason, whether of temperament or circumstance, they had never come into conflict with her will, and that with the passage of time conflict became less and less probable. But those who clashed with her, who took a course objectionable to her, who got a taste of her tongue, never forgot it. Her will was implacable; one did not argue with it, suggest a compromise to it, one either capitulated to it or got out of its reach. Its range was limited, largely because she was a limited woman. Had she had an intelligence to match it, she would have been a Medici or a Nightingale; or a Fry.

What her will was protecting, one can but conjecture. Was there in her mother a subtle possessiveness against which the proud daughter rebelled? The younger daughter had kept her faithful lover waiting many years, because she would not leave her ailing mother. But whatever Deborah Hofmeyr's will was protecting, there was much that it destroyed. She was unable to win the affection of her stepdaughters, nor that of her elder son. She knew only one deep relationship in her life, where love and domination were inextricably and bewilderingly intertwined; she had made it herself, she kept it for herself, she guarded it against any intrusion. It was of such a nature that neither party could form any other deep relationship outside it; she did not want to, he was not allowed to. So it happened that almost all those who visited the house in Wellington Square, and who had many bonds, of religion and homeland and other things, to bind them all together, felt for the mother a dislike, and for the son a coldness. Whether the son realized it then, we shall probably never know; he certainly realised it later.

Both the mother in her lodgings and the son in his college continued to live the simplest of lives. The Rhodes Scholarship was worth £300 a year, but in the first year they saved enough money to be able to visit South Africa for the long vacation, sailing from England on the *Walmer Castle* on 20 June 1914. Hofmeyr later told Haarhoff that he saved £240 in the three years he was at Oxford, and that was after he paid for all their travelling. Nor did they deprive themselves of holidays, as we shall see. But these holidays were austere in the extreme; both mother and son were able, to an extraordinary degree, to enjoy a holiday without extras.

For the short vacation between Hilary and Easter, they went to Margate. He had bought himself a bicycle, and did a great deal of cycling. All through his life he believed in the importance of physical exercise, until it became dangerous for him to take it. He played hockey at Balliol, and was selected for the second team; he played tennis in desultory fashion, but there is no record that in his first year he indulged his passion for cricket except from afar. When the war came and everyone was swept away, he actually represented the college against Balliol Boys' Club.

It was a wonderful year, that first year at Oxford.

Mother and son arrived in Cape Town to find glowing reviews of the recently published *Life of Jan Hendrik Hofmeyr (Onze Jan)*. The Dutch-language newspaper, *Ons Land*, gave a six-column review to the book, calling it a 'rich contribution to South African history'. In an editorial it said that it was a book 'written by an Afrikaner for Afrikaners'. The *Cape Times* gave it a seven-column review, and called it 'the work of a pious and discerning hand', and a 'most moving story'. It paid the young author the tribute that his judgement of Onze Jan would be the final judgement.

A more critical appraisal came from J. H. H. de Waal, who was a member of the committee which commissioned the book. He reviewed the book in *De Goede Hoop*, using the new language Afrikaans. He paid tribute to the thoroughness of the book—that was to be expected from such an industrious young man. But he criticised it for its purely factual nature, and its lack of insight into the character of its hero. He further thought it unfortunate that young Hofmeyr had given to Onze Jan's political character the same colour as his own, and said forthrightly that the young man had grown up in an environment which did not encourage passion for the Afrikaner cause.

De Waal's political criticisms were to be expected. However, his non-political criticisms were more penetrating than those of other reviewers; he considered that the biographer had failed to understand the *person*, and that much of Onze Jan's conservatism was in fact timidity. De Waal told the story of how, when the Anglo-Boer war was threatening, Onze Jan had said to President Steyn, 'You are going to fight, but do you see any chance to win?', to which President Steyn replied, 'We shall at least save our honour.' De Waal considered that Onze Jan, had he been President of the Transvaal, would have yielded to Chamberlain's claims one after the other. He was no admirer of Onze Jan's steady refusal to take governmental responsibility, and considered this a proof of his cautious and unadventurous nature.

These criticisms are important, because Hofmeyr was to say in later life that one must read the life of Onze Jan to understand his own politics.

Mrs Hofmeyr's pride in the long and complimentary reviews was boundless. Her son was now admired, not only for gifts which were God-given, 'but for the use made of them by steady and honest industry'. For her there was no greater virtue.

Mother and son received a great welcome from their many relatives and friends, and it would have been a visit of idyllic happiness had it not been for the fact that on 4 August 1914, Great Britain declared war on Germany. Nothing could have subjected the new Union of South Africa to greater stress and strain.

General Botha had not had an easy time as the first Prime Minister of the Union. His South African Party had entered Parliament with 66 seats, and the largely English-speaking Unionists with 39 seats, out of a House of 120. He himself had been Prime Minister of the Transvaal, and he took into his Cabinet representatives of the Cape, the Orange Free State, and Natal, though it is certain that he would rather have seen the Free Stater, General J. B. M. Hertzog, ascend the Bench. Botha was a big-hearted man, and was prepared to let things, under the guidance of his winning personality, take their course; but Hertzog was convinced that this would mean the final absorption of the Afrikaner people. While Botha therefore stressed the goal of unity among the white people of South Africa, and the need to overcome the bitterness of the past, Hertzog argued that there could be no real unity unless the parties to it were strong, virile, and self-respecting. Botha's personality appealed to those who wished to avoid further conflict, who were peace-loving by nature, who were satisfied with the new compact and wanted to give it a chance; Hertzog appealed to those who felt the deep injustice and humiliation of the Anglo-Boer War, and who were not only determined to resist any further decline of Afrikaner interests, but were also determined to advance them publicly, without undue concern to be nice and polite and forbearing about it.

On 7 December 1912, while Hertzog was still a member of the Botha Cabinet, he made his famous speech, in which he declared that imperialism was good for him in so far as it was good for South Africa. He declared that he was not one of those who always talked of conciliation and loyalty, for they were idle words that deceived nobody. He further stated that the reason he dwelt so much on the national feeling of Dutch-speaking Afrikaners was that they understood loyalty more deeply than most of the English, because their forefathers had come to South Africa 200 years earlier.

Hertzog's speech caused a crisis. What was one to make of a man who spoke of national unity at the same time that he spoke of a separate language, history, religion, and customs? And a man who, while he spoke of national unity, reserved all his fire and warmth and passion for the Afrikaner cause? What was more confusing, he used the word Afrikaner in its less usual sense (and as far as I know he did so all his life); he used the word to mean white South African, and not merely Afrikaans-speaking South African. But this was not always clear, and English-speaking people were always doubtful of him, and made anxious by his speeches, just as white people in Africa today are often made anxious by the ambiguous word African; for a black speaker may say 'Africa for the Africans', and yet mean by African any person who gives his love and loyalty to the new continent. In any event Hertzog's Afrikaner zeal was so warm and passionate that he evoked the love and admiration of those very zealots of whom the English-speaking were most afraid.

On 16 December 1912, Botha resigned, and asked by the Governor-General to form a new Government, excluded Hertzog from the cabinet. On 21 May 1913, the South African Party Provincial Congress in the Free State voted 47–1 in favour of the views of Hertzog. On 20 November 1913, the Party's National Congress in Cape Town voted 131–90 in favour of Botha. General Christiaan de Wet, beloved Anglo-Boer War hero, thereupon led most of the Free Staters out of the hall. On 7 January 1914, the National Party (invariably called by its opponents the Nationalist Party) was launched on its historic career, with General Hertzog as its unquestioned leader.

Such was the situation when Great Britain declared war on Germany. It was the view of both General Botha and General Smuts that South Africa, as part of the Empire, was automatically at war. Parliament was not in session, but Botha immediately offered to set free the Imperial garrison of the Union, and he mobilised the Naval Volunteers and portions of the Union Defence Force. Botha reminded his people of the noble action of Campbell-Bannerman, who in 1906 had restored responsible government to the Transvaal, and in 1907 to the Free State; and he told them that they could not be merely fair-weather friends of the Empire, and pointed to the aggressive nature of Germany's actions. These arguments fell coldly on the ears of many of those who twelve years before had lost their countries in what they too considered a war of aggression, and General Hertzog declared that he possessed no proof of the aggressive nature of Germany's action. Such was the confusion in South Africa that many a Boer veteran, including some of the highest rank, expected Botha and Smuts to take advantage of Great Britain's extremity and to declare South Africa a republic; and the story was told of one of Botha's trusted commandants that when he received a telegram from his old General calling on his services, he replied instantly, 'Certainly, on which side do we fight?' But what was most feared was an angry and uncontrollable reaction from Afrikaans-speaking South Africa when it learned that Botha expected its sons to fight for the British cause.

Botha and Smuts had another anxiety. On 7 August Botha had been asked by the British Government to proceed against South West Africa, but he was not at all certain that he commanded the loyalty of General Christiaan Beyers, Commandant-General of the Union Defence Force. Beyers, though born in the Cape, had gone to the Transvaal to practise law, and had served with distinction in the republican forces during the Anglo-Boer War. He had presided over the conference of delegates at Vereeniging in May 1902, and in 1907, when the Transvaal had received responsible government, he had been chosen as the first Speaker of the House, and had again distinguished himself. He was Botha's nominee for the speakership of the new Union House of Assembly, but the Free State and Merriman, fearing that the Transvaal wanted to control the whole of South Africa, had helped to elect J. T. (later Sir James) Molteno. Botha later appointed Beyers to be the first Commandant-General of the new Union Defence Force, and on a visit to Germany, Beyers had, according to Eric Walker the historian, 'been made much of by the Kaiser'.

Now Beyers was also a cousin of the Hofmeyrs, almost as distinguished as Onze Jan, and his photograph was given a proud place on the mantelpiece of the young undergraduate in his Balliol rooms. Although Mrs Hofmeyr could hardly have been described as knowledgeable or interested in politics, and although she observed a curious neutrality towards Nationalists throughout her life, she and her son were Botha supporters, and they were disappointed on their arrival to hear the rumour that the Commandant-General, who had first sided with Botha in the Hertzog dispute, was thinking of resigning his commandant-generalship, and of returning to politics as a supporter of the Nationalists, who now numbered 12 in the House. The Hofmeyrs were relieved when Beyers said publicly that he had no such intention.

Parliament was not in session, but on 10 August the Cabinet agreed to send an expedition to South West Africa, though Botha did not make it clear at the time that only volunteers would be sent. On 15 August Botha met his commandants, and Beyers and six others declared themselves opposed to the expedition. On the same day another of Botha's old colleagues, General de la Rey, fully intended to address a meeting of burghers at Treurfontein, and to urge them to rebel; but Botha by argument and kneeling with him in prayer persuaded the old man that such a course would be dishonourable. On 26 August the first Congress of Hertzog's new Nationalist Party condemned any proposal to attack South West Africa. On 9 September Parliament met and supported Botha's policies by 92–12, Hertzog being the leader of the minority, and saying, 'This war is a war between England and Germany, it is not a South African war.' On 15 September General Mackenzie occupied the South West African town of Lüderitzbucht, and that same day General Beyers resigned his commandant-generalship in protest. He met General de la Rey in Pretoria, and the two of them soon after left for the Defence Force camp at Potchefstroom. What was their purpose? No one has ever found the answer to that question, for they never reached their destination. Police were searching for the desperate and dangerous Foster gang, and had set up road blocks round Johannesburg; Beyers either did not hear the order to stop, or heard it and ignored it, with the consequence that the police fired, killing de la Rey almost instantly. The country was shocked by the tragedy, and so great was the distrust that even General Hertzog said that there was something strange about the whole business; however, Mrs de la Rey reported that she had asked Beyers why he had not stopped, and that he had replied that de la Rey had told him not to do so.

Generals Botha and Smuts made the long journey from Cape Town to Lichtenburg to attend the funeral of de la Rey on 20 September. Generals Beyers, de Wet, and Kemp were also there, three men who now regarded Botha and Smuts as traitors to the Afrikaner people. There was the car in which de la Rey had been killed, a silent accuser with its bullet hole and its blood. The great majority of those who attended had been commanded by one or other of the generals. So tense was the atmosphere, that Campbell-Bannerman's noble act of reparation now appeared like a cheap device, a stratagem to divide and rule. Botha suffered the painful experience of encountering the hatred of people who once had adored him, but he did not hesitate to move amongst them. He told them that he himself would assume the commandant-generalship, that he would lead the campaign against South West Africa, and that he would depend entirely on volunteers. The next day he made this information public, and not too soon, because simultaneously Generals Beyers, de Wet, and Kemp publicly demanded the dropping of the South West Africa campaign; they further demanded a decision by 30 September, failing which, a great gathering would be organised 'to compel them to drop it'.

It was on the day of General de la Rey's funeral, with General Botha moving gravely and heavily amongst his restless people, and General Smuts accompanying him, calm and confident amongst the hatred of many, that mother and son sailed out of Table Bay on the *Walmer Castle*, back to a country which, though at war with a deadly enemy, was at peace within herself.

It was a changed Oxford to which the Hofmeyrs returned. Of the South African Rhodes Scholars who had gone up with Hofmeyr in 1913, all except himself and Krige had decided to join the forces. Krige was a Hertzog man, and did not consider that South Africa had any moral obligations whatsoever; and that, for the time being, was Hofmeyr's own opinion.

The news from South Africa was disquieting. On the day after de la Rey's funeral, Smuts published Beyers' letter of resignation as Commandant-General and his own reply.

Beyers wrote: 'History teaches us, after all, that whenever it serves her interests Great Britain is always ready to protect smaller nations, but, unhappily, history also relates instances in which sacred rights and the independence of smaller nations have been violated, and treaties disregarded, by the same country . . . It is said that war is being waged against the barbarity of the Germans. We have forgiven but not forgotten all the barbarities perpetrated in this our own country during the South African war.' Beyers gave it as his opinion that the Defence Act did not permit South Africa to 'go and fight the enemy over the frontier and to light the fire in that way'. But should the enemy invade South Africa, it would be the people's duty 'to drive him back and pursue him in his own territory'.

Smuts replied to Beyers that the circumstances of his resignation left a painful impression, in that the Commandant-General had received all available secret information, and had actually drawn up plans for the operation against German South West Africa, thus leading Smuts to assume that he would continue to command the Defence Forces. He said that Beyers's reference to Britain's barbarity could 'only be calculated to sow hatred and division among the people of South Africa'. 'You forget to mention', wrote Smuts, 'that since the South African war the British people gave South Africa her entire freedom under a Constitution which makes it possible for us to realise our national ideals along our own lines, and which, for instance, allows you to write with impunity a letter for which you would, without doubt, be liable in the German Empire to the extreme penalty.'

General Botha rejected the demand by Generals Beyers, de Wet, and Kemp for the cessation of hostilities against South West Africa. At a meeting of 35 prominent commandants of the Boer War, whom he asked to serve under him in a voluntary campaign, he received unanimous support. But the country was restless. In the middle of October Salomon Maritz, who was in charge of the Union forces at Upington, near the border of South West Africa, having received from the German governor the promise of an independent South Africa, and permission to annex Delagoa Bay, went over to the Germans. Botha declared a state of martial law, and the Dutch Reformed Church in the Cape issued a warning against treason. Botha marched to crush Maritz, and defeated him on 24 October, Maritz escaping into South West Africa. But many of the men called up by Botha refused to comply, and gathered round Beyers, who was on a farm in the Magaliesberg. It was clear now that Beyers also meant to rebel, and on 27 October Botha scattered his commando near Rustenburg; Beyers and Kemp escaped, and Kemp eventually reached South West Africa. Meanwhile de Wet in the Free State announced his intention to join Maritz, but Botha, all the time using Afrikaner troops, routed him at Mushroom Valley, 60 miles north-east of Bloemfontein, and wept on the battlefield. Botha promised pardon to all who gave themselves up by 21 November. De Wet however would not yield, was captured in Bechuanaland on 2 December, and was sentenced to imprisonment. Beyers also would not yield, and on 8 December, trying to escape over the flooding Vaal River, was drowned, his death causing grief to both Botha and Smuts, his comrades of the Anglo-Boer War. The rebellion was over.

When finally it became known that Beyers had in fact rebelled, Hofmeyr took the treasured photograph off the mantelpiece. The episode was painful for both mother and son. Many years later, when her son had died, she did not consider that any biography of him should contain any reference to the Beyers episode. She did not approve of any biography that, to use her own words, 'raked up the past'.

Hofmeyr thought that Beyers' death by drowning was 'almost a merciful providence', for he questioned 'whether Smuts would have been able to rise above his personal animosity and to spare his life'. The young man's politics at this time were strongly influenced by his mother's neutralism. She never shrank from personal conflict, but she hated political conflict, and thought that under a great enough leader it would have been unnecessary. Her son was of the same opinion, and wrote to Cruse that South Africa needed a man like Onze Jan. He was extremely critical of Smuts, but at the same time he observed with apprehension the growing militancy of Hertzog's Nationalists. They had decided to launch a newspaper in Cape Town to be called *Die Burger,* with Dr Daniel François Malan, predikant of the Dutch Reformed Church at Graaff-Reinet, as editor. Hofmeyr wrote, 'The very name of the proposed editor is, I fear, sufficient condemnation.' He thought it good that the Government should be watched, he thought it bad that ministers of religion should enter politics, he thought that nationalism could not take the place of religion without detriment to the latter. 'Of course the Nationalist creed has much in it to attract the unthinking. In fact, if Smuts goes on making silly jingoistic speeches, I should be inclined to support the new party myself.'

Hofmeyr and Cruse argued for a year about the rebellion, and about parsons in politics. Cruse believed that the people in the Transvaal and the Free State had a right to rebel, and saw no reason why a parson should not pursue righteousness in politics. In the end he reproached Hofmeyr for his coldness, and said that with reference to the rebellion and indeed to the whole Afrikaner cause, he should try to feel, not merely to reason. Hofmeyr replied that Cruse had 'really hit off' his way of looking at things. 'I have been discovering more and more how unsentimental I am, and also that it is not quite so much of a virtue as I used to imagine.'

But he was not only unsentimental, he was also trying to maintain an almost impossible neutrality. Largely because of his neutralism, he had adopted a kind of pacifism, and this was encouraged by the presence in Oxford of a higher percentage of pacifists than usual, most of the warriors having departed. Like many young men of his time, he was revolted by the idea that each side should claim to be doing God's justice. His friend and mentor, D. C. Lusk, the Presbyterian chaplain, wrote to him from France that this revulsion was not a satisfactory ground for pacifism, because it was an objection to this war in particular and not to war in general. Lusk argued that pacifists placed peace before purity, 'which is not the order of wisdom that cometh from above'.

But Hofmeyr was just as powerfully affected by contrary influences. The great majority of his friends had only one thought, and that was to get into the war. Already news was being received of Oxford men who had given their lives for their country. The boys in the Balliol Club had the same thought. He himself wrote to Cruse that he would like to go too, but he thought it would be impossible. Six weeks later, he wrote to offer his services, 'military or otherwise'; but he feared his eyes would make military service impossible, and he expected a reply that his first duty to his country was to finish his course. He agreed with that view himself, but he wrote, 'I would like to be in things and doing something when so many friends are in the thick of it.'

In the end Hofmeyr rendered quite another kind of war service, which he was later to regard as one of the formative experiences of his life. He became the president of the Balliol Boys' Club. Of this appointment Secretan hoped the best, but he wrote privately that it would be idle to pretend that it was absolutely ideal. In fact there could not have been a better; Hoffers, alias Mr Hofmeyr, Hophmeyer, Hoffie, won the affection of the boys and the respect of his colleagues. The club was kept going throughout the war. He was at the club almost nightly, even though this was the heaviest year of his studies.

It is little wonder that the Balliol Boys' Club held such a place in memory, for there he was the recipient of that generous and unself-conscious affection that only the young can give. He was in some ways one of the least attractive of all the club officers; he was neither athletic nor debonair; but there was in him the ring of truth, of loyalty and steadfastness. He may not have found it easy to make friends, but no man in the world knew better what friendship was, no man would be truer to its rules. He may have been frugal, to some he even appeared mean, but to the Balliol Boys' Club and to its members he gave of himself, his gifts, and his time, with the most unselfish generosity.

Once Hofmeyr had made up his mind to complete his studies, he settled down to make the most of life in wartime Britain. This was his final year, and he applied himself to his studies and to the boys' club. He

was now, in pursuance of his classical studies, reading History and Philosophy with A. D. Lindsay, who became Master in 1924. The history in
particular was much more to his liking than literature. It was a strenuous
but happy year, filled with many joys—the work, the successful continuation of the club, the affection of the club members, the company at
Mansfield, the peaceful river. What was more, he rid himself completely,
as far as one knows, of the anti-Indian prejudice that he had brought
from South Africa. The victory was certainly in part due to J. Matthai of
Madras University, a freshman of 1915, later to become a Minister in
Nehru's first Cabinet. Matthai was a Christian, and he and Hofmeyr saw a
great deal of each other in the Christian Union and became friends.
Unfortunately there were no African students with whom he had anything to do, because undoubtedly he would have learned from these
relationships also.

He was now working harder than he had ever worked in his life. He
still kept the club open three nights a week, and he was determined to
keep that up till the end, but he was also determined to get his first in
Greats. No regular debates were held at the Union, and the informal
debates grew fewer and fewer. He would take his mother on the river,
but there were no organised sports. There were three firsts in Greats in
1916, D'Arcy of Pope's Hall, Scott of Queen's, and Hofmeyr of Balliol.

So ended the happy years. So happy were they, even in those unhappy
days, that thirteen years later, when Hofmeyr had already made his decision, known only to his mother, to enter politics, she, with a mother's
understanding of a son's nature, wished that he could rather have gone
back to Oxford. Despite the war, despite the frugality, despite the puritanical criticisms of Oxford's 'tone', despite the anti-English outbursts, no
one ever had Oxford more deeply in him. His mother, his country, Oxford—these were the three great loves of his life; and inseparably part of
Oxford was the Balliol Boys' Club.

Chapter 3

An Academic Career

WHAT was he going to do now? His first hope was that he would be given a job with the Students' Christian Association, where he could join Bull in the work that meant so much to them both. At the end of August 1916 he heard from the Christian Association. The Rev. G. B. A. Gerdener wrote, in the emerging written form of Afrikaans, that inquiries had been made 'from a responsible quarter' in regard to Hofmeyr's church affiliation. He himself had been under the impression that the young man was an adherent of the Nederduits Gereformeerde Kerk (the largest of the Dutch Reformed Churches), although he remembered his student activities with Ernest Baker, the well-known Baptist minister. In September Gerdener wrote that the church affiliation was not a stumbling block to him, but it might be to others, and a few days after that he wrote that such indeed was the case; further he wrote that the Separatists were working for a separate Dutch-speaking Students' Christian Association, and because of that danger the ministers of the NGK must not be alienated by a wrong appointment.

So Hofmeyr was not employed by the interdenominational association for which he had done so much, for the reason that he was an Afrikaner who did not belong to one of the Dutch Reformed Churches. This was in fact the religious counterpart of Hertzog's two-stream policy, the doctrine that the Afrikaner people must develop independently, with a church, a language, a culture of their own. It is difficult to define Hofmeyr's own attitude, because up to a point he himself believed in the independent development of the Afrikaner. When he was angered by English arrogance, he became an Afrikaner at once; but it was not a permanent condition. Nor could he really be enthusiastic about one's own Church, one's own language, one's own culture. Although a churchgoer, he himself belonged to no one church, but showed merely a preference for Presbyterianism after a Baptist upbringing. He championed Afrikaans, but his own language was really English. As for his culture, it was certainly not Afrikaans, but it was equally certainly not English; it was the culture of a man of the world (though not in a worldly sense), of a Christian and humanist, versed in the classics, and an admirer of British institutions. He was, however, no cosmopolitan—he was much more a South African. But narrow allegiances, especially when they were exclusive and intolerant, were distasteful to him.

He was therefore not attracted by Hertzog, whom he considered an apostle of a narrow nationalism, but all the same he held aloof from Botha's South African Party. He greatly respected Botha, but he considered that the Party was neglectful of Afrikaner traditions, and especially did he criticise Smuts for carrying his pro-Britishness to unnecessary lengths. Botha was in fact in no easy situation; in the 1915 elections he had lost 11 seats, securing only 54. The Unionist Party, largely English-speaking and strongly pro-British, had secured 40 seats. But the really important event, omen of greater things to come, was the advance of Hertzog's Nationalists from 16 to 27. In 1910 Botha had won 16 seats in the Orange Free State; in 1915 it was Hertzog who won them. Botha continued to govern therefore at the pleasure of the Unionist Party; his own Afrikaner support was declining, and Hertzog's 'two streams' were beginning to run with a vengeance. So Hofmeyr continued his policy of political neutralism as between Botha and Hertzog, and maintained his ambivalent attitude towards the war.

In the meantime and while the SCA negotiations had been pending, his old teacher at the South African College, Professor Ritchie, was looking for an assistant in the Department of Classics, and had naturally thought of his one-time pupil. Hofmeyr was appointed lecturer in Latin under Professor Ritchie, and in August began his teaching duties at the College. Apart from an uncharacteristic restlessness he found it pleasant to work under Ritchie, but he did not regard a lectureship at the South African College as anything more than a stepping-stone. His work left him a good deal of time to spare, and he could not bear to be idle, industry meaning as much to him as food and sleep. He therefore decided to compete for the J. B. Ebden Prize, which this year was being offered for the best essay on 'History and Control of National Debts with special reference to their liquidation'. He who had always had so little money, now began to study the control of big money. Without difficulty he won the Ebden Prize of £40 with an essay thought to be an extraordinary achievement for one whose main study had been the classics.

He was not satisfied to remain a lecturer. Up in Johannesburg the South African School of Mines had created nine new professorships, one being in the Classics. Hofmeyr applied for it.

In December the Senate of the School of Mines sent for Hofmeyr to see what he looked like. A friend urged him to buy a new suit, for he was wearing the jacket of one suit and the trousers of another. Hofmeyr's response was to buy a black Homburg hat, and resplendent in this, the jacket, and the trousers, he set out on his venture to the interior, from which he returned, at the age of twenty-two, a professor-to-be.

It was a tender age at which to be chosen a professor, even in a young country. The choice was determined partly by the brilliant record of the candidate, partly by the desire of the governing Council of the School of Mines to appoint South Africans where this was possible and profitable. Although the School was an English-speaking institution, and although many of its sentiments outraged Afrikaner Nationalists, being directed to Britain rather than to South Africa, yet its Council was ready to embark on a moderate policy of indigenisation.

Hofmeyr's appointment as professor at twenty-two was received with pride by his family and friends. It was of a kind with his earlier achievements, his Matriculation at twelve, his degree and Rhodes Scholarship at fifteen, his double first at Oxford. Where could such a talented young man be going? More and more people prophesied that he would one day be Prime Minister, but if they did so in Mrs Hofmeyr's presence, her voice would rise and the little stammer would come into it and she would say, 'Politics! Politics! when I'm dead he can go into politics.' She had reason too, for people were saying of Louis Botha, the big burly affable man, that politics were breaking his heart. And had not Onze Jan said, 'I am sick and tired of the whole business'? And did she not know what her son was like, with his gentle and upright and religious nature, and what would he be doing in politics, which broke much harder men? She still thought he would make his mark on the world; who could doubt it now? But she did not want it to be in politics.

Hofmeyr arrived in Johannesburg to find that city determined to have a university. The South African College had just become the University of Cape Town, and Victoria College had become the University of Stellenbosch. The Government had permitted a bequest of £200,000, which had been left for a future University of Johannesburg, to be diverted to the new University of Cape Town. The Johannesburg public was stung into action, and at a big meeting in the Town Hall on 17 March 1916, the Witwatersrand University Committee was set up. In 1917 the Council of the School of Mines created nine new departments in the arts and sciences, of which Hofmeyr's was one. It was a bold step, for there were only 171 students, fewer than half of them full time. The Witwatersrand owes much to that Council.

Among its members was H. J. Hofmeyr, a highly respected lawyer, with influential business and mining connections, who was a distant cousin of the new 22-year-old professor. He was a Cape Afrikaner—that could have been told from his names, Henry John—who 'understood the English'; his brother Willie was famous as a diehard Nationalist, but he himself accepted British rule without difficulty, and was himself so acceptable to the English that they made him mayor of Johannesburg. It is not known whether he smiled to himself when the Council granted leave of absence to its English-speaking members to go 'home', which meant of course to England, and when the Council decided to slow up the development of the embryo Medical School because it was impossible to get men from 'home'. Outwardly he took such things in his stride.

There was only one thing that could infuriate the Nationalists more than reference by English people in South Africa to England as 'home', and that was when born South Africans did it. That was not the only reason why the School was suspect; it brought too many teachers from England, it was loyal to King and Empire, and it had a high percentage of Jewish students. What was more, it was situated in Johannesburg, the town that had plotted mischief against President Kruger; and here it was that South African gold was taken out of the South African earth, and put into the pockets of *uitlanders* [foreigners]. And to cap it all, it was a wicked town. The hotels were rowdy and violent, there were sports and amusements on Sundays, and prostitutes walked about openly in the night streets, a thing unknown in Pretoria.

Nevertheless, although the Nationalists would hardly have perceived it, the School of Mines was already embarked on a process of indigenisation. The word 'home', meaning England, would eventually drop out of its vocabulary. Many of its students are today the most vigorous opponents of apartheid in the country, yet owe nothing of their opposition to 'imperialistic influences'. The Council of 1917 had appointed Hofmeyr to Classics, and J. D. A. Krige to German and Nederlands, and not long after would appoint Eustace Cluver, Margaret Hodgson, and Theo Haarhoff, all South

Africans. The members of that early Council knew really little about education, but they had vision enough.

Of all the new professors, the 22-year-old Hofmeyr, now almost twenty-three, was by far the youngest. His first salary was £850, which must be reckoned a considerable sum for those days. He and his mother took a modest house and although they lived unostentatiously, it was well known in the neighborhood who they were. The legends grew up around them, of the prodigious intellect, the fantastic achievements, the untidy dressing, the mutual devotion, the cats, including the one which was lost, and was found in the bathroom on Saturday night. When he left in the morning, Hofmeyr would caress the cats, and when he returned in the evening, he would lean his bicycle against the wall, and pick them up and stroke them. His name Hennie had now dropped out of use; at Oxford his mother had decided that Jan was to be used, and she herself called him by the diminutive Jantjie.

Mrs Hofmeyr soon gathered around her a new circle of friends. There were her neighbours the Joneses, Rheinallt and Edith. Mrs Rheinallt Jones was a wonderful hostess, and it became a custom for the Hofmeyrs to eat Sunday supper at her home in Saunders Street. Also frequent visitors to the house were the Henry John Hofmeyrs, and Herbert Le May and his wife. Through Henry John the young professor learned a great deal about the Council, and through Le May, a great deal about the school and its teaching staff. Most of the conversation took place around the tea table, accompanied by the eating of Mrs Hofmeyr's excellent cakes, scones, and biscuits; most of the conversation was about persons, and a great deal of it was about their weaknesses and lapses rather than their virtues. There is hardly one of us who does not like some gossip, even some scandal; but it must be said that in the Hofmeyr home, otherwise so frugal, so moderate, it became an excess.

It was natural that the young professor with the brilliant academic career should be much in demand as a speaker in Johannesburg and Pretoria. His themes revealed his interests: Augustus and the Empire, Imperialism and Liberty, Kruger, Rhodes and Hofmeyr. Empire was not something to be thrown away because of one's nationalism, nor was nationalism to be sacrificed to Empire. If Kruger stood for Separatist Republicanism, and Rhodes for Jingo Imperialism, then Onze Jan's greatness was that he bridged the gulf between them. This stuff was by no means

universally popular; *Die Burger* reported that at the Athenaeum Club in
Pretoria, 'Consternation was caused when one stately personage rose in
anger and exclaimed, "Such a bumptious little pup talking in that way
about men he has never seen or known", and stamped loudly out.'

One who was present wrote to Hofmeyr that such a thing had never
happened, but admitted that the English did not altogether like the lecture. The Nationalists liked it still less; they did not approve of this cold
and objective view of history; for them Kruger was a hero, Rhodes was a
rogue, and Onze Jan was a milksop who either did not recognise robbery
when he saw it, or was too afraid to say so. Discussion after the lecture
got warm, and according to the papers, Pretoria notabilities 'folded their
tents like the Arabs', and stole away rather than become involved. The
Minister of Mines, however, the Hon. F. S. Malan, joined in after coax-
ing, and said that Onze Jan's policy would triumph, and that 'the two
races would make one nation, peaceably flourishing under the British
flag'.

Afrikaner Nationalism had a mesmeric fascination for those who were
outside its sacred circle, and this fascination contained an element of fear.
Its opponents said that time would kill it, that no one could do without
the British fleet, that the Afrikaans language would die out, that the
Nationalists always fought among themselves anyway. But they were
fascinated nevertheless. The newly formed Eclectic Club in Johannesburg,
which was supported by Hofmeyr, Macmillan, and other members of
the staff of the School, concerned itself with many kinds of problems,
but it too was fascinated by Afrikaner Nationalism, and Cleaton Jones
persuaded Hofmeyr to give them his thoughts on Republicanism. Hofmeyr's address was an eye-opener to the members. He told them frankly
that for the overwhelming majority of Afrikaners, British policy had
been one of oppression, and that proof of his contention was to be found
in the title of Smuts's celebrated book *A Century of Wrong*. Hofmeyr
then proceeded as vigorously as any Nationalist could have done. He
called the annexation of the diamond fields by Britain in 1871 a robbery,
and the annexation of the Transvaal in 1877 a crime. He referred to the
fate of the 26,000 Afrikaner women and children who had died in the
concentration camps, and advised his hearers to go and contemplate the
sombre Vrouemonument at Bloemfontein if they wanted to understand
Republicanism. He told them that the British flag was hated by many as
the symbol of oppression, and that the benefits of British rule had not
availed to efface the very real and abiding scars of eighteen years before.

If there were any amongst his hearers who thought that the young professor was merely describing for them the emotions of others, their minds should have been disabused by his statement:

'It is a painful fact that to the ordinary Dutch-speaking South African the idea of an Englishman naturally arising (and I fear we could hardly expect anything better) is that of a fearfully superior individual who won't learn his language, who treats him, if not like a piece of dirt, then as a being in some grade between his exalted self and his native boy, and who is continually waving over him the glorious folds of the Union Jack.'

How deeply the arrogance of the British, especially the English, bit into the Afrikaner soul! How deeply it had bitten into the soul of this impassive, apparently unhurtable boy! And how deeply Afrikaner arrogance bites today into the souls of others. And this comment is no *tu quoque*, but rather the cry of the old doctor who watched Lady Macbeth walking in her sleep, 'God, God forgive us all.'

Hofmeyr warned his hearers not to try to crush Republicanism by direct opposition, and he put forward his own solution, that of an independent South African Republic, a member of a group of equal sister states. Thus the Englishman would lose his flag but save the British connection, and the Nationalist would have his own flag and President, and would perhaps find 'it not impossible to learn the lesson that the day of the completely isolated community enjoying full liberty is past'.

Hofmeyr's views of the future of South Africa were certainly Nationalist rather than Imperialist, and followed the Hertzog rather than the Botha line. It certainly was strong stuff for the English-speaking supporters of Botha to swallow at a time when the first Great War was still raging. If this was the kind of talk that one got in Johannesburg from a Rhodes Scholar and a Balliol man, what might the young men be saying in Pretoria and Potchefstroom, Bloemfontein and Graaff-Reinet!

But while Hofmeyr propounded these Nationalist views, he still remained a neutral. He was writing in Afrikaans to Haarhoff that Malan was an absolute failure. Both of them wrote scathingly about the imperialism of Smuts, whom they thought to be diabolically clever; but they were as fascinated by him as the Eclectic Club was fascinated by the Republicans. Smuts had been to England twice in 1917 on war business, and each time Haarhoff had gone down to London to hear him, each time reporting to Hofmeyr on his diabolical cleverness.

Hofmeyr wrote to his friends that he liked Johannesburg and his work, both of them being interesting. He had told Rheinallt Jones that one of the reasons he had wanted to leave the South African College was that the people there still treated him like a boy. But here at the School of Mines he was put on many sub-committees of the Senate, and discharged his duties on them not only industriously but also with an efficiency that showed he was not merely a scholar.

At the end of 1918, young Professor Hofmeyr informed the Senate that he had been appointed to the new Chair of Greek at the University of Cape Town, and that he would take up his appointment on the first day of April, 1919. His resignation was received with regret on all sides; he was regarded as an able head of a department, and being only twenty-four, he had doubtless a brilliant university career ahead of him.

Yet it is improbable that Hofmeyr was contemplating a university career. His real interest was politics, not classics. Had he not espoused the causes of Onze Jan, and taken Augustus as a model for rulers, and was he not now fascinated by Smuts, his diabolically clever kinsman-in-law? Was he not fascinated by the events that centred round the persons of Botha, Smuts, Hertzog, and Malan? His opponents often despised him for being not a 'true Afrikaner', and certainly in the sense in which they used the words, he was not. What they failed to understand is that he was in every bone a South African, and that Oxford and Balliol had not made him less of one. Although they did not know it, it was not his really non-existent Englishness that they hated; it was his growing belief, immature as yet and full of contradictions, in the brotherhood of all mankind.

South Africa differed sharply from older countries in 1917, in that there was no big career, no really important honour, outside politics. There were no high offices in the church to compare with Canterbury or York, no old universities, no famous public schools, no Army or Navy, no great titles, no public honours. If a young man was ambitious, and wanted recognition, he must go into politics. But in any event, people were already saying of Hofmeyr, 'There goes the future Prime Minister.'

The question was not whether Hofmeyr would go into politics, but when.

The Great War was at last over. In December 1918 Botha and Smuts left to attend the Peace Conference, leaving F. S. Malan as Acting Prime Minister. In January 1919 Malan asked Hofmeyr to become the Organising Secretary of the South African Party. Although Hofmeyr could see the political advantages of such a post, he decided to turn down the offer, partly because he was reluctant to commit himself to any party, partly because he wanted to become financially independent. Only a Hofmeyr would have thought of doing that on a thousand a year, but that was his intention; he meant to live on very little, and to build up a reserve. He had come to the conclusion that no politician could be honest unless he were independent.

Towards the end of February Hofmeyr returned to Johannesburg with his mother. The New Year was always a wonderful time at the Cape; the rains were finished, and would not begin again for some months. Day after day the sun poured down from cloudless skies. Both he and his mother were looking forward to their return to the gracious city and province where both of them had been born. They were leaving with regret nevertheless, she because of her many friends, he because he recognised that Johannesburg, for all its reputation for materialism, was the most stimulating, most lively place in the Union. The School of Mines itself was at the beginning of a period of great development. This year it would become a University College, and its Council would not rest until it had become a University worthy of the city. The Town Council had given a magnificent site of 90 acres at Milner Park, on a commanding ridge facing north, an aspect much to be desired in Johannesburg's sharp highveld winter. There must arise the finest university in the Union of South Africa. These new developments would now have to be put into new hands, for in January, after a long period of ill-health, the Principal Dr Corstorphine died. Even now the Council, and its members amongst themselves, were discussing what kind of man they were looking for, and where they would find him.

It took an astonishing decision. It decided to offer the principalship to the young Hofmeyr, who was 24 years of age. There were several reasons for this. It satisfied those who wanted 'a man from home'; it satisfied those who wanted a man from Oxford or Cambridge; it satisfied those who wanted a South African. Why look for an English Oxonian if you could get a South African one? And what a one! A brilliant scholastic record, a Rhodes Scholar, the J. B. Ebden Prize, and notable competence on the Senate sub-committees. There was the chairman's argument that the man to transform the School of Mines into a great university must be young, brilliant, and industrious, and Hofmeyr was all three. There was yet another possible reason, given by so many that one must attach importance to it, namely that the School was careless and irreligious, and that a man of strong Christian principle was needed to pull it together.

Hofmeyr was certainly not filled with vainglory by the offer of the principalship. He was in fact overwhelmed by it. His mother, while gratified that her son's brilliance was recognised, could see his unhappiness, and it was decided to seek the advice of J. L. van Eyssen, the trusted family friend. Van Eyssen wrote emphatically that Hofmeyr must accept the job; the members of the Council were 'hard-headed capable business men', who knew what they wanted and what they were doing. But the son still had misgivings; he prepared a humble memorandum for submission to the Council, expressing the hope that his name would not be pressed, saying that he had no such ambitions, and that the offer was unthinkable and remained unthinkable. He reminded Council that he was a great deal younger than all his colleagues, with an academic career inferior to many. However, if Council persisted, he would accept, provided that the University of Cape Town released him from his new appointment, and provided that the Senate assured him of its support.

On 15 March Hofmeyr was appointed at a salary of £1,350. The news caused a sensation in Johannesburg. Congratulations poured in on all sides. Mrs Hofmeyr told friends that her son Jantjie was 'a drop of sweetness in a bitter cup'.

He took his appointment with his usual apparent impassivity. But there can be no doubt that he felt conscious of divine leading, of the fact that he had 'been born for something'. He was impressed by the fact, and he impressed it on his friends, that he had 'done nothing' to secure this advancement, except, presumably, to work hard and do his duty. Certainly, there seemed to be no end to the divine favour, and he clearly seemed to have embarked on a road that would lead him somewhere. Why was he so insistent, not only at this time but later, that he had 'done nothing'? Why should one not actively plan one's future? The answer was not that he was averse to planning and preparing, but that he did not wish to appear as a vulgar and ambitious careerist. He liked the doors of life to behave like the doors of airport terminals, and to open while one was approaching.

Now that Hofmeyr had been appointed Principal, he gave up plans to take an Oxford B.Litt., for which no residence would be required. Reluctantly he also gave up his plans to take his mother to England in December 1919, and to visit Balliol and the club, 'before everyone has become stodgy and dull and married', so he wrote to Secretan. There was too much to do. On 1 August 1919, the School of Mines became the University College, Johannesburg. It now had 301 students, but on the morning of Inauguration Day, Hofmeyr told the assembled staff and students that the Witwatersrand could provide three thousand, not three hundred. The theme of his address was the nature of a university, which 'should know no distinctions of class, wealth, race or creed'. He discussed the mutual obligations of democracy and the university, and said that university institutions in South Africa still had much to do. In the evening a distinguished audience in the Assembly Hall heard Hofmeyr hint that the University College, Johannesburg, might soon become the University of the Witwatersrand.

It was a brilliant day and the most brilliant thing about it was the Principal's speech. On such occasions Hofmeyr was superb. He would start with a joke or two, always well chosen. Then he would develop his main theme, and conclude with a masterly peroration. He would throw his head back, and send his clear strong voice to the farthest parts of the hall, and that required energy and concentration in a day where there were no mechanical aids. But of course he had an abundance of energy. People who heard him often, and especially those who disliked him, accused him of speaking in clichés. One supposes that something of this was inevitable for a man who must have made a hundred speeches every year of his public life. But quite apart from the structure of his speech, he was saying things that people wanted to hear and believe; they wanted to be reassured of their validity, and here they heard them from quite the most brilliant man that South Africa had produced since Smuts, said with a sincerity that only the most hostile would have doubted. If older people were reassured, many of the younger were inspired, and were to remember such speeches their whole lives long.

Meanwhile Hofmeyr was turning out to be a planner in a thousand— even then perfecting the plans for converting the College into the University of the Witwatersrand. Massive Grecian buildings with great columns were to be erected at Milner Park, and hostels for men and for women.

The Council's vision was big, and Hofmeyr was keeping them busy with concrete proposals. They wanted a first-class university under a first-class principal, and they wanted to send Hofmeyr to the United States to study university development and administration. But Hofmeyr would not go because the funds which the Council proposed to use had not been collected for such a purpose. The Council took this moral instruction well; some members agreed with Hofmeyr, and others thought it was morality gone crazy. Dalrymple told Wylie that Mrs

Hofmeyr had said to him, 'I hope you're not thinking of sending him by himself, without me to look after him.' In any event, Hofmeyr was never to visit America.

Although Hofmeyr was proving so successful as organiser, planner, and administrator, he was finding difficulties with both students and staff. In May of 1920 his mother and he agreed, at the request of the Council, that until a Principal's house had been built at Milner Park, they would go into residence at the new men's hostel, provided 'he was in authority', and his mother was in charge of domestic arrangements. This was not a wise decision. Many of the students of the post-war years had served in the armed forces; they had talked soldiers' talk, lived soldiers' lives, and drunk soldiers' liquor. They liked noise and conviviality, just like the men at Balliol. Some of them reacted violently to Hofmeyr's discipline, unable to regard decorum as the point of living.

The atmosphere at the new College House was extremely unpleasant in those early days. When Macmurray and his wife arrived in Johannesburg in 1921, he formed the impression that Hofmeyr was trying to 'clean up' the university, and that his mother was going to help him. Neither Hofmeyr nor Macmurray found themselves as close to one another as they had expected. They had not seen one another for seven years, and in that time Macmurray had served as lieutenant in the Cameron Highlanders and had seen another side of life. In religion and friendship he had grown more tolerant and less dogmatic, less disposed to turn the world upside down, more ready to see virtue where before he would have seen none. Quite apart from that, an antagonism developed between him and Mrs Hofmeyr within the first week. The Macmurrays spent their first few days in Johannesburg at College House as the guests of the Hofmeyrs, until they could find a house, and Macmurray expected to renew the Oxford friendship and to enjoy some kind of men's talk. He soon learned that Hofmeyr did not have that kind of privacy; the apartment hardly allowed it, but neither did Hofmeyr appear to desire it. In fact Mrs Hofmeyr used to say, then and all through her life, in her shrill, emphatic way that was half joking and half serious, 'I don't live with my son, he lives with me.' It was with relief that the Macmurrays found a house and moved away.

Mrs Hofmeyr made no attempt to hide her opinion that the University College was a godless place. It certainly contrasted sharply with the more sedate South African College, now the University of Cape Town. Hofmeyr not only attempted to control the more unruly elements at College House; he also persuaded the Senate to appoint a standing committee to deal with matters affecting the women students, on the grounds that the behavior of some of them was unsatisfactory. It was said by an influential section of the students that he wanted to run the University College like a school, and many of them blamed Mrs Hofmeyr for this, and declared that she was really in charge. There was a cruel witticism on the campus, 'I am afraid that Mother will marry, and Mother's afraid that I shall marry.' The relationship of mother and son was often ridiculed. The students made fun of his clothes too, especially the cheap ready-made white suits which fitted him so badly. There was the story of the young woman student who after the first day of the academic year decided to go to Cape Town University instead, and applied for her fees to be refunded; but when Hofmeyr refused to consider a refund, she stormed out of the office crying, 'Keep the money then, and buy yourself a new suit.'

Yet while Hofmeyr had little in common with certain of his students, he exercised a deep influence over others, who still speak of him and his principalship with veneration. It would be superficial to say that he repelled the worldly and attracted the earnest, or to divide his students into gay and solemn, wicked and good, hedonists and puritans, drinkers and teetotallers. He already had the gift of being able to attract, especially through his speeches, those who wanted to find some satisfying use for their lives, who thought idealistically of man and society, who were already dimly sensing that something was wrong with South Africa, that the doctrine of the brotherhood of man posed tremendous challenges, which they in their youthful eagerness were ready to accept, especially when they were put by a man who had the gift of oratory. In fact this ability of Hofmeyr was to grow greater and greater, until he was putting these challenges, not to a college, but to a country. Two kinds of men and women listened to him, those who hated what he had to say, and those who knew that this man was in possession of a truth, the only truth, in fact, by which one might guide one's life. But there was a third kind too, namely those men and women who believed in the same truth but were quite unable to recognise that Hofmeyr was a custodian of it, because he seemed to them rather the champion of a morality that was narrow and joyless and, perhaps worst of all, pointless, because of which they came to hate or despise him or both. And when, in later years, Hofmeyr had discarded some of these lesser moralities, or admitted that he adhered to them out of taste and habit and nothing deeper, when he would sip a little sherry and play a Sunday game of tenniquoits (though never tennis or cricket), it was too late.

Between Principal and older, more rebellious students there came to be a kind of truce. They learned to behave more quietly than they had behaved in the army, and he permitted more horseplay at the graduation ceremonies than a good many people thought proper. Council decided, in spite of the stories of Sunday card-playing and idleness, that Sunday tennis would be undesirable. Dancing was of course permitted, and the Principal, though not a dancer himself, would put in an appearance at the functions. He did not like dancing; to Haarhoff he made the revealing remark that he himself would as soon take a pole and swing himself round it. But it revealed, not his attitude to women, but his mother's attitude to sex.

In the first year of Hofmeyr's Principalship, on 28 August 1919, the great Louis Botha died, worn out by his endeavours for the new and fractious Union of South Africa. His political ideal was simple, to unite the English-speaking and Afrikaans-speaking peoples in a new white South African nation. Yet that posed difficult problems. Where there are two racial groups in one country, and where their unity is the ideal, what language should be spoken, what flag flown, what national hymn sung, what foreign policy adopted? Botha would have been prepared to leave a great deal to time, but not so Hertzog's Nationalists.

The Nationalists were afraid of leaving things to time, for time would allow the Empire to eat up Afrikanerdom. It was all very well for Botha to talk of partners shaking each other's hands, but one had been victorious and the other had been defeated, one had gained and the other had lost. Surely it was sensible and just to build Afrikanerdom, so that there could be a partnership of equals. The only animal that could afford to embrace a lion was another lion. Yet every time Hertzog talked of building Afrikanerdom, some English-speaking voters took fright and went to Smartt's Unionists; and every time Botha made a gesture to the Empire some Afrikaans-speaking voters took fright and went to Hertzog.

Although weary of the tasks of mediation, Botha had gone off to the Peace Conference at Paris and Versailles, accompanied by Smuts. He opposed Lloyd George and his demand to 'Hang the Kaiser'. He opposed the plan for a triumphal march into Berlin. He opposed the plan of making Germany pay for the war. 'My soul has felt the harrow,' he said, 'I know what it means.'

He returned home and a month later he was dead. At his grave Smuts spoke immortal words. He called Botha 'the greatest, cleanest, sweetest soul of all the land—of all my days'.

So Hofmeyr's diabolically clever kinsman became Prime Minister of South Africa.

Just before his death Botha had declared that the reunion—*hereniging* —of his South African Party and Hertzog's Nationalists was essential; he emphasised that the Dominions were now independent members of the League of Nations, and voluntary members of the Commonwealth, so that there was nothing left to divide them.

Hofmeyr's position was enigmatic. He called the Nationalist agitation 'republican nonsense', and regarded Hertzog's trip to Versailles to ask for the return of the republics as amusing. Yet he had just prepared for publication his own article, 'The Republican Movement and the Problem of the British Empire', based on his address to the Eclectic Club, with its cry of protest against British arrogance. It appeared in the *South African Quarterly* for December 1919. The article expressed the view that a republican South Africa could effectively and heartily co-operate with a monarchical Britain in a Britannic alliance.

Today the word *imperialism* has an almost wholly unpleasant meaning, but even in 1919 it was a word and an idea hated by Afrikaner Nationalists. Hofmeyr's espousal of imperialism kept them at a distance, and it was a pity he did not find another word for it. He was really considering a bigger question, namely how to pursue simultaneously the ideals of international co-operation and national freedom. Why was it that Hofmeyr, holding the modern view that a republic might belong to the Commonwealth, was temperamentally incapable of working with the republicans in South Africa? Why was it that he was antipathetic to Malan and Hertzog? He criticised Smuts for not understanding the sentiment of the Afrikaner people, but he himself understood it only at second hand; he felt for it, but he did not feel it.

Why did he describe as 'republican nonsense' these efforts to achieve what he himself had recommended? Why was there this temperamental incompatibility? Of course his mother, his upbringing, his English education, his Rhodes Scholarship, all had something to do with it, and of course the Nationalists had noted them all. But part of the answer was that there was in Afrikaner Nationalism an exclusiveness, a shrinking from others, an isolationism, and ultimately a racial arrogance which did not accord with his deepest convictions. Perhaps if he had experienced what is known as Christian National Education, he might not have felt that exclusiveness and Christianity were irreconcilable. However, he had learned his religion in a church that was not much concerned with race.

He was not free of prejudices himself, but he was embarked on a journey of self-emancipation that would cease only with his death. To those of the left it was to seem too slow, hardly worth the making, to others it was to seem a journey made fifty, a hundred, a thousand years before its time. Whatever it was, it was a journey made by a man who tried to be true to his deepest convictions.

In March of 1919 he had sent a copy of his article on Republicanism to Patrick Duncan, a leading member of the Unionist Party, the official opposition to the South African Party of Botha and Smuts. Duncan commented at some length on the article, and his criticism was clear and to the point. He admitted that wrongs had been done, and even sympathised with the view that the Anglo-Boer war was in itself a wrong done by the British Empire to the republics; what he questioned was whether it was right for a public man to keep these memories alive. Furthermore, even if one admitted wrongs, one might only do further wrong by attempting to right them. The restoration of two republics and two British colonies would be disastrous, whether one's goal was republican independence or continued membership of the British Empire. It was South Africa as a whole that must be considered. If a South African republic were to come, it must be because a 'dominant majority of the people' wanted it. Duncan very much regretted the threat of his leader, Sir Thomas Smartt, that the whole of the Empire, including India, would be brought in to prevent South Africa from seceding. Lastly, he questioned whether republican independence was essential to the growth of a sense of South African citizenship.

Hofmeyr was delighted with Duncan's answer. He denied that he wanted to play on wrongs but he thought it would be good for the wrongdoers to remember them. The crux of his paper was that Botha took account of British sentiment, but Duncan's party did not take account of Dutch sentiment in the same way; for see how Botha and Smuts fought their own extremists, while the British leaders kept silent about theirs. Many Britishers were actually waiting for a moderate lead from one of their own. Hofmeyr urged the British openly to confess their guilt, and thought that much would come from it.

One should note that this conviction that the British must openly repent before any peace could come, was held by many extreme Nationalists at that time, though in truth nothing would really have satisfied them. How deeply did the unsentimental Hofmeyr hold it? He was experiencing in fact a struggle between reason and emotion, and for all we know he may have been surprised to find how deep resentment went in him. Nevertheless one must remember that his circle was not composed of those who held these extreme convictions, nor did he show any desire for it to be so. In the end he conquered his resentment, and one man more than all others was to be responsible. Emotion had to find some other channel of expression, and he was to become more and more devoted to the universal ideals of justice and love, or, to put it unequivocally, to that universal idea of brotherhood which was anathema to the Nationalists, and which they equated with promiscuity, mongrelisation, and sentimentality, a throwing away of one's God-given individuality out of mistaken obedience to commandments which meant something quite different. They treated Christ with respect, of course, but also with a certain amount of caution; they felt safer with God, who, in their opinion, had shown clearly at Babel that He liked separation of the races, but by his choice of Abraham had shown also that it was a good thing for one of them to be the Boss.

The man who above all others was to help Hofmeyr to conquer his resentment was of course Smuts. The new Prime Minister had just emerged from the disastrous election of March 1920. His South African Party had dropped again, this time from 54 to 41, with three independent supporters. The Unionists had dropped also, from 40 to 25. But the Nationalists had risen from 27 to 44, and the Labourites from three to 21. Many of Smuts's rural supporters wanted to be reconciled with their fellow-Afrikaners, the Nationalists. Was not *hereniging*, reunion, one of the last wishes of Louis Botha? What was more, many of the Nationalists would rather have been reconciled to Smuts's Afrikaners than ally themselves with Labour and its socialist rather than nationalist ideals.

So a reunion conference was held at Bloemfontein in September 1920. The key question was the position of South Africa within the Commonwealth. All agreed that the interests of South Africa should come first, but the South African Party was suspicious of the Nationalist goal of sovereign independence, and even held the now obsolete view that a Dominion could not secede. It therefore was unable to accept the Nationalist view that a reunited party must permit its members to make active propaganda for secession. The conference was a failure, though sovereign independence was accepted by all nations of the Commonwealth only eight years later. Smuts continued to govern at the pleasure of the Unionists and the Independents, but the Unionists, terrified by the thought that the Nationalists might come to power, were beginning to consider amalgamation with Smuts.

Hofmeyr himself was bitterly disappointed by the failure of the re-union conference. His neutralism in politics was a sign, not of neutrality, but of the difficulty of choosing between the broad tolerance of Louis Botha and the sturdy independence of the Afrikaner Nationalists, which Onze Jan had championed 20 years before, and which the young Hofmeyr admired and shrank from. Mrs Hofmeyr too was disappointed over the failure of *hereniging;* the new cleavages in Afrikanerdom, between Botha men and Hertzog men, were splitting Afrikaner families in two, setting son against father, and brother against brother. *Broedertwis*, strife between brothers, is always the greatest crime that a nationalist can commit.

There is no evidence that before 1920 Hofmeyr had ever met the great Smuts, State Attorney to President Kruger at 28, Boer War general, Transvaal Minister of Education, South African Minister of Defence, member of the Imperial War Cabinet, consulting architect of the League of Nations, and now Prime Minister of the Union. But now he was to meet him, for in October 1920 Smuts invited the brilliant young Principal to visit him at Doornkloof. Hofmeyr was then 26, Smuts 50.

The house at Doornkloof, near Pretoria, was made of wood and iron, part of a British army cantonment erected during the Boer War. Smuts bought it cheap, and lived in it till he died. It had no grandeur about it, but it attracted the notables of the world. One can hardly imagine anything less fashionable than the Smuts home and the Smuts family. Mrs Smuts went about without stockings, and with her shortish hair in a wild tousle. People did what they liked, and the Smuts grandchildren were once discovered on Smuts's bed, shining a torch into his mouth. When Smuts was not with his family, or in his wood-and-iron library, he liked to be about the farm, or to walk in the veld amongst the flowers and the grasses. Smuts had the gift of recreation, and climbed Table Mountain until past the age of 70. He had a contempt for Bridge, but liked reading and study. He was not an orthodox churchman, but once called himself a Christian, a Christ-man.

Although many people thought he was an atheist, or at least an agnostic, Smuts had a faith that the universe was good, and headed towards a good end. His faith was far however from the fundamentalism of Hof-

meyr. Smuts was not only a believer in the human future, he was fascinated by the human past, by the new theories of man's origins, by the
various estimates of the length of true human existence. The evidence of
bones, rocks, weapons, enthralled him. He was in fact in thrall, but to
the creation rather than to the Creator. If he enjoyed communion with
God, it was through the medium of the creation, for there his own
creative mind was excited by the evidences of a supreme creativeness. It
was excited by the contemplation of man, and of his history and his
prehistory. Sarah Gertrude Millin wrote epigrammatically, 'Smuts's
enemies say it is Smuts's great defect that he does not understand men.
He has a greater defect. He believes in them.'

Yet Smuts's belief in men was to a large extent the secret of his power
over them. Like Hofmeyr, he too, though in a different fashion, could say
things that people wanted to hear and believe, things of whose validity
they wanted to be reassured; when the world looked black, it was
good to be told by men like Smuts and Hofmeyr that truth, beauty, and
goodness could never be lost. It was true that Smuts could not speak quite
like Hofmeyr, not with that same force and eloquence, nor, if he spoke in
English, with that absence of an accent. On the whole, however good his
speeches, he did not speak them well; his voice was higher than Hofmeyr's, and far less powerful. On the other hand, Hofmeyr was a mere
boy, and his idealism came from books, student movements, church, and
his mother, whereas Smuts's idealism had met every trial in the world.
Hofmeyr was prodigy, student, university professor. Smuts was General,
Prime Minister, world statesman, and the darling of the British people.
Had he not gone to Tonypandy, where the Welsh coalminers were on
strike in the dark days of 1917 but had curiosity enough to come in their
thousands to listen to the Boer general from South Africa, and had he not
asked them to sing 'Land of my Fathers', and when they had sung it, had
they not just stood, so that Smuts could see that the whole thing was
over? And had they not given him a banquet in the Royal Gallery of the
House of Lords, in those same dark days, to thank him for all that he had
done, and had not Asquith, Haldane, Milner, Reading, Bonar Law, Gladstone, Robert Cecil, Churchill, and many others with famous names come
there to honour him?

So mother and son set out for Doornkloof to visit their famous kinsman. Mrs Hofmeyr was not overawed by the occasion. Although she had
been poor, this was not the first famous man with whom she had been
connected by marriage. In fact, she had, even before this occasion, got

into the habit, whenever Smuts was discussed, of making a joke about the connection. She would say with demure pride, which she could assume as well as any actress, 'Of course you know we are relations'; and when the hearer showed surprise, she would add, 'Yes, we are the p-p-poor relations.' In any case, why should she be overawed? Was her own son not famous? And did not people say that Smuts and Hofmeyr were the two great geniuses of the Afrikaner people? And was her own son not still a very young man, merely at the beginning of his career? If she was at all nervous about this visit, it was for quite another reason: the invitation had the smell of politics.

After the preliminaries were over, Smuts took the young man to the library, and there he asked him at once what he thought of the failure of the reunion conference in Bloemfontein. Hofmeyr told him that he thought it had been a tragedy, that Afrikaner Nationalism, instead of being brought back into a moderating alliance, would now pursue a more intransigent and uncompromising course, with consequences that he thought would be disastrous for South Africa.

Smuts asked him whether he did not think that the gap had already become too great to bridge, and Hofmeyr replied that it might be so, but that merely proved his often-stated opinion, that the attempt should have been made before the election, before the Nationalists had become the real opposition. Smuts made no reply to this, but the young man came to the conclusion that reunion had failed because Smuts had wanted it to fail, that coalescence with Thomas Smartt's Unionists was more palatable to him than reunion with General Hertzog and Editor Malan and their Nationalists. The truth is that Smuts had made up his mind, and that Hofmeyr had not; and another thing is true too, that Hofmeyr had a greater fear of Afrikaner Nationalism than Smuts had, and therefore hesitated to drive it out completely.

Smuts then discussed amalgamation of the South African Party and Smartt's Unionists. He wondered if Hofmeyr would become Chief Organising Secretary of the new party, with assistants in the provinces; in a few years he would be in the Cabinet. But the young man was not overwhelmed. He said he would have to be satisfied that in such a job he could work 'for the realisation of certain ideals', a satisfaction which was assured in his position as Principal of the University College. He did not want to run the danger of 'giving up for party what was meant for mankind.' But he was going to think over the proposition.

What else they talked about one does not know, but it is probable that it was on this occasion that Hofmeyr promised to send Smuts his republican article. A few days later Hofmeyr had a letter from Smuts, written in Nederlands. The Prime Minister thanked 'Friend Hofmeyr' for his article, which he had read with great interest.

'Freedom as objective, yes—but reached by the road, not of isolation and perhaps violence, but constructively—as an equal and free partner of the British and World League. South Africa as a part of mankind, acting to promote great human ideals . . .'

While the Nationalists were saying that Smuts had sold out to the Unionists, he regarded amalgamation as an historic step. 'The disbanding of the party of Rhodes and Jameson is one of the greatest victories yet gained on the road of South Africanism.'

Smuts hoped the Afrikaner Nationalists would realise the true meaning of what had happened. But they did not. By South Africa they meant an independent republic, in a League or out of a League—who cared, whichever was convenient—and ruled by Afrikaner Nationalists. Smuts ended his letter with cordial greetings to Hofmeyr and also to 'Poor Relations'.

Some five months after his visit to Doornkloof, Hofmeyr wrote a short account of his talk with Smuts in the library, and of the offer that Smuts had made to him. By that time Smuts was again secure as Prime Minister. The new South African Party, formed by amalgamation with the Unionists, won 79 seats in the election of February 1921. This victory was at the expense of Labour, who fell to 9. Hertzog's Nationalists more than held their ground, and advanced from 44 to 45.

Hofmeyr added a note to his account; he reported that he had heard nothing more about the organisership. But it did not really matter. He had made up his mind not to accept it. In any case it was reasonably clear that Smuts had his eye on him; and Hofmeyr, in his own modest and impassive way, had his eye on Smuts too.

The Senate had not adapted itself easily to Hofmeyr's elevation. Many heads of department could not accept with grace the appointment of a young man of 24 as Principal. Hofmeyr himself had no talent for overcoming this hostility. Macmurray, hoping to renew the Oxford friendship, found him bafflingly aloof, and so did many others. To make things worse, Hofmeyr and his mother, far from overcoming the hostility, added to it. They showed plainly which staff-members they liked, and these chosen ones were regarded by others as informers. Many thought Mrs Hofmeyr an interfering busybody, and there was the joke that Mr Hofmeyr and the Principal had been seen strolling round the grounds together. It was widely said that Mrs Hofmeyr had set herself up as a judge of the conduct and morals of staff and students, and that she passed judgement and he executed sentence. One thing is certain, that Hofmeyr did not at that stage of his life realise the danger of the gossiping round the tea-table. Margaret Hodgson, who later as Margaret Ballinger was renowned for her honesty and outspokenness, said, 'No one was safe from their tongues, not even the dead.'

There was certainly no considerable body of opinion amongst the staff which regarded Hofmeyr as a great principal. He was certainly not loved, though that was doubtless irrelevant. Nor was he widely respected, although his intellect and ability were admired. Some regarded him as arrogant, especially when some opinion or decision of his was questioned. Nor did his carelessness about his dress do anything to moderate the dislike of his critics. As for the students, most of them had no inkling as to what was going on above them. Some thought Hofmeyr narrow and sanctimonious; others, especially the idealistic and the impressionable, thought he was wonderful, especially after they had listened to one of the great speeches. However, few formed any appraisal of him, being, in general, concerned with their own affairs.

Hofmeyr was well aware of these tensions, some of which led to open disagreements, and he wrote to the Council, renewing his offer to return to an ordinary professorship, which he said would give him more opportunity to devote himself again to those studies in which his main interest lay. A week later the Council unanimously asked him to accept the appointment for another three years, and he accepted, provided the Senate agreed. Ten days later, the Senate unanimously approved of the Principal's re-appointment. What is more, it thanked him for his 'very considerable services', it recommended that the University should bestow on him the degree of D.Litt., and resolved that the Senate itself should present him with the robes. The Principal was then recalled to the meeting, told of the approval, the thanks, the recommendation, and the resolution, to all of which he replied suitably.

Two days later he took a step which alienated the Senate for ever.

Professor E. P. Stibbe, head of the department of Anatomy, and Dean of the Faculty of Medicine, was an amiable man. His students had the greatest affection for him, and his colleagues found him a pleasant though not strong personality. There was a story that he wanted to have full control of the Medical School but that the Principal thought it important to keep it in his own hands in those early days of expansion and development. There was also the story that when Stibbe first arrived in Johannesburg, the Principal had met him at the station, and Stibbe had given him the heaviest bag to carry, thinking he was a handyman from the College. However, no one ever suggested that either of these things had anything to do with the drastic action which the Principal took against his Professor of Anatomy.

Stibbe's wife and children, some time in 1921, went away to the coast for a holiday, and it was said that it was Mrs Stibbe herself who arranged that her husband should stay in the boarding-house kept by the mother of two of the College typists. Before, during, or after this holiday, people commented that Stibbe was more than casually friendly with the elder of the two girls; he would go into her office more frequently than most Professors of Anatomy go into the offices of administrative typists. He was seen walking to work with her, waiting for her to come out, and during his wife's holiday they had been seen at the cinema. There were those who believed that it was nothing more than an unconventional friendship, and there were those who believed the contrary, though no one ever offered evidence of it. All we are concerned with here is the effect that this unconventional friendship had on the Principal.

There can be no doubt whatever that an unconventional friendship of this kind, no matter if it had been nothing more than friendship, would have been highly reprehensible to Hofmeyr. Not only evil, but also the appearance of evil, must be avoided, especially by one who taught the young. People talked about this kind of thing, and that was bad for the good name of the College, which was in his keeping. The idea of a university wholly devoted to the truth, but indifferent to any other kind of virtue would have been to him incomprehensible. Hofmeyr was not a believer in absolute freedom, and indeed very few heads of institutions ever have been; nor is it a Christian value, except in a poetic and Augustinian sense. Therefore Hofmeyr did what he considered to be his duty. He wrote, two days after the Senate had showered honours upon him, on 16 November 1921, and told Stibbe that the appearance of evil must cease; and if it did not, steps might have to be taken against him. Whether he had an interview before or after the letter is not known, but one thing is known, that there was an interview during which Stibbe denied Hofmeyr's right to interfere in his private affairs, and refused to be directed by him in regard to his private conduct.

Therefore on 2 December, with Hofmeyr's letter and Stibbe's reply before it, a not very full meeting of the Council resolved that 'Dr Stibbe's connection with the College should be severed; that he be informed of this, and that, if it is his desire to do so he may bring the matter to the notice of the Senate'.

This was the time of the long College vacation, and many of the teaching staff were away. But some Council members who had not been present at the meeting were taken aback by the severity of the decision; some were disturbed even more by the suggestion that the Council had exceeded its powers, and had no right to dismiss a university teacher, except on the grounds of grave misconduct, without giving him, not mere permission to report to the Senate, but the opportunity to appeal to it against the decision.

Another and fuller meeting of the Council was held a few days later, and it was apparent that some members were extremely unhappy about the decision and would be glad to see it rescinded. But Hofmeyr had had no second thoughts; he made it clear in unequivocal terms that the Council had to choose between Stibbe and himself. Sorely pressed, the Council adopted an ancient stratagem, namely to persuade Stibbe that it would be in his interests to resign rather than to be dismissed. A committee was given this task. It was also decided to lay down more detailed procedure in regard to staff dismissals, so that unhappy events of this kind could be avoided. Finally it was decided, either at that meeting or a later one, to destroy the minutes of the meeting of 2 December, with its record of Stibbe's dismissal. Grave indeed must have been the Council's predicament when it consented to this action. Had Stibbe only known it, he was no longer dismissed. But he did not know it, and he yielded to the arguments of the Council's committee. On 23 December Professor Young reported to the Council that Stibbe had resigned as from 1 July 1922. The Council expressed appreciation to Professor Stibbe for his work, and agreed to advertise his post at once.

Drennan was one of the first to see the advertisement, and he was astounded. He knew Stibbe well and had never heard from him any talk of resigning. He showed the advertisement to Macmurray and they went at once to Stibbe, who said that he had resigned because he had been told that the alternative was dismissal. He also told them that the offer of the opportunity to resign had puzzled him, because on 3 December he had received notice of dismissal. Drennan and Macmurray were outraged by this information, and by the failure of the Principal to consult his Senate; but they were also determined to unravel the mystery of the dismissal and the resignation. They enlisted the powerful support of Dalton, and it was agreed that Macmurray would lead the campaign for Stibbe's reinstatement, because he had already accepted an invitation to return to Balliol as Senior Lecturer in Philosophy and could afford to challenge Principal and Council. He went to Hofmeyr and asked for the Stibbe affair to be put on the Senate agenda. Hofmeyr replied that Stibbe had resigned, that the Council had accepted his resignation, that it was a Council matter, and that it would not be put on the Senate agenda. Macmurray and his colleagues promptly requisitioned a special meeting of the Senate, and this was held on 27 February 1922, a tense, excited meeting attended by all members.

[The friends of Professor Stibbe came to his support and a bitter controversy ensued. This is recounted step by step and in precise detail in the definitive biography of Hofmeyr. Involved primarily were the validity and circumstances of the dismissal and resignation. But inevitably this spread into a larger and broader area. The affair became a classic jurisdictional struggle involving the status of and the relationships between the Principal, the Council and the Senate—in the American University structure, the President, the Trustees and the Faculty. The significant stages in the long drawn-out struggle were first, an arbitration which substained Professor Stibbe's right to appeal to the Senate but held that, since he had resigned, he could not be reinstated, and second, the intervention in the matter at a later stage of the South African Minister of Education which added fuel to the flames of controversy between Hofmeyr and the Senate. Of this later phase, the author wrote: 'The Stibbe affair had eaten up the whole of 1922; this new struggle ate up the year 1923.'

With the foregoing in mind the following excerpts selected from the original account will serve to point up the drama and poignancy that were involved in the affair. D.L.]

Hofmeyr was pale but impassive. Only the tell-tale twitch on his face revealed his knowledge that he was facing a crisis. By now he knew that his action had antagonised the most powerful members of the Senate. But he knew also that he had antagonised some of them already, that some of them had never forgiven him for his youth and success.

Stibbe was also pale and determined. He had had an experience granted to few men who are struck down by authority, for after many weeks of misery, there had suddenly come to him mighty champions, brilliant, angry, resolute men, as militant over his future as he had been resigned, thrusting their manifold gifts upon him to be used in his defence, confident that they could put right what had been put wrong.

Encouraged by all this, Stibbe addressed himself to the Principal, and said that he intended to raise the matter of his dismissal and resignation. Hofmeyr apparently ruled that such a discussion would be out of order; it was a Council matter and did not fall within the province of the Senate. Macmurray intervened at once on a point of order, and claimed that Senate was competent to overrule the Chair. That was true too, and Hofmeyr had no alternative but to put it to the vote, whereupon the Senate decided that Stibbe should be allowed to proceed.

Stibbe said that the Principal had given him an ultimatum that no self-respecting man could accept. Some two weeks later he was dismissed; but some days after that he was visited by a Council committee which gave him an opportunity to resign. He stated emphatically that it was clear to him that the alternative to resignation would be confirmation of the dismissal. He did what most men would have done; he accepted the chance to resign. But now he accused the Council of having got him to resign under duress, and of having been prepared in any event to dismiss him, not because of any proved offence, but because he had refused to allow the Principal to dictate to him in what was a private and personal matter.

Stibbe was filled with emotion and was trembling with his sense of bitter injustice. He considered he had done his best to be a loyal servant of the university, and to build for it a medical school of which both university and city could be proud. His return for that was to be forced into resigning for an offence of which no proof had been offered, no verdict given. Suddenly the Senate was electrified. They saw Stibbe, overwrought by it all, turn to the principal and declare that his mother was at the bottom of it all, because of her love of scandal and her malicious tongue. She was not only at the bottom of this, but of other things as well. What these other things were, the Senate was not to hear, because Hofmeyr was on his feet immediately, telling Stibbe that under no circumstances could he continue unless he undertook to leave Mrs Hofmeyr's name out of the discussion; and Stibbe, with not only Hofmeyr's ruling but also the expostulations of Macmurray and others of his champions in his ears, was suddenly overwhelmed by the misery of it all, and by the pitifulness of his own state, and sat down.

. . . . . The truth was, and it could hardly have been concealed, that Stibbe's dismissal had been cancelled, not by rescinding it, but by cancelling the very meeting at which it had been decided, and by destroying any record that the meeting had ever been held. This decision to destroy must have been taken by the Council itself, and it was Macmurray who eventually compelled the Council to admit the truth. This had one harsh consequence, namely that men of substance were to say of Hofmeyr the Principal that he was not to be trusted, and that it was wiser to get things from him in writing. Few generalisations are exact, and the generalisations of the hostile are less exact than most; this one certainly was. Yet the fact remained that whoever had ordered the destruction of the minutes, and that whoever had assured the Senate, after Stibbe had been dismissed, that the Council had made no decision, and that even if the Council of 2 December had no quorum, Hofmeyr must have consented to the order. If the destruction of the minutes was perfectly legitimate, that is, if they had been the minutes of an invalid meeting, then it was legitimate but unfortunate, and certainly highly unusual. But if the destruction had been the destruction of the minutes of a valid meeting that had taken a wrong or unjustifiable decision, then Hofmeyr had consented to something worse, and one can only believe that he must have felt threatened in his very self and being.

. . . . . Those members of the Council whose experience had been confined to big business were both angered and disturbed by the attitude of the Senate. They were angered because these men were their employees, in receipt of trifling salaries, yet they spoke to the Council as equals; and what is more, many of them could speak with a clarity and a command of language that few members of the Council could equal. It was a new idea, and took getting used to, that the University in some important way belonged to men who had not raised a penny towards it; and that they who had not raised a penny could be so truculent towards those who had. But perhaps more disturbing than all this was the fact that while the University was appealing to the people of the Witwatersrand to make their university the greatest in the country, here were its Council and its Senate locked in an ugly struggle. If things went on like this, the whole city, and perhaps even people outside the city, would be brought in.

. . . . . It was a tense Senate that met to hear Hofmeyr read the arbitration award. Cluver remembered that when Hofmeyr had finished reading it, he said, 'I am sure we are glad that the matter is settled.' Cluver decided that Hofmeyr had no conception of the anger and contempt with which the award was received, and no conception of the width of the

gulf separating him from his colleagues. The majority of the members of
the Senate were outraged to think that Stibbe might well have been reinstated had he not resigned, and that he had, according to R. B. Young,
and to himself, resigned because he was told that the alternative was to be
dismissed; but most of all they were outraged to think that the Council
had made use of this legal quibble. With bitter feelings the Senate recommended the appointment of Dr A. L. Macgregor as temporary Professor
of Anatomy and agreed to make a recommendation for a permanent
successor to Stibbe. But what had been an engagement had now become a
war. The Senate was now determined to define exactly the relationship
between itself and the Council, particularly in the matter of dismissals. It
was also going to fire at almost every meeting a few volleys in memory of
Stibbe. And the brunt of the fighting was going to be borne by Hofmeyr.

Hofmeyr had to attend this bitter series of Senate meetings. He
had to sit there and listen to the hard things being said, for though
personalities were now barred, it was his treatment of Stibbe that was
being attacked as harsh, over-zealous, arrogant, unmerciful, unjust. The
assault was launched always against the Council, but it was meant for him.
His old Balliol friend was leading it, and his new Professor of Classics,
Theo Haarhoff, his boyhood friend, had joined in it. His friendship with
Eustace Cluver had fallen to pieces. True, the relationship between himself and Margaret Hodgson had never been intimate, but now it was non-
existent. Moss, who was laying out the grounds at Milner Park, decided
that he could no longer continue with it. Gentle Mrs Hoernlé, who
conceded a Principal's right under certain circumstances to be concerned
with the private lives of the staff, wholly disapproved of the way he had
done it; and her genial husband, Alfred, with his fine presence and compelling voice and devastating judgements, said when he came out from
Harvard in 1922, that Hofmeyr had acted wrongly and stupidly and had
used the gallows to punish a peccadillo, simply because he knew too little
of men and the world. Hoernlé went further and said that by Christian
standards it was really Hofmeyr who was the sinner, with his coldness
and lack of mercy.

Hofmeyr and Rheinallt Jones also broke with each other. The wonderful Sunday suppers prepared by the genius of Edith Rheinallt Jones came
to an end. The Stibbe affair had been discussed in Jones's office, and
Jones had expressed his own opinion that Stibbe had been unfairly
treated. In his own way he had tried to moderate the fury of the Senate's

wrath, for he feared it would force Hofmeyr into such a position that he would have to resign. But one day Hofmeyr had come into his office, and charged him with being one of the leaders of the opposition. Jones was shocked and had said, 'If you believe that you'll believe anything.' Then he too told Hofmeyr that it was time for Mrs Hofmeyr to stop interfering in university affairs; so the great friendship ended. For some years there was no communication between the Hofmeyrs and the Joneses. Later, as the Joneses became more active in welfare, and Hofmeyr more powerful in government, circumstances and good sense brought the two men again together. But the old intimacy was never restored. Thus were alienated the Rheinallt Joneses, the Hoernlés, and Margaret Hodgson, five of the outstanding South African liberals of the time, all dedicated to the same cause as Hofmeyr, and the same principles, all alienated by the Stibbe affair from the man who was to become the spearhead of the revolt against the policies of white supremacy and apartheid.

. . . . . Hofmeyr, however, had one champion, untiring and quite indomitable, his mother. Her will was in any event exceptional, but when it allied itself with some great cause, as she thought this cause to be, and when, on top of that, it was her son's cause, and he was in danger because of it, then she would have died rather than yield. One had only to look at her at those times to realise that she was indomitable; it was impossible to think of her fleeing from any situation, or from any person; it was impossible to imagine what fear would have looked like on her face. Of these times she said, 'We did not walk on velvet.'

She knew of course better than anyone what her son was suffering. She could interpret his speech or his silence, his news or his lack of it. But never would it have been her prime purpose to save him from suffering, only to support him in the doing of his duty. Her love for him was hard as well as tender. This fire in her was to be abated only by time, and never by any circumstances save one, and that was his death.

She knew herself to be, by God's providence, of harder stuff than he. Yet he had courage, too, of another kind, for where she was fearless, he had to be brave. He was no weakling, this young unworldly man who had had an older man thrown out because he had been careless about the appearance of evil, and who had brought down the wrath of his own immediate world upon him. He said to his mother, 'I must stand or fall by this,' and she applied all her will to see that he did not fall. He was to live through a more tragic year than this one, but never one so full of suffering. At some time during the Stibbe affair, he felt that he could bear no more. He was literally ill, and could not eat or sleep. She had to take him away from his work, and they took a train into the country where they walked about the veld. 'I had a terrible time with him,' she said. Whether she meant she had to persuade him to continue, or whether she was grieving over his physical and mental distress, one does not know. But when they returned from their expedition, he was confirmed in his decision to 'stand or fall' by what he had done.

There was one judgement that might have gone to the bone: not that he had been harsh, or arrogant, or puritanical, but that he had been just plain foolish, a green inexperienced boy rushing in where wiser men would have trodden more cautiously. More than one person said, Macmurray amongst them, that before the matter had even gone to Council, Hofmeyr could have settled it with Stibbe 'over a cup of tea'. Of an older Hofmeyr that might have been true; it was certainly not true of the Hofmeyr of 1922. But it would have been strange if Hofmeyr had not at times been haunted by the possibility that an action which had plunged the university into such desolation must *ipso facto* have been rash and unwise. There were those who thought that he was arrogantly self-sufficient, but they were looking at the armour, not at the man.

. . . . . The crisis caused by the arbitration award was a frightening one. Some members of the Senate wanted the teaching staff to withdraw from every activity except teaching, from every committee, every voluntary service to the University. Macmillan and others tried to make peace; they wanted Senate to drop the whole Stibbe affair, and to defer discussion of the award for at least three months, but they could find little support. Their colleagues were determined to hear the report of their representatives at the arbitration, and they discussed it for some bitter hours before adjourning for a few days. When they met again, they received astonishing news: the Minister of Education, Patrick Duncan, had read the award and asked permission to attend a meeting of Senate to discuss the whole situation.

This was surely the heaviest blow that Hofmeyr had thus far borne; there is no greater humiliation for the head of an institution than to have an outsider come in to put things right. To make things worse, Duncan's request to intervene came just at a time when Hofmeyr was feeling a new anxiety. His colleagues were beginning to attack on another front, and were wanting to know exactly what charges he had levelled against Professor Stibbe. Should a man not be told the nature of his offence when he is advised to resign or is threatened with dismissal? And surely the Senate had a right to know also? Or had he been dismissed simply because he had told the Principal that he should mind his own business? Surely a man would not be dismissed for that? Hofmeyr knew too well the legal dangers ahead; he was fortunate in one thing, he had never charged Stibbe with more than the appearance of evil. But now his colleagues were saying he must do better than that; how could Stibbe be allowed to go out from the University having had no trial, having never been proved guilty of any offence, but with this shadow over his name? And must the young woman not be considered too? And Mrs Stibbe also, because it was known that the whole unpleasant business was threatening her marriage? There was something else as well: there was a growing opinion that the affair had been magnified out of all proportion. Hofmeyr must have seen the quicksands that opened out before him. What he had done with such a feeling of rightness, was appearing more and more unjustifiable. Therefore under pressure from his colleagues he stated, 'I have nothing to say against the moral character of Professor Stibbe.'

Then what had the whole thing been about? Was it for this Stibbe had lost his job, and suffered damage to his good name? Was it for this that the relations between Council and Senate, and Principal and Senate, had gone to pieces?

. . . . . The Senate decided to invite the Minister to a meeting, and the subject of discussion was to be the new constitution of the University, which, if it was to be workable, must give to the Senate greater responsibilities and powers. August 1922 was the most desperate month of Hofmeyr's life. Except for the support of his mother, he was virtually alone, and fighting for something more than life. He had always been cold towards Duncan, regarding him as a man who could have done more to forward Botha's work; now he felt even colder. But he could do nothing to stop the Minister's intervention, for even members of the Council were becoming tired of the struggle.

. . . . . Duncan's next step was to invite Council and Senate to meet him in joint session, so that the future working of the new constitution could be discussed. For Hofmeyr this was the bitterest meeting of them all. Dalton, Macmurray, Drennan, all were advocating direct advisory functions for the Senate. Hofmeyr expressed his view that any such concessions would make the Principal a mere mouthpiece for the Senate, but in spite of that the Council agreed to discuss such suggestions with the Senate. For the first time the Council could clearly see that he stood almost alone. It was decided that Council and Senate should each appoint committees which would confer together on the question of the constitution, so as to obtain that harmony which was essential for the welfare of the University.

. . . . . In the farewells and presentations to Stibbe, Hofmeyr had no part. The hero of the day was not the Principal, but the man he had got rid of. One presumes that neither Hofmeyr nor Stibbe had any parting word to say to each other. Stibbe went off with his career in pieces, leaving Hofmeyr behind with his University in pieces.

. . . . . Hofmeyr did no moaning over his fate. He thought he had done right, and that he had had to suffer unjustly for it. He had taken a great beating, and had thought more than once of getting out of it all, but he did not. Some people said it was insensitiveness but a great deal of it was courage. He had been given a job, and he meant to carry it through. Some of his colleagues he thought to be unprincipled men, and no words from Macmurray would persuade him to think otherwise. To think of trusting himself to their generosity was absurd; they had to be fought and he intended to fight them. He was the Principal, and he had the support of the Council, even although the nature of its support had subtly changed. In a personal sense, except for his mother, he fought alone. Bull visited the newly formed branch of the Students' Christian Association at the University and Hofmeyr told him the whole story. Bull found the situation baffling, and so it was; Bull wrote, 'I only regret being helpless on the touch-line—but I will pray.' There was literally nothing else to do.

Very few of those who attended the brilliant ceremonies of the inauguration and first graduation of the University of the Witwatersrand knew anything about its internal crisis. Three thousand people crowded the Johannesburg City Hall to see the first graduates and the first honorary graduates, Smuts and Reunert, capped and robed. After the Chancellor had opened the convocation, Duncan delivered the inaugural address. Surely he had the crisis in mind, and surely his words were in part for the Principal?

'In the ordinary business of mankind and especially in matters of government it is seldom possible to follow the straight line of principle. You have to veer and tack and compromise, and to realise that the better is sometimes the enemy of the good. But if policy is to be more than opportunism, and the art of finding it the way of least resistance, we must at least know what principle demands of us, and keep that in view amid the varying shifts of circumstance.'

The Minister then congratulated the Principal and his staff on being privileged to be present at the birth of a university and to lay down the lines along which it is to live and grow.

The day was a great one. The University of the Witwatersrand was growing and flourishing. So many new activities were planned that it was hard to imagine how Johannesburg had got on so long without a university. It was common knowledge that the brains behind it all, the planning, the skill, the drive came from that incredibly youthful-looking Principal at the dignitaries' table. He was a genius, that was the long and short of it, and was destined to go far.

After the festivities were over, the struggle was resumed. The joint committee had done a great deal of work, but Senate would not accept Council's conditions of appointment of staff. It insisted that no member of the academic staff should be dismissed without consultation with the Senate; and any member dismissed should have the right to appeal to the Minister. Council accepted the second proposal, but not the first. Advised by Hofmeyr, it demanded the right to dismiss as the right of an employer. Macmurray was gone, but his successor, Alfred Hoernlé, was an equally determined champion of the status of the academic staff; the relations between himself and Hofmeyr were correct and cool.

It is said by many that, with the exception of Hofmeyr's own friends, personal relations between Principal and staff had ceased to be. His heads of departments complained of his stubbornness and unapproachability; and since the Stibbe affair, many distrusted him. Margaret Hodgson, who did not like either mother or son, began to dislike them actively when she took on the wardenship of the new women's residence at Milner Park. Although the university year opened early in March, some of the women students had to return in February, and for that month they and Miss Hodgson lived in the men's residence with the Hofmeyrs. The divided control did not work and Miss Hodgson had to swallow a good deal of pride before she would approach the older woman. She was glad to move into the new but near-by residence, but then received notes from the Principal, asking her to see that her girls drew their curtains when dressing and undressing, to which she finally replied tartly, 'What's the matter with your men?' Things got so bad that she would not communicate with Hofmeyr except by note. She was a young woman of spirit, and she wrote a strong memorandum to the Council saying that she was a warden, not a housekeeper, and complaining that Mrs Hofmeyr had undermined her authority. For this she was brought up before the Council for insubordination; Dalrymple was in the chair and said to her testily, 'What's all this nonsense between you and the Principal? What are all these notes? Why don't you go and see him?' But Dalrymple could not be hard on a woman, and he told her to go away and be more sensible.

Hofmeyr and Margaret Hodgson, by then Mrs Ballinger, were to be in Parliament together. They were to be regarded by many as the two outstanding liberals in the field of politics, yet neither was able to see much good in the other. Certainly they saw little good in each other in 1923.

So the year 1923 came to its end with little improvement. Council and Senate sent back and forth their proposals for defining and perfecting their own relationship. Otherwise communication between them was non-existent. The Senate thought that the Council did not understand the true nature of a university, and the Council thought that the Senate was too big for its boots. At the end of 1923, the gulf between Council and Senate was almost unbridgeable. Little wonder that Council, replying to a question from Grey University College as to whether the Witwatersrand University favoured opening its Council meetings to the press, replied, 'Under no circumstances.'

It was a deadlock, a tug-of-war, with the danger that if nobody won, the whole University would come to a standstill, and if somebody won, everything might collapse. Here were two teams which should have been pulling together for the sake of the University, pulling against each other for what they thought was the sake of the University also; for each held the belief that it was vital for the University that its own side should win. There was only one solution left, and that was for a new event to happen, something that would make the struggle different, and convert it from a personal conflict into a search for a solution of an administrative and constitutional problem.

It was General Smuts who provided the solution, although that was not his purpose or intention.

Chapter 4

Administrator
of the Transvaal Province

EARLY in 1924 Smuts was faced with a by-election in the rural constituency of Wakkerstroom. He decided to make it a trial of strength and accepted the resignation of A. G. Robertson, the Administrator of the Transvaal Province, who wished to step down from his lofty position to fight for the seat.

The administratorship is a distinguished office; in his own province the Administrator takes precedence over any person except the President of the Republic and the Prime Minister. There are four Administrators, one of the Cape, one of the Free State, one of Natal, and one of the Transvaal. He is a kind of junior governor. He presides over an elected provincial council, and is chairman of the provincial executive. He and his three colleagues are the four senior public servants of South Africa, though they are seldom chosen from the public service; more often they are politicians, and the appointment is usually a reward for political services. Yet, once appointed, the Administrator is presumed to become non-partisan, and his loyalty is no longer to the party, but rather to the State on the one hand, and to the Province on the other.

Robertson's resignation was therefore a big event, and aroused hope in many a political breast. Amongst the first persons to know that these hopes would not be satisfied were the members of the University Council, who met to consider the astounding news that the Prime Minister proposed to elevate their 29-year-old Principal to the administratorship.

The news had a marked effect on the University Senate. Whereas Hofmeyr had been almost completely isolated, many began now to think better of him; it was hard to regard with contempt a man in whom the great Smuts had such faith. A number of members wrote to him on the day his appointment was made known hoping that he would not resign the principalship and saying that they needed his help; Hoernlé was one of those who signed it, but not Drennan, Haarhoff, Dalton, Lehfeldt, or Moss. However, Drennan, Haarhoff, and Moss were three of the one hundred and sixty-four people whose letters of congratulation he kept till his death. Senate gave the retiring principal a farewell dinner at the Carlton, and passed an unopposed motion thanking him for his 'distinguished services'.

Two of the messages he received had especial meaning in showing that there were in 1924 those who felt that South African politics were avoiding more fundamental issues, particularly those of race. Edgar Brookes, Professor of History at the Transvaal University College, wrote, 'All who would write ourselves down as Liberals, were there a Liberal Party in South Africa, were delighted.' Theo Haarhoff wrote, 'I hope still that you will one day found that Liberal Party; you have a chance that no one else has.'

Smuts wrote:

> As I last told you at Groote Schuur it was my plan to get you away from pure academic work as soon as possible, and to introduce you to the political life. With an eye to the future I thought it would have been wrong if you developed too academically. Fortunately the opening came sooner than I expected, and I thank you for not hesitating . . .
>
> Where I can help you and thereby help the country, I shall not hesitate for a moment.
>
> Warm greetings to Poor Relations.
> Always faithful
> J. C. Smuts

So there it was. Hofmeyr had already consented to be introduced by this great sponsor to the political life. He was during the next few years to remind many people on many occasions that he was not a party man, and was even to be reported as saying that he hoped never to be one. Certainly he observed a strict impartiality while he was Administrator, and would smile when asked his politics, so that he was portrayed as a Buddha, affable, benign, rotund and enigmatic.

In April he and his mother moved to Bryntirion, in Pretoria, into a house which, while not so grand as the present official residence, was the biggest they had yet lived in. He liked living in a big house; it gave more room for the cats and his books. Further, it enabled him to have some privacy. A new custom began to grow, namely that, when he had visitors who had come to talk about business and affairs, his mother would leave them alone, but would either join them or have them join her for tea. He had his own tennis friends too, and spent Saturday afternoons with them; he was a vigorous player of slightly more than average skill, and played with a pugnacity that added zest to the game. Play was enlivened by dispassionate praise for one's own brilliance, and hypocritical sympathy for one's opponent's weaknesses. Those who did not like him thought he took a mean delight in beating people; those who liked him enjoyed every minute of those games.

He and his mother no longer lived so frugally, but they did not live extravagantly. His salary was now £2,500 a year, and he began collecting the private means which he thought indispensable for an honest politician. Yet when Bull had a hard time with family illnesses, it was Hofmeyr who collected £120 for him, to which he was the biggest contributor. Of all the adjectives that were used to describe his spending of money, *careful* was certainly the fairest one, and *responsible* was the truest; and this responsibility was to him a Christian responsibility, the sense of being steward of his own possessions.

These five years were to be the most satisfying of his life. His elevation to the administratorship had come as a miracle. At the University he had had to grit his teeth every day, and waste half his energy in the futile tug-of-war. Many people thought, and some had said openly to him, that he had failed as a principal. Then in the twinkling of an eye, his prestige had been, not only restored, but doubled and trebled. What was more, he was doing the job for which he was born. He was happy because he was successful. No one knew better than he how to manage an administrative machine, and in a few days he had mastered it.

There would never be any question as to who ran the Transvaal. He had suddenly become a great man, and his mother an important woman, and both of them enjoyed it. From the public servants in the Transvaal he received a deference such as one does not experience at universities. He was still extremely careless about his dress; although he was one of the best-paid men in South Africa, he continued to buy the cheapest of ready-made suits and to wear boots, but he made the same conventional gesture as he had made in 1916, namely, he wore a dark hat.

He was so quick to master the provincial machine that he soon knew the machinery better than some of his officials; his manner of correcting errors was brusque rather than rude, but he offended some of his subordinates, especially those who were twenty to thirty years older than he. Although he never quite lost this brusqueness, he was to grow more considerate of those who were not so quick as he. Equally quickly he mastered the functions of a provincial council and its place in the constitutional machinery of the country. Many of his councillors were grey-beards, and he told them what councils and councillors could and could not do; nor was the crime of his youth mitigated by the fact that he was always right. The leader of the Nationalists in the Council was the redoubtable C. H. Stoffberg, who was devoted to the cause of his people and the education of their children. He welcomed Hofmeyr formally on behalf of the Nationalists, but determined to watch him closely, for in spite of the new Administrator's early assumption of the most magnificent impartiality, everyone knew now that he was a Smuts man, and had been brought up in English.

In fact Hofmeyr now used more Afrikaans than ever before or ever after in his life. He knew the simple domestic idiom, but not the more literate idiom in which the language is rich; therefore his more literate Afrikaans bore a strong resemblance to English, and he found some difficulty in remembering to use the double negative, which came into the language from French and not from Nederlands. Hofmeyr's use of Afrikaans did not in any way lessen the Nationalists' suspicions of him; it was not only the question of his background, there was also the question of that Provincial Finances Commission of which he had been a member, and which had produced recommendations which showed that the Commission had more concern for mechanical efficiency and economy than for what Stoffberg would have called 'the soul of the people'.

Hofmeyr's predecessor A. G. Robertson had no luck in the by-election at Wakkerstroom. The Nationalists won the seat, and Smuts decided to appeal to the country. When he had absorbed the Unionist Party in 1921, the new elections had given him a majority of 22 over all parties. But now three years later the Nationalists increased their total from 45 to 63, and having a pact with the Labour Party's 18 members, had now a substantial majority over Smuts and his South African Party of 53. It was 1924 that made it finally clear that, for better or for worse, Afrikaner Nationalism had become the greatest political power in the land. Something had gone wrong with Botha's policy of conciliation, and from this time on the trend was clear, subject to temporary deviations, namely that the Nationalist Party became more and more the party of the Afrikaner, and the South African Party (and later the United Party) became more and more the party of the other white races, and of the Cape coloured people also, until they were removed to a separate roll.

Hofmeyr wrote to the new Prime Minister, General Hertzog, saying that he did not regard the Administratorship as party-political in nature, but he acknowledged that the Administrator should be someone who could co-operate with the government of the day. 'As far as *I* am concerned there is so far no information available which makes me feel that I am compelled to answer this question in the negative.'

Nevertheless the Prime Minister might want to have a little more certainty than this! Therefore in order to give freedom to him, Hofmeyr added, 'Unless it is your wish that I should remain on as Administrator, I am ready to place my resignation in your hands.'

The Prime Minister delicately declined to express such a wish, but wrote that it was for Hofmeyr himself to decide whether he would be able to give and receive that amount of co-operation necessary to the carrying out of his responsible duties. Hertzog concluded, with a generosity of feeling that has now quite disappeared from the South African political scene:

'This question is so personal a one, as far as you are concerned, that you will recognise at once that I cannot help you with advice, without running the danger either of being unjust to you, or of going counter to the interests of the Province.'

Hofmeyr replied to this that he had not been seeking advice from the Prime Minister, but rather offering him freedom of action. However, it appeared from his letter that the Prime Minister did not wish the Administrator to resign. Therefore, Hofmeyr intended to remain in his post, and was ready to work with the Prime Minister for the good of South Africa.

Much was to be made later of the fact that the Prime Minister at no time expressed a wish that Hofmeyr should remain in his post, and that therefore Hofmeyr should have handed in his resignation. These facts were known because Hofmeyr had made them known to the Provincial Council when he was asked whether he intended to remain in his post now that Smuts had been defeated. Then *Ons Vaderland* took it up, and maintained that Hofmeyr had promised to offer his resignation; it also argued that of course the Administratorship was party-political, and quoted the case of Dr Ramsbottom, who, when his term as Administrator of the Free State came to an end in 1915, was not reappointed by Botha, presumably because he was known to be a friend and supporter of Hertzog.

Hofmeyr was stung by this imputation of dishonesty and was not at all soothed by the fact that the paper had called it 'political dishonesty'. He took advantage of another question in the Council to state his case, and said he was satisfied that the Prime Minister did not wish him to resign. He denied that he was influenced by considerations of personal ambition or material advantage. The Prime Minister's view of the functions of the Administrator and his own views coincided. Therefore he would remain in office unless removed by the Government.

General Hertzog gave what appeared to be the final blow to the opposition to Hofmeyr's appointment; he was asked in the new Parliament, and by one of his own followers, whether it was Government policy to leave the Administrators as they were, and if not, whether the Government would inform such persons. The Prime Minister replied that the post was not political; all that was important was that the Administrator at the time of his appointment should enjoy the confidence of the majority, and that he, in any case, should co-operate in a spirit compatible with the political feeling of the majority. So that was that.

Yet the whole matter was to be reopened in a few months, and in a tricky manner. Sir John Adamson, the English-speaking and British-born Director of Education in the Transvaal, handed in his resignation. His obvious successor was H. S. Scott, his second-in-command, generally considered a competent, sound, acceptable, and well-qualified man, of outstanding character and personality. But Scott was also English-speaking and British-born, and there was a strong feeling in the Transvaal, especially now that the Nationalists ruled the country, that it was time for one of their own people to look after the education of their children. What is more, Scott had also been a member of the Provincial Finances Commission, whose recommendations on rural education many Nationalists found disquieting. It is true that the white population of the Transvaal was fairly evenly divided between the two language groups, but after all they had just had one Britisher as Director; surely it was time to have an Afrikaner. Stoffberg had already made known to the Administrator the deepest longings of the Nationalists of the Transvaal and had prophesied the gravest unrest if another English-speaking person were appointed.

Now before such appointments are made by the Provincial Executive, the Public Service Commission makes a recommendation, and the Executive may disregard this only if the Government agrees.

Hofmeyr approached the matter with the greatest caution and foresight. He was in a ticklish situation; his Executive consisted of four members, two Nationalists and two South African Party. Should they take sides—and they often did—the Administrator had to make the decision. He knew that feelings would run high over this new appointment, and he consulted each of his Executive members separately and proposed to them that Scott should be appointed to act temporarily while Adamson was on leave before his resignation took final effect. Then both Administrator and Executive would be able to see how Scott measured up to the new position. Meanwhile the matter would be referred to the Public Service Commission, whose job it was to look at the matter from a national rather than a local point of view, and to see that the claims of seniority and efficiency were balanced as far as it was possible.

When Stoffberg made known this decision to the Nationalist Party caucus, they immediately sent a deputation to Hofmeyr, and asked him to give his deciding vote for the appointment forthwith of Dr N. M. Hoogenhout, who was Principal of the Normal College in Pretoria, as Director of Education. Hofmeyr regretted that he could not oblige them. If the Public Service Commission recommended Scott, on what grounds could he reject him? On the grounds that he was British-born? That was unthinkable. There was only one condition that was important, and that was whether Scott was able to do justice to the aspirations of the Transvaal Afrikaners. That was why he was given the acting appointment, so that his ability could be tested. Hofmeyr assured the deputation that he understood the depth and sincerity of their feelings.

But he went a step further. He told them that if the Commission recommended Scott when Adamson finally retired, and he the Administrator agreed with them, then he would discuss the whole matter with the Prime Minister. If General Hertzog wished him to vote against Scott, and he felt unable to agree, then he would certainly seriously consider resigning his position as Administrator. Hofmeyr made it clear, however, that he was not promising to resign.

It took the members of the Public Service Commission a long time to make up their minds, but in November they recommended Scott. Hofmeyr had already made up his own. He was satisfied with Scott and was not prepared to commit the injustice of rejecting him. That for him would have been a real injustice, whereas the injustice towards the Afrikaner people was problematical. But there was already a possibility that he would not need to act; Pienaar, one of the South African Party men on the Executive, was wavering in his support of Scott. The political atmosphere was becoming emotional, and some of his own supporters wanted an Afrikaner. If then the Executive voted three to one against Scott's appointment, Hofmeyr decided that he would not vote at all; in the first place because of the impartiality of his position, in the second place because to vote would destroy the impartiality to no purpose.

Stoffberg was beginning to acquire a reluctant respect for the young Administrator, as also were the other Nationalist councillors. This trust from both sides was very pleasant to Hofmeyr, and accorded well with his temperament. It would have been easier, therefore, if the Executive had voted three to one against Scott, and the Administrator could have remained silent. But Pienaar decided to vote for Scott, and Hofmeyr therefore had to give the crucial vote. He wrote to Stoffberg and told him that in his opinion Scott was the man for the job, but he would in accordance with his promise take the matter to the Prime Minister. He assured Stoffberg that he understood the gravity of his decision, and hoped it would not cause any change in their relationship.

The Prime Minister again showed his quality. He said that he did not wish to be drawn into the affair, but told Hofmeyr that had he been the Administrator he would not have seen how such a recommendation could be ignored; it was a pity that in such an important case, the Public Service Commission had to recommend, but that was the law and one must take the law as one found it. He himself would find it impossible to justify to Parliament the passing over of a man merely because he was not an Afrikaner.

Speaking to the Executive, Hofmeyr said (according to his own notes):

'. . . it is never easy and often unwise to neglect popular sentiment. But those who are called to a position of leadership as are members of the Executive Committee must have the strength to be able to set such sentiment aside in those cases where it is wise to do so. They can never justify their actions merely by reference to the existence of popular sentiment—they must at least be able to find an adequate ground for its existence. If they are not satisfied that they are able to find such a ground, then it is their duty to refuse to give way to that sentiment. And it is because I for my part cannot find such an adequate ground in this case that I refuse to vote for the rejection of the Commission's recommendation.'

So Scott was appointed Director by three votes to two, and Stoffberg and his Nationalist colleague walked out of the executive meeting in protest.

Hofmeyr's visit to the Prime Minister was the second within a few days. Hertzog's Minister of Justice and Deputy Prime Minister, a corpulent, genial, astute Transvaaler called Tielman Roos, had spoken at the Free State Nationalist Congress the previous week, and had said categorically that the only honourable thing for the Administrator to do was to resign, also the members of the Public Service Commission and a few other bodies; the Government carried a heavy burden and these persons did nothing to help it.

There is such a thing as Cabinet responsibility, and Hofmeyr called at once on the Prime Minister to make sure that he had not changed his ground. Hertzog assured him he had not. The *Rand Daily Mail*, commenting editorially, thought that Hofmeyr need not have offered his resignation in the first place. This editorial moved Roos to take the unprecedented step of writing to the *Rand Daily Mail*, and reaffirming that 'a sense of self respect' should have led certain officials to resign.

Roos wrote:

'You are entirely in error in saying that one of the Administrators placed his resignation in the Prime Minister's hands.

'He did not. His letter said that he would resign unless he was asked to continue.

'He was not asked to continue.

'He has not resigned.'

The Opposition tried naturally but unsuccessfully to blow up the Hertzog-Roos disagreement into a crisis. It was known that Hertzog was not an intimate of Roos's; he had made him Deputy Prime Minister more because of his power in the Transvaal than for any other reason. Roos was the more spectacular figure and was called the Lion of the North; he was bigger, more hearty, and the kind of speaker who could keep an audience listening to him, whereas his chief had a poor voice and made no concessions to the popular taste. One thing was clear, that at this point neither of them wanted to quarrel in public, for the pleasure of their political opponents. Hertzog said he had already made his position clear in Parliament, and Roos said he had nothing to add to or subtract from the opinions he had already expressed. Nor did the Prime Minister pay public attention to the resolution of the Transvaal Nationalist Party Executive, giving full support to Roos. The crisis failed to ripen.

The Transvaal Nationalist resolution was the work of Stoffberg, who was incensed to think that though the Government was Nationalist, it was impossible to get an Afrikaner as Director of Education. One could not rely on Hofmeyr, that was clear; he denied that he was a Smuts man, but he certainly was no Nationalist, for no Nationalist could ever have said that one 'must have the strength to be able to set aside sentiment where it was wise to do so'. Where Afrikaner sentiment was concerned, wisdom was irrelevant. Both Stoffberg and Roos were still determined to get rid of the Administrator.

As for Hofmeyr, he was thoroughly enjoying himself. Whether he remained on as Administrator, or whether he were forced out, his reputation would be enhanced by it. His handling of the controversy had received much praise from politicians and non-politicians, from Nationalists as well as from Smuts men. This crisis was very different from the university one, for one thing he had not made it, for another he had tremendous support. Meanwhile he went on imperturbably with his work, making plans for expansion and improvements in every department of provincial affairs. It was this compound of detachment, humanity, and efficiency that kept his critics somewhat in awe of him. If their cause had been less important, they would have come to terms with him. But their cause was nothing less than the strengthening of the Afrikaner people, in preparation for the great struggle which lay ahead of a white people on a black continent. Anyone who did not identify himself with the struggle must be pushed aside, no matter how honourable, how efficient, how impartial, how punctilious in the use of both official languages. It was a pity that General Hertzog was being so legalistic, but wait until the Provincial Council reassembled!

Hofmeyr had written to Secretan and given him an account of the exciting events of the year, written in his usual dispassionate manner. He predicted a break in the Nationalist Party. Hertzog would not be able to stand the strain of office for long, but Roos was physically stronger, and would lead the extreme Republicans and oust his leader. In fact, Roos died long before Hertzog, and died a sick and discredited man. It was left to other extreme Republicans to do the ousting of the man who had, more than any other, built Afrikanerdom.

Hofmeyr's reputation reached a new high point in the second year of his administratorship. Stoffberg moved that the Administrator should resign because he neither had the confidence of the majority of the Council, nor did he represent the political views of the Government. Stoffberg said that although the South African Party was in a minority, it had a majority on the Executive, by which he meant of course that the Administrator was a partisan. He had nothing personally against the Administrator; if he would join them they would welcome him with open arms. There was loud laughter and applause at this, which became yet louder when a South African Party man called out, 'He hasn't joined *us* yet.' Then a member of the South African Party asked what lay behind the motion, and whether it was not the appointment of Mr Scott as Director of Education? Would Councillor Stoffberg confess it?

Hofmeyr listened to this debate with the keenest enjoyment. So often impassive, or apparently so, now he was alert, fully participating, snorting with laughter when the jokes were good. It was a comic-opera affair, with Stoffberg trying to eject a man he couldn't help approving of, knowing that he would get support from the Deputy Prime Minister and the cold shoulder from the Prime Minister, with the English-speaking Labour members putting up a half-hearted show of fierceness, because they knew that half of the trouble was that Scott was English-speaking, with the South African Party guffawing at every crack by the Administrator, almost as though he were really one of them after all, and the Administrator with punctilious impartiality piloting through a resolution he intended to take no notice of. It was carried 26-19, with Nationalists and Labour for and South African Party against; the Nationalists greeted the result with enthusiasm, but everyone knew that Hofmeyr had won.

Two days after Hofmeyr's triumph, the discomfited Nationalists loosed their bomb upon the country from Parliament in Cape Town. Most of the Nationalist and Labour members of Parliament for the Transvaal, including three Transvaal Cabinet Ministers, signed a document supporting the Transvaal Provincial Council resolution, and calling on Hofmeyr to resign.

This second indiscretion on the part of Roos and his friends was much more serious than the first. They defended it on the grounds that it was the Prime Minister himself who had laid down that an Administrator should have the confidence of his Council, and Hofmeyr had now clearly lost it. Some of the big papers called it a crisis, and Smuts, speaking at Stellenbosch, compared the situation with that of 1912, when Hertzog made his famous 'two-stream' speech, after which Botha resigned as Prime Minister and reformed the Cabinet without his determined colleague. But even in spite of the seriousness of Roos's second indiscretion, the two situations were not really similar. Roos was disagreeing with Hertzog on a matter of constitutional procedure, while Hertzog had disagreed with Botha on a fundamental issue, namely whether Afrikaner resurgence or Anglo-Afrikaner co-operation was the big political task of the day.

Nevertheless, although there was never the crisis that Smuts and the newspapers claimed there was, Hertzog's behavior was baffling. He appeared to be on the best of terms with Roos, almost as though he were allowing him a romp that must go no further. It now became clear that the protesting document had never been formally presented to the Prime Minister. Furthermore it was now said that the three Ministers had signed, not as Ministers, but as members of Parliament. But most interesting of all, the newspapers were now fascinated by the news that the document had got lost. At first it was reported that the Chief Whip of the Party had taken it to Klerksdorp to electrify an election meeting, or alternatively, had taken it to Klerksdorp to get it lost again; but the Chief Whip laughing heartily, denied this, and said that the document was in a drawer in Cape Town to which Roos had the key. Dr H. H. Moll later told Hofmeyr that the Prime Minister had threatened to resign if Roos did not drop the matter. It was then that the document got 'lost'.

Hofmeyr had no lack of champions in the debate. Patrick Duncan said that the attacks were indecent, and would only strengthen the Administrator in his position; he argued that Hofmeyr was acting with perfect correctness. If the Government wanted to get rid of him, it could use its powers under the law; and so long as it did not wish to use these powers, it was indecent to attack him.

The Prime Minister thanked Duncan for his speech. He too regretted the attack, but he blamed Smuts and his previous appointments for the belief that Administrators must represent the Government.

'I understand the position that the administrator is appointed by the Union Government, but when once appointed he is not a representative of the Union Government, but responsible to the people of a province for which he is appointed, and then it is his duty to remain on according to the provisions of the law, and there is no reason why on a change of Government he need resign, unless he feels that he in the altered circumstances can no longer fulfill the duties of an administrator.'

Hertzog concluded that an end must be made of these attacks on the Administrator, who should be in a position to act in the interests of the province, and who should receive proper respect.

Hertzog's speech marked the end of the campaign. But it was not only that that brought it to an end. It was Hofmeyr's own achievement as Administrator, and his reputation for fairness. He took one last step which again demonstrated that 'considerable agility' of which one of his critics had spoken. Anticipating that the Nationalists might win the 1926 provincial election by an absolute majority, he wrote out his resignation for the Prime Minister, on the grounds that while he had thought it his duty to stay on where there were three minority parties, he would think it better for the Province for him to resign if there were a majority party. But he did not need to send in his resignation, the Nationalists failing to reach their goal.

There is one last thing to be said about the anti-Hofmeyr campaign. Never once during it did Hofmeyr say one word that would have reflected on the integrity of his opponents. When Stoffberg moved his motion of no confidence, Hofmeyr said that he was satisfied as to the honesty of the mover, which put Stoffberg into the terrible position of having to deliver mortal blows against a man who could make him feel so good.

Some of Hofmeyr's critics—who were by no means always his political enemies—thought that he was mean and petty. These were what one might call trace elements in his character. Basically he was a generous and big-minded man, but like all of us, he needed the right environment in which his nature could flourish and be evident.

After the agitation had died away, Hofmeyr settled down to three years of hard work, enjoyment, and being appreciated. He had at one time made fun of Rheinallt Jones's saying 'one does like to be appreciated', but he liked it too. It was a perfect life. Apart from the absence of personal conflicts, it gave more leisure than the university had ever done. On Saturday afternoons he would play tennis with his friends, on Saturday evenings he and his mother would go out more often than not. On Sunday mornings they went to service, usually but by no means always at the Presbyterian church, and when they returned he liked to sit on the *stoep* or in the garden, or to take a short walk to see his boyhood friend, Jackie Louw. On Sunday afternoons there would always be visitors, and in the evenings he wrote letters, and when Schlesinger started his African Broadcasting Corporation in 1927, he would join in the hymns in his own private fashion, his favourites being 'Lead, kindly Light' and 'O Love that wilt not let me go'.

It was the first big garden Mrs Hofmeyr had had since her girlhood days at her mother's home in Stellenbosch, and she was a good gardener. Her son's knowledge of gardening was like his knowledge of music; he claimed to know only two kinds of flowers, one was a rose, and the other wasn't. And he claimed to know two kinds of roses, the white and the red. He opened the flower show of the Eastern Districts Horticultural Society, and he expressed his greatest admiration for gardeners; he admired them as he admired the ladies, at a distance, with an admiration not likely to lead to action or to imitation. Hofmeyr's enjoyment of gardens, like his enjoyment of nature, was in the highest degree vague, though none the less real for that. As Administrator he was seeing more of South Africa than he had ever seen before, and he would talk often of the beauty of the Eastern Transvaal, especially at Kowyn's Pass, where the highveld stops abruptly at the edge of the escarpment, below which is a rich and luxuriant countryside, given over to the cultivation of almost every kind of sub-tropical fruit.

A subtle change was taking place at this time in the relationship between Hofmeyr and his mother. For one thing, there was the privacy afforded by the big new house. For another, the Transvaal was bigger than the university campus, and gave him more freedom. What is more, he was maturing; it was late, because great things had held him back, but now great things were pulling him forward. Many a boy had never been able to break from his mother because he had never been able to leave her world; but Hofmeyr was entering a big world where he was a big man meeting big people. He had become someone in his own right, and was in fact undergoing his weaning. It was never to be complete, because for one thing it was late, and for another, he was bound to his mother by deep and powerful bonds. She was the only one who knew of the agony of the Stibbe affair, and she was the one who had helped him through it. Nevertheless it had opened his eyes to one thing, the danger of her interference. She would cry out to him, when he had discussed some problem with her. 'No, no, you can't p-p-possibly do that,' when he had already decided that he could possibly do it, and that made it awkward.

Genuine maternal bossiness he did not mind, as at the time when the Administrator had cut himself severely on the tennis court, and was rushed to the near-by chemist's shop; and when he jumped at the iodine she called out, 'Jantjie, don't jump like that, how can the lady help you if you jump like that?' And Jantjie replied, 'It hurts, Ma, it hurts.' Or the time when they had dinner with the Chinese consul, and Hofmeyr was struggling with the chopsticks, and she had called out to him, 'Jantjie, use your spoon like a sensible being.' He genuinely did not mind this bossiness, but in other matters, of a gravity and an intimacy that she did not understand, it was necessary for him to decide for himself. So came into being his saying that she often repeated, not jokingly but rather when there was the suggestion that she dominated him, 'I am the master of the house.' When he said it, why he said it, whether he said it so pithily and unequivocally, no one will ever know; but in declaring that he said it, she was herself acknowledging that some such point had been reached. In any case she could see with her own eyes that he was growing up. He was moving amongst the greatest in the land with confidence. If she was the most important woman in the society of Pretoria, it was because of him.

There was another rumour about this time, known to more than one of his friends, that Mrs Hofmeyr was now wanting him to get married, and that she had selected a Miss L— of H—, whose father was a respected minister of the Nederduits Gereformeerde Kerk. Rumour had it that Miss L— had been too shy ever to get near being married, but would make an excellent wife for any man however distinguished; rumour also said that Hofmeyr cried off after reasonable progress had been achieved by the leading negotiators, who were afflicted by the timidities of the two junior parties. However in the end it was timidity that won, although one does not know if it was one timidity or two.

At this time Hofmeyr was more in demand as a speaker than ever. He was already the regular after-dinner speaker at the banquets of the Chemical, Metallurgical, and Mining Society of South Africa, and was now entering the field of engineering; electrical, civil, chemical, it made no difference to him. Occasionally he found himself paired with Smuts at these banquets, and once with the Prime Minister himself, who at the banquet of the South African Institute of Electrical Engineers, issued a stern warning to outside meddlers:

'There is no other question in which the South African, no matter whether he be a citizen of the Union or Rhodesia, so much resents interference from outside. The reasons are obvious. He will not allow his country's future, his home and his happiness, to be wrecked at the dictates of maudlin theorists whose national interests are 6,000 miles away. Such interference caused the Great Trek; it all but caused Natal to revolt, not many years ago. Unless that irritating practice is dropped, it will cost the British Empire one day the greater part of that which is included in Africa.'

In those days, not only Hertzog, but also Smuts and Hofmeyr, entertained an idea of the white man's role in Africa which has proved erroneous. Only six days later Hofmeyr, speaking at yet another banquet of engineers, said:

'We have a common opportunity—to build up here in South Africa and Eastern Africa a great European civilisation which will, by virtue of its strategic position, be able to play a great part in the world's affairs.'

The *Rand Daily Mail* said it was incontestable and finely said, whereas it would appear now to be nonsense. But at least it can be said on Hofmeyr's behalf that he was to change his categories of thought, whereas Hertzog died holding them; as for Smuts, no one knew his thoughts because of the barrier of optimism behind which he concealed them.

At this second banquet Hofmeyr said yet another thing which today is seen to be meaningless. 'The Native problem', he said, 'is no problem for South Africa. It is a problem for Africa.'

It is now almost universally accepted that these are the categories of thought of the white supremacist, that they exist only in his own world, and that his own world exists only in his own imagination. It can be cleverly said that what was once called the 'native problem' has turned out to be a white problem. But in a way that is what it is; can the white man who brought about such tremendous changes in Africa, himself adapt to the yet greater changes that are coming? It is pretty certain that at the age of 30 Hofmeyr had not yet thought of asking such a question.

There was another field of public speaking which Hofmeyr began to make peculiarly his own. As he acquired a reputation as a reconciler of white racial and language groups in the Provincial Council, so every white minority group in the country began to clamour to hear him, the Jews, the Caledonians, the Sons of England, the Cambrians, the Greeks. His popularity with white minority groups was immense, and his message to them consistent, namely that it was good for people to belong to groups and be proud of them and work for them, so long as they remembered that the diversity of these riches belonged to something yet greater, and that was the unity called South Africa. He told the Zionists that they would be all the better South Africans because of their concern for Israel, which caused many to inquire why he could show this enthusiasm for Jewish nationalism and so little for his own. It was noticeable that almost never was he invited to address an Afrikaner language or cultural group. Unity in Diversity, that was in a sense the great theme of his life; but his offence in extreme Nationalist eyes was that his real interest in the parts was the way in which they contributed to the whole, to which he gave his final devotion. This does not mean by any means that he was anathema to all the Nationalists; but it does mean that he was anathema to the extremists who were more and more controlling Afrikaner thought and culture. They might well have said to him, as a modern African national-ist might well say to a liberal, 'You talk about liberty, but we want to hear about liberation.'

There is available to us one striking picture of Hofmeyr in these years of his greatest success and self-confidence. It came from Hector Bolitho, the English journalist, writing in the *South African Nation*.

'Mr Hofmeyr came in, a man careless of appearance; a man so clever that he could make an Anderson and Shepherd suit look like a Moss within a few days. I present that as a genuine tribute to him. He offers little to the casual observer; he might be one of twenty people packed into a railway carriage with you. But examination floors any accusation of his being like the next man. His eyes are almost terrifying. He is the only person I met in Africa to whom I wouldn't tell a lie; mainly because it would be useless. Scholarly without being academic, humorous without being frivolous, he rather urges one to silence. I felt mentally nude in front of him. Prone to entertain with weak-kneed epigrams, I felt that here at last was a man who would see through any half-baked jokes or humours; so I remained silent. He said little, but when he did speak it was as if solidly thought out commandments were being delivered to the world. When anybody else spoke and he chose to add anything to the discussion, he drowned their efforts at being wise, by being damned wise. I have heard people say that General Smuts's cloak will fall on his shoul-ders. May one submit that the cloak will be lifted to his shoulders? There is a slight difference.'

Bolitho's vignette was thought extravagant by many; others thought it discerning, though some of these rejected the comparison with Smuts as either absurd or uncalled for. Hofmeyr was certainly attracting a grow-ing number of people because they saw the ideals they cherished trium-phant in him. Churchmen and religious men and women of all kinds, leaders of charitable and humanitarian causes, even those whose philoso-phy was vague but who desperately wanted good to keep ahead of evil in the perennial struggle, all these people were beginning—in the Transvaal at least—to say, 'Hofmeyr is the man,' and by that of course they meant the man for the future. Only the worldly-wise were sceptical; they would have liked to have seen a little more of their worldly wisdom in him, and a little more worldliness too, a good cigar after the food and wine, a flutter on the races, an occasional 'damn', a good story, and a little less of Mrs Hofmeyr. They related, with perverse pride, tales of his phenomenal powers, but they regarded him as a kind of Sunday School giant.

Of the many groups of people who were being drawn into the orbit of his influence, one was in Natal. George Gale, later Union Secretary of Public Health, had founded a vigorous branch of the Students' Christian Association at the University College of Pietermaritzburg. It was supported by young men and women, many of whom became prominent in the educational and missionary fields.

A number of these, the author among them, launched the boys' camps in Natal, with the powerful aid of Oswin Bull from Cape Town. Except for a virtually one-man preliminary effort by Bull at Illovo River, the first camp was established at Umgababa, on a flat piece of ground at the foot of the railway bridge. The aim of the camps was to win boys to an allegiance, or to confirm in them an allegiance already held, to Christ as the Lord of life, and to Christian principles in life and in society.

Hofmeyr came to the second camp at Umgababa, and then year after year to the new camp site on the Idomba River at Anerley, which site he helped the Association to buy and develop. He was a camper of the first class. He wore a canvas hat of uncertain shape and great antiquity, a khaki shirt and shorts, and discoloured sandshoes, known as tackies. He subjected himself in every detail to the discipline and programme of the camp, though he put on a show of subversiveness, and through this seduced more than one problem boy into developing a liking for obedience. He played every camp game. To oppose him at rugby football was a profound physical experience; this was one of the few activities for which he discarded his spectacles, without which he could see nothing but night and day. If he got the ball, he would charge for the goal line, two hundred pounds of concentrated material. If one knew no oriental arts, it was a clear duty to keep out of his course, for not to do so was to risk total disablement. If some extra-heavy camper should try conclusions with him, the air would be full of cries, of agony from the one, and of uncontrollable giggling from the other. It was strange that one who almost certainly in the whole of his life had never struck a living thing in anger, should revel in this gross physical combat. At any idle moment of the day, especially before and after meals, boys would gather round him for a game. After a day or two they all called him Hoffie.

It has been said that Hofmeyr lacked gifts of personality. It is truer to say that not every environment could bring them out. He often felt constrained with people, so that they never saw the real personality. With boys he felt no constraint; and as a consequence he was for them the most important, the most zestful, the most loved personality, in the camps. As for the young men who staffed the camps, they came to feel for him a deep trust and abiding affection. He could easily have chosen some other kind of holiday, yet he did not. One can only conclude that in the camps he was renewed and restored in some especial way; so the knower of the rose and the not-rose came to camp, for it was there that he himself blossomed.

Many of these boys and young men wrote to Hofmeyr. He had at one time a habit of carrying all unanswered letters in his inside pocket; this he said compelled him to answer them promptly. They found no coldness in him; he would remember a boy's name, the address of his home, the name of his school, and many other things which more demonstrative persons might forget. If a camper visited Pretoria, he could always see the Administrator; and when Hofmeyr became a Minister, many a youngster had tea with him in the Houses of Parliament in Cape Town, in a room filled with notabilities. One of his godsons, Gordon Wells Blake, who camped once with him at Umgababa, received a letter of advice and instruction from his godfather when he went to boarding-school for the first time.

'Make it your aim always to play the game, and that not only on the cricket field or the football field, but in every part of your school life. Play the game by your school-fellows, play the game by your parents who have given you so much, and above all, try to play the game by our Lord Jesus Christ, to whom we owe so much, and whom we must do our best not to let down by failing to do and be what he expects of us.'

Another group which came near to Hofmeyr in those days were the cricketers of Pretoria. Hofmeyr organised an Administrator's Eleven and captained it. This team used to play Saturday afternoon matches against the high schools of Pretoria and Johannesburg. Hofmeyr was no more of a great performer than he had been in his student days, but the purity of his devotion was so manifest that no one could resist it. He never stayed long at the wicket, and when his innings was over he liked nothing better than to take over the scorebook. He did not wear a cap, but a sort of floppy white hat. He would sit at the scorer's table, and those who liked to talk to him would come and sit by him. Serious matters were not excluded, but the main talk was about cricket and cricketing friends. Cricketers are pleasant and simple fellows, and what could be better than to sit with one of them in the summer shade, listening to his unexacting but interesting conversation, and to the incomparable sound of ball on bat, interrupting him now and then to comment on some fine piece of play or to ejaculate on some narrow and totally undeserved escape? For Hofmeyr it was the purest and completest of joys, and a slight smile would play about his lips, so that in later years, when he had such deep and hidden griefs, the sight if it could touch one to the heart. And for yet another thing, cricket satisfied utterly his moral sense, for here was a human activity, governed by the rule of law, competitive in nature, yet devoid of rapacity or fear or cruelty, and pleasurable to enjoy.

Not so completely felicitous were his relations with the University of the Witwatersrand. His prestige with the Council was higher than ever; he acted for several months as Principal, and was put on a committee to select his successor.

The Senate had already by unopposed motion recorded its appreciation of Hofmeyr's distinguished services. It appointed Maingard as its acting chairman, and he, towards the end of 1924, when the new Principal was due to take over, proposed that the honorary degree of LL.D. should be conferred on the Hon. J. H. Hofmeyr. It was a dangerous step for Maingard to take without making sure of his support. Senate declined to recommend their previous Principal.

Hofmeyr knew he had been rejected, and he knew because he had been told. He took the decision hard. He wrote on a piece of paper the names of all the members of the Senate, and wrote plus and minus after them; what is more, he left the piece of paper for any biographer to see, whether or not with intent, no one knows. His guess as to the voting was reasonably accurate; most of his extreme opponents in the Stibbe affair voted against him. He did not know that one of the most violent abstained. But he knew, because he was told, that his old teacher Alfred Hoernlé had thought him unworthy of an honorary degree. That was a nasty pill to swallow.

There was another pill too. At the time he received the news that the Senate had not recommended the honorary degree, he was actually waiting for an invitation to the annual graduation ceremony of the University on 4 April, which was only a fortnight away. But he did not receive one. On the evening of the day that the ceremony was held, Hofmeyr informed the new Principal and Vice-Chancellor that he had received no invitation. Nearly three weeks went by before he received any reply. Then the Registrar wrote to express the deep regrets of all concerned;

there was only one explanation he could offer, namely that the omission was an oversight plain and simple. He then wrote personally, hoping that Hofmeyr would be 'able to forget' the incident. Hofmeyr wrote:

'I naturally accept your apology and also your explanation of the oversight. But though the blame is quite probably not yours, I cannot help remarking that the salt of the apology has lost a good deal of its savour during the eighteen days that have elapsed since I drew the attention of the Principal, the Vice-Chancellor, and I think the Chairman of the Council to the omission.'

In spite of these experiences, Hofmeyr accepted the position of Government nominee on the Council, and in February 1926 he was elected as Vice-Chancellor. He was now appointed to the Honorary Degrees Committee, and usually took the Chair at its meetings; but though he was later to accept the highest honour of the Chancellorship, he would never accept an honorary degree from the University of the Witwatersrand.

Tielman Roos, who had accused Hofmeyr of lacking in self-respect, now came angling for him. He explained to Hofmeyr that the attacks on him were merely to keep the Nationalists together, and that there was nothing personal in them; he was sure Hofmeyr had seen this, and had not taken them seriously. Hofmeyr made no direct reply to this, but said urbanely that the attacks had afforded him much amusement. Roos then sent two of the Boer generals who had rebelled against Botha in 1914, to see Hofmeyr and persuade him to join the Nationalists. Both of them told him that the day of Smuts and Hertzog was done, and that the future lay with Roos, Hofmeyr, and the new rising star of the Transvaal, Advocate Oswald Pirow.

Hofmeyr refused to commit himself; he said that he wanted to keep his hands free. Roos accepted this with great affability, and said he could get Hofmeyr a second term as Administrator if he wanted it. He also said that his first impression of Hofmeyr was that he was 'too English', but now he knew him better, he found he was a good Afrikaner. Mrs Hofmeyr could sum up the whole situation better than anybody; she would say, 'We thought T-T-Tielman was our enemy, but we were m-mistaken, all the t-t-time he was our very good friend.' Then she would say, with that slight change in tone which heralded her shafts, 'T-T-Tielman was mistaken too, he said Jantjie had no self-respect, but now he says he is a good Afrikaner.'

H. H. Moll, then one of the most promising of the young Nationalists, quite fell under the spell of Hofmeyr's reputation. He wrote to Hofmeyr and said he wanted to be one of his lieutenants, because Young South Africa was looking to him. But some of Hofmeyr's speeches troubled him; this incessant talk of human brotherhood, this hobnobbing with Scots and Welshmen and Jews and Greeks, that surely was unwise. Afrikaner Nationalists felt just as generously about all these people (well, nearly all), but they didn't speak about it so incessantly, in fact they didn't really speak about it at all, not because they didn't want to, but because there wasn't time for it, there being so much of their own to speak about. And one had to admit that Hofmeyr spoke very little about *that*. There was always the danger that Hofmeyr might go to Smuts after all. 'Be careful', wrote Moll, 'that you do not take a step in such a way that we could not follow you.' He repeated the prophecy, 'The time of Hertzog and Smuts is past. The future is with Tielman and you.'

Dr Malan had sent an invitation to Hofmeyr to serve on a commission which was to suggest a suitable design for the new South African flag. The whole of white South Africa was in a ferment about the flag, and some of the bitter memories of the Anglo-Boer war were being re-awakened. Some demanded that the British Union Jack should be part of the new flag, others demanded it should not. Roos sent a special message by Moll, urging Hofmeyr to have nothing to do with the business, and both Roos and Moll were delighted to find that he had already refused the invitation.

In October of 1927, after months of wrangling, a new flag was decided upon; it was the flag of the House of Orange, with three parallel bands of orange, white, and blue, and on the central band three miniature flags, the Union Jack and the flags of the two lost republics. Malan hated the compromise, but Hertzog and Roos had been against him. Later Malan called the group of miniature flags a scab, and said that it would one day fall off.

Moll took away with him a copy of Hofmeyr's anti-republican essay, the one towards which Smuts had been so cold. Moll wanted to show it to doubting Thomases who found it hard to believe that Hofmeyr was really an Afrikaner. These doubters distrusted Hofmeyr because they distrusted H. S. Scott, his Director of Education, who thought that parents should be allowed to choose the language through which their children should be educated, and that English-speaking and Afrikaans-speaking pupils, even if they were taught in two different languages, should learn under one roof. Both these views were anathema to the true

Nationalists, led by the tireless Stoffberg, who was now a senator. They believed that compulsion should be applied to Afrikaners to have their children taught through the medium of Afrikaans, because large numbers of parents, believing that English was essential to success in life, sent their children to English schools. There was a saying, 'Learn only English, Hollands comes by itself,' which angered all true Nationalists. And as for teaching all children under one roof, that was merely another way to assure the ascendancy of English, and to distract Afrikaner children from pride in their own by a lot of sentimentality about brotherhood and reconciliation.

Hofmeyr had to make up his own mind about these matters, and he chose to support own-language instruction, provided both groups were taught under the same roof. But although this made him suspect amongst the 'true Afrikaners', he still had many Nationalist admirers. There were places in the Transvaal countryside where he was regarded as God's gift to the Afrikaner people, the man to whom God had given special talents so that he could consolidate Hertzog's work.

'*We Nats as Afrikaners out and out have a right to you. You are our share, our inheritance.*'

So, underlining each word separately, the old gentleman, Chris Hofmeyr, an influential Nationalist, urged Hofmeyr to declare himself. Hofmeyr wrote to him, explaining the nature of the Administrator's office, and the need for him to stand aside from the storms of politics. This did not satisfy the old man. Old Chris would be honest with him; did he not see now that Scott's appointment was a blunder, because he was not an Afrikaner? People say the young Hofmeyr is an Imperialist. Does young Hofmeyr give old Hofmeyr permission to deny it, to go to General Hertzog and say with authority, 'Young Hofmeyr is a Nationalist'? Ah, that he wants with his whole heart; for a long time he and his friends have been discussing it!

But the young Hofmeyr is stubborn. So long as he is Administrator, he is neutral, and nothing moves him from that, not even the promise of reappointment. As for his Imperialism, he is perfectly satisfied with the present position (which is clever, because Hertzog has said he is satisfied too).

He would appreciate it if the older man spoke to General Hertzog, but under no circumstances must the older say one word to the General which would lead him to think that the Administrator was a Nationalist; 'This is my final opinion and resolve.'

From another part of the rural Transvaal, came a simple letter from eleven Boer farmers, breathing the most humble trust in the Administrator. He is for *hereniging*, and so are they. They, like him, want to see Afrikanerdom reunited and *broedertwis* brought to an end.

Whatever Hofmeyr lost because of his neutrality, he gained because he was becoming the obvious architect of *hereniging*.

At the annual banquet of the South African Institute of Engineers, he made a speech. He warned the country against the present political struggle, and called for a re-alignment of the parties. Although he was holding talks with Roos and his friends at this time, his speech was quite clearly aimed at Hertzog and Smuts, neither of whom paid any public attention to it. Hofmeyr was not deterred by this, because his popularity was at its height, and both Hertzog and Smuts knew it. Six months later, on Union Day, 31 May 1928, on the occasion of the first hoisting of the new flag, Hofmeyr appealed for 'the coming together of the two larger parties in South Africa, and the formation of a great new party of all those who have the same general outlook'. He hoped that South Africa would have such a party before the next Union Day was celebrated.

His speech brought more letters from all parts of the Transvaal, especially from those who were still trying to heal the Botha-Hertzog breach of 1912.

A Nationalist of substance travelled to Pretoria to see the maker of this important speech. He told Hofmeyr that things were humming on the 'platteland', a word for countryside as opposed to urban areas. People were sick and tired of conflict, and wanted reunion. Down in Potchefstroom they had already formed a vigilance committee from both parties. Hofmeyr made it clear to him that when he made his speech, he expected nothing to come of it before the election; now however he was not so sure, and he now had hopes that a bitter struggle might be avoided. But how? Not through his intervention, because he was Administrator. The answer was a *volksbeweging*, a people's movement, that would compel the leaders to listen. Here was Hofmeyr's plan—let a manifesto go out from the vigilance committee, let the committee call on other constituencies to form committees; if that happened, then 'the veld would catch fire, and nothing would stop it'.

The Nationalist went back to Potchefstroom and his committee issued a manifesto. It saw communism as a danger to the world, and it was high time that Hertzog men and Smuts men united against it; now was the time, because after the strife of the election, reunion would be harder. It was urgent to reunite so that the 'Native problem' and the 'Indian problem' could be dealt with. He wrote to Hofmeyr that Smuts and Hertzog must call all their followers together. They must first choose a leader, 'and there is already a man towards whom the finger of Destiny is pointing'. Then Smuts and Hertzog could retire, with full honours from a grateful and united people.

However, Smuts and Hertzog had no thought of earning honours in this way. Though both of them knew Hofmeyr's importance, neither of them had any intention of making way for him. Smuts assumed that Hofmeyr would join him in the South African Party, and would become his lieutenant and finally his successor. Smuts had a habit of wanting to retire from politics and then of being persuaded to return to them. About 1928 he was tired of them, and wanted to leave them as soon as he had found a leader for the party; and that leader as he told several people, including Hofmeyr himself, was the young Administrator.

There seems good reason to believe that the understanding between Smuts and Hofmeyr was far from clear. Smuts seemed to take the younger man's acquiescence as a matter of course; after all, Smuts was 58 years of age, and a world statesman, whereas Hofmeyr was a young man of 34. Both Hofmeyr and his mother resented his being taken for granted; it was true that Smuts had made Hofmeyr Administrator, but it was certainly not Smuts who had made him such a good one. This understanding, that Hofmeyr would support Smuts and that Smuts would advance Hofmeyr, never assumed the status of an undertaking. There were however people who considered that Smuts did not keep faith with Hofmeyr in later years; yet the last few months of Hofmeyr's administratorship provide sufficient evidence that they had no kind of contractual obligation to each other.

At the time of his retirement Hofmeyr would have completed, with holidays far shorter than most senior public servants, a period of five hard-working years. He was determined to have a good holiday, and in February 1929 to take his mother up the East Coast of Africa to Kenya, Palestine, Athens, and Rome, and then England and Oxford. Smuts thought that Hertzog would hold an election in August 1929, and he wrote to Hofmeyr, 'You will have to be back at that time and will have to arrange your holiday so that you will be back at the end of May or in June.' Yet

Hofmeyr had more or less already decided that he would not be back in time; he had no desire to take part in the election, but he and his mother kept this fact to themselves.

A few months later, in April 1928, Smuts wrote again, saying that the 'friends at Barberton' wanted an early announcement of their candidate for the election. 'It seems to me you will have to do this before your departure.'

But Hofmeyr knew that the Nationalist members of the Transvaal Provincial Council were planning to go to the Prime Minister to ask him to give Hofmeyr a second term as Administrator, and what is more, Hofmeyr wanted such an offer to be made to him, although he had more or less decided not to accept it. He wrote to Smuts that he did not wish there to be any rumour of his candidature while he was Administrator. Smuts then suggested that some kind of hint should be given that Hofmeyr would be the man, so as to frighten off local competitors. Hofmeyr resisted this too, and Smuts then suggested that the hint should be quite unofficial and Hofmeyr could ignore it and it would do him no harm.

It was about the middle of 1928 that Hertzog ('affability itself', said Hofmeyr) made confidential offers to the Administrator; he could either take a second term as Administrator, or he could go to London as High Commissioner for South Africa. Hofmeyr asked for time to consider the offers, but in fact he had more or less decided against both. He thought that as High Commissioner he would be out of sight, out of mind, and if one meant to become a politician, one could not afford that. Nor did he want another term as Administrator; he thought the provincial system was dying, and he may have thought—though he did not say so—that in the Transvaal there was nothing left to conquer. He had two other reasons; he thought London would be too cold for his mother, and he thought that the second term would interfere with his holiday, on which his heart was set.

Hofmeyr told Smuts about his talks with Hertzog, and said that, if the second term were offered, he would be hesitant about accepting it. This seems to dispose of the idea that he had reached any kind of firm understanding with Smuts about the future. Both men seemed agreed that neither choice was advisable; the only question was whether Hofmeyr should declare himself before the election or after. It seems certain that Hofmeyr concealed his reluctance to have anything to do with the election. As for Smuts, he was of two minds, and agreed the problem was difficult. He told Hofmeyr that he wanted him in political life as soon as possible, with the intention of making way for him later. On the other hand he thought that *hereniging* was coming nearer, and Hofmeyr might be more valuable if he came in after the election 'with clean hands'.

Hofmeyr's memorandum on the interview between Smuts and himself stated that the question of his contesting or abstaining from the election was left undecided. But only a few days after the interview, Smuts had written again to say that the 'friends at Barberton' were pressing for an answer. Hofmeyr in his reply reminded him of the attempts being made to get him re-appointed; it would be unpleasant if there were rumours of his seeking a parliamentary nomination. A few days after that, 'friends at Carolina' pressed Hofmeyr to stand there for the South African Party, and a few days after that, the Rev. J. H. Batts of Grahamstown wrote to remind him that the ambition of his childhood had been to enter the Baptist ministry, and now was the great opportunity. And there was the rumour that he was to be appointed Chairman of ISCOR, Hertzog's new Iron and Steel Corporation, which was to make South Africa independent of world steel. Hofmeyr told of his excitement in a public speech; he knew nothing of iron and steel, but was told it didn't matter!

Supporters of Hertzog and Smuts who thought that Hofmeyr's preference might decide the whole election were angry that he would give no sign. Nationalists who agonised over the perpetual crisis of Afrikanerdom were shocked that he took Afrikaner survival so lightly; Smutsites who agonised over racial tolerance amongst white people were shocked that he would not fight for the things he was always talking about. And they had an additional cause for anger—here was Hofmeyr playing the big man, but who had made him one?

And what about Hertzog? Most observers thought that he wanted to keep Hofmeyr away from Smuts but was not anxious to have him himself. That was why he had offered him two cold-storage jobs. At least rumour said that he had. And rumour was proved right on 30 October, when it was announced that Hofmeyr would accept neither the Commissionership nor a second term as Administrator.

Whatever Hertzog thought of this, his supporters were furious. The Nationalist members of the Provincial Council felt they had been made fools of. Here they had gone to the Prime Minister to ask for a second term, fully confident that Hofmeyr would accept it, as he had never even hinted that he would turn it down. Had they known that he would, they would never have gone to the Prime Minister. The National Party of South Africa did not offer gifts to be rejected. *Ons Vaderland* accused

Hofmeyr of exploiting the widespread interest in his future intentions 'in an improper manner', and said that an end should be made to these offers. The honeymoon was over.

Did Hofmeyr, if by nothing more than silence, or by expressing appreciation, encourage the Nationalist provincial councillors to ask for a second term, when he knew that he would not accept it? It seems that he did. And if he did, was that in accordance with his own high standards? It seems that it was not. He was, though this was not apparent, in a divided state of mind. He was asked, after he had refused both of Hertzog's offers, whether he would take up politics on his return from Europe, and he replied, 'I have not yet made up my mind.' The *Rand Daily Mail* told him not to play the mystery man too long. The *Star* predicted that he would come down on the side of Smuts, and hinted that he would stand for Barberton. It mentioned a lesser possibility, namely that he would wait until after the election and then fight 'with a Centre Party as a slogan'.

In fact the 'friends at Barberton' had approached him again, after the news that he would soon be free. Hofmeyr then took a surprising step; he not only decided not to stand, but he wrote to Smuts, enclosing a copy of his letter to Barberton:

'I just want to add—it was inappropriate to say it to them—that at the moment I am unwilling to commit myself definitely to the South African Party, because I think that there is still a chance to reach the desired goal by another road. But as soon—which is very possible in the course of time—as it becomes clear to me that there is no such chance, then I shall place myself at your disposal.

'I hope my decision will not disappoint you—it seems to me the right choice now.'

Smuts was more than disappointed. He was, to use Mrs Smuts's word, 'peeved'. By what other road did Hofmeyr expect to reach his goal? Did he take Tielman Roos seriously, that feather-weight Lion of the North? Could he not see that there were only two factors of any account, the Nationalists and the South African Party? Smuts did not think for a minute that Hofmeyr would ever dream of launching a centre party. He pushed it aside and turned to his books and his flowers.

Now came the round of banquets. Innumerable welfare and patriotic organisations, schools, municipalities, wanted to do Hofmeyr honour. Critics may have carped at his jokes and his mysteriousness, but people were unanimous about his administratorship, and said it had been magnificent. Raikes, the new Principal of the University of the Witwatersrand, wrote a generous letter to him and asked him to accept an honorary degree when he came there in 1929 as the newly elected president of the South African Association for the Advancement of Science.

'I know your feelings were injured four years ago, and, as far as I can understand the circumstances, you were justified in being injured. But do forget all that is past, and start out on your new career, whatever it may be, with no barrier, however imaginary, on either side between yourself and the University, the creation of which may very well be shown to have been one of the greatest triumphs of a not uneventful and triumphal life.'

But Hofmeyr could not. He had taken the Vice-Chancellorship from the Council, but this gift, which in reality came from the Senate, he could not take.

So, in a burst of applause and a blaze of glory, the illustrious five years came to their end.

Chapter 5

Entry Into Politics

HOFMEYR and his mother set out on their holiday with the keenest anticipation. It was easily the most extravagant adventure of their lives. Hofmeyr was, to see for the first time, not only the continent of Africa, but
the three most important cities of his life, Jerusalem, Athens and Rome.
There was nothing to do except eat, read, sleep, and play games, or sit on
the deck and watch Africa go by. Hofmeyr had taken on only one job,
and that was to write articles for the *Pretoria News*, what he called 'the
idle thoughts of a (for once) idle fellow'.

His articles confirmed that he shared with Livingstone, Rhodes, and
Smuts, the dream that the highveld of South Africa, continuing north-
wards through Rhodesia, Tanganyika, and Kenya, would be successfully
settled and developed by the Europeans. He and his mother visited Eldoret,
where the Kenya Afrikaners lived, and he and the minister sat on the
stoep and spoke Afrikaans, so he said, 'to our hearts' content'. He noted
that the settlers were bitterly dissatisfied with a policy that put the interests of the indigenous people first; perhaps the Afrikaners would trek
again, to Northern Rhodesia; who knew?

He wrote in one of his articles for the *Pretoria News*:

'In 1923 when the settlers of Kenya were in the thick of the struggle
over the Indian question, they looked to South Africa for help. It is to our
advantage as well as to theirs, that the Europeans in East Africa should
regard us as a potential source of assistance in the present and the future.
It is of real interest to South Africa that European civilisation should be
established on a firm basis throughout the Highland belt which stretches
through Eastern Africa. It is of real interest to South Africa that policies
in regard to native questions should not be initiated to the north of us,
which in these days of shrinking distance cannot but complicate our own
handling of such questions in the future.'

It is clear that Hofmeyr used the categories of the white thinking of
those days. The overwhelming majority of white South Africans spoke

then, not of the problems of race relations, but of Indian problems and 'Native' problems. In those days many white South Africans, and many other white men, thought of a great federation stretching from Cape Town to the northern border of Kenya. In 1929 white South Africa took it for granted that she would have an important say in the political development of Africa.

In Jerusalem Hofmeyr received Smuts's cable asking him to stand in the elections, which were to be held on 12 June; to this he replied, 'Candidature unlikely, writing.' He was still determined not to stand, but he found it difficult to say No to Smuts in a firm voice. He wrote that at that moment he felt that it would perhaps be better if he took no part. But he had not decided finally. He would do so when he reached London. 'Only sound reasons would move me to say No, if indeed, I do so decide.'

When he reached London, he wrote a final No, and said he thought it would be important, when *hereniging* drew near, that there should be 'someone on our side who had not taken part in the struggle'.

Meanwhile Reuters cabled South Africa that although Hofmeyr adhered to his oft-repeated opinion that the gulf between the parties was a narrow one, and though his aim was co-operation between them, he indicated that on the chief election issues his sympathies were with the South African Party, even though he would arrive back too late to help it.

It was not only Smuts who was peeved. All those who believed that Smuts was the only bulwark against Nationalist isolationism were peeved too. Some of the Nationalists felt that Hofmeyr had made a fool of them, but even they could laugh at the South African Party, whose famous new recruit, after having abstained from all the fighting, would arrive back in time to give them one vote on election day.

What did Mrs Hofmeyr make of all this? By this time she knew that it was to be politics after all. There can be no doubt that she, with her political neutralism, powerfully reinforced his decision to 'keep his hands clean', and gave him strength to keep their powerful kinsman at arm's length. Behind his reluctance to return was her own. And she was afraid of politics, lest it turn out like the Stibbe affair, and bring him suffering and despair. She had seen his joy in Balliol revisited, and in old friendships renewed, with Secretan and Jacks and Underhill and them all. To go to Mansfield College was like going back home. Oh, the joys of those quiet days, when his greatest responsibilities had been his books and his boys' club! If only he could return there, and take up the life of a scholar behind those ancient walls, and leave others more suited to it to wrestle with the fears and the hates, and the harsh history so full of wrongs! She told him so, that she would have liked him to do that. But both she and he knew it was only a dream. Even in his childhood, when they had learned how great were his gifts, they had known they must be used for his country.

Though Hofmeyr might not be able to recapture the past, the present was surely enough. London, Oxford, old friends, and—strangest of all, something he did not really believe in, but found very pleasant—freedom without responsibility. Both he and his mother were enjoying it, and were reluctant to give it up. So they resisted the return to Smuts, she stubbornly, he with indecision. This vacillation must not be taken to be fundamental to his character. It was something to do with Smuts alone; Hofmeyr, even while he resisted him, stood in awe of him, as indeed might any modest young man. Hofmeyr had had a career that was steadfast and brilliant, and there was no reason to suppose that the rest of it would be different. Some people now called him a fence-sitter, but he considered he was keeping his hands clean to tie the knots of *hereniging*. Other people called him the future Prime Minister, but he was not aiming at that either; three years earlier he had read Raymond's *Disraeli*, and had considered the question whether political success comes to those who do not seek it.

He even wrote a memorandum on it which made it clear that he would do nothing to attain the Premiership as such. He had set himself a course, and that was to serve his country in accordance with his principles. If the Premiership lay at the end of it, well and good; if not, then well and good too. He asked himself whether he had political ambition. His answer was that by temperament he was fitted to be, not a Gladstone, but a Bright, influencing the policy of the government, 'especially on questions of moral bearing'.

In all this Hofmeyr showed considerable insight into his own nature. It would have saved others from too great expectations had they known that he thus thought of himself. Many awaited a lead from him while he awaited a lead, or even a push, from God. It was clear that if he was to be Prime Minister, God would have to do it; for he himself had already decided that the Premiership was not only not essential, but would almost certainly be burdensome, to the kind of political course he meant to follow. It was Onze Jan come back to life again.

It seems certain that man is so made that if he is to reach some high goal, he must have some kind of personal ambition, not only an aspiration, but an intensity of ambition to be the one who achieves it. J. H. H. de Waal had a name for this lack of intensity in Onze Jan; he called it timidity. There are no doubt intimate connections amongst the several qualities of timidity, modesty, loyalty, gentleness, and lack of ambition; but one's enemies will use one word, and one's friends another.

Hofmeyr admitted at once that he wanted to be a participant in politics rather than an onlooker, but not a responsible minister or one of the leading men of the party, only a private member with influence in the House. 'Therein would lie great satisfaction, and I am not sure if it is not the kind of political role which my outlook and temperament best fit me to fill.' These words he wrote when he was in what might justifiably be called the prime of his life, with his ears full of praises.

Hofmeyr was beginning to learn that in human conduct, the 'will to do' is not everything. The prizes do not always go to those who work for them, nor to the virtuous; they go, especially the biggest of them, to those who are fitted, by no act or virtue of their own, to receive them. The University had taught him that he had limitations, which no amount of virtue or industry could overcome; and now he was being taught it again by his great kinsman, before whom he often felt like a child.

Meanwhile he was having a wonderful time in London. The Royal Empire Society gave him a luncheon, and he gave it a speech to remember. Speaking as one who had not a drop of British blood in his veins, he told his audience that South Africa had come to regard the question of its relationship to the British Empire 'as definitely and finally settled'. To its member nations the Empire gave status, to the world it was a bulwark of peace.

On Smuts's birthday, which was also Empire Day, 24 May, mother and son sailed for Cape Town. A few days before they landed, a statement by Hofmeyr was published. It covered well-trodden ground. Again he drew attention to the unimportance of the issues separating the parties; this would have made him a half-hearted contestant, and he looked forward to a realignment of the parties. He repudiated the suggestion that he was waiting to see which way the cat would jump; he thought it would jump in Smuts's direction, but even had he thought it would jump in the other, he would not have jumped with it. He had three reasons for not supporting Hertzog.

He thought Hertzog should not have made an election issue of his solutions for the 'Native problem'; such solutions involved constitutional changes and required a two-thirds majority in both Houses sitting together.

He objected to the trade treaty with Germany, which he reckoned would weaken Commonwealth bonds.

He was revolted by Hertzog's 'Black Manifesto', which accused Smuts of wanting to see white South Africa swamped in a black sea, and called all voters to the defence of South Africa as a white man's country.

Hofmeyr therefore came down on the side of the South African Party, but kept the door open for co-operation. As for the Labour Party, he hoped it would be destroyed, as it had sold its soul for the loaves and fishes of office, and had abandoned the 'protection of the interests of the real underdog in South Africa'.

Hofmeyr's election forecast was wrong. In the previous election the Nationalists had won 63, SAP 53, Labour 18, Independent 1. Now the number of constituencies had been increased from 135 to 148 and the Nationalists secured for the first time an absolute majority in the Lower House. They secured 78, SAP 61, Labour 8 with 1 Independent. Hofmeyr wrote to Underhill that it was not so much the result that was disquieting, as the fact that it was won by an open and unashamed appeal to colour prejudice; Hertzog himself spoke from every platform of the 'native menace'; Hofmeyr's letter of 1929 reveals the same fears as are strong in 1964. He wrote of the increasing tendency among Africans to write off Christianity as a fraud, and said that the creation of a sullen hostile population was a poor foundation for a policy of preserving European civilisation. As for himself, he said that the election had left him high and dry.

Although Hofmeyr had declared for the South African Party, he was still resisting it. He wrote to Roos, who was undergoing treatment in Germany, lamenting that the election had been fought on racial lines, which, he said, 'seems to me to hold the seed of great evil for South Africa'. He was still convinced that the future depended on white racial co-operation, and asked whether Roos would be willing to work towards that end. He asked Roos to be quite frank about the matter, and if he would rather not commit himself, to destroy the letter and leave it unanswered. Roos replied that the consolidation of the two parties was essential, not only to the economic development of the Union in peace, but to bring about the incorporation of at least the two Rhodesias in the near future. Hofmeyr replied that there was a good deal of pressure on him to take a definite party line, but he thought he would continue to resist; and in any case he would not commit himself until Roos's return.

But while he was contemplating working with Roos and simultaneously giving praise to the South African Party, he took part briefly in yet another adventure which seemed to show beyond doubt that he did not know his mind. On 22 June 1929, Mr Ludwig Japhet, a Johannesburg attorney, 39 years of age, whom his friends thought vigorous and his enemies pushing, wrote a letter to the *Star*, maintaining that a young country should be governed by young people. They would not shirk 'the Native problem'. He, Ludwig Japhet, would advocate equal pay for equal work, and could assure his readers that 'the native does not wish to fraternise with the whites'; he wanted only equal opportunity. Japhet declared that a new party must arise, representative of both Boer and Briton; 'when it does, South Africa will find a solution to its problem'.

Japhet's writing might have ended there had Hofmeyr not responded to it in the next issue of the *Star*. He agreed that youth longed to close the old chapter and make a fresh start; 'it must mobilise itself against the day when the call will come to it'. Hofmeyr wrote:

'Now, when we have a reasonable prospect of political stability with no general elections threatening us, is the time for young South Africa, the younger folk of all parties, to come together in such an effort. . . . Will not Mr Japhet take the initiative?'

On the next day it was announced that Hofmeyr would take the chair at a public meeting in Johannesburg, and that a new party would be launched. But on the day following, Hofmeyr denied that there was any question of a new party; Japhet declared that talk of a new party was a 'happy anticipation', and that Hofmeyr's support for his views was great encouragement. In the afternoon Japhet declared that a new party was the goal, and Hofmeyr declared that the goal was to get young people of all parties together, 'to think things out a bit'.

Hofmeyr came under scathing attack for his part in the Japhet episode. The *Star* described talk of a new party as 'froth'; Smuts was indispensable. The *Rand Daily Mail* said the whole thing was Hofmeyr's biggest blunder. His first blunder was to be absent from South Africa during the general elections; his second was to lead the public to expect from him an important pre-election announcement and to give them instead a complete misreading of the situation. *Die Volksblad* said that Hofmeyr had no conception of the pride and self-confidence of Nationalist youth; it wanted no centre party. The *Natal Advertiser*, in an editorial called 'Japhet in Search of a Party', asked what kind of example Hofmeyr was for youth.

What was Hofmeyr doing? Japhet had in his first letter clearly asked for a 'new party'. Hofmeyr had just as clearly asked Japhet to take the initiative. Yet four days later he announced that he withdrew his consent to act as chairman of the meeting, and would not attend in any capacity whatever. Japhet was left with no choice; he announced that he had abandoned the project. The *Rand Daily Mail* showed Alchemist Hofmeyr staring with horror at a chemical retort labelled 'Elixir of Youth Party', from which not a drop was coming.

The newspapers liked to give Hofmeyr a drubbing, but most of them liked to make it up to him again. Their chance came soon. In 1927, after hesitating over his lack of qualifications, and after receiving encouragement from Smuts, who said he was the best man for the job, Hofmeyr accepted the presidency of the South African Association for the Advancement of Science. Smuts wrote, 'You know what my wish and plan is, and this unique honour will do much towards their fulfilment.' So in July, after a week at the boys' camp at Anerley, he went to Cape Town to deliver the inaugural address to the joint meeting of the South African and British Associations, one of his distinguished hearers being the Prime Minister himself. His theme was the development of science in South Africa, and the great opportunity that lay before South Africa of helping forward the scientific and economic development of the whole continent. The newspapers were agreed that it was a remarkable performance. It was the kind of speech at which both Smuts and Hofmeyr were adept, and, to do them justice, the kind of speech that was expected of them; they both could see in public great visions of the future, and persuade their audiences that they were within grasp, when the hard truth was that a South Africa whose rulers thought of the majority of their people as a menace, would never be able to offer any kind of leadership to the continent at all. The *Cape Times* asked what reflection there was of Hofmeyr's vision in the public life of South Africa, whose white people despised vision and built altars to a despicable racial fear, and wondered what General Hertzog was thinking while he listened.

The University of Cape Town used the great occasion to honour its guests, and who more deserving than the most brilliant of her sons? What Hofmeyr had refused from the Witwatersrand, he took from Cape Town: an honorary degree. He became a Doctor of Science, but he would not be called by the title except on academic occasions. He had by now almost completely succeeded in shedding the title Professor. Both titles he regarded as damaging to a politician, and thought Professor Doctor Hofmeyr the most damning of all.

When he returned to Johannesburg, he had three tasks awaiting him. The first was to write a chapter on South Africa for the Cambridge History of the British Empire, and the second was to write a book on South Africa for the Modern World series. The third was the most immediate, and had come out of a discussion with E. B. Woolff, the Johannesburg physiotherapist, and Herbert Frankel, one of the most brilliant graduates of the University of the Witwatersrand, and a man who was devoted to Hofmeyr, and willing to be his disciple. The year 1931 was the year of the coming of age of the Union of South Africa, and the proposal was for a group of young South Africans to examine the achievements and the problems, and to chart a course for the future. Oliver Schreiner wrote quite independently to Hofmeyr to suggest to him a similar scheme that Ronald Currey had put to himself and Hal Ramsbottom. Currey was keen because he thought that English-speaking South Africans were being driven, or felt they were being driven, into becoming *uitlanders*. Currey wrote to Hofmeyr that whereas in 1900 his father's attitude had been dubbed pro-Boer, today it seemed 'vaguely Jingo'. Edgar Brookes, Professor of History at the Pretoria University College, an English-speaking liberal who tried to understand Afrikaner Nationalism, was brought in and also J. D. Rheinallt Jones, who was now the adviser to the newly formed Institute of Race Relations. The Institute had been founded by the Hoernlés, Loram of the Native Affairs Commission, the Rheinallt Joneses, Professor Jabavu of Fort Hare, and other liberals, and while its task was to gather and disseminate objective information about all racial affairs, this was to be done from the point of view of those who believed in a common South African society, and who regarded segregation as both impossible and unjust. It was agreed to call the book *Coming of Age*, and the group settled down to decide the topics and prepare the material. Hofmeyr was chosen as chairman, and Frankel undertook to do all the secretarial work.

Meanwhile, however, a little post-election drama was being played in the constituency of Johannesburg North, which was going to complicate Hofmeyr's life. Lourens Geldenhuys had won the seat for the South African Party by beating the Labour candidate, John Duthie, by one vote. His majority was challenged, and one of his votes declared invalid.

According to the electoral law, the issue should then have been decided by drawing lots, but before that could be done, Geldenhuys died. The seat was then declared vacant, and the divisional council of the party, headed by the same Colonel Stallard who had acted as arbitrator in the Stibbe affair, decided to ask Hofmeyr to stand for the South African Party.

One thing seems clear, and that is that up to this point Hofmeyr did not feel himself committed to Smuts, not even by the statement he had made a few days before the election. Whether he saw Roos on his return from Germany, or whether Roos had by that time returned, one does not know. Roos had been elevated to the Appeal Bench, and it was said that he was both too ill to be a politician, and too political to be a judge; he may well have felt physically unable to go chasing with Hofmeyr after the will-o'-the-wisp of *hereniging*. Therefore when Colonel Stallard came to the Hofmeyr house, both mother and son knew that the hour had come.

She used to say thereafter that Stallard persuaded her son, but in fact he needed no persuasion. He was satisfied that no *hereniging* would come from outside Parliament, therefore into Parliament he must go. He wrote to Underhill that he had no political ambitions and would as readily have washed his hands of the whole thing. But it was to be a kind of test. 'If I win, full steam ahead! If I don't, I am going to keep quiet for a few years and find other things with which to occupy myself.' He was already thinking of the law, which he could have studied in his spare time, and for which his gifts so clearly qualified him.

Of all this his mother said, 'It was a nail in my soul.' She and he made an agreement that there would never be politics in the house; by that was meant no political arguments and no polemics, but of course it did not exclude conversations between him and others, provided she was not present. It was a necessary arrangement, because her friends came from both parties, to her tea-table and dinner-table, and to sit on the *stoep*. Then she shrugged the whole thing off, saying that politics was in the Hofmeyr blood. But the real fear she put away and would not speak of, that they would do again to him what they had done at the University, and that this time they would break his heart.

By many others Hofmeyr's decision was received with joy, especially those who were disturbed by the tendency of white politics to become more and more obsessed with racial fears and the struggle for survival. His colleagues in the writing of *Coming of Age*, though they had barred all politicians, would not now let him go, because after all he was going to *do* the things that they were merely writing about.

Hofmeyr announced that he was entering the battle as a humble musket-bearer. He believed that Anglo-Afrikaner co-operation was essential for the welfare and prosperity of South Africa and all its people; therefore he supported the South African Party which had the same idea. But he was going to work for the modification of the present lines of party division.

People wondered how the classroom prodigy, whose worldly knowledge was acquired behind college walls, would face up to an election. They still looked upon him as a child, and were continually wondering how he would succeed in a new situation. The answer was that Hofmeyr was as magnificent a candidate as he had been an Administrator, and that throughout his parliamentary career no candidate ever surpassed him, for industry, thoroughness and efficiency. His committees worked with a will because he himself was tireless. The Rev. S. R. Hattingh, the Nationalist stalwart, who prophesied a victory for Duthie, caused much amusement by saying about Hofmeyr, 'We have not got to do here with a remarkably strong and wonderful man. We have to do with practically a dead man.'

It was precisely the kind of remark which delighted Hofmeyr. He told the story of the young dominie who played mediocre golf against his ageing beadle, and was beaten at the eighteenth hole. The beadle was indecently delighted, and exclaimed, 'It's ma hole, it's ma hole!' The dominie said that such behavior was unseemly in one so near the grave, and that he would say so at the burial service. And the beadle said, 'Dominie, you can say what you like, but that will be ma hole too.'

'And so,' said Hofmeyr, 'when the Rev Mr Hattingh comes to read the burial service over me, he will find that Johannesburg North is ma hole.'

That brought the house down. The *Rand Daily Mail* said Mr Hofmeyr might not aspire higher than a musket-bearer, but he was a deadly shot with the instrument in question.

Hofmeyr increased the party majority in Johannesburg North from 1 to 305, in spite of the fact that the Prime Minister himself came there to speak against him. Three other by-elections took place at the same time, and the Nationalist young hope, Oswald Pirow, won Gezina with an increased majority. Pirow had fought against Smuts at Standerton in the general election, and had lost. The Prime Minister however was deter-

mined to have him in the Cabinet to replace Tielman Roos as Minister of
Justice. It so happened that there was a vacancy in the Senate, for a
Government-appointed Senator whose qualification must be that he was
acquainted with the reasonable wants and aspirations of the coloured
people. The Prime Minister therefore appointed Pirow to the vacancy.

Pirow's appointment in this way had a powerful effect on Hofmeyr.
Though he may at that time have thought in categories unacceptable
today, the direction of his evolution was already plain, and he was revolted that the Prime Minister should use this sole instrument of non-
white representation for his own purposes. The appointment was made
still more objectionable because Pirow had shown, and was to show
throughout his political life, no sympathy whatever for the aspirations of
non-white people. He spoke contemptuously of *koelies* and *kaffers*, and
described the coloured people with that contemptuous word, *mengelmoes* [mixture]. Pirow believed in white superiority, 'and in its preservation
at any cost'. But he was an intelligent man, and even in those far-off days,
he knew how to speak of the white man's moral responsibility for others,
especially for the *mengelmoes*, which the white man himself had made,
even to the extent of a contribution of blood. He was also absurd, and
believed in the partition of Africa between black and white till as late as
the end of the Second World War. This is the tragedy of Afrikaner
politics that the most able men devote their lives to drawing blueprints
for the impossible.

It was already being said that the future lay with Pirow and Hofmeyr.
They represented two distinct though not diametrically opposite views.
Pirow stood openly for white supremacy, for what later came to be
called *baasskap*. Hofmeyr believed in white responsibility for a just order,
later called trusteeship.

In his election campaign Hofmeyr was challenged by Pirow to state
his views on racial segregation. He replied:

'With regard to segregation, this is, in my view, the most logically
satisfactory, in fact the ideal policy, but we should not forget that it is
not an easy policy to give effect to, and that it calls for sacrifices on our
part . . . [it is] an urgent matter to face the position and to consider
whether we are willing to pay the price.'

What did Hofmeyr and Pirow mean by 'segregation'? It seems clear
from the context that they were talking about territorial separation, later
to be called apartheid, and still later, separate development. That was the

way Hofmeyr was thinking on the eve of his entry into Parliament; and it was Pirow, with his absurd dream of dividing Africa between black and white, who as much as any person helped Hofmeyr to clarify and modernise his ideas.

Hofmeyr's Labour Party opponent, John Duthie, called on the voters to vote for a white South Africa; meanwhile Hertzog's Minister of Labour, Mr Sampson, said in Durban that Indians would be admitted to the Typographical Union. Hofmeyr made great play with this, and it is a popular election tactic to this day for the main opposition party to attack the Nationalists when they relax their apartheid policies and do something humane. Oliver Schreiner did not like it, and he was one of the few South Africans who could write to Hofmeyr, and tell him that better could be expected. 'I feel that the platform is not the place for compromise,' wrote Schreiner; 'it is the place for saying what one really feels and what one hopes to persuade other people to feel.' Many people would not have kept such a letter, but Hofmeyr did, this seeming to indicate some kind of humility in him, some determination to set his standard higher, and to listen to those whose own standards he respected.

One consequence of Hofmeyr's victory was that he became immediately a South African figure. As a speaker he was in demand everywhere. A feature of these speeches was his cordial references to the Prime Minister, who was now asking publicly for co-operation in settling once and for all the 'Native question'. Hofmeyr referred sympathetically to Hertzog's anxiety about 'agitators who are inciting natives to follow a course which can only lead to lawlessness'.

'The position is unsatisfactory and legislation necessary. There is a certain number of people, though certainly not so many as we sometimes suppose, whose activities should be checked. Such activities will only embitter racial relations; they do positive harm to the individuals and expose natives to the penalties of lawlessness to which they were incited. Moreover, they excite the hostility of Europeans who otherwise might be well disposed towards them.'

Another feature of Hofmeyr's speeches was that, after having won a seat for the South African Party, he kept on calling for realignment. In some places he stated specifically that although he had come to discuss political questions, it was not as a politician. What the party bosses thought, no one knows. Smuts was away in England, talking about his dreams for the White Highlands of Africa.

Hofmeyr took great trouble over his maiden speech. He chose to make it on Dr Malan's Immigration Quota Bill, which proposed to allow unrestricted immigration from certain countries and to set a limit for others. Among the countries limited were those from which most of the Jewish immigrants were coming, seeking to escape not only the ghettos of Eastern Europe but the economic distress of the Western world.

Hofmeyr memorised his speech and knew every word in it from the first to the last. He was more nervous about his first speech in Parliament than he had ever been about any as Administrator. The House was full and expectant, but after a few minutes the expectancy had died away; members began to drift out of the House. Hofmeyr, knowing that he had lost, stuck it out for forty minutes, giving the strange impression of a reciter who wasn't enjoying reciting, but who, having started, must go on to the end. John Cope, parliamentary correspondent of the *Natal Mercury*, another of Hofmeyr's admirers and potential disciples, sent him a note, 'Dear Mr Hofmeyr, you're going to get a bad press. It was a completely memorised speech. Don't be discouraged.'

The House was not only expectant; some of its members were hostile. It would have been useless to try to disarm them with a joke or two. Many not hostile were critical; this was Parliament, and even ex-Administrators must pass the test. Yet others were crestfallen; they had boasted about their new recruit, and he had failed. Hofmeyr put on his armour, and went out into the lobbies, where he admitted to Cope his nervousness and the fact that he had known his speech by heart. It was very difficult for Hofmeyr not to know a speech by heart if he had once rehearsed it. There is only one hope for a speaker with such a memory, and that is to speak extempore, with or without notes; but that one cannot do well unless one is unconstrained. On this occasion he was full of constraint; he was not speaking to a jolly group of well-fed and well-wined engineers, but to the toughest audience in the country, and he had failed. He did not recover from his speech for the rest of the session.

The whole purpose of the 1929 election had been to save white South Africa from being swamped by Smuts's great African dominion, and to give the Nationalists a mandate to settle the 'Native question' once and for all. Yet the Prime Minister yielded to Smuts's persuasion to refer his race policies to a select committee, and Hofmeyr was appointed to it. So now at last there was a chance for Hertzog to secure agreement, and thereafter the two-thirds majority required for alteration of the entrenched clauses of the constitution. Hofmeyr was hopeful about it, and wrote to Underhill that there was 'a determination on both sides to come to a settlement which the native can accept as reasonable and which will satisfy the conscience of the civilised world'.

Hofmeyr liked committee work, and excelled at it. He made no further attempt at a big speech. He certainly liked the parliamentary life. Parliament itself, the procedures, the etiquette, the precedents, fascinated him, and soon no one was to know as much about them as he. Something else fascinated him too, and that was Smuts in the caucus. Whatever one thought of his policies, Smuts was a great man amongst men; there were those in his party, not eager young boys any longer, but men, who would have died for him. His leadership was beyond questioning, even by those loyal monarchists who wanted him to repudiate utterly every Nationalist move towards greater national independence. His party may have contained intriguers, but no one intrigued against him. Himself free from personal hates and grudges, he did not excite them in others, excepting the Prime Minister, whose bitter attacks told more of himself than of Smuts. Hofmeyr, who had known him only at Doornkloof and on the public platform, began to cease to resist him. He gave to his leader a respect that was akin to veneration, and that was easier to do, and more difficult not to do, when all his associates had done it already. Smuts won Hofmeyr, as he won many others, not by charm or argument, but by the simple expedient of being himself. So he was able to hold in one party men of diverse interests and beliefs, Afrikaners willing to move slowly for the sake of racial peace, English monarchists not willing to move at all, big money and big business, intellectuals and hardheaded practicalists, the warm-hearted and the clear-headed, countrymen and townsmen, white supremacists and negrophiles.

And then on the other side of the House, the Nationalist freedom fighters. Hertzog, with his ascetic face and plain speaking, charming and unapproachable, at the height of his power. Havenga, one of the few who could approach the Prime Minister, loyal to a degree, untutored, yet the model of an able, conservative Finance Minister. Malan, Interior and Health, with implacable face and determination, an excellent administrator, second only to his leader in Nationalist esteem. Pirow, Justice, the rising young man, able and vigorous, feeling for Hertzog as a son for his father, Afrikaner with German affinities, for ever thinking about the destiny of the white man in Africa. They were worth watching. None of them was to like Hofmeyr, he was to like none of them. Their nationalism repelled him; and they, though they could not say then precisely how or why, saw in the new Smuts man a danger to their precious cause.

It was Hofmeyr's first personal encounter with men who placed the survival and strengthening of Afrikanerdom above every other value. He had met Nationalists aplenty, and seen them in action, but that was in the kindergarten of a Provincial Council where there still prevailed a convention that the primary concern was provincial welfare and not national policy. But here in Parliament it became clear that justice and mercy and truth and all those things called rights and freedoms, while certainly not to be ignored, were to be placed in a hierarchy in which survival was supreme. There was a theory of course that the pursuit of survival and the pursuit of justice were really one and the same, and that underneath any apparent injustice there was really a greater and more fundamental justice; but it was unsatisfactory for any believer or humanist when the injustice was flagrant and the justice unseen.

Perhaps it was this encounter with the freedom fighters of those days, or perhaps it was the encounter with the order and majesty of parliamentary government, that caused Hofmeyr to qualify sharply though privately the praise that he had given publicly to Hertzog six months before in the matter of laws to control agitators. He wrote to Underhill:

'We have also passed a Riotous Assemblies Bill which gives the Government dictatorial powers (without redress in the Courts) over those whom it regards as agitators among the natives. We have all grown acutely sensitive about so-called communistic agitators, in fact communism is as much a bogey with us as Russia is with you.'

When the session was over and he had seen his mother safely back in Pretoria, Hofmeyr went to the Native College at Fort Hare to open the Bantu-European Student Christian Conference, the first gatherings of its size to be held in South Africa. One hundred and thirty African and sixty white students, together with one hundred and fifty senior people, met together to study and discuss Christianity and its social implications for South Africa. They met, as Bull said, in a time of danger and anxiety, when relations between white and black were a matter for concern. And they ask the same questions today as they asked at Fort Hare in 1930, 'What are black hopes, what are white hopes, and can they be hoped together?'

There was no doubt where Hofmeyr stood. We with our hindsight can note, with smugness if that pleases us, his use of words and ideas that have no meaning today, but there was no doubt where he was moving to. He chose one of his favourite themes, Unity in Diversity, the theme which more than any other divides the one kind of South African Christian from the other; for the one believes it is his duty to maintain diversity, and the other believes it is his duty to achieve unity. Some of those who shrink from Christian unity in any visible manifestation maintain that it is something spiritual and invisible, and will even argue that it is precisely the maintenance of diversity that will achieve it, so that theology, which should be the fruit of man's deepest searching, becomes instead the fruit of his deepest fears.

Though white and black slept separately at the conference, they ate together, the men at Fort Hare, the women at Lovedale where they were housed. On the Sunday morning there was a joint Communion service, which may have been the first ecumenical and interracial service of that size ever to have been held in South Africa. To some it was the deepest experience of their lives; they could hardly control the tumult of emotions that threatened to overwhelm them. Spiritual and invisible unity is very fine, but visible unity stabs at the heart and takes away the breath and fills one with unspeakable and painful joy, unspeakable because glory is unspeakable, painful because it is all a dream, and who knows how many years must pass and how many lives be spent and how much suffering undergone before it all comes true. And when it all comes true, only those who are steeped in the past will have any understanding of the greatness of the present. The emotion of joy was all the deeper because all fear had gone, the white fear of the black, the black fear of the white, gone at the sight of black and white kneeling humbly before the Lord of them all, here in this very countryside where their forefathers had fought implacably against each other in the bitter frontier wars. 'There is undoubtedly a rising tide of liberalism among the younger generation in regard to native questions,' wrote Hofmeyr to Underhill. 'One only hopes that it may assert itself in time.'

Sleeping in separate hostels is quite unexceptionable. Eating at the same tables is tricky, of course, but at least men sat with men and women with women. Discussion together, well, if you think any good will come of it, carry on. There was not really much that the Nationalists could say against the whole affair. But the students, young and eager, gave them something. They decided to play a game of rugby football, Fort Hare versus the rest. If it had been chess, no one would have worried, perhaps no one would have known; any indoor game. And if it had to be out of doors, then tennis; or if one really had to, a game of soccer. But rugby, where men grappled with each other, and threw each other to the ground, and scrummed together head to head! It was a scandal.

It was a scandal indeed, even though the game was finally called off. What young white men wanted to do in the eagerness of their budding love, what they had thought to be some kind of witness for Christ, some message of hope to the country, was looked upon as foolish, indecent, even wicked. Their action was condemned by leading white people all over the country. This was not Christianity, it was liberalism; not love, but sentimentality. And the Nationalists did not neglect to note that the conference had been opened by Hofmeyr, with one of those brotherhood-of-man speeches that were his stock in trade, but which had so little relevance to the hard realities of life.

This whole year 1930 was an important year in Hofmeyr's life. He was, on 20 March, thirty-six years of age, yet new thoughts were moving in his mind. It was not just Parliament that was responsible; it was the association with Currey, Schreiner, Brookes, Ramsbottom, and Haarhoff. His old student, Herbert Frankel, was full of new economic ideas. Hofmeyr was beginning to re-examine his terminology, and discussion with his friends was helping him to remedy the disadvantages of too analytical a mind. Rheinallt Jones, though not himself an original mind, was quick to assimilate the clear thinking that Hoernlé and others were bringing to race questions, and to pass it on.

Back in Pretoria after a visit to the boys' camp at Anerley, Hofmeyr settled down to discussion with his collaborators in the writing of *Coming of Age*. Both Schreiner and Currey noted that he did not play a vigorous part in the discussions. That was not surprising; he was hearing new ideas. For years he had been speaking, now he was thinking. It was decided that he would write the introduction, and also one of the studies, that dealing with the relatively uncontroversial subject of 'Provincial and Local Government'. It was agreed that he was not committed to the views expressed, especially on the controversial matters dealt with by the other writers, and this partly because of his party affiliations, but more specifically because of his membership of the select committee on Hertzog's Native Bills.

His introduction was to the point, although written from a white point of view. There was, he said, an uneasiness, a *malaise*, in South Africa, and for three reasons, the first being the delay in achieving national union, accompanied by the waning of the influence of the English language and men of English speech. The second reason for uneasiness was economic, the race against time to industrialise the country before the mines gave out. The third was the 'Native problem,' the white man's fear of the economic advance of the black man, and of the growth of his political rights, the fear of the black revenge which prevents the white man from making any concession of power, the fear that one day 'little brown children will play among the ruins of the Union Buildings'.

Hofmeyr saw the task as that 'of making South Africa safe for European civilisation without paying the price of dishonour to the highest ideals of that civilisation'. That seems to be still the question, and there are still two white answers to it, as there were in 1930; the first is that only white power can preserve civilisation, the second is that only shared power can do it. And in 1930, as now, each group finds the answer of the other dangerous.

Although Hofmeyr had already used the phrase 'Native problem' in his introduction, he declared that he and his fellow-writers found it invalid, and that the problem was one of how white and black could live together in peace and harmony to their common advantage. The very use of such words, 'live together', 'common advantage', indicated the trend of his thought, for barely twelve months before, he had replied to Pirow that segregation was the ideal policy, if only one would pay the price; but in his introduction, segregation as a policy was not put forward at all. Why, even that new Lion of the North, the future Prime Minister Johannes Gerhardus Strijdom, said in the House that very year, 'It is universally acknowledged that rightly or wrongly, total segregation is no longer possible in South Africa.' But while Strijdom moved reluctantly away from segregation, Hofmeyr was moving slowly towards a shore but dimly seen, of that country called by some Utopia, and by others the Never-never-land, and by modern liberals the Common Society. It was a voyage into the unknown, and he had as compass nothing but his own convictions, and now the convictions of others who were seeking the same country. He was to be called impractical by the hard-headed, but he was as practical and as hard-headed as they. Was it they who understood the world too well, and he too little? Or was it they who understood too little, believing that fear and self-interest drive men along the hard road of life, with love and justice but pretty flowers that grow along the way?

Besides his writing, he had agreed to do a great deal of public speaking for the Party, and he declined the offer of a Carnegie grant to go to the

States and study problems common to both countries. Although he still hoped actively for *hereniging*, he had become a loyal Party man, and began to attack the Nationalists in a vigorous fashion. He accused Malan of exploiting racial fear in order to get conservative white farmers to give the vote to white women, and he reminded Malan, as many others were to remind him for some twenty years, that only two years earlier he had said that he personally would like to give coloured women the vote. But he was on several public occasions very generous to the Prime Minister. Hertzog had scored another success in Britain in 1930, where he had expressed his satisfaction with South Africa's constitutional progress, but wanted it defined in both British and South African law. He had stilled British fears of the German trade treaty by seeking closer economic relationships with Britain. Hofmeyr praised Hertzog for this, and said he hoped that the Prime Minister would persevere along the path of Commonwealth co-operation. Hofmeyr made it clear once and for all that although he was a liberal, he was working for *hereniging*, and not for the formation of a new liberal party, which he said was not practical politics.

Coming of Age was published at the end of 1930, and was well received by the press. Its success was modest, and its readers were confined to a highly select public, of whom less than two thousand bought the English edition, and only one hundred or so the Afrikaans. *Coming of Age* was the product of the liberalism of the thirties. Currey and Haarhoff stated that until national unity between the white races had been achieved, the question of the extent to which non-white peoples were members of the nation must be held over, a view that liberals no longer hold, believing that a call for white unity is either a call for the continuance of white domination or an excuse for indefinite delay. Haarhoff looked to the day when the English-speaking South African would value Afrikaner tradition, and the Afrikaner would value English literature as his own. Currey thought that the introduction of the idea of hereditary monarchy had brought South Africa a great advantage, and Ramsbottom thought that South Africa and Southern Rhodesia should have a joint policy for the development of their native peoples. Schreiner and Ramsbottom tackled the franchise, and took the modern view that the economic situation of the non-white people was intimately connected with their votelessness. The writers thought it was incontestable that Hertzog's proposed Bills were animated by a desire to curtail parliamentary representation; the Bills were based on the belief that white and non-white interests were in conflict. Clearly the writers did not believe in territorial segregation, either as an ideal or as a possibility; they believed in some kind of common society and a common electoral roll, and they laid down three possibilities for franchise, namely the enfranchisement of all adults, or the enfranchisement of all adults irrespective of race who possess certain qualifications, or finally, the enfranchisement of all white adults irrespective of qualification and of such non-white adults as possess certain qualifications. Schreiner and Ramsbottom decided that the second form of franchise was morally superior to the others; but because it was hopeless to expect it, they decided in favour of the third, which, if white fears of swamping increased, could be amended.

Such was the liberalism of 1930. What did Currey and Haarhoff mean by national unity between the white races? They meant that a considerable majority of the white people should agree on a plan for achieving South African harmony; they did not say what white people should agree about, but simply that they should agree. Quite clearly Schreiner and Ramsbottom did not think that Hertzog's Bills offered a sound basis for this agreement; yet for Hofmeyr at least they offered a sound basis for discussion. It is fair to conclude that the liberalism of the thirties, inadequate as it may now appear to be, was slightly ahead of Hofmeyr; his main political aim was still *hereniging*.

The prospects for *hereniging* were improving. On his return from the Imperial Conference Hertzog rebuked the Nationalist intransigents, who wanted nothing less than republican independence. Some of them were saying that in his decline he was becoming a second Botha, while Smuts said that he had been converted in London. Neither of these judgements was just, for neither recognised the Prime Minister's peculiar and stubborn honesty. Hofmeyr was nearer the mark when he wrote to Underhill that Hertzog had caught the South African Party bathing and had stolen their clothes, but Hofmeyr believed, on this occasion, that he was sincere.

Hofmeyr's second session was more successful than his first. He established himself as one of the foremost debaters of his party by delivering two speeches which were regarded as two of the most remarkable of the session. The first was a brilliant appraisal of the budget, made by one of the few members competent to criticise Havenga. Its brilliance lay in its mastery of the material and its reliance on memory, but it contained no oratory; indeed it could not, for Havenga and Hofmeyr were too much alike, and had the same attitude towards public finances, both being thrifty and conservative, both believing that a budget ought to be balanced, both seeing no virtue in an unexpectedly large surplus and only shame in an unexpectedly large deficit.

Hofmeyr's second speech was on Malan's Higher Education Control Bill. It was his first big clash with the leader of the Cape Nationalists. Malan was dissatisfied with the amount of time that was being taken to equalise the opportunities offered to English-language and Afrikaans-language universities. He proposed to confer on the Minister powers to veto any appointment of which he disapproved, and powers to disapprove items in the university budgets, which must be submitted in more detailed form than before. Hofmeyr resisted these proposals, not only out of unsurpassed knowledge, but out of his real belief in academic freedom. In committee Hofmeyr scrutinised every clause, and he and Smuts 'saved for Parliament much that Malan desired to take for his office'. But though Malan made these concessions, he strengthened his control over university finances.

Nothing could have shown more clearly than this debate the difference between Malan's nationalism and Hofmeyr's. Malan was concerned always for the unity, independence, security, and general well-being of the Afrikaner people, and such an ideal as academic freedom, no doubt worthy in itself, could not be allowed to interfere. Hofmeyr on the other hand believed that the free pursuit of knowledge by those best qualified was one of the guarantees of the well-being of a people. He attacked Malan as he never would have attacked Hertzog, accusing him of trying to make himself 'the Grand Inquisitor of the institutions of higher education, a role which he would very aptly fill'.

Hofmeyr, by complimenting Hertzog and attacking Malan, was playing a political game. It was well known that Hertzog, especially since what Smuts called his 'conversion', found Malan's intransigence irritating, while Malan found Hertzog's new reasonableness dangerous. It was also well known that Hertzog had allowed Roos to outmanoeuvre Malan on several occasions, notably during the flag controversy; most people shrank from challenging Malan's inflexibility, but Roos sailed past it, all charm and joviality, defeating by bonhomie what was in fact great force of character. Hofmeyr was therefore not endangering *hereniging* by attacking Malan; it is even possible that Hertzog himself may have disapproved of Malan's desire to interfere with the universities. Hofmeyr's speech, full of knowledge and conviction, made a deep impression on the House, causing the Malan men to wonder again how any Nationalist could have been so foolish as to imagine Hofmeyr would join them.

H. H. Moll, who a few years earlier had wanted to become Hofmeyr's lieutenant, said he was sorry to attack Hofmeyr, because he had had such high hopes of him; but he had never made a single speech or done a single act in the interests of justice and right for the Dutch-speaking South Africans, nor had he ever made an important speech in Afrikaans, which was not true and Hofmeyr denied it. When Hofmeyr joined the South African Party, the Nationalists had hoped for better co-operation, but the very opposite had happened.

Moll's bitter speech caused anger on the other side of the House. The speaker himself later faded away, but on behalf of the 'true Nationalists' he had declared war on Hofmeyr, who was a danger to Afrikanerdom, because Afrikaner survival was not the supreme goal of his life.

While the select committee was considering Hertzog's Native Bills, the Prime Minister brought before the House a measure which if passed would enable him to change radically the value of the Coloured and African franchise in the Cape without altering the franchise itself, for which alteration he would have required a two-thirds majority of both Houses sitting together, this franchise being protected by one of two entrenchments in the South African constitution, the other being the equality of English and Afrikaans as the two official languages. In 1930 the Prime Minister, opposed by many of his own party, including two of his Ministers, but supported by the South African Party, had enfranchised, on the basis of unqualified adult suffrage, every white woman in the country. Now in 1931 he proposed to extend the unqualified male suffrage of the Transvaal and the Free State to the Cape and Natal, where men had enjoyed only a qualified suffrage. In 1930 the Prime Minister had virtually doubled the white vote; now in 1931, by extending the unqualified franchise to all white men, he strengthened it still further. Therefore without touching the non-white vote, he was not only halving its value, but was undermining the equality principle implicit in the Cape non-racial franchise.

Hofmeyr strongly opposed the Bill, not only because of its undermining effect, but because he thought it was being done in a discreditable manner. He challenged the Government to say openly that it was abandoning the equality principle of the Cape. Hofmeyr often appeared evasive when dealing with the question of advancing towards the shared society, but he always knew where he was in regard to existing rights, and resisted any attempt to change them.

One realises better the intensity of Afrikaner fear of 'swamping' (which has since infected more and more English-speaking people), when one remembers that in 1930, after Hertzog had enfranchised white women, African voters were less than 2 per cent of the South African electorate, some 15,000 out of 892,000. In the twenty-four years after 1903, the Cape African vote rose from 8,117 to 14,912, which was an increase of 295 per annum, while the Cape white vote rose from 114,450 to 162,323, which was an increase of 2,081 per annum. The fearful could hardly claim that they were being 'swamped'; therefore they pointed to the fact that these 14,912 African voters 'decided' the vote in so many Cape constituencies, which was shocking because it meant, first, that they were deciding important white issues, and second, that they were being drawn into white quarrels. They also pointed out that while the actual annual increase appeared to favour the Cape whites, in actual fact in 1903 the African voters formed 7 per cent of the Cape total, and in 1926 they formed 9 per cent of the total. But there were many to deny that fear was operating at all; what was operating was the desire for racial separation, the desire to give a different kind of representation to Africans, more suited to their genius and state of development, the desire to retreat from the repugnant notion that black men did have and should have any part in white society.

Whatever was the case, Hofmeyr was thought by the 'true Afrikaners' either too sentimental or too naïve to make proper allowance for the fear, and too Anglicised to understand the fierce desire to hold nothing whatsoever in common with any non-white people, certainly not Africans or Indians, except those things that God in His Providence had made it inevitable to hold in common, like air, disease, and currency. They admitted that he was Afrikaner by blood but they declared that of the spiritual essence of Afrikanerdom he knew almost nothing at all.

His book *South Africa*, which was published at the end of the 1931 session, did nothing to change these opinions. In his chapter on 'South Africa's National Future', which was really on the future of Anglo-Afrikaner relations, he hoped for a realignment, and added that 'the possibility of the coming into being of a strong Republican party will need careful watching', and that 'such an eventuality might present a grave threat to the peaceful development of South Africa'. He was thinking of Malan and his men.

It is easy for us with our hindsight to criticise Hofmeyr's *South Africa*, but our present duty is to do so. Hofmeyr's vision of the relations between South Africa and the North, of increasingly closer bonds, has been falsified by time. His own suggestion, repeated by Smuts in the Rhodes Lectures, that South, Central and Eastern African governments should meet to shape common policies, was stillborn; and the reason why it was stillborn was because the attitudes of the British and South African governments towards the future status of African people were quite different. His hope that South African science would play a part in Africa's development has to some minor extent been realised, but there is today little likelihood of more, and much likelihood of less. His vision of the Commonwealth, his assertion of the strength of its bonds, could not keep South Africa within it. But which of us could have foreseen our present isolation?

Hofmeyr in his discussion of the 'Native problem'—a phrase to which he had returned—expressed clearly a view which is still held strongly by the United Party—the heirs, in a way which we shall later understand, to the South African Party. That view was that the political aspect of the 'Native problem' had acquired an entirely false emphasis, and should be regarded as subordinate to the question of economic adjustment; Hofmeyr, stimulated by Frankel, had come to hold strongly the view that the raising of African living standards was the key to the future prosperity of the country. But Hofmeyr in his *South Africa* was more specific about African development than he had ever been before. He rejected the 'equalisation' of the missionaries, and the 'repression' of some of the colonists, and declared for 'differentiation', that is development 'on distinctively native lines'. Hofmeyr appeared to approve of the Native Trust and Land Act of 1913, which was to prevent Africans from buying any more land in the 'white' areas of South Africa, and to confine them forever to areas, constituting one-seventh of the Union, which had been set aside for them, although they contributed two-thirds of the population; but what Hofmeyr approved of has been for subsequent generations of Africans one of the cruellest deprivations they have ever been made to suffer. 'Behind all these things looms the problem of the land,' wrote Hofmeyr, for self-development of the African depended on that. But complete territorial separation he ruled out as impossible, though he would have favoured it. 'Too late,' he wrote, 'and therein is South Africa's tragedy.'

Did Hofmeyr understand fully what he was writing about? Was it really development along one's own lines that the Fort Hare conference had talked about, or was it the need for community? Is the whole

Christianising process compatible with development along one's own lines? And if it is, what about the philosophical and political ideas that owe their inspiration to Christianity? The truth is he had been caught in a cliché, in the days before he began to think. Yet he understood in part, for he wrote that if differentiation proved to be no longer practicable, 'then difficult, indeed, will be the path which South Africa must tread, between a policy of repression and subjection on the one hand and a policy of identity and equality on the other. It will have great need of vision and of faith, if it is to find the road.'

He concluded his book by detailing all the things that South Africa 'would' do, using *would* in the sense of having a will to. It would make itself safe for European civilisation, without paying the price of dishonour to the highest ideals of that civilisation. It would be the bearer of civilisation in Africa, and contribute, by virtue of the very greatness of its racial difficulties, to the solution of the outstanding political problem of the twentieth-century world. 'In the opportunities of service beyond its borders is South Africa's high calling. It will not yet fail in giving diligence to make its calling and election sure.'

May it yet be even so.

South Africa had a generous reception from the national press, particularly because of its impartiality. It strengthened Hofmeyr's attraction for the peace-lovers, with its calm survey of past conflicts, its hope for a new white South Africanism, its recognition of non-white aspirations, especially towards a better material life. It apportioned praise and blame with fine impartiality, praising missionaries for this but blaming them for that, praising farmers for this but blaming them for that, praising administrators when they sided with the missionaries or the farmers when these were praiseworthy, and blaming the administrators for siding with them when they were blameworthy. *Punch* said that the author applied 'tactful discretion so lavishly that one may almost hear it drip from the gearbox on to the track-way of his narrative', and said that he kept the reader guessing as to what bits of least-forgotten history he would leave out next. The *Sunday Times* of Britain said that he used 'tact in excess' to the point in some cases of *suppressio veri*. The *Christian Science Monitor* said that he hardly made vivid enough 'how profound and dangerous are the anxieties and bitternesses which are already surging around the bases of South Africa's political and economic life'.

But it was the *New York Times,* in a Book Review, that wrote most penetratingly. It said that Hofmeyr 'avoided the falsehood of extremes', yet also evaded their truth. It took Hofmeyr's statement that it was too late to apply a policy of differentiated development, and quoted his remark 'Therein is South Africa's tragedy'.

'The word *tragedy* shows how difficult it is for the Cape Dutch to emancipate themselves from the slaveholding sentiment of the past. The fact that the Negro has ceased to be a serf and refused to be a segregated captive, insisting on the position of "co-worker in the building up of South Africa's economic life" is not "a tragedy" but an opportunity. That opportunity, including education, is what the missionary, despite all his blunders, realised far ahead of time.'

Hard words, but true. But it is not only the Cape Dutch who find it difficult to emancipate themselves, it is almost every white South African. This is fear speaking here, the fear of the white South African whose mind cannot encompass and whose soul cannot rejoice in the idea of the liberation of his non-white fellow citizens from every restriction of true liberty. Hofmeyr wrote that South Africa would need vision and faith, and he meant, even if he did not know it, that he would need them too.

If it was fear that so blinded Hofmeyr that he could not see opportunity but only tragedy, and made him speak as a white man and not as a Christian, it was fear also that opened his eyes and helped him to see clearly the danger that a party might emerge that would be a grave threat to the peaceful development of South Africa. He meant the emergence of a party that would put the welfare and survival of the Afrikaner people above any consideration of liberty and justice.

He saw clearly the danger of Malan and his men, more clearly than the great Smuts himself.

Chapter 6

Coalition and Fusion

SOUTH AFRICA, like many other countries, was having bad times. The United States, in deep depression, was buying no diamonds, and the price of wool dropped all over the world. To make it worse, the end of 1930 and the opening of 1931 was a time of severe drought; rain usually comes to the high interior in October or November, and then follow ploughing and planting, so that the crops can ripen before the winter comes again. But with planting time almost over, the interior plains of the Free State and the Transvaal still lay parched under the burning skies of the worst drought for over 60 years. Hofmeyr, by no means a countryman, never failed to mention drought when there was one; it was his nearest approach to natural description.

In 1931 Havenga taxed townsmen heavily to keep farmers on the land, and the prices of maize and wheat were fixed irrespective of demand. The trade of Europe went into a decline, and there was a run on the banks. Great Britain, on 21 September, left the gold standard. Smuts, who was in England, sent cables home urging that South Africa should leave the gold standard immediately. He had the support of nearly all those who had goods to sell, except the farmers, who were torn in two between their desire to make a living and their desire to demonstrate the economic strength of their now independent country. But the powerful Chamber of Mines supported Havenga in his determination to stay on gold, because although they stood to benefit by a rising gold price if the country left the standard, they knew that it would also mean a rise of wages, difficult to lower when the standard returned.

The position continued to get worse. Among farmers and exporters the dissatisfaction was intense, and capital was leaving the country. Hertzog called Parliament together in November 1931, two months earlier than usual, and had to face a demand by Patrick Duncan, in Smuts's absence, that the country leave the gold standard immediately. Hertzog declared with passion that the Government would stand or fall with the standard which for him was the symbol of South Africa's economic independence, the loss of which would endanger its hard-won sovereignty. The pressure on him had increased because the Chamber of Mines had changed its ground, and now supported the abandonment; it was now prepared to face the prospect of deflation in the hopes of increasing the life of the low-grade mines. But Hertzog refused to yield. The House gave Havenga tremendous powers to regulate currency and exchange.

When Parliament resumed after a Christmas recess, Hertzog faced a dismal situation. In spite of Havenga's measures, farmers were still deserting the farms and going to the cities. It was clear that taxation would have to be increased, and public expenditure restricted. Although capital was beginning to return, some of the older mines had closed down, an event which always chills white South Africans, for the gold industry has been the stay of the state since Union in 1910. What is more, Smuts had returned from abroad, and had been up and down the country during the recess, telling the voters that leaving the gold standard would reopen mines, increase profits, reduce taxation, restore imports, and rehabilitate the farmers. Further, for the second year in succession the sun burned down on a rainless land.

But Hertzog still refused to yield. His bitter attacks on Smuts continued, making sometimes even his opponents embarrassed for him. Hertzog said of Smuts that in 1922 he incited men so that he could shoot them down, and that he was unconcerned about innocent people being killed; his footsteps dripped with blood. He said that South Africa was too small for Smuts; he wanted to stand on a mountain instead of an ant-heap, and to have his feet in two continents.

Was Hertzog jealous of his great antagonist, of his world fame, of his intellect, of his journeys and his honours? Whatever it was, it was a considerable defect in a man of considerable quality. Under these attacks Smuts sat silent, and frequently did not refer to them when he replied; nothing caused his followers to stand in awe of him so much as this. Hofmeyr could sit imperturbable under attack, but he was the recipient of baiting rather than of bitterness, and he could snort at it and rise to give thrice what he received. He could not, if he had wanted to, withhold his admiration from this extraordinary man, with the blue eyes of innocence and wisdom, and the self-containment that is given to or achieved by few; who not only forbore to reply but forbore also to taunt his tormentor for so revealing himself, this man who, although he believed that to cling to the gold standard would ruin South Africa, allowed his juniors to speak for it, and took no offence. In his speeches, Hofmeyr began to refer to Smuts as great.

It was nine o'clock in the evening when Hofmeyr rose to speak on the Prime Minister's motion to appoint a select committee to consider the gold standard. The debate was flagging, but when he rose the House came immediately to attention, because it was known that he disagreed with his Party. Members filed in from the lobbies, letter-writers put away their letters, the Prime Minister put away his book. Hofmeyr, his face white under the influence of emotion, said that he still believed that 'South Africa should remain on gold unless the price to be paid becomes too heavy'. The Nationalists laughed ironically at this. Hofmeyr did not think the price had become too heavy, but he refused to vote for the Prime Minister's proposal to appoint a select committee. He thought it was a national issue, and that the Prime Minister should have gone to his opponents and asked for their co-operation, instead of which, speaking on Dingaan's Day—the anniversary of the day when the Voortrekkers had defeated the Zulus, the holy day of Afrikanerdom— he had found for his followers the rallying cry for which they were looking, namely 'economic independence'.

Hofmeyr was loudly applauded by his own Party when he sat down. The setback of the maiden speech had finally been overcome. Why was he so under the influence of emotion? It was partly because he was doing a dramatic thing, differing openly from his own Party. But it might also have been the influence of Smuts's magnanimity. Hofmeyr told the House that he was proud to belong to a Party that allowed him the right to differ. 'It is to me unthinkable that I should belong to any other Party.'

When Hofmeyr was under the influence of pugnacious emotion, he was a dangerous opponent. His retorts were instant and biting. His impassivity quite left him, he was fighting, for his principles, for himself; his English became refined of all pomposity and floridity.

These personal victories in the House, while they enhanced his reputation, did not alter his temperament. After them his impassivity returned; he accepted compliments formally, for he had already retreated into himself. John Cope, his friend and admirer, wrote that Hofmeyr sat aloof in Parliament, and that, like General Smuts, he was lonely and had no real friends among his fellow men. 'The tragedy of it all is that by nature he is companionable, and longs to be able to unburden himself, but his sensitive mind can never quite find its parallel. Probably, it never will.'

Cope was right, but not altogether. Hofmeyr's mind could have found parallels. Though he was a genius, he was not primarily a thinking genius. It was his self that could not find a parallel. He was sundered from his fellows, not so much by his intellect, as by his incredible childhood.

Quite another person was Oswald Pirow, who was supposed to be to Hertzog what Hofmeyr was supposed to be to Smuts, a kind of lieutenant-heir. Pirow had brains too, but he boxed, shot, flew planes, and wrestled. He was proving a strong but impulsive Minister of Justice; Patrick Duncan, as a compliment, called him turbulent. He was not quite so approachable as Tielman Roos, not quite so opportunistic, but oppor-tunistic enough. Whereas Roos had had few doctrines, Pirow had some; one was the doctrine of white superiority, which he held not only be-cause he was white, but also because he was sure of it. With his German affinities and his assurance of superiority, he eyed with approval the new man Hitler and his promises to use power without sentimental inhibitions when he got it.

No sooner had Pirow become Minister of Justice than he did an extraordinary thing; instead of acting decorously from Pretoria, he led his police in person against the pitifully paid black dock labourers on strike in Durban. He was responsible for the Riotous Assemblies Amendment Act, which gave him dictatorial powers; he later complained that Smuts allowed these powers to fall into disuse. Now in 1932 he introduced the Native Service Contract Bill which gave the State new powers over the African tenants of white farmers. On each white farm lived labour ten-ants who in return for the use of some land gave so many months' labour every year to the farmer, either free or for a very small wage, each member of the family contributing. But often it would happen that the tenant might want to send the growing child to school, or that the grown child would go to the towns and not return when it was time to give his labour. Pirow, strongly supported by the Afrikaans-speaking farmers of the Transvaal and the English-speaking farmers of Natal, intended to put an end to these derelictions. It was already a criminal offence for a ten-ant's children to break a contract, but now sons of 18 or under could be whipped for it by the courts. Now also if sons or daughters broke a contract, which they often did in defiance of their parents, the whole family could be ejected. The power of farmer over labourer was made almost absolute.

Not all tenants were labourers; some were squatters, and paid rent to the farmer, thus avoiding labour obligations. Their breadwinners often worked in the cities, thus angering neighbouring farmers. Pirow proposed to tax farmers £5 per annum for each male able-bodied squatter, which would have compelled them to give up the practice; and if the squatters left, where could they go, and what could they do, but give up their little freedom, and become labour tenants? Farm labour is, with commendable exceptions, the most backward and depressed labour in South Africa; and it is difficult for anyone to break out of its bonds, for where is he to go? Many a bright child has stayed in these bonds, never to know his powers, or perhaps only dimly to sense them; sometimes his parents free him, and take the consequences.

Smuts's party unanimously opposed the squatting tax, but his farmer members supported the collective responsibility clause and the whipping clause. Many church leaders denounced the Bill, but it was carried. Hertzog remaining silent throughout the debate. Such was Pirow; he believed in white superiority and he legislated to preserve it. He, like all extreme Nationalists, regarded such things as human rights and dignities as obstacles that impeded the majestic advance of the State, especially if the sufferer were not one of the elect; the word *elect* he used in a Hitlerian rather than a Calvinist sense. It was clear that there could be nothing in common between Pirow and Hofmeyr. To Hofmeyr, however lonely and guarded he was in personal relationships, the person was all. Yet sometimes his friends wished he could have thundered about persons as he did about principles.

At this time he was writing regularly for the *Manchester Guardian* on South African topics, and his articles were marred by this impersonality. Of the Native Service Contract Bill, with its inhuman conditions smelling strongly of slavery, he wrote 'on the principles of the Forced Labour Convention adopted at Geneva in 1930, it would indeed be difficult to justify it'. But his friends were longing to hear him say that the Bill was unjustifiable because it offended not against the Convention but against the teachings of Christ and the highest ethics of man. Of the pernicious clause which permitted an African parent to bind his child to a contract, usually under economic pressure, he said that it savoured almost of the farming out of children, whereas it *was* in fact the farming out of children. What made it exasperating was that he himself would rather have died than be responsible for such a bill.

Pirow himself said of Hofmeyr that he lacked aggressiveness, and was therefore better at resisting than attacking. There was another big difference between them. Pirow loved the press, Hofmeyr was always uncomfortable with it. When Cope wanted to do a sketch of Hofmeyr, what is today called a profile, Hofmeyr refused to help him. One concludes that Hofmeyr was very like T. E. Lawrence, who liked publicity only when he had some control of it, when he was on a platform making a big speech, or being interviewed on something in which he had the initiative. But other publicity he disliked; it came too near the deep and private self. Look what Cope wrote—that he was lonely, yet wanting nothing more than friends. One could hardly snort at that.

Hofmeyr attacked the Native Service Contract Bill on the grounds of its cruelty to those people who would be ejected from homes, and have nowhere to go.

'Does segregation merely mean forcing the native out from where he is today, so that he has to work for the white man, or does it mean giving him an opportunity to develop on his own lines? Does it mean developing on his own lines, or on the lines of working for the white man? If . . . the affirmative, I ask him (the Minister) to assist in getting that principle [opportunity for development] enshrined in this legislation. If that principle is not enshrined, this clause is going to be nothing short of a breach of faith with the natives.'

It was a difficult session for the Government. There was much dissatisfaction in those rural constituencies where Hertzog had his strength. What is more, his majority had declined by six, and he was not looking forward to a by-election in the constituency of Colesberg. Havenga went to Ottawa in July, and laid the foundation for trade preferences which were to last for nearly thirty years, besides making a reputation for himself as a sound, conservative, decent negotiator. Yet not even his successful debut overseas could give his party more than a narrow win at Colesberg, where embattled Nationalist Afrikanerdom exploited to the full the two relentless enemies of the people, the blacks and the English.

There was another by-election pending in Germiston, the industrial and mining town just outside Johannesburg. In 1929 Smuts had not been able to find a candidate willing to fight. In 1932 Strauss, the Smuts nominee, defeated his Nationalist opponent by over a thousand votes. Labour polled an ignominious 132. It was clear that the gold standard was losing its grip.

The Smuts victory at Germiston was followed by a second at Roodepoort, in a Transvaal provincial by-election. The electorate, frustrated by the Smuts-Hertzog stalemate, was filled with excitement and expectancy. Most restless of all was Mr Justice Roos, who had not been six months on the Appeal Bench before he had wanted to get back to politics. No one knew this better than Hertzog, and when he learned that Piet Grobler, his Minister of Lands, had promised to make way for Roos if he returned, he told him that under no circumstances would he take Roos into the Cabinet, and he wished Roos to know it. On principle Hertzog did not approve of judges returning to politics.

Tielman Roos was unsnubbable. He approached his young friend Pirow, who had made a similar promise, and was quite ready to carry it out until he realised that the Prime Minister was adamant. Roos also approached his old enemy Dr Malan, who took the story straight to Hertzog.

This was Roos's reputation, a man who wanted power, and would use any means to get it. On the holy day, Dingaan's Day, 16 December of 1932, he was the chief speaker at a Transvaal hamlet Haakboslaagte where, with a slight bow to the Voortrekkers, and no bow at all to the Appeal Bench, he told his hearers that it was madness to stick to the gold standard, and imperative to get a National Government. Six days later he came down from the Bench. The result was spectacular: money began to pour out of the country in a flood, in the hopes that it could soon be brought back at a premium. But if the voters looked forward to a relief from their economic frustration, they looked forward to political salvation as well, to a breakaway from the Hertzog-Smuts stalemate, and who could do it but Roos, that confident jovial fellow whose cheerful face looked up from every newspaper, and who, if he was a Nationalist, was obviously one of a most delightful kind? Roos put up at the Carlton Hotel in the heart of Johannesburg, and received an endless stream of callers, some of them very important. Six days after he left the Bench, came the ultimate event. Warned by the banks that the outflow of money was bringing the country to disaster, Havenga announced that South Africa had left the gold standard. Hertzog refused to resign, maintaining that he had been forced to yield. In his New Year's message he spoke with bitterness of the triumph of the money power, that had humbled Afrikanerdom with the help of an old friend who had once been so active in the Nationalist cause.

Most countries that go off gold do so to keep going. But South Africa now entered the most exciting period of her economic history. Gold, that had been worth £4 an ounce, went up to £6, then £7 an ounce. Mines that had threatened to close down began to earn £2 to £3 an ounce. Dying mines came alive. Rich mines stopped working rich ore, and worked only the poor. Gold shares doubled, trebled, quadrupled in value. Johannesburg pulled down its old buildings, and began to remake itself. Money from taxes, customs, luxuries, and especially from the mines themselves, began to pour into Havenga's treasury, making complete nonsense of his budget. The gold-mining industry, that had kept the country going during the crisis, now made it possible to rehabilitate farmers, establish industries, reopen businesses. All the public servants in the country were jubilant when Havenga announced that he would restore the salary cuts that they had suffered for two years; to many of them it was like coming into a fortune.

Full of a sense of power, Roos called on all parties to unite under him, meaning the South African Party and those unnamed and unnumbered Nationalist M.P.s who were prepared to follow him. No one knew just how many there were, but ten of them sat on his platform in the City Hall, at one of the most wildly enthusiastic meetings Johannesburg had ever seen. That same evening in Germiston, Smuts was saying a cautious word of welcome to Roos; but in Johannesburg Roos was speaking of Smuts with contempt.

It was Hofmeyr who had advised Smuts to be friendly towards Roos. No one could yet tell what havoc Roos might cause in the Nationalist ranks. By this time Hofmeyr had joined the inner circle of the Party. Smuts had been away botanising when Roos resigned, and it was Hofmeyr who said publicly that if there was to be co-operation between the Party and a minority of the Nationalists, it would be Smuts who would lead it.

Early in the New Year Roos had planned a monster meeting in Pretoria, and Ivan Solomon, the 35-year-old Mayor of Pretoria, fearing another attack on Smuts, urged Hofmeyr to get Smuts to approach Roos before the meeting. But Hofmeyr said it was impossible; unless Roos showed some change of heart, no one should expect Smuts to approach him. Hofmeyr himself went to Roos's meeting, and exchanged a few friendly but non-political words with him in the Mayor's parlour. He thought Roos looked a very sick man; Roos said to him, 'This thing is going to kill me.'

The inner circle met again the following day. Smuts told his colleagues that he had decided to approach Roos, and was prepared to offer him the Deputy Prime Ministership and three seats in the Cabinet. He would even agree to the appointment of a third party as Prime Minister, provided he was an SAP man. Smuts's colleagues refused categorically to agree to this. They accepted Smuts's first proposal, and appointed Hofmeyr as negotiator. But they met again the next day, at Duncan's request. Duncan told them he did not like the idea of negotiating with Roos at all. What real policy had he to offer except that Hertzog must be ousted, and Roos take his place? Duncan said he would far rather negotiate with Hertzog. Smuts, who had so often sat silent under Hertzog's attacks, said emphatically that he could not work with him. So Hofmeyr's dream of *hereniging*, faded away.

Meanwhile Roos was the man of the hour in Cape Town. All over the country the coalition fever was spreading, and coalition committees were being formed in all the big cities. At Ventersdorp a tremendous meeting of maize farmers called for coalition; old enemies shook hands, and sent a deputation to Pretoria to urge Hertzog and Smuts to sink their differences. Smuts was gracious to them, but Hertzog stubborn.

On 10 January Roos returned to Johannesburg, and in the afternoon at the Carlton Hotel, he met Hofmeyr and Esselen. Roos proposed a cabinet of five Nationalists, five SAP men, one Labourite, with himself as Prime Minister, Hofmeyr put the blunt question to Roos, 'What support have you got in Parliament?' Roos said he was not prepared to discuss it, but support was a certainty. Hofmeyr said that in politics there were no certainties; if the South African Party formed a coalition with a minority of the Nationalists, that minority could hardly expect to have the premiership. To that Roos replied bluntly, 'You could not swing a dog into the movement from the Nationalist ranks unless there is to be a Nationalist Prime Minister.' When no agreement could be reached, Roos asked for the counter-offer. Hofmeyr gave it to him, Roos to get the deputy prime-ministership and three additional seats in the Cabinet. Roos said he wanted to consider it, and the meeting ended. Hofmeyr made a statement to the press; it merely said that negotiations were proceeding favourably, but that out of consideration for Mr Roos, he could give no details. The next day, he announced that Mr Roos did not wish to negotiate any further; having taken a certain line, he refused to budge from it, and therefore must be held responsible for the breakdown.

Smuts was in Cape Town, and he wired to Duncan, Reitz, and Hofmeyr to join him there. Smuts reported that pro-coalition feeling in the Cape was intense, and he felt that he should not stand in the way of it. He put forward a suggestion that they should accept Roos as Prime Minister, or perhaps Roos's nominee. Smuts's colleagues resisted the suggestion so strongly that after a day or two Smuts abandoned it. On Friday 19 January, Roos met Hofmeyr and Smuts at Smuts's house in Cape Town.

Roos said he realised Smuts's difficulties in accepting him as Prime Minister. But he also had difficulties; what would be his standing if he succeeded in doing no more than bring over true Nationalists to Smuts? He would be regarded as a traitor to the Afrikaner cause, and his influence would be ended. He was prepared to agree to a cabinet of ten, five SAP men and five of his supporters, one of whom would be a Labour man, this second five to choose the Prime Minister. He said frankly he could not promise that he would be able to turn out the Government. His parliamentary position was weak, but he thought it would become stronger.

The meeting ended, Roos saying that they must accept that agreement was not possible for the time being. Speaking later, in the Transvaal on 3 February, Roos announced that he had since offered Smuts seven SAP men in a cabinet of eleven, with Roos as Prime Minister; had Smuts accepted, the Government would have fallen before the end of January. But Smuts would not accept, the reason being of course that his closest colleagues would not hear of Roos as Prime Minister.

But Smuts's rank and file came very near to accepting Roos in caucus. Hofmeyr wrote:

'At first the tide was against us but during the four days several members swung over to our side—at the end we were just about equally divided. At the end the General summed up magnificently, stating that he could not accept the Roos offer. The caucus unanimously affirmed confidence in him, and left further negotiations in his hands.'

It was Smuts's statesmanship that conquered the caucus. After two days of silence he asked them some quiet questions. Could Roos really bring a worthwhile contribution to a coalition, and if he could, what would be the price of it? Would it not be an election more bitter than any before? And if the Party won, how sullen would be Hertzog and his Nationalists, thinking only of revenge, and plunging the country into new bitterness? No, he would not consent at such a price.

No wonder the caucus supported him. Some of them must have been ashamed, to think that they had been prepared to exchange this man for Roos.

While the South African Party was hesitating between Smuts and Roos, Smuts had a motion before the House, calling on Hertzog to resign, and to make way for a National Government. It was not a motion of no confidence; it was rather a proud man's way of asking for reconciliation. The speech was not a masterpiece of tact. Smuts reminded Hertzog that he had said there would never be devaluation so long as the Nationalist Party was in power, yet here were they all, 'clinging to their seats'. He went on, 'We bring our whole public life into contempt and shame when we do this sort of thing.' Smuts said his motion was an appeal for a new start in the politics of the country; the people were sick of party wrangling, and longed for it to come to an end. They had suffered the biggest economic loss of that generation, and they longed intensely for a new government, a coalition government, call it what one would. Smuts predicted that his Party would win the next election resoundingly but the bitterness would remain, and it would be an empty victory. He urged Hertzog to bow to the will of the people.

Hertzog replied to Smuts with a bitterness of invective that the House had rarely heard equalled. According to Pirow, Hertzog did this because he did not believe that Smuts's offer was sincere, especially as he believed Smuts to be then negotiating with Roos. He likened Smuts to an 'evil spirit'; he said that in England in September Smuts had 'resumed his historic role . . . a role which has already caused much blood and misery'. He accused Smuts of trying to incite people to the use of 'force and possibly to crime in order that he might become Prime Minister'. He warned Smuts that he would pay the penalty, and he, Hertzog, would see to it; otherwise through the member for Standerton the country would once more be 'plunged in blood'. Smuts had 'slunk round the country' to delude ignorant farmers about the gold standard, but the campaign had failed.

Hertzog called Smuts a 'political intriguer', but this was thought to be too strong, and he was forced to withdraw it by the Speaker. But he was able to accuse him of 'shamelessly and irresponsibly misleading the people', and of being arrogant and a presumptuous boaster. Smuts sat silent under the attack, but Piet van der Byl could not endure it, and called out angrily to the Prime Minister, 'Are you finished now with Smuts? Tell us a little about the gold standard.'

Hertzog rejected Smuts's proposition. He dismissed the idea of a heterogeneous coalition, in which there was no community of ideals, convictions, and objects. Coalition was only possible between spiritual allies. The prospects for *hereniging* were now certainly at their lowest ebb.

During the time that the South African Party caucus was still debating Tielman Roos, and the House was still debating Smuts's National Government proposal, Hofmeyr fell into casual conversation with Pen Wessels, Nationalist M.P., one of the eleven who had followed Hertzog into the wilderness in 1912. Wessels referred to the SAP's caucus troubles, and Hofmeyr replied that he hoped the party would reject Roos once and for all, thus leaving 'the way open for the bigger thing'. Wessels responded immediately that he thought something could be done about it. He admitted he had no authority for saying so; therefore either he did not know, or he knew only through rumour, that the Prime Minister had already discussed, first with his intimates Havenga and Pirow, and then with his Cabinet, the possibility of reconciliation. Perhaps also Wessels did not know that Havenga and Pirow had supported the Prime Minister strongly, and that Dr Malan had as strongly opposed him. Wessels promised Hofmeyr that he would keep in touch with him.

Next day Wessels told Hofmeyr that the time was ripe for an advance. He gave Havenga and Pirow as his authorities, and said that Hertzog would welcome an approach by Smuts before the winding up of the National Government debate. Smuts had already left the House and was climbing the mountain, and when he reached home, he found Hofmeyr waiting for him with the unbelievable news.

Hofmeyr never forgot Smuts's reaction to it. The younger man was not gifted with much psychological insight or acute powers of observation, but he knew that his leader, who could sit silent under bitter attack, and who seemed immune to many human emotions, was deeply affected. He watched Smuts struggling with the thought that he would have to serve under Hertzog, under the man whose narrowness and pettiness he had found at times almost unendurable, then struggling with the quite different thought that here within grasp was a miracle, thinking perhaps that here was not only a miracle for the country, but also for two men whose enmity had become a legend, so that no man dreamt they could ever come together. Then Smuts would return to the earlier thought, that he would have to serve under a man who had spoken of him with such contempt; not with mere political invective, but with some deep and private emotion, akin surely to hate. There was nothing for Hofmeyr to do but to watch Smuts struggling, and he knew that what he was watching no man might ever see again. Then Smuts asked him, whether it would not be possible to secure a National Government, to which he would give his blessing, while he remained outside it.

Some of Hofmeyr's detractors said that Smuts was always the general, and that he was always Jantjie, the small boy. There was a partial truth in it, but not in matters of duty. In such matters Hofmeyr was small boy to none. He told Smuts it was impossible for him to remain outside; what would it be like for Duncan and Reitz to enter the Cabinet without him? Smuts listened to him, and said he would think it over, but in his heart he knew that it was his pride that was talking, telling him to take a path other than that of duty. Why, was he not at that very moment calling for a National Government, and now that it was here, how could he stay out of it?

The following day he told Hofmeyr that he was willing to see Hertzog, but still uneasy, he asked first to see Havenga, who for reasons of his own would not see him. Smuts then put it off until he had wound up the National Government debate. His speech was more conciliatory than before. He acknowledged that he might have handled the debate unskillfully, for he had not meant to start a dog-fight. The Prime Minister had not banged the door, but he had come close to doing it. Smuts again appealed for co-operation, but he could not forbear to remind the Prime Minister that some of those who kept him in power had openly declared, even in the House, that they had no confidence in him.

After the debate he told Hofmeyr that he would speak to Hertzog the following day, but when the time came he said he thought it would be better to 'let things simmer for a bit'. Hofmeyr got the impression that he doubted Hertzog's sincerity, and wanted some overture from him. But perhaps it was the pride again. Perhaps he was remembering that he had held out his hand more than once before, and it had been refused, sometimes in words not easy to forget; should not Hertzog now offer his own? Perhaps he was afraid to meet Hertzog face to face. They had spoken to each other across the floor of the House; they had spoken at each other from a thousand platforms. Yet they had not met face to face for many years, and had grown out of it. Perhaps Hertzog was the one man with whom Smuts ever felt constraint.

That week-end Hofmeyr took the fast train to Pretoria to fetch his mother. He had had to leave her behind because of the sudden call to Cape Town. When he returned with her, it was to find that Charlie Malan, Hertzog's Minister of Railways, had died, so that further negotiations were suspended. Smuts attended the funeral, and there was a story that he accepted a lift home from Hertzog, leading some, who did not know what was already afoot, to believe that reconciliation was born in the Prime Minister's car. Meanwhile Wessels told Hofmeyr that there need be no further steps from the Smuts side; Hertzog would be communicating with Smuts after the Nationalist Party caucus on the fourteenth.

What had happened was that Hertzog had decided, in view of the division in his Cabinet and caucus, to take his own line. He had informed his Party that he could not let Smuts's offer go unanswered. His biographer was later to describe this action as that of a true leader, while Dr Malan was to describe it as that of an autocrat. Hertzog also told his caucus that the Nationalists would lose the next election, which Malan deplored as a statement 'unworthy of true Nationalism'. It was clear that Hertzog and Malan had reached the parting of their ways; it was also clear that Malan felt that the destiny of Afrikanerdom had passed into his hands.

Malan never withheld his praise for Hertzog's twenty years of service to the Party and the people; but when Hertzog faltered, it was Malan who took over. What Hertzog contemplated, Malan called *vereniging*, a union of parties; whereas *hereniging* was a union of souls. And what soul-community could there be between any true Nationalist and Smuts, the handyman of the British Empire; or Reitz, the colonel of the Royal Scots Fusiliers; or Hofmeyr, Rhodes Scholar, and the champion of every small nation except his own? When Hertzog made up his mind, no one could change it. Therefore, with the ever-present danger that he might lose the support of twenty to thirty members of his caucus, he sent coalition proposals to Smuts on 14 February.

Soon after Hertzog's statement arrived, Smuts sent for Hofmeyr, and asked him what he thought of it. 'He seemed to be very much afraid that he was being led into a trap'; but Hofmeyr reassured him, saying that despite all the verbiage Hertzog was sincere. Duncan drafted a letter for Smuts, asking the Prime Minister for elucidation. This Hertzog agreed to at once, and finally, at eleven in the morning of 15 February, Smuts, his movements known to almost every person in the buildings, left his office to walk round the corner to the office of the Prime Minister, carrying with him the silent good wishes of many. There the two men talked for an hour; Smuts's last doubts of Hertzog's sincerity were removed.

That sincerity is clearly seen in the notes Hertzog made at this time. He was prepared to talk to Smuts because the country-wide feeling for *hereniging* was stronger than it had ever been; but also he did not wish to drive Smuts into the arms of Roos, or of those Natal men who wanted independence for their province—the Devolutionists as they were called. Hertzog, who was afraid of so little, was afraid that if Smuts and they made common cause, it would deal 'the Afrikaans language and Afrikanerdom an irreparable blow'. Hertzog may well have had another reason, but it was too private and personal to set down. Was it his secret hope that Malan would resign and that Smuts would lose his Devolutionists, and leave a stable majority in the centre? It seems probable. His first meeting with Smuts was, in his own words, 'very friendly and promising'.

Negotiations now passed into higher hands. The caucus appointed Smuts and Duncan to negotiate with Hertzog and Havenga. Hofmeyr made way, but he had done his work well. What is more, he had strengthened Smuts's confidence in him, not only as a negotiator, but as a follower of unquestionable loyalty. What he had waited for ever since he became Administrator, had now come true. He had not sat on the fence for nothing.

Why was Hofmeyr so set on *hereniging?* His mother had a great deal to do with it; for years they had talked to each other about the shame of the divisions of Afrikanerdom, that set members of families against their parents, their children, their brothers, their sisters. There was no prouder woman in all South Africa than Deborah Hofmeyr. Politics she did not like, but here was her son, after only three years of it, bringing together two men whose reconciliation was thought impossible. Politics had suddenly become noble, and who could doubt that her son had ennobled it? His enemies had called him a child, but it was the child who had led them. Whatever he had done in his life, he had done well. This would open the eyes of those people in Johannesburg who had thought he had no understanding of men and their affairs. There was talk that it was Duncan, with his patience and his courtesy and his aristocratic ways, who had really made the coalition. Friends told them that, and she would say emphatically, 'Don't worry, the t-truth will out.' As for her son, he would give his snort; somehow he could never get to like Duncan, and never gave him his proper due. But neither did he brood over the fact that Duncan got the credit; there were big days ahead, and he looked forward to living in them.

Hofmeyr had other reasons for welcoming *hereniging.* One was that he hated the waste of uneconomic strife. The other, and that was his most important political reason, was that he believed that *hereniging* was an essential prerequisite for the planning of a 'native policy' which would still the fears of white people, meet the aspirations of black people, and satisfy the watching, critical, sometimes hostile world. In the excited, feverish, confident atmosphere of the House in February 1933, one could hope for almost anything.

From all the excitement, the fever, the confidence, one person was totally excluded. When he came down from his bench Tielman Roos had been a man of power. With this power he brought the gold standard crashing down. But once it was down, his power was gone. He had nothing then but himself to offer and no one wanted him. If Smuts and Hertzog had failed to agree, Roos might still have had a following; but rather than work with Roos, they chose to work with each other. Beside these two men, Roos weighed too light. The roar of the Lion out of the North had electrified the nation, but now no one listened any more.

Malan wrote sternly of Roos. 'I opposed the Smuts-Hertzog coalition, just as I had spurned the unprincipled manoeuverings of Roos.' Roos had been ready to destroy the Nationalist Party for the sake of economic prosperity. Hertzog was ready to destroy it for the sake of a spurious *hereniging*. There was only one kind of *hereniging* that Malan cared anything about. That was the reunion of all true Afrikaners.

The Afrikaner could be said to have maintained himself in South Africa in the face of two enemies, the British and the black men of the tribes. The politics of Afrikaner Nationalism had therefore two main aims, and they were, to achieve complete independence of the British, and to maintain complete mastery over the non-white population; there were therefore two roots of Nationalism, the constitutional and the racial.

There was some struggle between the coalition negotiators over the constitutional issue; eventually Smuts, in the opinion of Sarah Gertrude Millin, his biographer, 'in effect' accepted the Hertzog formulation he had rejected in 1920, and Hertzog, according to Malan, capitulated to Smuts.

What really happened was that Smuts's English-speaking supporters were becoming, if only by passage of time and the rise of new generations, more South African in outlook, while Hertzog's supporters were becoming, largely because of the Imperial Conference decision of 1926, more reconciled to association with Britain. What is more, both were bowing to the desire of the electorate for *hereniging*. Even Malan, who derived sardonic amusement from the sight of Hertzog and Smuts each assuring their supporters that their respective parties were sacrificing nothing, was too clever to appear to resist the electorate's will.

So strong was this will that one crucial question was left unanswered. What would South Africa do if Britain went to war? Smuts's English-speaking supporters were not yet so South African that they would leave

Britain to fight alone, and Hertzog's supporters did not regard association with Britain as meaning that they would go to war for her. Smuts and Hertzog decided that the question could be left unanswered.

It was from the racial, not the constitutional, root of Nationalism that the greatest difficulty sprang. Hertzog wanted coalition so that the 'Native problem' could be settled once and for all, and he wished the main provisions of this settlement to be decided upon before coalition was finally agreed to. The most important of these provisions was the one relating to separate political representation, which meant in so many words that the Cape non-racial franchise would be amended to exclude Africans.

Hertzog's and Smuts's senses of obligation were different. Hertzog was intent on nothing less than the total replanning of the political structure of South Africa, and having such a purpose, he was not prepared to let any of the experiments of the past stand in his way. On the other hand Smuts, although he had been State Attorney in a republic which in its constitution forbade racial equality in church or state, was reluctant to abolish any right that had once been given. A strong personal motive also operated. He was known throughout the world as the champion of rights, and he shrank from the thought of becoming known as a filcher of rights in his own country, and especially from a voiceless people. So deep was his reluctance and so obvious his unhappiness that Hertzog wrote in his diary, 'It appears to be an insuperable difficulty.'

Smuts called Hofmeyr to consult with Duncan and himself. 'He was obviously very much upset and talked of the possible breakdown of the negotiations,' wrote Hofmeyr. He had tried to persuade Hertzog not to make the provisions a condition for coalition, but rather to seek agreement after the coalition. Duncan and Hofmeyr tried together to find a new formula. Smuts wanted the Bills to be decided on by the two parties in coalition. His proposals were finally put to the Big Four. After the meeting Smuts called Hofmeyr into his room, and said, 'Die ding is deur,' meaning, the thing is done. So after twenty-one years of strife Hertzog and Smuts were reconciled. Had they had another twenty-one years of working together, many things that happened in South Africa might have happened differently. In that time the unanswered question about war might have answered itself. But no time was given, for six years later Fate prematurely demanded that it should be answered immediately.

Smuts now told Hofmeyr that he wanted him for the Cabinet. The next day Hertzog had agreed to six SAP seats in a Cabinet of twelve, and Smuts now told Hofmeyr that five of these seats would go to himself (Smuts), Duncan, Hofmeyr, Stuttaford of the Cape, and a man from Natal. The sixth place would go to Reitz or to a second man from the Cape. Hofmeyr supported the idea of a second man from the Cape, but Smuts would not hear of it. Smuts then decided on Clarkson from Natal and Conroy from the Cape. Conroy was an Irish Afrikaner, a great big farmer, full of vitality and devoid of tact, a jovial friend and an unpleasant enemy. He loved Smuts, and Smuts was blind to his faults, especially his hobby, the most dangerous hobby to choose in South Africa, of attacking the Dutch Reformed Church (Nederduits Gereformeerde Kerk), especially when it entered the field of social welfare. Hertzog told Smuts that Conroy would be too much to bear, and would quarrel, particularly with Kemp; Smuts then decided to risk having only one man from the Cape, and went back to Reitz, whom he had wanted all along. Reitz had been his Minister of Lands in 1920, and was known for his diligence in visiting the remotest parts of his domain, especially where the hunting was good, and there was plenty of sun, fresh air, and open space; he hated sitting in an office, and left the work of his department to its permanent head. It was for quite other qualities that Smuts wanted him; he was a rich personality, loyal and honourable. There was a deep bond between the two men quite apart from soldiering; they were Afrikaners in a natural fashion and could not be intense about it. They felt inferior to no nation or person, and were therefore able to be big-hearted to a degree which Hertzog found reprehensible, and Malan downright traitorous.

On his side Hertzog chose Havenga, Grobler, Pirow, Kemp, and Fourie. Malan declined to serve in the Cabinet, and issued on behalf of himself and some twenty-nine supporters in both Houses, a manifesto strongly critical of his Prime Minister. He stated that Hertzog had acted on his own in beginning negotiations with Smuts, and had brought about coalition without referring to a single Party committee. He went further and characterised the promise of a solution of the 'Native problem' as a bait held before the Nationalists, though he did not say by whom. The rift between Hertzog and Malan was now virtually unbridgeable but Malan concluded that there must be no personal antagonism to leaders, especially to General Hertzog, to whom so much was owed.

The electorate gave thunderous approval to Hertzog and Smuts. Seventy-five Nationalists, sixty Smuts men and one Smuts woman, and two Cresswellites, endorsed coalition. Six Independents did the same. Of

150 members of the Lower House, only six were in opposition. At Johannesburg North, Hofmeyr was returned unopposed.

Hofmeyr was again a man of considerable importance. Hertzog gave him Malan's portfolios of Education, Interior, and Public Health. Hofmeyr immediately dropped his law studies, considering it improper for a Minister of Education to sit for examinations. He took over Malan's private secretary. He never regarded the private secretaryship as an office in his gift, nor as an opportunity for grooming some future political leader. Never in the course of his political career did he advance a friend for reasons of friendship. This was often attributed to his integrity, but it had much to do with his reluctance to put his hands on any other man's life, which reluctance in itself was complex in nature. Hofmeyr was prepared to leave the selection of political leaders to the rough and ready methods of the electoral machinery. The idea of preparing or encouraging young men and women to follow in his footsteps, except in a general way by means of public speeches, was foreign to him. This had no doubt something to do with his frequent statement to his friends that he had 'done nothing' to win his present position. Others must do the same. If they could not catch the eye of Smuts, they must catch the eye of God.

Hofmeyr soon showed again that he was a genius at administration. He mastered the business of his three departments in as many days. He was no longer a free man when the session was over. After a week in the new camp of the Students' Christian Association at Anerley in Natal, he had to return to Pretoria to attend to his three departments, and also to join his fellow-Ministers in commending coalition to the electorate. Of course it was no longer coalition that had to be commended, but something more far-reaching, namely the fusion of the two big parties. Hertzog put it forward in August, at the Transvaal National Party Congress, but his final pronouncement he made in September in his own constituency of Smithfield, where he always made his important speeches.

Hertzog's dilemma was very clear. He did not want to disown Malan; like all 'true Afrikaners', even the opportunistic Roos, he could not afford to appear to break with Afrikanerdom. Nor did he want Malan to gain influence over the Orange Free State. As for Malan, he was still urging *hereniging*, the union of souls, and opposing *vereniging*, the union of mere bodies. It was not an easy time for Hertzog; if he agreed with Malan, Smuts would come rushing to see him. It was not an easy time for

Smuts either; if he agreed with Hertzog, Stallard and the Natal men would come rushing to see him.

In October of 1933, at the Cape congress of the National Party in Port Elizabeth, 170 delegates met to discuss the Prime Minister's plan for a union of parties. Of the Cape delegates, 142 out of 172 voted against fusion of the parties. A week later, in Bloemfontein, at the meeting of the federal council of the party, Hertzog carried the other three provinces with him, but the Cape decided to remain outside of any fusion. Van den Heever wrote that this was a 'great blow' for Hertzog. It was indeed; Hertzog was prepared to lose Malan, but the loss of the Cape Province was disquieting.

Yet the Cape was not yet finally lost, nor was fusion finally assured. When Parliament reassembled in January 1934, Malan visited Hertzog for 'friendly talks'. Malan knew the weak spot of the coalition, and he kept on probing it. Could South Africa be neutral? Could South Africa secede? Could not the right of appeal to the Privy Council from South Africa's highest court be for ever abolished? Could it not be laid down that the next Governor-General would be a South African? Then Malan praised the Prime Minister in public for all that he was doing to reach agreement. Both Hertzog and Malan appealed to the Nationalists to bury the past, and Hertzog said that he had never doubted South Africa's right to secede or be neutral. That was enough to bring Smuts to the Prime Minister's office; surely the agreement was to be between Hertzog and himself, not between Hertzog and Malan! According to Hertzog's own account, Smuts said he had decided to write a letter to the Prime Minister to inform him 'that he was no longer prepared to negotiate fusion'. The following day the letter was brought to Hertzog, with the accompanying message that it would be given to the press that afternoon. Meanwhile Esselen had been trying to persuade Smuts not to do anything of the kind. The letter was withdrawn by Smuts the next day.

Whatever may be the truth as seen by the Olympian observer it is clear that once the excitement of coalition was over, the road to fusion was rough and full of obstacles. Although coalition had been made more difficult by the 'Native problem', fusion was being made more difficult by the constitutional problem. It was the old difficulty of reconciling nationalism and imperialism, to use Hofmeyr's own terminology.

To use another terminology, it was the difficulty of reconciling freedom with co-operation. Could South Africa be free while remaining in the Commonwealth? Malan was being drawn more and more to the side of those who believed that the answer was No.

It was Smuts however who was having the most difficult passage. He had won the confidence of almost the entire white English-speaking population of South Africa, and he knew with what anxiety they watched the constitutional evolution of their country, partly because they had strong pro-British sentiments, partly because the ideal of national independence seemed to have become an almost Afrikaner monopoly. While Smuts accepted wholeheartedly the new sovereign status, he was embarrassed by all the corollaries deduced from it, because the very mention of them angered and terrified his English-speaking supporters; above all he did not want these corollaries embodied in any statement of principles. Hertzog could well understand Smuts's position, and he consented to state publicly that while his views remained the same, and while members of the new party would be free to advocate a republic, the Party itself would stand for the maintenance of the present constitutional position. This in turn made Malan so angry that he declared only seven days after his public praise for Hertzog, that fusion was dead.

Hofmeyr was very satisfied with this turn of events. He had seen clearly that Malan was not really seeking reassurances from Hertzog. He was trying to kill fusion, and to return to the old party divisions. Failing that, he was trying to frighten half of Smuts's supporters out of fusion, in which case he himself would go into it. In either case he would preserve the Nationalist Party. If he failed to reach either of these objectives, there was only one other thing to do, heroic maybe but quite inevitable, and that was to begin the Nationalist struggle all over again, and strive to recapture the gains that, in his opinion, Hertzog after twenty-one years of fighting had so misguidedly thrown away.

Hofmeyr's phlegmatic temperament fitted him well to advise Smuts in these difficult times. He was not given to panics or hot-blooded decisions. Esselen and he were at hand to prevent any action that would have alienated Hertzog, and brought the whole fusion movement to an end. They were equally determined to keep Malan out, because they feared that if they did not, many of Smuts's supporters would break away and form a wholly English-speaking party; but they knew that only one person could safely break with Malan, and that was Hertzog himself. Smuts had already made it clear to the Prime Minister in private that his party would not fuse with Malan.

There was another considerable obstacle in the way of fusion. In 1931 the autonomy of the Dominions had been guaranteed by the Statute of Westminster. Now in 1934, by agreement between Hertzog and Smuts, South Africa was to recognise this new situation by passing a Status Act. The gift of Britain had been generally approved, but the legal acceptance of it by South Africa caused disquiet in the breasts of many an English-speaking person. It was further evidence to them of Afrikaner determination to loosen every bond; 'Give a finger, and they take the whole hand.'

The Status Bill was entrusted to Pirow, who handled it with distinction. Now was the time to settle the constitutional question, he said, while such amity prevailed. South Africa was a sovereign independent state, united by a common allegiance to the Crown, and freely associated as a member of the Commonwealth. That fact had already been recognised by every member of the coalition; it was in fact the first clause of the coalition agreement.

Hofmeyr in his speech, after paying tribute to the Commonwealth as an instrument of peace, tackled the tricky questions of the Crown and of neutrality, about which Hertzog and Smuts had agreed to differ. He was witty about the first.

'Those of us who were once classical scholars will also be able to tell the House of the desperate struggle waged for centuries over the question of the divisibility of the poet Homer. I am glad to say that the trend of criticism today is to make Homer much less divisible than he was at one time.'

He then dealt with the question of war. There would be three courses for South Africa, active participation, passive belligerency, and neutrality. In his opinion a declaration of neutrality would mean that she had seceded from the Commonwealth.

Stallard, Coulter, and Marwick opposed the Bill with determination. Smuts in a great speech tried to still the doubts of others. He said emphatically, 'Whatever can be said in human language to affirm the British connection, is said in the Bill.' He referred to the two roots of division, the racial and the constitutional. The racial root was withering; now let the other be cut.

Only seven M.P.s voted against the Status Bill: Stallard, Coulter, Marwick, and four Labourites. The debate was characterised by great ovations. Two young men, Hofmeyr and Pirow, were clearly potential Prime Ministers. One of the most contentious Bills in the history of Parliament was passed almost unanimously. The road to fusion was wide and open.

Everything was fine, except that Dr Malan chilled many a heart by saying that now the British Empire was dead. But for that, it was a famous victory.

Yet the verdict of history must be otherwise. The unanswered question remained unanswered. Smuts and Hertzog continued to differ about an issue which had power to destroy the coalition. Hofmeyr's contention about secession and neutrality was not replied to. He succeeded in reconciling the irreconcilables in the extraordinary phrase, 'passive belligerency'. One thing should have been plain; that Smuts believed that membership of the Commonwealth meant united action in wartime, and that Hertzog did not. But Hertzog kept silent during the debate. It was true that his throat was troubling him, but someone could have spoken for him. The fact was that although sovereign independence was important to him, the settlement of the 'Native problem' was important also. For that he needed the coalition.

Hofmeyr's misgivings about the Status Act were quite different from those prevalent in his party. He left amongst his papers a note which showed his anxiety lest legislation for sovereign independence should derogate in any way from the entrenched provisions of the South Africa Act, which laid down that the status of the official languages and the Cape non-racial franchise which could not be changed except by a two-thirds majority of both Houses sitting together. Many Nationalists were now arguing that sovereign independence made Parliament independent of any such entrenchments, and that it could now alter the Cape franchise by simple majority. Hofmeyr's misgivings were groundless. Hertzog announced publicly that 'the movement to reach solution of our Native problem by such means deserves our disapproval in every respect. As for me, I must repudiate it absolutely.'

On 5 June 1934 the terms of fusion were published. Two weeks later the federal council of the National Party met in Pretoria, and accepted Hertzog's principles for fusion by 12 votes to 8. On 25 July the Cape Nationalist Party decided by 164 votes to 18 to continue as a Nationalist Party, and were supported by anti-fusion minorities in the other three provinces. The Party was constituted in Bloemfontein on 4 December, and became known as the Purified National Party.

Meanwhile the South African Party, whose constitutional arrangements were somewhat different, met in National Congress in Bloemfontein in August 1934, and by a majority of 453 against 8 accepted fusion. Stallard, after shaking hands with Smuts, left the meeting to establish the

Dominion Party, which had a strength of four M.P.s; its purpose was to cherish and strengthen the bonds which bound South Africa to the Commonwealth.

The final step was taken in December 1934 at Bloemfontein. Hertzog without the Malanites, and Smuts without the Stallardites, formed the United National South African Party. The new United Party, as it came to be called, commanded 117 seats in the Lower House as against 19 Purified Nationalists under Malan. Hertzog was now assured of the two-thirds majority in both Houses which he required before he could amend the Cape franchise. He now prepared in earnest the legislation which was to decide the future of South Africa for generations to come. This was to be the work for which he would be remembered.

Hofmeyr allowed himself a prediction, that as far as Hertzog and Smuts were concerned, there was not one chance in a hundred that they would ever be antagonists again. Most South Africans who thought about these things at all, would have predicted the same. The meaning of Hitler was not yet fully seen.

Chapter 7

A Minister Dissents

WHEN Hofmeyr became a Minister, he and his mother moved to the house that was to become so well known to many of their friends. It was an official residence, with large, high-ceilinged rooms, a fine level garden and a tennis-court. Its front door opened on to a long, wide passage down which his cry of 'Ma! Ma!' would echo when he arrived home from work.

Something of the aura of the Patrick Duncans dwelt in the house. They had lived there when Duncan was a Minister in the Smuts Government. While they were there, Mrs Duncan, who was very proud of her china, persuaded the Public Works Department to make her a special cupboard for it. Now as one of the senior members of the new Ministry, Duncan had been promoted to Bryntirion. The Duncans arrived back from Cape Town before the Hofmeyrs, and Mrs Duncan's first thought was to get back her special cupboard, and she persuaded the PWD to move it from Schoeman Street to Bryntirion before the Hofmeyrs arrived. But alas, somebody blundered. When the PWD arrived, Mrs Hofmeyr was already in command, putting things to rights in the house. When she heard that the man had come for 'Mrs Duncan's cupboard', her anger was magnificent. 'Does the cupboard belong to this house, or does it not?' she asked, and when it was admitted that it did, she said, 'Then it will stay where it b-belongs.' Mrs Duncan, when she heard of it, was not only appalled by the magnitude of the blunder, but also felt guilty of wrong-doing, and sent Christmas flowers to Mrs Hofmeyr for nine years, after which she ceased, having made no impression whatever.

Hofmeyr began the day's work at half-past eight; he liked to walk to his work with the crowds of public servants going to the Union Buildings, and was unique not only in this, but also in his dress, which was inferior both in cost and taste to that of most of his subordinates.

He dealt with his correspondence with the greatest dispatch and then

160

turned to his engagements, which were numerous. His training in punctuality served him well, and he was intolerant of unpunctuality in others.
He reacted to it not with outward but with inward anger, which expressed itself in the coldness of the greeting; if he gave a rebuke, it was
quietly given, but was as uncomfortable to bear as the lashing tongues of
others. Unless the matter was of tremendous and unexpected urgency, he
would guide the business to its conclusion a minute or two before his next
caller was due. Forgetfulness or poorness of memory he came very near
to despising; sometimes even his friends thought him arrogant in such
matters. Not all of them had the courage of van der Brugge, who had
been his registrar at the University of the Witwatersrand. Seeing van der
Brugge open the telephone book, Hofmeyr said, 'Can't you remember the
number?' to which van der Brugge had replied with some heat, 'I use my
brain for better things.'

Professor M. C. Botha, who was Hofmeyr's distinguished Secretary
for Education, later Principal of the University of Pretoria and Chairman
of the Board controlling the South African Broadcasting Corporation,
was once guilty of a serious act of forgetfulness. It had been the custom
since Hofmeyr's childhood to celebrate his mother's birthday with a tea-
party, but when he came to Pretoria as Administrator in 1924, the party
had grown into one of the social occasions of the year. It was attended by
Cabinet Ministers, members of the diplomatic corps, civic personalities,
high civil servants, and almost anyone of importance. The house was
filled with people, flowers, and gifts. It was one of those unforgettable
occasions, but M. C. Botha forgot it. The next day he phoned the Minister. 'Mr Hofmeyr,' he said, 'I've done a terrible thing. I forgot your
mother's birthday.' Hofmeyr said, 'I know.' Botha asked him, 'What can
I do? Do you think a nice box of chocolates would help?' Hofmeyr
snorted and said, 'You can try.' So the Union Secretary for Education left
his office, and went down into the streets and bought a nice box of
chocolates; he got into his car, and with a wry grin at himself, drove to
743 Schoeman Street. When Mrs Hofmeyr opened the door, she looked
at him as though she had never seen him before. 'Mrs Hofmeyr,' he said,
'I've come to ask for forgiveness, and to bring you a peace offering.' He
held out the box of chocolates to her, but she made no attempt to take
them. Instead she said, 'We have m-many chocolates.' So they stood
eyeing each other, perhaps for a second or two, but too long for Botha.
He was tempted, but he was wise too; he said humbly, 'I know, it was a
disgrace.' Then she smiled. 'Yes, it was a disgrace,' she said, 'but I'll take

the chocolates.' He went in and had tea with her, and she said to him, 'You mustn't kill my son.'

Botha thought Mrs Hofmeyr was a remarkable woman, but that she had spoiled her son's life. It was a misfortune for the country that Hofmeyr had not grown up on the *platteland*, gone to war, married, and had children; this lack of knowledge of life inclined him to refer everything to principle, and to ignore personal and human factors.

Hofmeyr felt safe in relaxing with Chris Dames his first private secretary. Once at Zanzibar, watching a woman climbing the gangway to the ship, Dames had remarked that she had a beautiful body, and Hofmeyr had said, 'Do you think so?', and had observed her critically. These were interests that he never revealed at home, and that may have been the reason for his mother's jealousy. In 1936, during the famous Representation of Natives Bill debate, Hofmeyr was taken ill in the House and was sent to hospital. Esselen and Dames went to see him, and then reported to Mrs Hofmeyr. Esselen said to her jokingly, 'Don't worry about him, he's got a pretty little nurse looking after him, he'll be quite all right.' Two days later Hofmeyr was out of the hospital, though still confined to bed.

Mrs Hofmeyr's jealousy of other women was well known in Pretoria. Mother and son were guests at many dinners, but it was the cocktail parties that were dangerous. Neither mother nor son drank any alcohol at that time, and Hofmeyr was well known for his choice of ginger-ale, which he said could so easily be mistaken for a whisky or brandy with soda. But the parties were dangerous nevertheless; tongues were loosened, eyes flashed, and Pretoria had some beautiful women. People moved about, as if pursued, wit lifted the lids of convention and peered into unusual places; who could deny that her son was witty, and that wit between a man and a woman was first cousin to flirtation? If he became too animated, if his conversation became too particular, if his companion looked too much into his face, as if to wrest secrets from behind those thick lenses which helped him to look out and hindered others from looking in, then she would move over to him, not crudely but with design transparent to anyone observant. The brief encounter would come to an end. The lady would take her graceful departure, sped by a ministerial bow; or if the wit continued, it would have lost its flash and fire, and that faint hint of breathlessness that comes with cut and parry between a man and a woman.

That is why she preferred dinners; the rules were stricter, the atmosphere less frenetic, the drinking more orderly, the conversation less intimate. At the cocktail parties it was easier to become jealous, because of the very feeling of excitement and looseness in the air. Some thought she was jealous without reason, but they were wrong; the truth is she was jealous beyond reason. There were times when she went and stood before him, and said outright, 'I'm t-tired, t-take me home.' Nor did he ever refuse; the very thought was unthinkable. Rebellion was impossible, and resentment was improbable; regret was the probable emotion.

Their relationship was a recurring theme of conversation in Pretoria. At the Smuts home, someone asked the question, 'When will Jantjie marry?' And someone who knew the old joke replied, 'He's going to marry Helen Bull,' which moved Smuts to rejoin, 'How can he marry Helen Bull, when he's married already?' Smuts may have found pleasure in saying that, because in as far as he could be afraid of anyone, he was afraid of her.

But the relationship was imperfectly understood. Some saw it as a straightforward domination, which of course it was not. Their relationship had lasted throughout many years, like a bridge put together by Isaac Newton, without nail or peg or dowel, so that if one piece were taken out the whole thing would fall to pieces; but to take out the one piece was virtually impossible, not only because superhuman effort would have been required, but because each of them knew the consequences, and he especially knew that his freedom would have meant her destruction and her destruction would have destroyed his freedom. The truth was that they were inseparably joined together, like Siamese twins of the spirit, whose separation would have been catastrophic. Yet he would have lived after her death, just as she lived after his for ten long years. He wrote to one of his friends, 'If my mother died, I should like to marry.'

Yet the elements of domination were there. There were things in which her word was absolute, such as, for example, his diet. There were things in which her word was absolute but unspoken, for example, his friendship with women, and in a much smaller degree, his friendship with men. There were things in which his word was absolute, but taken for granted rather than spoken, for example, his work and his responsibilities. There was also a world in which his freedom was uncontroversial and traditional, the world of camps, boys' clubs, recreation, and to a large extent, his holidays. There was the last world where they were both subject to contract, the world of politics, in which she would never interfere with his plans and obligations, and which he would keep out of their domestic life. They moved easily in their different worlds, because they had long been used to them; but the mere existence of this complexity, and the fact that few understood it, led to the most extraordinary explications of their relationship. Some thought that she ruled great areas of his life, and some thought that she ruled none, except those that a mother of a bachelor could appropriately and lovingly rule. Some thought her the perfect mother, and some thought her a wicked woman, who had possessed her son in childhood and would never let him go. Some thought that she more than anyone else had been responsible for the misery of his life in Johannesburg, and others thought that but for her he would have been broken.

Smuts was right, it was a kind of marriage. It was not a common one, yet one not uncommonly seen where the man or the woman, or even both, control areas in which one asserts the mastery, and would die rather than surrender it. So there may come times even in marriages of long standing, where the two bared natures are uglily revealed, to the horror of those who thought they knew them. Such times never came in the Hofmeyr home, and that must be ascribed, not only to the strength of their affection, but to the docility of his filial nature.

Nevertheless at this very time, in the middle nineteen-thirties, some changes were taking place in their relationship. Had he been a nobody, they might never have happened. He might have become one of those men of whom one reads, who, though fully grown, obey their mothers like children. But Hofmeyr was not a nobody; he was both a genius and a man of great authority. It was this second thing, his ministership, which was modifying their relationship, much more than the administratorship had ever done. Pretoria was the Administrator's capital, but it was also the administrative capital of the nation, and when the Ministers returned from Parliament in Cape Town, it was they and their houses which were the centres of attraction. Few people could pass such a house without looking in, wondering what it was like to live in a place so charged with power; some would have the experience of reaching the gate just as the big black car, flying the ministerial pennant, took the great man out to, or brought him back from, some majestic occasion. All this Mrs Hofmeyr enjoyed, but it would have been foolish not to know through whom this power had come; yet in a way, since he was so uniquely hers, it had come through her as well. When Stanley Jones, the Christian missionary, and author of *Christ of the Indian Road*, visited Johannesburg, a big meeting was arranged for him in the City Hall, and it was right, of course, that from the whole Transvaal Hofmeyr should be chosen to thank him. William Janisch, whom Mrs Hofmeyr had almost revered for his gentleness and saintliness in the old days of the Wale Street Baptist Church in Cape Town, had made all the arrangements except one, and that was to reserve a parking place for the Minister's car. Hofmeyr drove his mother over from Pretoria in their own private car, for he was scrupulous in not using a government car, or a government chauffeur on non-government occasions. They arrived, as they invariably did, in time for the Minister to come on to the platform on the hour, but there was no parking place, they had to drive a further couple of blocks, and when they reached the City Hall, eight o'clock had already struck. William Janisch was there to meet them, white-haired and proud, never even thinking of the fact that the meeting would start a few minutes late. Hofmeyr was friendly and smiling, but his mother, her face carrying no hint of warmth or recognition, said to Janisch, unsmilingly, 'Why did you not make a place for the Minister's car?' Janisch apologised, but her face did not change. For him the great occasion was spoiled, for he could not keep his thoughts away from his hurt and humiliation. The meeting was successful, the speeches were good, but he could see only those unsmiling eyes, not of the woman who had once revered him, but of one of whose existence he had not known till now. Although her territory was petty, she moved in it with a terrifying power.

The weaning process which had begun during the administratorship continued during Hofmeyr's first few years as Minister. But because it had come so late, it brought no fundamental change. It was as though they had turned from each other a little, yet still lay side by side in their symbiotic shell. But he was also becoming more guarded about the things he told his mother. When people tried to get information from her, her voice would rise in complaint, part simulated and part real, who knows? And she would say, 'Don't ask me, he never t-tells me anything.' Then she would look round as if daring anyone to contradict her, and when no one did, she would say, 'Jantjie is now s-silent as the grave.' If the inquirer pressed her to fill out her meanings, to say what it was that Jantjie would not tell, to say when he had decided to tell no more, she would look at him with that expressionless expression which said so clearly that he was exceeding the bounds of the proper; she would say, 'Beggars c-can't be choosers,' and whether she referred to herself or inquirers in general only a fool would have tried to discover. But it was not all play-acting; it was said so often that it seemed to have something of the nature of a plaint.

They had both become Pretoria-lovers. They enjoyed the five or six-months in Cape Town when Parliament was meeting, but they were always glad to get back. The northern capital has not the majestic surroundings of the southern, but the central part of the city, and most of its white suburbs, are very pleasant. The heart of Pretoria is Church Square, the Kerkplein, a fine open space of lawns and trees and flowers, now containing Anton van Wouw's statue of President Paul Kruger in his famous top hat, and surrounded by splendid buildings, including the historic Raadzaal, the Council Chamber. The white town was, as it still is, a gracious one of wide tree-lined streets and beautiful public and private gardens.

The city is famous for many things, one of them being that its streets are lined by thousand upon thousand of the jacaranda trees of Brazil, which in October and November are covered with mauve flowers. Hofmeyr the unpoetical wrote to Underhill:

'I wish you could be in Pretoria now—it is really amazingly beautiful. Not only is it a town of very fine gardens which are at their best at this time of the year, but most of the streets are planted with a tree called the jacaranda which comes out in a blaze of purple for about three weeks in October. When the petals begin to fall you have a purple carpet on the ground and a purple canopy above—there is something deliciously Eastern about the effect.'

In the first years of his ministership there begins to emerge new evidence about Hofmeyr and his work, of a strange and disturbing kind. Hofmeyr had more than once written to Underhill that his work was strenuous, but in 1934, at the age of 40, when he was about to go to the annual camp for a week, he wrote that he could do with a longer spell. A few months later he wrote that he wished he could get away from everything, and just do nothing. He had been three times from Pretoria to Johannesburg the previous week, and this week he would have to go four times; of this he used the word 'exhausting'. This thought runs like a thread through the letters of this time. Why was he working so hard? Was there some compulsion at work in his personality, quite apart from his belief in work as the fruit of faith and the duty of man, and quite apart from the Prime Minister's inclination to make use of his colleague's great ability? He had three portfolios, Interior, Public Health, and Education, and he was frequently entrusted with those of Ministers who were ill or travelling abroad. Why did he do it? It seems improbable that he did it merely to exhibit his great abilities; the newspapers certainly publicised his genius, but he was outgrowing the need for such praise. It is a question we shall have to consider again, for later in his life he assumed burdens beyond all reason; had he known it, he was beginning to do that even now. Was work a kind of anodyne, and if so, for what? In the first years of his ministership, there was no urgency, no crisis; the country had never been on so easy a course. Why did he work so hard?

One person realised it of course, the one who had said to M. C. Botha, 'You mustn't kill my son.' There was something desperate in her voice, because she was powerless in the sphere of work and duty. There he ruled his own life, and she herself had made him so. It was she who had taught him that duty was to be set above all other considerations. There was only one thing that she could do, and that was to feed him more carefully, more fortifyingly, than ever. And he for his part exercised violently to make up for the pitiful holidays that he took for himself. There was always tennis, but now he took up tenniquoits, playing it, not with a rubber ring, but with a heavy medicine-ball, so that he could get his exercise in concentrated form. He wrote of the game, 'Very strenuous, but it gives you all the exercise you want in half-an-hour.'

It was a pity that he could not have had a little of Reitz's luck, which gave him opportunity to sit on camp-stools instead of platforms, under the lights of heaven, listening, not to speeches, but to the calls and cries of the wild. Hofmeyr regarded Reitz with an amused tolerance that he felt for few people, largely because Reitz had qualities of heart and spirit that were not inconsiderable. And in this tolerance there was the hidden element of envy, not because Reitz did not work, but because he never pretended to like it.

Hofmeyr's humility told him that Smuts and Reitz had qualities that he would never possess, and he told a story of Reitz, that he was once sitting next to him in the House, when someone put a question that had been placed on the order paper. Reitz was flustered, because he had forgotten all about it, and had thrown his departmental chief's answer into the wastepaper basket; in a second Hofmeyr had it out, and Reitz had it in his hand and was answering the question. When Reitz sat down, he said to Hofmeyr, 'You saved my life.' And Hofmeyr replied, 'The Reitzes always have Hofmeyrs to find their papers for them.'

It was only occasionally that Hofmeyr made such remarks about himself. They revealed, not only unsentimental self-knowledge, but his growing awareness that the proverb 'Where there's a will there's a way' had no absolute validity. Meanwhile his reputation as a Minister and a parliamentarian was increasing year by year. Early in 1936 Arthur Barlow, of the

Sunday Express, after commenting on his brilliance as an Administrator, went on, 'I believe that Hofmeyr will yet develop into one of the greatest Parliamentarians the Union has ever had. His natural destiny is the portfolio of Prime Minister of the Union.'

Just how Hofmeyr was to become Prime Minister, Barlow did not say, for he picked out five of Malan's younger men as Cabinet Ministers of the future. They were C. W. M. du Toit, Paul Sauer, J. G. Strijdom, F. C. Erasmus, and C. R. Swart, all men uncompromisingly hostile to everything that Hofmeyr stood for. Already they were beginning to hold him up, especially on the platteland, as a man whose political and racial ideas would mean the doom of Afrikanerdom. They were able to embarrass the members of the United Party too, especially its ex-Nationalists, by asking them why they, whose supreme loyalty was to white South Africa, kept such a man in the Cabinet.

Meanwhile Hofmeyr was making fresh ammunition for them. It is of no use to ask whether he did it willingly or unwillingly, because he was guided by quite other considerations. His life was moving into new and deep waters. He had all his adult life longed for *hereniging,* and had played his part in bringing it about. Apart from his hatred of strife, one of his main motives had been to bring white people together to do something about their country's problems. Now they had come together to do something, he found himself gravely questioning what they wanted to do. He who had hated strife, found himself in danger of arousing it. The waters were not only new and deep; they gave every promise of being turbulent.

In 1929, it was Smuts who had prevented Hertzog from securing the two-thirds majority which was necessary before the franchise enjoyed by Africans in the Cape could be altered.

In 1933, it was Smuts who nearly brought the coalition negotiations to an end because he would not consent to the abolition of the Cape African franchise. It was eventually agreed that the whole matter would be decided after coalition.

Now in 1935, after sitting for five years, the joint select committee on Hertzog's Native Bills submitted its report to Parliament. The committee's proposal was to exclude Africans from the franchise in future, but three Ministers, Smuts, Hofmeyr and Stuttaford, and the old Cape Liberal F. S. Malan, had voted against it, while Patrick Duncan supported it.

Hofmeyr wrote to Underhill explaining that he was not against separate political development as a matter of principle, but he thought that the time for it had passed by. His real objection now was to the destruction of an existing right; yet if African opinion accepted the Bills as a whole, he would feel obliged to do the same. If, on the contrary, African opinion opposed the Bills, he would oppose also, and would be prepared to face a serious cabinet crisis. Of this possibility he used the adjective 'interesting'; to describe situations in this way was one of his habits, and many of his supporters found it irritating, feeling that it showed a dispassionateness that no good man should feel.

Hertzog's planning of the national future was originally based on four Bills, one concerned with the coloured people and three with the African. The joint select committee now reduced these latter three Bills to two.

The first of these was the Representation of Natives Bill. It proposed to admit no more Africans to the parliamentary roll, but to leave the 11,000 existing voters as they were. In compensation for this it divided black South Africans into four constituencies, Cape Western, Cape Eastern, Natal, and Free State–Transvaal, each of which would return a white representative to the Senate and the first two of which would each return one white representative to the Cape Provincial Council. These constituencies would return three Africans each to the Natives Representative Council, where they would be joined by four nominated Africans and five white Chief Native Commissioners without vote, all under the presidency of the Secretary for Native Affairs.

The second Bill was the Native Trust and Land Bill, which would provide for the purchase of 15,000,000 acres to add to the existing 22,000,000 acres of the Native Reserves. Although the total available for African ownership would then be only one-seventh of the land area of the Union, the aim of the Bill was to make the practice of segregation more easily justifiable and more practicable. Segregation in South Africa has always been a mixture of white idealism and white supremacy, and each is used to justify the other. The idealism of the Native Trust and Land Bill was sharply modified by the embodiment in the Bill of the drastic provisions of the Native Service Contract Act, which Hofmeyr had opposed in 1932, namely the taxing of squatters, the empowering of African parents to send their young children to labour in any part of the Union, the holding of whole families responsible for individual breaches of contract, and the empowering of the courts to order whippings for breaches of contract by boys under eighteen.

When Parliament assembled in January 1936, Hertzog presented his Representation of Natives Bill, which would have brought to an end the

Cape African franchise. Public reaction was strong and immediate. The Cape Native Voters Convention and several other officially convened conferences of Africans had already condemned the proposals. So had the All-Africa Convention at Bloemfontein under the presidency of Professor Jabavu, the most representative meeting of non-white South Africans yet held in the country. Now many church leaders joined in the general condemnation. Sir James Rose Innes, retired Chief Justice of the Union and a born South African, presided over a large protest meeting in the Cape Town City Hall, largely attended by white people. Even then Hertzog, whose determination, by some called stubbornness, was massive, would have gone on; what deterred him was the possible failure to obtain the two-thirds majority and the possible break-up of the United Party. He was perhaps influenced by the representations made to him by a responsible deputation of African citizens who urged him rather to return to his own proposals of 1929. They also asked to be heard at the bar of the House. Hertzog, in moving the first reading of the Bill, referred to this African request:

'I then said to them, my friends, I am sorry. I would like very much to do it, and I will do my best to meet the Natives, but it would be very unreasonable to ask the joint session to do such a thing. I have already been engaged on this for fifteen years and we have all been trying to make the Natives and the whole population of South Africa clearly understand what our intentions are.'

Hertzog now proposed a compromise to the United Party, namely to allow the Cape African franchise to continue, but to place all African voters on a separate roll, and to allow them to elect three white representatives to the lower house, which would then consist of 153 members. Smuts decided to accept the compromise, which was in its essence similar to the one which he and the South African Party had opposed so strongly in 1929.

Hofmeyr wrote that he was against the abolition of the Cape African franchise, but he was prepared to vote for abolition if African opinion was agreeable. In January 1936, no doubt because African opinion was not agreeable, he came out openly against abolition, but in February Hertzog proposed communal representation for Cape Africans.

Hofmeyr's interview with the Prime Minister was not characterised by the unpleasantness that he feared. Although Hertzog was renowned for his courtesy, he was cordial towards very few people, and Hofmeyr was not one of them. Nevertheless he told Hofmeyr that he would not regard opposition to the Bill as a vote of no confidence. He said he was prepared to keep Hofmeyr in his cabinet, and Hofmeyr said he was prepared to stay in it. Hofmeyr's next task was to tell Smuts. They had doubtless discussed the matter before, but it was not until the day before the second reading that Hofmeyr told Smuts that he would not only vote, but that he would speak against the Bill. He did not record that Smuts made any attempt to reason with him, only that he 'was very much disturbed'.

Just as Hofmeyr had slowly been breaking away from the possessiveness of his mother, so it is certain that he had been growing more critical of Smuts. Sarah Millin had encouraged Hofmeyr to talk about his leader. In 1935 Hofmeyr had written to her:

'About Smuts: his dilatoriness—the tendency to let things develop . . . He shows a tendency to put off doing things which are a little unpleasant . . . combined with his dynamic energy he has today a kind of occasional indolence of mind which makes him tend to shirk issues which . . . seem to him unimportant . . .

'I am puzzled by the obvious conflict going on between the old Boer attitude and the British Liberal attitude. You describe him as essentially the old Boer in this regard—you may be right . . . But last year when he returned from England . . . it was clear that the whole idea of any additional colour bar was hateful to him. And yet I feel it in my bones that, although he has stood out for the Cape native franchise so far, he will let it go without a struggle next year.'

Smuts certainly let the Cape African franchise go the following year. It is true that he accepted a new kind of Cape franchise, but he certainly let the old one go. Smuts could well have been disturbed when he heard that Hofmeyr had decided to speak and vote against the Bill, and not merely because he and Hofmeyr would be on opposite sides. It would in any case have been hard to explain his own acceptance of the compromise to the outside world, which had come to look upon him as the supreme champion of liberty. But now it would be harder, because the cause that Smuts had thought not necessary to fight for, his young lieutenant Hofmeyr had espoused; and this could occasion, not only feelings of unease, but also of jealousy, even in so great a man.

Why did Smuts behave as he did? Some said that rather than see the Cape African franchise destroyed, he consented to see it modified. Others said that he realised that if he resisted any modification of the franchise, then the United Party itself would have been destroyed.

Pirow, who was an intelligent observer biased by a strong point of view, was unimpressed by the first explanation, but was ready to accept the second. He reckoned that having in the interests of Imperialism split the Nationalist Party at the time of fusion, Smuts had no intention of endangering his achievement over a black man's vote. Smuts had just returned from Scotland, where he had been installed as Rector of the University of St Andrews and had delivered a great address on Freedom. When he walked into the Lord Mayor's reception in London, the whole company rose as if for Royalty. 'He left for home,' wrote Crafford, 'in a blaze of glory to face and acquiesce in the somewhat inglorious native bills.'

After the passage of twenty-five years, one might essay a judgement. It was true that Smuts was a Boer in respect of the 'Native question', and a world citizen in respect of almost everything else. By now the danger of Hitler was clear, and Smuts saw it. There can be no doubt that if Britain had gone to war with Hitler, Smuts would have wanted South Africa to be at Britain's side. Smuts was prepared to swallow many things in the hope that the United Party could be held together, until the grave logic of events convinced it that the country which had once overwhelmed the republics was now the champion of liberty, in a time dangerous and grave. How else can one explain the local acquiescence? Was he giving Hertzog his head in national affairs—and indeed it was hard to do any-thing else—so that he himself could lead when the real crisis came? There seems reason to adopt this view.

Hofmeyr found it difficult to accept it as completely valid. He could see, with the clarity of vision that he possessed in every ethical context, that Smuts the Rector of St Andrews and Smuts the Deputy Prime Minis-ter were two different persons, that Smuts found it impossible to apply his universal ideals to his particular situation, not merely because the situation was so difficult, but because of psychological difficulty within him-self.

In his youth Hofmeyr had exchanged with Haarhoff views on his diabolical kinsman which were robust and superficial. Throughout the administratorship Hofmeyr had resisted him. But when Hofmeyr became a member of his party, most of these resistances broke down. Smuts knew how to lead a party; for all his faults, he had qualities that stamped him as one of the great. There seems little doubt but that Hofmeyr had been under the spell. But now, after some years of close association, he had become more critical. Just what he really thought about Smuts no one ever knew, except possibly his mother. Especially when Smuts was the Deputy Prime Minister, and later the Prime Minister, Hofmeyr would seldom criticise him and then only to his closest friends. Sarah Millin was certainly one of the exceptions, but then of course Smuts was her subject. This growing reticence was partly due to Hofmeyr's loyalty to Smuts, partly to his more and more evident maturity.

It was on 24 February that Hofmeyr told Smuts that he would speak against the Bill at the second reading. But in fact he did not. He was suddenly attacked by a fierce pain in the kidneys, that doubled him up and drove away what little blood there was in his sallow face, giving him the appearance of death. He was hurried off to hospital, where, as Esselen reported to Mrs Hofmeyr, a pretty little nurse was looking after him. It was Hofmeyr's first illness since infancy, except for an attack of influenza while he was at Balliol. Why was he ill? It was said of course that he was ill because he could not face the second reading. The truth was that quite apart from any psychological factor, he had a bacterial infection of the kidneys. He wrote to Underhill that the infection was made active by a chill but there seems no reason to doubt that he was more prone to physical attack because of his nervous condition.

What was Hofmeyr doing? It was as though in venturing into these deep waters, he had left the harbour of *hereniging*, in which his life would have been safe and its lines cast in pleasant places, and had embarked on a voyage into the unknown. Except for the Communists, no one in a political sense had made this voyage before. One difference between the Communists and Hofmeyr was that they knew where they were going and Hofmeyr did not. At that moment he was not going anywhere. He was not setting out on any new course. He was not setting up new values, he was fighting in the defence of old ones, that he had learned from his mother and the Bible and the church and the Greeks; from Bull and the Christian Association and Oxford and the Balliol Boys' Club. Probably it was his mother who most clearly saw his situation, for she saw him through the eyes of love, not as a man but as a boy, the small boy whose life she had cherished and whose character she had formed, docile, obedient, gentle, affectionate, challenging now for the first time principalities and powers, challenging the ideals and beliefs of his own Afrikanerdom, that could spew out so cruelly those who did not conform.

While Hofmeyr was ill, Hertzog was telling the joint session that the two great fears of white South Africa were the intermingling of blood and black domination. He said that continued postponement of a solution was 'a canker that was eating into the souls of the white population'. He rejoiced that a time had come when English-speaking and Afrikaans-speaking people were able to consider these matters calmly and quietly. He welcomed the appointment of a Natives Representative Council, which would be able to bring complaints quickly to the attention of Parliament.

He said he respected those who opposed the Bill on conscientious grounds, 'but they must not forget that the Europeans have the fullest right of seeing that their continued existence in South Africa shall be secured. And when they appeal to me as has sometimes been done recently on the ground that it is not Christian, that it is in conflict with Christian principles, then I say, Oh no, now I do not understand at all what you mean by Christian principles.'

Hertzog then went on to utter one of the most plausible of Christian heresies; he said there was a principle of self-preservation for a nation, 'the principle which causes everybody to sacrifice his life in time of war'.

'It is a sacred principle, a Christian principle just the same as any other principle, and it stands equally high—I place that principle still higher, it is the only principle, that of self-preservation, that of self-defence, by which humanity itself and Christianity itself will ever be able to protect itself.'

So Hertzog placed the defence of the good higher than the good itself, and made Christianity one of many warring factions, the survival of which was in the last resort dependent on the use of power.

Smuts gave as his reason for supporting the Bill the very one that Pirow had pooh-poohed. He had decided that rather than risk abolition of the Cape African franchise, he would work for separate representation, although he did not like it and had voted against it previously. Speaking amidst numerous interjections he said:

'Of course I could have died in the last ditch so to say, I could have said, I fight to the bitter end for the Cape Native Franchise, but what would have been the result? It would not have been I who died, but the Natives, metaphorically speaking.'

He was glad that after years of wrangling—'bitter years for me, some of the bitterest years of my life'—settlement had been reached, not ideal, but containing 'the elements of justice and fair play and fruitfulness for the future'. He concluded that it was a measure 'which I can ask my fellow men of black colour to accept, and to work on as a basis for their advancement in the years to come'.

Hofmeyr from his bed followed the debate with his usual interest and outward impassivity. Hertzog's argument about a principle higher even than Christianity itself, Smuts's argument about yielding something in order not to lose all, both affected not at all his view that the white man was breaking his word. He spent nearly two weeks in bed and had a painful time. When he was able to move, he and his mother went off for a week at Somerset Strand, where he enjoyed the warm, cloudless days. When he returned to Cape Town he decided that he would oppose the Bill at its third reading which took place on 6 April.

The House was tense, having heard that Hofmeyr would oppose his Prime Minister; members recalled the great speech he had made on the gold standard when he had opposed Smuts. Hofmeyr was tense too. His hands, never supple, were tight and swollen, and his face was twitching; he was not only opposing both Hertzog and Smuts, he was opposing white South Africa; he was laying himself open to the half-contemptuous, half-fearful dislike, of those who are told that what they believe to be politically magnificent is in fact morally wrong. The papers reported that he looked pale and nervous, that he sat with his head bowed, hardly listening to the earlier speeches. But few people knew that his infection had returned, and that he was in considerable pain, and but for the debate, would have been back in bed. But once he was on his feet, all sign of pain and nervousness left him. He said:

'I do very sincerely regret that I cannot on this occasion align myself with my leader the Prime Minister. I appreciate the Prime Minister's sincere desire to further the best interests of white men and black men in this country. I recognise that his knowledge and experience of native affairs are greater than mine and that this Bill represents a life-work to him. I am most grateful indeed to him for his forbearance and tolerance in this matter to an errant colleague. But . . . there is a fundamental difference in this matter between my outlook and that which underlies this Bill. While that is so, I can do no other than oppose it, and I must do so regardless of what the political consequences for myself might be.'

Hofmeyr referred in strong terms to the intention of the Bill, once the entrenchment had been set aside, to re-entrench the separate roll under which the African people of the Union would have three representatives out of 153. He said:

'It is now proposed to put up an entrenchment of a two-thirds majority not only against any deterioration in the Natives' position but also against any improvement in the Natives' position. The National Convention did not think such a double entrenchment necessary. Why not? Because the White man was put in the constitution into an impregnable position, they thought there was no necessity to protect the White man. They did not think it necessary to protect the White man against the possibility of his own generosity. Today we are asked to do both. I have heard one of my friends say that it is only just and fair that, if we give entrenchment on the one side, we should also give it on the other, and that reminded me of the first recorded definition of justice. *Justice is the interest of the stronger*. I am afraid it is from that conception of justice that a good deal of the support of this Bill is derived.'

Hofmeyr again asserted that the Bill was no more acceptable than its predecessors.

'It is called a compromise, but if we look back to 1926, then from the point of view of the Natives, it is the Natives who have done all the giving and none of the taking. Let us see what this Bill does. The central feature is to give to the Natives an inferior, a qualified citizenship which has the marks of inferiority in clause after clause of this Bill and which bears the added stigma that whatever may be the advance of the Native in civilisation and education, to all intents and purposes he is limited for all time to three members in a House of 153. That surely is a qualified, an inferior citizenship.'

Hofmeyr referred to Senator F. S. Malan, who had voted against the second reading because he believed in common citizenship.

'May I make my own position clear? I am not one of those who would necessarily stand or fall by the ideal of common citizenship as an absolute thing. I do not go with the Right Hon. Senator Malan to that extent. If we were starting with a clean sheet, it would certainly be possible to devise a system of separate representation in separate assemblies which would be fair and just and sound. I am not saying that it is impossible to do so today. But we are not starting with a clean sheet. We are starting with the existence of a vested right which has been in existence and which has not been abused for more than eighty years. And I want to say this, that once franchise rights have been given and exercised by a section of the community, then no nation save at the cost of honour and ultimate security should take away those rights without adequate justification.'

Hofmeyr then went on to ask what justification there was for this proposal.

'Attempts have been made to answer that question. Some have sought to find that justification in terms of high ethical and political principle. Some have used those blessed words and phrases, segregation, trusteeship, the Native developing along his own lines. The Native developing along his own lines—that means for most who use the words the same as the Native being kept in his place.'

Of trusteeship he said:

'I have always regarded trusteeship as implying that at some stage or another, the trustee is prepared to hand over the trust to his ward. I have yet to learn that the European trustee in South Africa contemplates any such possibility. And that being so, I find it very difficult to reconcile the use of the word trusteeship in relation to a Bill for which it is claimed that it is going to make South Africa safe for European civilisation. But we are also told that we can justify the Bill because once the political question is removed the Native will receive better treatment. There will be more sympathy with their development. I know that is sincerely meant, but I know too that, in the case of many people, that is simply a conscience-salving argument which they are laying to their souls.'

Hofmeyr strongly objected to the principle of communal representation, and regarded it as dangerous, 'not least of all from the point of view of the European in this country'.

'Communal representation of different races implies a divergence of interests, and in South Africa there is no real ultimate divergence of interests between Europeans and non-Europeans. There is a far greater community of interests in this land. We have on both sides a contribution to make to the welfare of South Africa, and the weakness of this Bill, from my point of view, is that it emphasises the differences, it stimulates hostility, and it pays no regard to the ultimate community of interest.'

Hofmeyr gave a warning to the House.

'By this Bill we are sowing the seeds of a far greater potential conflict than is being done by anything in existence today. Let me explain. To my mind, as I have always felt, the crux of the position is in regard to the educated Native. We have many educated and semi-educated Natives in South Africa. Many of them have attained to and many more of them are advancing towards European standards. They have been trained on European lines, they have been taught to think and act as Europeans, we may not like it, but those are the plain facts. Now what is the political future for these people? This Bill says that even the most educated Native shall never have political equality with even the least educated and the least cultured White or Coloured man. This Bill says to these educated Natives: "There is no room for you, you must be driven back upon your own people." But we drive them back in hostility and disgruntlement, and do not let us forget this, that all that this Bill is doing for those educated Natives is to make them the leaders of their own people, in disaffection and revolt.'

Hofmeyr said that the Bill was born of fear, of the desire to achieve self-preservation, but he did not believe that self-preservation could be attained in such a way; he did not believe that white civilisation could be preserved except with the consent and the good will of the non-European people. The fear was unreasoning, and it was that fear together with sentiment based on tradition that lay behind the Bill.

'These are the facts that made the Prime Minister recede from the relative liberalism of the Bill of 1926; these are the facts that made the Bill of 1929 worse than the Bill of 1926, and made this Bill again worse than the Bill of 1929. And there is no finality. There is no more finality than there was in 1892, when Sir James Rose Innes supported the Bill of that date because it might bring finality. That tide of reaction is still flowing forward. I know that those of us who are opposing that tide cannot hope to check it. The puny breastworks that we put up must be swept away, but I do believe that the mere putting up of those breastworks is going to accelerate the day when the tide will turn, as turn, I believe, it some day will . . . I know perfectly well that I am speaking against the feeling of the overwhelming majority of this House. I know I am speaking against the feeling of the great mass of the people of this country. I know how my remarks will be described as "academic" and quixotic and unrealistic. I am accustomed to that. I can see all the adjectives that will be used. But these are matters on which the future must be left to judge. I expressed the belief that the tide of reaction will turn, and I base that belief on what I know of what is going on in the minds of some at least of the younger people in South Africa, especially in the universities. I believe that there is also a rising tide of liberalism in South Africa. It is mostly the younger people who are in the forefront of that tide. It is they who are the custodians of the future. And whatever we may or may not do today, it is by them that the ultimate issues in connection with this matter will have to be decided.'

Hofmeyr sat down in what was almost a silence. There were murmurs of admiration, even from some who opposed him, and an attempt at clapping in the public gallery was immediately silenced. No one, not even Smuts, had expected such a wholesale rejection of the Bill. By his impassive demeanour Smuts gave no sign that he had even heard the speech, nor did he ever speak of it afterwards; yet in its general substance, its defence of the ideals of Western civilisation, in its call for courage rather than fear, it was brother to the speeches Smuts made overseas. The trouble was that Hofmeyr was more and more inclined to relate the universal to the particular, and Smuts less and less.

When Hofmeyr sat down he knew that his speech had gone home. How a speaker knows this when he is not cheered one does not know. He did not look about him. Of his colleagues on the ministerial benches not one was for him. He had given some of his fellow members an uncomfortable time. Many of them had never heard these views advanced before, and they had already promised their support to the Bill. Now that they had heard Hofmeyr they were filled with misgivings. The Prime Minister was also impassive and Pirow was busy preparing to reply to the debate. But Kemp and Grobler must have been thinking of what the Malanites would say, how they would ask how Kemp and Grobler could possibly stay in a party that gave high position to such a man. As for the Malanites, they were satisfied. If Hofmeyr stayed in the United Party more ex-Nationalists would desert to Malan; if Hofmeyr were expelled from the United Party, that might be the end of fusion.

The speech itself angered them. It was unthinkable to attack it point by point; its whole basic philosophy was un-South African, un-Afrikaner and alien. Hofmeyr revealed his usual obsession with rights, and talked as though the preservation of a black man's vote was a cause more important than the preservation of Afrikanerdom. He was so blind that he could not see that the Cape franchise was a British imposition, an incubus laid by the Imperial power on the shoulders of the unwilling Afrikaner people. Most distasteful of all, showing the depth of his ignorance of the Afrikaner soul, was his concern over those black men who had been taught 'to think and act as Europeans'. Under the Nationalists there would be no such tragic people. As for the rising tide of liberalism, let him go to the young people of Stellenbosch, and Potchefstroom and Bloemfontein and Pretoria; the idea was laughable.

But it was not only Nationalists who were angered. J. J. van Rensburg, a member of the United Party, deplored Hofmeyr's speech. 'The knowledge he has of the natives he has acquired between four walls but of the practical condition of the natives he knows nothing . . . Not five per cent of his party will agree with him in what he said here this afternoon.'

The heaviest attack of all came from yet another member of Hofmeyr's own party, the beetle-browed Heaton Nicholls who, though he had not come to South Africa until the age of 36, was regarded as an expert on the 'Native question' because he was not only a farmer, he was a farmer in Zululand.

Nicholls attacked Hofmeyr fiercely, not only for condemning the Bill after voting for it at the first reading, not only for attacking inferior and qualified citizenship after proposing it in the select committee, but for speaking in such a way that the white people of South Africa were made to appear dishonest and dishonourable. He then delivered himself of a powerful attack on all those who stirred up racial dissension in the name of justice, a classic speech which even today can be regarded with envy by all who aspire to be regarded as authorities on the 'Native question'.

'What is the difference between a communist protagonist who believes that human happiness can be better furthered if people will only adopt his tenets and the bishops who go around the country telling the natives that if they will only join together and agitate sufficiently, and believe that Parliament is animated by the worst possible repressive intentions, they will be the happier for it? . . . Is a manifesto issued by an ex-chief justice to receive more immunity than a manifesto by a communist when both aim at sowing dissension between the races?'

The task of replying to the debate Hertzog entrusted to Pirow, to whom he now entrusted so many things. Pirow made no mention of Hofmeyr's speech or any of his arguments, and therefore had little to reply to. With an eye on Heaton Nicholls' bishops, he appealed to the churches to use their influence to see that the settlement was given a fair trial. He gave the black people of the country the traditional promise and warning:

'Once the political question is settled, once the political aspect of the relationship between black and white has been placed on a firm basis, the white people of this country, including the north . . . are prepared to be more than fair. But I am very much afraid that this attitude of being fair and being generous is going to be affected by the attitude of the natives, if the natives are going to allow themselves to be persuaded to stand aside in a sullen and hostile manner.'

When the final vote was taken, after midnight on 7 April, Hertzog secured a majority of 169 votes to 11. Out of a total of 190 M.P.s and Senators, he required 127 votes to change the franchise, but he had received 42 more than that. When the count was announced, an unprecedented thing happened; members defied the rules and burst out into cheering in acknowledgement of Hertzog's achievement and the crowning of his life's work. Four days earlier he had reached the age of 70, and many regarded the passing of the Bill as his birthday present. The Speaker, Dr E. G. Jansen, who also felt that Hertzog's achievement was a great one, upheld the dignity of the House by rebuking those who had cheered the Prime Minister, for their 'unseemly behaviour'.

Party politics has strange effects on moral decisions. Stallard and Marwick voted against the Bill and Heaton Nicholls for it, yet all three were very much alike; they were devoted to King and Empire, and thought that the strong should be just to the weak. All three exhibited the characteristics of English-speaking South Africa, which is torn (though not in a very painful way) between Boer policies of self-preservation and British ideals of justice and fair play. In this case, when the rent came, Stallard and Marwick were on one side of it, and Nicholls on the other; party membership was undoubtedly the deciding factor. Stallard, who in the select committee had voted for the abolition of the Cape African franchise, now voted against any change in it. By such imponderables are men's destinies decided.

The effect of Hofmeyr's speech on what could be called the liberal elements in South Africa was tremendous. It turned, as great speeches are able to do, despondency into resolution. Men and women who might have been expected to be discouraged, took new courage because Hofmeyr was there. He himself had said—with a slip of the mind that showed where he had come from rather than where he was going—that he was speaking against the feeling of the great mass of the people of the country, meaning of course the great mass of the white people. That was true; hundreds of thousands of white South Africans were quite unaffected by his arguments, and certainly felt no guilt because of them. Even a man like the Speaker, E. G. Jansen, a gentle, honourable man, while sensing that Hofmeyr was equally honourable, was baffled by his politics, which seemed related to nothing in the Afrikaner soul, nor to Afrikaner history or tradition or religion or political struggle; Hertzog offered a road, and one might not like everything about it, but at least one could travel on it, whereas Hofmeyr was like a man launching himself ineffectually at Heaven. Jansen said of him, wistfully, as though he wished it had been otherwise, 'We spoke a common language, but all we had in common were the words.' Strange that one gentle, honourable man should not know what another was talking about! But all those white South Africans who felt that something was wrong, that their own people were retreating step by step from any kind of common life with their non-white fellows, that an all-white Parliament enacted law after law that affected the destinies of non-white people, that justice—to use Hofmeyr's own words—was the interest of the stronger, all these took heart that after twenty-six years of Union a voice was raised for the right. They poured in their messages upon him, old friends, schoolmasters, old colleagues at the University of the Witwatersrand, leaders of the churches.

It is interesting to read what one publicist wrote about what he called 'this memorable speech'.

'From that moment may be said to have begun the steady, insistent and ever-growing opposition to Hofmeyr within the ranks of the United Party, mainly from the Platteland.'

If history remembers the Representation of Natives Act of 1936, and if it remembers Hofmeyr's great speech, which will it praise? Of that there seems little doubt. It will remember also that the Representation of Natives Act, which was to lay such honourable foundations for the future, was repealed in 1960, and replaced by an Act which abolished altogether the representation of Africans in the South African Parliament. History will also record that in 1956, it was the turn of Coloured voters to be given a separate roll, with representation by four white members of Parliament. History may also well record that even this separate Coloured representation was itself later abolished: already a separate Coloured Affairs Department has been established, and it may not be long before the existence of M.P.s representing Coloured interests will be regarded as a monstrous interference with separate development.

What was it that Hofmeyr said on 6 April 1936? 'And there is no finality. There is no more finality than there was in 1892, when Sir James Rose Innes supported the Bill of that date because it might bring finality. The tide of reaction is still flowing forward.'

The *Rand Daily Mail* expressed its belief that history would be on the side of Hofmeyr. The paper which had found itself irritated by Hofmeyr's coyness in 1929, paid him in 1936 a tribute that has seldom been equalled, either for its generosity of sentiment or its economy of words:

'New lustre has been added to the honoured name of Hofmeyr in

South African politics by the speech of the Minister of the Interior on the final reading of the Native Bill. It was an utterance all compact of courage, and generations yet to come will hold his name in honour because of its deliverance. The making of such a speech in such an atmosphere was an exhibition of intellectual and moral integrity that has probably not been excelled in South Africa in our time.'

George Heard, the political correspondent of the *Rand Daily Mail*, went yet further, and ventured to prophesy. He wrote of Hofmeyr:

'Today he is misunderstood because he represents a new outlook in South African politics—a liberal outlook that is foreign to the old order of fear-conditioned politics in our country. The old battle cries do not stir him; they belong to an age that is passing. Mr Hofmeyr belongs to a new age that is just coming to birth. The young men in Parliament will, I believe, be with him in the day of its fulfilment.'

And his mother? She was a proud woman. For the politics of the affair she cared little, but that her son should stand for the right, she cared for more than anything in the world. She was an Afrikaner, as much as any Hertzog or Malan, and she hated *broedertwis*, but never would she put self-interest above the right. Visitors came to see her to bring their thanks and their congratulations, and she would receive them like a queen, regally and not with little jests that were sharp and dry, for one should bear oneself with dignity in momentous days.

There was another woman too who mattered a great deal to Hofmeyr in 1936: she was Sarah Gertrude Millin. They had known each other since 1917, but in 1936 their friendship blossomed. She objected to his calling her Mrs, so he called her Sarah, which must have been one of the rare occasions in his adult life that he had done such a thing. She spoke and wrote to him as no other woman had ever spoken and written before. In February 1936, in a letter asking his permission to use his name in her biography of Smuts, and to tell the story of how he took to Smuts the amazing news that Hertzog was ready to co-operate, she wrote, 'Your last letter was discernibly human.'

Sarah Millin had undoubtedly sensed in Hofmeyr, behind all the well-known shortcomings, a quality of greatness and had noted the swift march to maturity since his days as Administrator. A bond between them was his consistent championship of the Jews. Sarah Millin was a novelist of repute, used to the study of character; she discovered in Hofmeyr hidden qualities, and she longed to bring them out, to help him to break through his diffidence and his reserve. That was no doubt why he loved her.

Hofmeyr's speech of 6 April, and the sensation that it caused in many circles, and the nobility of its ethics, were very exciting to Sarah Millin, who knew drama when she encountered it, especially the drama of prophets. Now she set herself a surprising task, to persuade Hofmeyr, not merely that he is a bigger man than he thinks, but that he has it in him to be the biggest of them all. But he must overcome his uncertainty. She uses of him the same word that de Waal had used of Onze Jan, timidity. She hears him speak at the Rand SACS dinner in November, and she asks herself, 'Why can't Jan Hofmeyr lead people away from the Devil?' She adds, 'Your speaking last night made me surer than ever . . . that South Africa's future lies in your hands—if you will take it.' He replies:

'Your letter . . . has caused me a good deal of searching of the heart. Am I uncertain and timid? Or are you over-estimating my powers? It may be that I have a gift of speech but is it not of the kind that appeals only to intellectuals, and does not really stir the masses? I wish I could see myself leading people away from the Devil—but when I realise the strength of the forces arrayed against whosoever essays that task, I can, at best, only foresee a more or less splendid failure.' He reminds her of his modest wish to be a John Bright, leading a liberal wing. But that is 'a good deal short of what you are thinking of'.

'If the other thing were really possible, if there were a chance of leading South Africa from the Devil, I would readily sspend myself in the process—but is it? Or is it possibly that there is something lacking in my make-up?'

Even in 1936 Hofmeyr was writing to her that he was dangerously near to accepting the fatalistic Greek apophthegm—what must come will come. Yet 1936 was the year that he had expressed the belief, in the course of his great speech, that the tide of reaction would turn, largely due to those very same intellectuals, the young people at the universities.

It is clear that one must not look for consistency in these day-to-day statements, which appear, even in the case of the great, to be powerfully coloured by the mood of the moment; and by the need of the moment too, whether people at that moment need to face stark reality or need to be encouraged to hope, therefore to work, for something better. Hofmeyr clearly oscillated between believing that right would triumph and doubting that it would. The consistency of character that one might expect from him is therefore to be found somewhere else, namely in his love of righteousness whether it triumphed or not. It was that same love which comforted the Jews when literally there was nothing else to comfort them, so that the words of the great prophets, which had failed to save the old Israel, are yet heard with cries of joy by the new; and with tears too, because righteousness at times appears both powerless and ineffable. Nor must one look for consistency in the beliefs of Sarah Millin. She had once made the famous epigram that people said that Smuts's great defect was that he misunderstood men; but, she added, he had a greater defect, he believed in them. Now she wants Hofmeyr to believe in them also, and to save them from the devil. She writes:

'Since ever I've known you the thought has been in my mind that you had it in you to be the great man of South Africa. I have watched you struggling against your uncertainties and hoped you might come out on the high side. You have done so.'

She deals with his fear that he cannot stir the masses. She reassures him, and tells him that when he is not rhetorical, he is the most moving speaker she knows. She, who knows all about man and his frailty, she, who knows as well as anyone that fear is at the bottom of white politics, she writes to him, 'You *can* appeal to the masses.'

She appeals to him in the language of the Bible:

'Show thyself, Jan. Unless all your party go down, you can't go down. You are too valuable, too necessary—worth half the Cabinet and I bet the Cabinet knows it. Forgive my daring to say all these things to you. I say them in deep admiration and faith.'

He replies to her that she acts like a gadfly! He acknowledges having become rhetorical! He still has his doubts but he is conscious of growing strength of late. He feels too that the time for independent action will come, but he does not see when. He writes, 'You adjure me (somewhat rhetorically) to show myself but you are not very precise in giving your ideas as to what you regard as the immediate action that I should take.'

He tells her that if one takes a stand, it must be on a really big issue. 'So it is not just caution and timidity that makes one choose one's ground carefully.'

Is one to deduce from these letters that he had decided to challenge the Government? And was the ground of the challenge to be—in general —that the Government was evil?

All through 1937 she encourages him. In August she discovers something. 'Are you a bit shy, I wonder? You don't altogether trust people, do you? You're a little uncomfortable, aren't you, about yielding too much of yourself to anyone?'

He sends her a copy of Paton's study of him in *South African Opin-*

ion. She is not sure whether his concern for detail is valuable or danger-ous. 'Your friend, for instance, says you promptly answer the letters of the veriest whippersnapper.' She disapproves of this, and writes, 'You give yourself too equally.'

This friendship was to last till his death, but it was also to change greatly. The shadows of Hitler, of anti-Semitism both abroad and at home, the disappointment that her husband was not sooner made a judge, the horror of war and the tragedy of the Jews of Europe, began to lie dark and heavy over Sarah Millin's life, so that she could spare less and less thought for others. As for Hofmeyr, there began to lie shadows over his life too, so that their friendship began to lose the excitement of its first discoveries. Yet he was never to know another friendship like it, nor was he ever to enter again into such intimacies. Was he in love? In his own Hofmeyrian way he was. But she was right when she wrote, 'You're a little uncomfortable, aren't you, about yielding too much of yourself to anyone?'

Chapter 8

Champion of the Voiceless

HOFMEYR had started on a voyage from which there could be no return. If he had offered resistance to Hertzog's Bill on the narrow ground that it wished to remove an existing right, he might have been dismissed as quixotic. But he had gone much further; he had attacked the Bill on the ground that it was an abuse of white power, that it offered inferior citizenship, and would stimulate hostility. He was attacking the whole concept of segregation, which was as much part of Afrikaner Nationalism as was sovereign independence.

There was one thing he could have done. Softened by Hertzog's patience, he could have settled down and become a tractable Minister, but he did not do so. Even if he had, he would not have been left alone. Malan, Strijdom, Swart, Erasmus, du Toit, saw that he was the Achilles heel of the Government, and lost no opportunity of attacking him.

On 10 March 1936, the House gave leave to Major F. J. Roberts, once United Party, now an Independent member to introduce a Bill to control interracial marriages. When it became clear that this Bill would never see a second reading, J. H. Grobler, United Party member for a rural constituency in the Transvaal, asked for a select committee to investigate the matter of Indians who married white wives, so that their wives could own land in areas closed to their husbands. Grobler also wanted the committee to find out how many white girls were employed by Indians, and he recommended steps to forbid such employment. He chilled the blood of many by picturing the white girl who worked behind the same counter as an Indian, coming into touch with him shoulder to shoulder, until any proper feeling against Indians disappeared.

Malan and his men registered grief and horror at these revelations, but in fact they were occasions of joy to them. Such debates subjected the United Party to severe strain, especially when they were initiated by its own members. If Malan took advantage of this, no United Party member would dare to shrug it off as politics, for these things were life and death to the Afrikaner countryside.

Hofmeyr replied to Grobler with cold logic. There was only one case of a mixed marriage in which land was held by a white woman. From 1925 to 1934, there were only thirty-nine marriages between white persons and Indians. Therefore it did not seem necessary to appoint a select committee, but he would not object if the House thought it desirable.

Major Roberts, whose own Bill had so languished, seized his chance and moved to prohibit all mixed marriages. He said that in the last ten years there had been 517 mixed marriages of all kinds, and in eight years' time there would be 2,000 more coloured children as a result. Strijdom, du Toit, and Luttig all joined in the attack.

Hofmeyr replied that the Government would not agree to Roberts's Bill. For one thing it was impracticable; it was difficult to distinguish White from Coloured people in some parts of the country. Further, if mixed marriages were prohibited, the number of extra-marital relationships would increase. His reply outraged the Nationalists. Du Toit said he had never before heard such a speech from an Afrikaans-speaking Minister.

One of Malan's outstanding lieutenants, C. R. Swart, speculated in the *Sunday Express* on Hofmeyr's future. He wrote, 'When he refused to accept the motion by Mr Jannie Grobler on the Asiatic question and made a speech that sent thrills of horror down spines of members from northern provinces, he sealed his doom as an influence in his party.'

Swart mentioned rumours that Hofmeyr would lead a so-called Liberal Party, and other rumours that he would complete his LL.B., resign from the Cabinet, and build up a practice in Johannesburg. There was no truth in any of these. What was true was that Hofmeyr, fortified by conscience and many fellow-believers, had embarked on a course which endangered his membership of both Party and Cabinet, and that he knew it.

He had no difficulty over Hertzog's second big Bill, the Native Trust and Land Bill. He was fully in favour of increasing the area reserved for Africans by some 15,000,000 acres. He had lost the battle for the Cape African franchise; now he was prepared to support the making of reparation. His support of the Bill helped to restore his standing with his own party, but the Nationalists were determined not to let his past be forgotten.

The Rev. C. W. M. du Toit attacked Hofmeyr as Minister of Education. There were four non-white students at the University of the Witwatersrand, and forty-four at Cape Town, and they were not segregated. He told the House that at one of these universities a white liberal-minded student took an African friend home, and his friend and his sister fell in love and became engaged. It was a very good family, and it took two years' struggle to break the engagement.

Du Toit wanted to know what Hofmeyr was going to do about maintaining segregation. If he was going to do nothing, let him get up and say so; then the Government could not blame the Nationalists if they went to the country and told them the position.

Hofmeyr's reply was clear. He had no power to prevent universities from admitting non-white students. He could ask for such powers, but he did not intend to do so. He regarded it as a matter for the universities.

Such a reply both angered and gladdened the Nationalists. Here was a Minister who put university freedom above the principle of segregation and the purity of Afrikanerdom. He declared that race mixture was repugnant to him, but he did nothing to prevent it.

Hofmeyr again earned the disapproval of the Malanites when as Minister of the Interior he introduced his Transvaal Asiatic Land Tenure Amendment Bill. So restrictive were the laws relating to the ownership of land by Indian persons outside certain congested areas, that they resorted to many stratagems. They formed impersonal companies to buy land, or bought land in the name of some trusted white person, or in one rare case, an Indian married a white woman and she bought the land. Now Hofmeyr presented a Bill to relax some of these restrictions, and to condone some illegal occupations. It was widely regarded as an extraordinary achievement for liberal forces, and *Round Table* declared that, having regard to Transvaal history and sentiment, it was 'an important advance towards a more liberal society'.

Hertzog's country members were again restive. Commandant W. R. Collins said he did not want to hold up the Bill. If it meant that the Indian community would now behave itself, he would be very happy, and he would not say one word on the Bill. But he did not believe it for a minute. He said:

'My considered opinion is that within a very short time there will be no trade in the hands of the white man in the Transvaal . . . outside the big cities.'

J. H. Grobler, another United Party man, reinforced the warning. He said, 'The antipathy existing against the Indians today is largely attributable to the fact that Indians in the past have done everything in their power to evade the law. The white population is getting tired of this sort of thing.'

It was a weary Hofmeyr who returned to Pretoria on 17 June after the long session had ended. He had recovered from his illness, but he was tired, both by his multi-ministerial duties and by the need to reply to the attacks directed against him. William Janisch saw him hurrying in a Johannesburg street, and detained him for only a moment to say, 'Lots of us are praying for you,' to which Hofmeyr replied, 'You'd better,' and hurried on. In spite of his tiredness he did not rest, nor as far as one knows did he change his diet. Within a day or two of his return to Pretoria he was speaking in Pietermaritzburg in Natal, and after returning home flew to Cape Town for an evening engagement, and back the following day; at that time he was still marvelling at the wonder of air travel. His health seemed quite restored, and his energy immense.

In Pretoria he took up a task that was important to him, and that was to set down his political thought, in an address entitled 'The Approach to the Native Problem', which he intended to deliver, first at Rhodes University College in Grahamstown, and then to the Bantu Studies Society of the University of the Witwatersrand. This address can be taken to represent Hofmeyr's thinking of 1936, and one of its preliminary assumptions was that Hertzog's Bills did not solve the 'Native problem'.

In his address Hofmeyr declared that Cape liberalism was fighting a losing battle. It could not allay white fear of the black man's numerical superiority, of his constantly accelerating advance, and of 'the revolting possibility of ultimate social equality and the mixture of the races'. To be able to defeat white fear, idealism must be grounded in knowledge and nurtured in understanding. This new liberalism would accept the same broad principles as the old, but would couple it with 'sympathetic first-hand acquaintance with the Native peoples', by which Hofmeyr meant study and investigation. The new liberalism would be restrained, and 'content to hasten slowly'. He felt hopeful, because while the old liberalism had been defeated in Parliament, there was abundant evidence outside Parliament that the new liberalism was growing.

Hofmeyr made an important political statement at this point. He said he regarded the question of the Cape Native franchise as an issue which had been adjudicated. 'I certainly have no intention of reviving it. All that I am saying this evening is based on the assumption that the present position in regard to the representation of natives is to continue.'

As in 1930, so in 1936, Hofmeyr rejected the two extremes of white supremacy and racial equalitarianism. The first he rejected on moral grounds, the second because it was repugnant 'to the South African'. He wrote, 'French policy formulates the identity of all subjects of France whatever the colour or race. To the South African of course the notion is repugnant. We are revolted in particular by the notion of social equality, with its corollary, it seems to us, of intermarriage and miscegenation.'

Having rejected white domination, black domination, and equality, Hofmeyr asked what came next. Was it segregation? He rejected what he called 'crude segregationism', because it was really white domination. He then examined 'constructive segregationism', as advanced by Smuts in his Rhodes lectures, but decided that the white man would never pay the price for it, in money or land. In any case it was too late. 'The policy of constructive segregation may have been a practicable one for the last generation. In our own we can apply it in bits and fragments: the chance of using it as a solution of the problem is lost.'

What was there left to do? He gave a twofold answer to the question. 'White South Africa could encourage distinctive Native development in Native areas, even though this is only of partial applicability. White South Africa could show practical sympathy for the economic aspirations of the residual urban Native.'

Would economic advancement lead to social equality, and so to inter-marriage and miscegenation? Hofmeyr thought there was little ground for such a fear. He gave as example the United States, where intermixture was on the decline, according to a 'competent observer'. His other example was the Cape Province, which had a 'Native policy . . . broadly sympathetic', and produced per 100,000 people only half of the offences against the Immorality Act, and only one quarter of violent sexual offences.

Would the approach he had adumbrated make South Africa safe for European civilisation? His answer was that no 'Native policy' could be guaranteed to do that, but that the dangers of a policy of repression would be far greater than those of any other. He concluded:

'It is on the note of faith and confidence that I would close. The problem of which I have been speaking presents to this small nation of ours a cruelly severe test. But when I have regard to our nation's past history, when I see in that history proof at once of the fundamental soundness of its instinctive reactions in times of crisis and of its genius for constructive statesmanship, I have confidence that it will in this matter also, in the long run, not be found wanting. And the measure of its success will be its capacity to make faith triumph over fear.'

Hofmeyr's slogan of development—he once said, 'Development is the keyword'—offered to many people a way to escape complete frustration. It did not satisfy the white conservatives of the United or the Nationalist Parties; they wanted it clearly stated that if there was to be development, it must be development in a pattern of segregation. Nor did it satisfy the left, who considered that Hofmeyr was fruitlessly seeking a compromise between segregation and equality. What was his new liberalism but a mixture of the old liberalism and a bit of study? They neither liked nor understood his categories of faith and fear. Their own categories were more materialist, more directly political and economic; they had no time for metaphysics.

Hofmeyr's address disappointed even some of his own supporters. Why should he declare that he regarded the Cape franchise issue as adjudicated? What development could there be in society if one accepted a retrogressive law as its foundation? Did such acceptance not commit Hofmeyr to a system of communal representation which he once declared would promote racial hostility?

And why must he say, 'We are revolted by the notion of social equality?' Was that the sort of thing he would have said at Fort Hare? Was that the sort of utterance that would help faith to triumph over fear?

To this biographer, who often heard Hofmeyr speak of the white South African repugnance for race mixture, it seemed that he was talking of something felt by others, by his mother perhaps, or his relations, or by the man in the street, something that a politician could not ignore. It was Hofmeyr who had declined in Parliament to ban mixed marriages, showing a detachment that angered the Malanites and even some of his own party. It was Hofmeyr who had refused to take powers to prevent 'White' universities from admitting non-white students.

In all these matters Hofmeyr had the characteristics of many white South Africans. He wanted justice and economic equality, but not social equality or race mixture. He said that the new liberalism must include 'sympathetic first-hand acquaintance with the Native peoples', but it is unlikely that he ever meant, for himself at least, ordinary personal acquaintance. There is no evidence that any non-white visitor ever entered the Hofmeyr home except as a special visitor, coming either because he was of great importance or because he had special business; nor is there any evidence that this special exception ever occurred. It is certain that no non-white person ever entered the Hofmeyr home in the same way that white persons entered it, to enjoy Mrs Hofmeyr's teas and a pleasant gossip. There is no evidence that any non-white South African ever called the adult Hofmeyr by his first name. The Ballingers, the Hoernlés, the Rheinallt Joneses, had overcome many of these inhibitions, and still more had the white people of the left, the Communists and the strong Socialists, who, even though they held an incomplete view of man's nature, were not guilty of the white Christian heresy of judging him by his colour and his race. Hofmeyr's life was not the life of an angel or a paragon, but of a white South African painfully inching his way towards emancipation, with fear and caution, but not without courage.

Late in the year 1936 Hofmeyr went to India on an official good will tour, and when he returned, anti-Semitism was raging. Malan had once argued, and Hofmeyr had approved, that he wished to curb Jewish immigration for the sake of both South Africa and the Jews. Now he declared openly that Jews were unassimilable, and that South Africa wanted no more of them. It was said that Malan was never personally anti-Semitic, whatever that phrase may mean, but it seems beyond doubt that he was prepared to use anti-Semitism if that would help the Nationalist Party. The Chief Rabbi took the unprecedented step of saying this publicly. Malan's old paper, *Die Burger*, although a paper of repute, published interviews denying that there was any persecution of Jews in Germany.

Malan may well have felt compelled to use anti-Semitism, because if he did not, others would. All over the country were springing up the Greyshirts, the Blackshirts, the Brownshirts, all of them rivals, if one were not careful, to the Nationalist Party. Malan, though no equestrian, rode on a black horse into Lichtenburg, and praised the Greyshirts.

The Nationalist Party did not lag behind the 'Shirt' movements. Dr Eben Dönges, assisted by Dr Hendrik Verwoerd, Professor of Psychology at Stellenbosch, spoke to one crowded protest meeting, and Erasmus to another. Verwoerd threatened that the country would march on Parliament if it received no satisfaction. Malan was the guest of honour at the Transvaal Congress of the Nationalist Party, and declared that the Government was not able to do anything about Jewish immigration, because that would mean that Smuts and Hofmeyr would have to sacrifice their principles.

South Africa was an ugly place for Jews at this time. It had once seemed a haven in a cruel world, but now one could not be so sure. Non-Afrikaners have always been afraid of Afrikaner Nationalism, even at its weakest; but if it did this at its weakest, what would it do in the days of its power? Jewish parents were afraid that their growing sons and daughters would read the papers and learn that the centuries-old enemy of Jewish peace was not confined to Germany, but was now, in the words of the Book of Job, going to and fro in the earth.

The Government was in a quandary. Every new batch of Jewish immigrants added fuel to the anti-Semitic and anti-Government flames. Hofmeyr therefore introduced interim regulations, and promised a new Aliens Bill for 1937. But before the regulations could take effect, 500 German Jews, fleeing from Hitler before the last doors closed, arrived at Cape Town in the *Stuttgart*. Verwoerd and five other professors from the University of Stellenbosch protested vehemently against their entry. Hofmeyr condemned the professors at the annual dinner of his old school in Johannesburg; he declared that the scientific spirit no longer lived in them. Verwoerd and his five colleagues accused Hofmeyr of being grossly intolerant towards them while so tolerant towards Jews, and they reminded him that he had voted for the Quota Act in 1930. Why did he not as Minister of Education write to the University Council instead of denouncing them at a school dinner? On 25 November yet another 75 German Jews arrived in the *Guilio Cesare*. Verwoerd and Dönges addressed another protest meeting where Verwoerd spoke sarcastically of Hofmeyr. At this time it was noticeable that anti-Semitic public servants and teachers felt bold enough to refer publicly to the 'Jewish menace'.

Suddenly the pressure on Hofmeyr was relieved. The King agreed to appoint Patrick Duncan, Minister of Mines, as Governor-General. Hertzog now gave Hofmeyr the two departments of Mines and Labour, and relieved him of the Interior, with all its problems of Jewish immigration, Indian land purchases, and mixed marriages. It was widely believed that Hertzog had seized his opportunity. Malan told his constituents that at the last United Party congress there had been a protracted battle behind the scenes to get Hofmeyr out of the Party. But there is no evidence whatsoever that Hofmeyr thought that Hertzog had taken the opportunity to push him out of the Interior.

A few days after the shuffle, Hofmeyr, speaking to a meeting of his constituents in Johannesburg North, denied that he had lost the confidence of the Prime Minister. He told them he would rather leave politics than give up his principles, and the meeting applauded him warmly. A parliamentary observer wrote of him, '. . . there is a somewhat pathetic doggedness about this short untidy man, who looks on the political war with bewildered scorn and clings to a vision of true democracy in South Africa.'

This sketch had a certain validity in that it reflected the opinion of many. But Hofmeyr was neither bewildered by nor scornful of the political war. There was no true pleasure unless one worked, and politics was his work. He had chosen it, and he wanted no pity for that. And when the work was done, he liked going back home, to the cats and the newspapers and the books, and to her with whom he had lived so long, in whose company he could sing the hymns of boyhood, in a voice that had no music at all, and who would care?

There was another pleasure too, one of those which seemed to make reparation for any loss. That beautiful Cape house, the Woolsack, which Rhodes had built for Kipling, reverted on the poet's death to the Groote Schuur Estate, which was controlled by the Government. Hofmeyr asked for it, and it was allotted to him. This house with its white walls and gables, and its window-frames of oiled reddish-brown wood, surrounded by old and giant oaks, lay under Table Mountain, and looked out over the Cape Flats and the distant mountains of Stellenbosch and the Hottentots Holland. Doves called in the trees and squirrels ran across the lawns. There was continuous traffic on the road above, but here one could hardly hear it. Hofmeyr called it 'an almost incredibly lovely place', and in the midst of all the attacks on him, wrote to Underhill that because of this house, life seemed very good to him.

On 12 January 1937, Richard Stuttaford, the new Minister of the Interior, introduced a Bill to control immigration, and to allow for the screening of all immigrants except born subjects of the King. Aliens would be forbidden to change their occupations for three years, and the changing of surnames was forbidden, 'except in accordance with well-established custom'. The Bill did not mention Jews, but everyone knew it was meant to check Jewish immigration. The Malanites taunted Stuttaford because he would not say so. The Bill did not satisfy Malan. He moved to prevent all further Jewish immigration, to abolish Yiddish as a recognised language for immigration purposes, to close certain occupations to aliens, to issue special trading licences to them, and to prevent the changing of surnames.

Hofmeyr called Malan the admitted leader of the anti-Semitic party in all its intolerance. He was on less sure ground when he declared that it was not the intention of the Bill to keep out the Jew as a Jew, and that the difference between Government and Opposition was that the Opposition was dissatisfied because the Bill did not definitely state that its intention was to keep out the Jew as a Jew. Walter Madeley was sarcastic about Hofmeyr's speech and said:

'I being a blunt man, perhaps dull of comprehension, cannot understand how this legislation is not anti-Jewish, when they, the progenitors of the legislation, confess that the practical result is going to be a diminution of Jewish immigration. And I want to ask them to cut out the cackle and stop all this verbiage surrounding their real intentions and say frankly and outspokenly that they are anxious to prevent Jewish immigration.'

Madeley was right. Though Hofmeyr might deny that the Government's intention was to keep out the Jew as a Jew, its intention was clearly to keep out the Jew as an immigrant.

Malan was himself attacked for inconsistency. In 1932 he had written to the Rev. S. Michelson, who was writing a history of South Africa in Yiddish, and had welcomed the project, 'because such an important section of the population is of Jewish origin and they have fully identified themselves with the country and its people'. The House poured ridicule on Malan, but he was apparently unmoved. Strange that a man whose life was one of massive consistency, should have cared so little in 1937 what he had written in 1932, and seemed to care so little who knew it. He went to his grave full of honours, the most successful Prime Minister of them all, the man who above all, even Hertzog the great pioneer, had 'saved Afrikanerdom'. Yet as one moves forward to do homage to him, one also shrinks from him, the Christian minister who made safety and survival the supreme moral values of his people.

When Malan spoke against the third reading of the Bill, he gave praise to a future Prime Minister, Professor Hendrik Verwoerd, for showing such courage on the public platform. Malan said that Verwoerd's action would be remembered long after Hofmeyr's rebuke had been forgotten. Malan asked, not only how white South Africa could keep Jews out, but how it could protect itself against those who were in.

Hertzog's tactics at this time were baffling. His Aliens Bill was passed without difficulty, and now, although aware of the division amongst his Ministers, he allowed General J. J. Pienaar, leader of the United Party in the Transvaal, to bring in a private Bill against mixed marriages. Was he trying to pacify elements in his own Party? Or was he trying to force Hofmeyr out? This seems unlikely, because when Stuttaford went off sick for three months, he recalled Hofmeyr to the Interior. It seems probable that while Hertzog agreed with Hofmeyr that legislation was not the right way to deal with mixed marriages, it was not for him a matter of any principle. If Parliament decided to ban mixed marriages, he would acquiesce.

Thus Hertzog was led into a situation unseemly for a Prime Minister. While the Government held one view officially, Cabinet Ministers and members of the Party were allowed to say openly that they held another. There is no evidence whatever that Hertzog thought the situation unseemly.

Pienaar reminded the House that in 1936 Hofmeyr had told Roberts that his Bill was impracticable because no one could separate white from coloured in the Cape. But one could separate white from African, and white from Indian. Pienaar spoke with urgency, not only because of his strong emotions, but because there were three by-elections pending in the Transvaal, and Malan intended to fight them all.

Hofmeyr's reply was hailed by the English-speaking press as a masterpiece. He repeated his arguments. He disapproved of mixed marriages, but he objected to controlling them by law. One could not deal with every social evil by legislation. What was more, the percentage of mixed marriages was both infinitesimal and declining. Why stigmatise the nation for so little reason? He begged the House not to insult India, 'a nation with a great heritage and a sensitive pride'.

He admitted that he found it difficult to oppose a ban on marriages 'between Europeans and Natives'. He would oppose it however because it placed a stigma on white South Africa, and advertised to the world that only by making laws could they keep their race pure.

Although Hofmeyr claimed to be speaking for the Government, his colleague, Piet Grobler, Minister of Native Affairs, said, '. . . he is no more expressing the views of the Government than I am, and I support this Bill from A. to Z.'

It was a long time since the Malanites had enjoyed themselves so much. When the vote on the adjournment was taken, Grobler and Kemp voted against it, and Pirow had discreetly disappeared. The voting was close, 66 ayes and 43 nays, and so many members were absent that Swart cried out it was a scandal. What the Malanites enjoyed was not so much the agreeability of the Bill as the spectacle of their old colleagues of prefusion days, bowing regretfully to the Speaker as they hurried away to other more pressing duties.

Feelings ran high after the adjournment. In the Transvaal it was Hertzog's own United Party that held meetings of protest. Pienaar, having virtually lost his Bill, gave notice of another, this time to debar non-white traders from employing white persons. J. H. Grobler gave notice of a Bill to prevent the white wives of non-white husbands from acquiring property. Meanwhile Hertzog, who was going overseas with three other Ministers for the coronation of King George VI, proposed to take one of the two days allotted for private business. Thus he made it unlikely that either Grobler or Pienaar would get time for their Bills. He carried his proposal by 68 votes to 23, but many of his supporters disappeared before the count was taken.

It was a fantastic situation. Hofmeyr gave an emphatic assurance to the parliamentary correspondent of the *Natal Mercury* that the Government opposed these two new private Bills, and would not give time for them. It was common talk in the lobbies that Grobler, Kemp, and Pirow would all vote for the Bills, and that they had in fact advised Pienaar to bring them forward. Hofmeyr reminded the *Natal Mercury* that the Government had offered a select committee in 1936, and that offer was still open.

So firm was Hofmeyr's stand that Pienaar and Grobler agreed to ask the House to refer their Bills to a select committee. To this private motion Hertzog gave priority over Government business. But now Pirow predicted to *Die Suiderstem*, the pro-Government newspaper in Afrikaans, that before the end of the session Asians would no longer be able to employ white girls, and the paper said that Pirow's prediction gave the impression that both Pienaar's and Grobler's measures had the Government's blessing. Malan asked the Government for an assurance that the Bills would be on the statute book before the end of the session, to which Hofmeyr replied, 'On behalf of the Government I am not prepared to give such a guarantee.'

Then Swart rose his full six foot six and demanded a guarantee that the Bills would be dealt with before the end of the session. Then occurred a dramatic event. Pirow scribbled a note and passed it to the Prime Minister. There seems little doubt that this hard-headed Minister had allowed himself to become emotionally involved, whether on his own account or because he could see the damage that the Malanites were doing to the United Party. He could control himself no longer and wished to get up and say that he himself supported the Bills with all his heart, no matter what the Acting Minister of the Interior said on behalf of the

Government. Hertzog read the note, and leaned over to speak to Smuts. Smuts then left the Chamber, and no sooner had Swart ended than the Prime Minister was on his feet and moved the adjournment. It was an act that had no precedent. The Prime Minister had moved the adjournment of a debate to which he himself had given priority. His motion was carried by 65 votes to 18; if it had not been moved by the Prime Minister, many of his own followers would have voted against it.

An emergency meeting of the Cabinet was called for the next morning. While those outside declared that either Hofmeyr or Pirow must go, those inside could see at once that Hertzog and Smuts wanted a compromise, namely that Hofmeyr should be supported in respect of the select committee, and Pirow be supported in that the proposals of the select committee should be considered that session. What would the Government do if the select committee proposed to prevent Asians from employing white persons, and the white wives of Asians from acquiring land? That was the issue that Hertzog had for the time being avoided.

Pirow was not disposed to accept any evasion. Backed by Grobler and Kemp, he insisted that the Cabinet itself should have a policy, and that if it did not, many right-wing fusionists would desert to Malan. Hofmeyr declared that if the Cabinet itself adopted the Pienaar-Grobler policies, he would be compelled to resign. Neither Hertzog nor Smuts cared to face such an event, for it could have spelt the end of the great experiment of fusion. Hertzog made his view clear that his short-term solution was the only one possible. Pirow, Grobler, and Kemp came to heel, and Hertzog entrusted to Pirow and Hofmeyr the task of drawing up the final formula. When their colleagues had left them alone, Pirow said to Hofmeyr, 'What shall we say to save the country?'

In 1926, under Hofmeyr as Administrator, the Transvaal Provincial Council, by Ordinance 12 of that year, resolved to demand of all Indian applicants for trading licences a certificate of fitness issued by the local authority. But the Hofmeyr of 1937 was beginning to find such racial restrictions unpalatable, and, since his visit to India, he felt particularly sensitive about restrictions on Indians. Such is the growth of a white South African, who, brought up in the fortress of privilege, is nevertheless urged by reason, morality, and religious belief to seek a wider air, and in doing so, takes now and then the backward glance that shows from whence he came.

Hofmeyr was now prepared to accept the open vote of the House on the select committee proposals; but he had decided to resign if the Government itself sponsored them. He thought the select committee would produce watered-down proposals, but he was not prepared to accept them for himself. He wrote that, in spite of the doubts of some, he was satisfied that he was doing more for the liberal cause by staying in than by getting out.

'But it is difficult to know what the future holds in store. A few months ago a definite attempt was made to push me out—then at the critical moment those responsible for it trembled on the brink; they realised that, especially with a general election in the offing, I have a nuisance value. The position may be different after the election, which will take place probably in June of next year—I shall not be surprised if things develop in such a way that an issue becomes inevitable. For my own part I shall have no hesitation about going into the political wilderness, but it is difficult to see what will be the outcome for the causes and ideals one has at heart . . .'

It was in those days always a matter for debate whether Hofmeyr should have stayed in or got out. But one may ask, was it because of timidity that he stayed in? Or loyalty to Smuts? Or was it what he himself thought it to be, that he could do more for the liberal cause by staying in? *Timidity* seems the wrong word to use here; he was anything but timid in those days. It was possible that he did not see himself as a leader of a liberal or Liberal Party that would be of any consequence. It seems reasonable to believe him when he said that he stayed in the Cabinet because he thought that was the most useful thing to do, and because he believed that in defending him, his fellow-Ministers had had to adopt a more liberal position than they would otherwise have done.

It was definitely not loyalty to Smuts that kept him in the Cabinet in 1937. Hofmeyr received a letter in March from Sarah Millin, hurt and bitter because Smuts had just appointed new judges, and Philip Millin was not amongst them. Hofmeyr's reply revealed some of his inner thoughts that were in all probability known only to his mother.

'I spoke to Smuts, but the only result was to show me how weak he had been in this matter of lying down to anti-Semitism. I am ashamed of the Government of which I am a member. Smuts was just as weak over me, just as ready to let the wicked triumph and the forces of reaction prevail . . .'

The true inwardness of the relationship between Smuts and Hofmeyr will never be known, but in 1937 the gap between them was wide and growing wider. One thing is certain, that in all Hofmeyr's stubborn defence of existing rights, and his resistance to encroachment on them, he had, in human terms, no strength to call on but his own. Another thing seems reasonably certain, that Smuts, knowing the threat of Nazism to the freedom of mankind, thought that the best way to prepare for it was not to defend freedom in South Africa, but to keep the United Party together. Between his and Hofmeyr's point of view there was little hope of reconciliation.

While the gap between Smuts and Hofmeyr widened, Malan told a crowded public meeting that it was Smuts who was keeping Hofmeyr in the Cabinet, because if Hofmeyr went Smuts would have to consider his position and also the future of the coalition; Hofmeyr was the champion of Jews and non-white people, and Hertzog was afraid to touch him, because 'the Jews have the vote, and in the Cape the Coloureds have the vote and their votes count'. Malan declared, 'We want in South Africa a strong Nordic front of English- and Afrikaans-speaking people.' Throughout 1937 Malan and his Purified Nationalists continued their anti-Jewish campaign unabated. Dr Verwoerd, writing as editor of *Die Transvaler*, declared that the Jews were the group that stood in the way of the Afrikaners' economic well-being. It was another frightening year for South African Jews, but many of them took courage from the short, thick-set, untidy man, who, in spite of an almost unbelievable ministerial burden, was here, there, and everywhere, championing in that ringing and unwearying voice what he believed right.

In March of 1937 he went to the graduation ceremony at Fort Hare, to deliver the speech that made Sarah Millin exclaim that he was a great man. Fort Hare exercised a strong influence on Hofmeyr, and it was there that he took some of his most daring leaps into the unknown. This was not surprising, for it was in respect of black South Africa that his white South Africanism was most hesitant, most fearful, most inclined to shelter behind the emotionalisms that he himself so strongly condemned in other spheres. Just as there were two Smutses, the Holist and the Boer, so there were two Hofmeyrs, the Fort Hare Hofmeyr and the Hofmeyr who might have consented to legislation against white-black marriages except that it would place a stigma on white South Africa.

It was in 1930, during the writing of *Coming of Age*, that Hofmeyr had found the term 'Native problem' invalid, and had recognised the problem as one of race relations. Yet in his book *South Africa* he returned to the term, and had gone on using it for many years. Now at Fort Hare he said, 'I see no solution of what I refuse to call "the Native problem",

what I shall call the problem of race relations, save on the basis of the
recognition that white man and black man are possessors of a common
humanity.'

He also rejected the phrase 'the development of the native on his own
lines' as a cloak for hypocrisy, with the meaning of either no development or as little development as possible. He quoted Dickens:

> O let us love our occupations,
> Bless the squire and his relations,
> Live upon our daily rations,
> And always know our proper stations.

That verse, he declared, revealed the real thought which underlay
'development on one's own lines'. He was prepared to accept that under
present circumstances African and white education could not be the
same, but he did not want his audience to think that he either desired or
believed that it would always be so.

Hofmeyr went on to quote with approbation what Smuts had said at
his recent installation as Chancellor of the University of Cape Town.
These were ultra-strong words, going as far as can ever be gone, and one
can but wonder that they were spoken by the same man who had, to use
Crafford's words, come back from Europe in a blaze of glory to 'acquiesce in the somewhat inglorious Native bills'; the same man who had, to
use Hofmeyr's recent words to Sarah Millin, been so ready 'to let the
wicked triumph and the forces of reaction prevail'. Smuts had spoken in
Cape Town of the fundamental recognition of all men, to the extent of
'racial indifference', as the very foundation of our human culture. Terrible
words, 'racial indifference', not only providing Malan with fresh ammunition, but spurring him on to use it with contempt and anger, and to organise
against Hertzog and Smuts, but especially against Hofmeyr, not only the
most bitter white racists, but also the outraged believers in that heretical
Christianity which had made racial separation the highest of all goals, and
racial difference a God-given gift, which no ordinary man could set aside.
For that is indeed the just indictment of white South African Christianity, that its most cherished values are not to be found in the Gospel, and
had no place in the mind of Christ.

Hofmeyr was not the only one who foresaw the possibility that his
opposition to racial separation as a political policy might lead him into the
wilderness. John Martin, the powerful chairman of the Corner House, the

man who could and did break editors who would not yield to him, the man who had vastly more influence with Prime Ministers than his successors have today, watched Hofmeyr with some anxiety. Martin did not share the views of many of his less powerful associates that Hofmeyr was no proper man to succeed Smuts. On the contrary he regarded Hofmeyr as Smuts's only possible successor. Martin shared with Smuts the belief that the great political task of the time was to keep the United Party together, against the day when Hitler would turn on Europe. Martin had just been elected to the Court of the Bank of England, and Hofmeyr had written to congratulate him. Martin replied that Hofmeyr was much in his mind, especially as he knew that Hofmeyr was uncertain about the future. Martin hoped that the younger man would exercise 'patience and more patience'. 'There are dangerous days ahead as you yourself well know. Disintegration might well spell disaster.'

Martin was a conservative, and on the whole preferred stability and order to reform and change; yet both his head and his heart told him that reform and change were urgently needed. Therefore he watched Hofmeyr with anxiety, for if reform and change there must be, he would rather they were in Hofmeyr's hands than in those of Malan or the Leftists.

Hofmeyr always enjoyed the reluctant admiration of the Chamber of Mines. He believed, died believing, that the mining industry was the backbone of the South African economy; but he also believed that it should be taxed to the limit that it could bear, without making future development impossible. He was opposed to high dividends, and was curt to those who complained that low dividends meant loss of new capital. Besides that, he had another belief of his own, namely, that a Minister of Mines should not hold mining shares, and therefore he got rid of those that he had. His attitude to the industry came under much sharper fire from the Left, and that was on the question of labour and wages. The mining industry, the backbone of the economy, was very spectacular, with its world-famous efficiency, its towering headgears, its great dumps that ran like a mountain chain along the whole Witwatersrand, its hundreds of thousands of employees, its massive blocks of city offices, its ramifications into secondary industries, its stately homes of big directors, and the metropolis that it had created, the restless city of Johannesburg, which never stopped growing and threw out new suburbs every year on its sprawling periphery.

Yet it was the truth—the plain truth, not a political or ideological one—that all this grandeur and power and wealth was only made possible because hundreds of thousands of black men went down into the depths of the earth for a wage of just over three shillings a day. The entire industry was ruled by a legal colour-bar, the Mines and Works Act of 1911, that confined non-white workers to the lowest occupations. As the years passed, African mine-workers were given better accommodation, better food, better medical care, and today few die from disease or accident; but the daily wage which was 2s. 2.1d. in 1921 was only 2s. 3d. eighteen years later. The question may well be asked, how does one justify the continuance of an industry whose great wealth comes, not from gold, but from small wages? And which paid to white miners wages which were from six to ten times as high as black wages, after allowance had been made for accommodation, food, and medical care?

Hofmeyr was not a reformer of the drastic kind. Yet even after his own fashion, he could have done more to secure a rise in African wages, both in the mining industry and elsewhere; there is no record that he ever put forth sustained effort in that direction. In one way he accepted his society, in another way he wanted to change it, but he would have changed it in accordance with his own temperament. For him it would have been just as easy to run naked down Schoeman Street as to denounce the mining magnates as blood-suckers, murderers, and robbers. He could see clearly that society needed reform, but his faith in his power to do it fluctuated with his fortunes; and this book is very little about what he might have been, and very much about what he was. John Martin was afraid that Hofmeyr might be too impatient, and the Left thought that he was over-patient, and from their own points of view both were justified. In fact, Hofmeyr's temperament was neither patient nor impatient. Though he knew well enough that the white man's time for negotiating change was running out, he was not really impelled by that knowledge. The force that impelled him, the only force that he trusted, the only force under whose impulsion he felt secure in action, was his sense of the right.

That and that alone sustained him through the difficult days of his chairmanship of the select committee on the contentious Bills in the early part of April 1937. Except for J. G. Derbyshire, a member of the Dominion Party, he stood alone in his convictions. A remarkable cleavage of opinion was revealed between those who gave evidence before the committee and those who heard it, most of the first being against the Bill, and most of the second for it. Syed Sir Raza Ali, the Agent-General for India, asked to be present at the discussions, but permission was refused. After hearing evidence, the committee turned to Pienaar's delicately named Provincial Legislative Powers Extension Bill, and called it forthrightly the European Women's Restriction of Employment Bill. The Bill provided that:

> No white woman might be employed by Asians except by authority of the Minister of Labour.
>
> No white woman might be directed or supervised by Asians.
>
> Six months after the Bill becomes law, no white woman might remain in Asian employ, except by authority of the Minister.
>
> The Minister must be satisfied that no such white woman would be housed on Asian premises, or come into contact with any Asians except customers.

However, Japanese were to be excluded from these restrictions. The Consul-General for Japan had warned the committee that if the Bill applied to Japanese, that would mean the end of Japanese trade. Therefore the Bill provided that the restrictions did not apply to Japanese 'while there is in force an agreement between the Governments of South Africa and Japan to facilitate trade'. This degrading provision the Japanese were willing to accept. Hofmeyr and Derbyshire fought every clause in the proposed Bill, but on every important occasion were defeated. So finally Hofmeyr, as chairman, was given the unpleasant task of laying before the House proposals which ran counter not only to most of the evidence received, but also to his own convictions.

Meanwhile a powerful ally came to his aid. The Government of India registered an ominously strong protest against the Bill. The press of India was unanimous in condemning it. In South Africa, A. I. Kajee, secretary of the South African Indian Congress, said that the Bill insulted both white and Indian women, and assumed that Indians employed white women to become intimate with them, or to marry them in order to acquire land. He said that fifty-eight white women in the Transvaal and six in Natal worked for Indians. There were three white women married to Indians in the Transvaal who owned property; one had first been married to a white husband and had bought her property from him, the second had married her Indian husband in Scotland thirty-six years earlier, and the third owned only three properties worth altogether £3,000.

Kajee then announced that the South African Indian Congress would enter into a gentleman's agreement to do all in its power to eliminate the employment of white women if the Government dropped the Bill.

Hertzog was in an embarrassing situation. South African governments, especially those kept in power by the platteland, are always caught between world opinion and the approval of the rural electorate. The greatest and noblest statesman in the world would be shouted down at Marico and Wakkerstroom, if he advocated liberal or non-racial policies. The European Women's Restriction Employment Bill might sound magnificent in Marico, but when it was reported in the world press, it was downright embarrassing. What made it more embarrassing to Hertzog was that the select committee evidence gave the Bill no support whatsoever; the Reddingsdaadbond, an organisation for the economic rehabilitation of the Afrikaner, could quote only one instance—in 1920—where the employment of a white girl by an Indian led to marriage.

Hertzog grasped at the offer by the South African Indian Congress, and announced amid jeers from the Malanites and cheers from the Dominionites that the Government would drop both the Employment Bill and the proposed Bill to control land ownership by white wives of Asians, and would accept the gentleman's agreement.

Syed Sir Raza Ali paid diplomatic tribute to Hertzog for his farsightedness, and praised both press and Parliament. But his real tribute was to Hofmeyr:

'Mr Hofmeyr is a really big man. He is a spiritual disciple of Gladstone and hates all injustice, but between him and the Gladstonian Liberals there is a marked difference. The hardships of the latter in connection with the Irish question pale into insignificance, as compared with the ridicule and scorn to which the enlightened and just whites are subjected by their own people in this country for befriending the coloured communities.'

What was a victory for Hofmeyr was an inglorious episode for Hertzog and a downright defeat for Pirow, Kemp, Grobler, Pienaar, and the young Grobler. Nothing had come of Pirow's promise that by the end of the session no Asian would be able to employ white women.

Hofmeyr's victory was a victory for Malan also. Every time that the liberal view triumphed over the conservative in the United Party, just so often did some right-wing fusionist decide to leave Hertzog the vacillator, and go to Malan the resolute. Malan was only secondarily concerned with preventing mixed marriages; his tactics were to use mixed marriages to break the United Party. He did not cease to exploit these racial issues, but he turned now to another profitable field, the constitutional issues, the issues of King, Crown, war, neutrality, flags, anthems, republic, on all of which English- and Afrikaans-speaking people were, for the most part, deeply divided. No one knew better than Malan how and where to aim arrows tipped with the poison of history; if it was a skill to be praised, then who more praiseworthy than he? And who less praiseworthy than Hofmeyr, who, had he had such a skill, had also a quality of soul which would have made the use of it impossible.

It is a difficult thing for the great majority of white South Africans to break with the habit of looking on the African people as people to be ruled. The better the white man, the more justly he will want them ruled. Hofmeyr had shown in his Fort Hare speech that he was breaking away even from this class of would-be-just paternalists; he said at Fort Hare that while he accepted that African and white education could not be the same, he did not want his audience to think that he either desired or believed that it should always be so. He was indeed moving closer and closer to the idea of a common society.

That his progress was slow, painful, characterised by advances and retreats, and that his reasoning was often inconsistent should by now be plain; in the space of a few weeks he could both praise 'racial indifference', and yet say he was tempted to consider a ban on marriages between black and white. His experiences at Oxford, his trip to India, his defence of the rights of Indians in South Africa, had brought him relatively close to Indian people. His ignorance of African people was still great, his knowledge of them gained from a few outstanding personalities like Jabavu and Z. K. Matthews; of those less known figures whose fight for freedom was just as courageous as any that any Afrikaner had ever waged, Hofmeyr knew nothing.

Hofmeyr's inconsistency was shown when after emerging with honour from the fight over the anti-Indian Bills, he failed to appreciate the iniquity of the Native Laws Amendment Bill. This was the third Bill of Hertzog's great legislative programme and its purpose was, in the interests of the whole policy of segregation, to control the movement of Africans from the country to the towns, and their residence in the towns. The control of African movement has always occupied a central place in so-called 'Native policy' but the urban authorities, largely English-speaking, had shown reluctance to use the Urban Areas Acts, and had allowed missionaries and others to build schools and churches in the so-called white areas. The presence of such buildings had always been offensive to white racists, and to other white people corrupted by living in a racist society. Now the new Bill empowered magistrates and Native Commissioners to give or refuse leave to Africans to quit reserves and rural areas, and empowered local authorities not only to deny them entrance to the towns but to subject to innumerable restrictions those who were already there. Municipalities were empowered to forbid African worship and education in these white areas, and to surround locations by fences if they so desired; this fencing was often justified on the grounds that it was in the interests of those who lived in the locations, and protected them from white and Indian exploiters, liquor sellers, and womanisers. Tremendous power was put into the hands of local officials, who, if they were so inclined, could destroy the livelihood and happiness of men and their families. If a man lost his job in the town, a merciful location superintendent might give him time to find another; but a hostile or indifferent superintendent might secure an order for the deportation of man, wife and children to an ancestral home they had never before seen.

If a man had strong political views which were distasteful to the authorities, or if he did not behave himself with seemly docility, pressure could be put on his employer to sack him, and then he could be ejected without further ado. This has been the lot of many African people, who, when they have shown the same zeal as a Hertzog or a Malan, have found themselves thrown out of home and employment, and condemned to a life of exile and despair. One thing can be said about this kind of legislation, that not in three hundred years of South African history had any white person ever been subjected to anything like it.

There were many white people, and Hofmeyr was one of them, who, however opposed they were to harsh laws, dreaded the thought of uncontrolled African migration to the towns, which not only choked up the locations, but spilled out on the veld, where there rose villages of tin, without light, water, sanitation, or any kind of authority. With these things in mind, such white people consented to the control of migration.

But there were other arguments, equally powerful, against control. When poor white people had come flooding into the towns, no law was passed to prevent them; rather every effort was made to improve their economic situation. Was the real cause of the migration not the mean life of the black labourer on the white farm, the growing impoverishment of the reserves, the increasing population pressure, the eroding land, the lack of any industry except agriculture? Were these not the real problems to be tackled? Did not the passing of harsh laws distract the attention of rulers from the real needs of the ruled, and postpone yet further the day of change?

There was another disquieting argument. Was it possible to control migration and over-population without putting almost unlimited power into the hands of quite small men? Was it possible to avoid the almost continuous asking for papers, the stopping of people in the street, the arrest of servants outside their employers' houses because they did not have their papers on their persons, the venting of petty spites by petty officials, the ejectment of decent and established families from their homes because the father had lost his job? A man, his wife, his daughters and his sons could all be in employment, bringing in a reasonable income to the home, buying furniture and insurance and educating younger children, and the whole family could be thrown out if the man lost his job. Ninety per cent of African convictions were for offences which had no counterpart for white people; and every year one African out of fourteen was convicted of such statutory offences. And now came a law fiercer than any that had been passed before.

But it was not Hofmeyr who was to be the champion on this occasion of that sanctity of personality of which he had spoken at Fort Hare. The champion this time was C. W. Coulter, a member of the Dominion Party. He clung determinedly to outworn ideas of sovereignty and empire, but he knew repressive legislation when he encountered it. When the Bill had been first introduced some three months earlier, he argued on a point of order that it should first have been referred to the Natives Representative Council, which should already have been set up under the Representation of Natives Act of 1936. The fact that the Council had not yet been set up did not affect his argument. The Speaker rejected the argument, but Coulter moved the adjournment of the debate so that the Natives Representative Council could be consulted; otherwise the House would be deprived 'of the benefit of the views of the Natives on so important a matter as this, although I know in this House the Native is regarded as little more than a muscular machine by a great number of honourable members'.

A month later Coulter attacked vigorously the notorious clause 21, which gave local authorities extraordinary powers to refuse entry to and order expulsion from the towns. An African wife whose husband had died in the location had no right to enter it, but had to apply for a permit. An African man whose aged father had died in some other place, could not of right bring his aged mother to live with him, but had to apply for a permit, nor could his adult children visit him except with a permit. When a boy or girl reached the age of 18 years, he or she was an adult, and if not in employment, could be ordered to the ancestral home. These were the laws against which Coulter fought so passionately, but which the majority of the House regarded as essential to the proper control of migration. It is one of the immutable characteristics of segregation that the most ineffable of goals can only be reached by the harshest of laws, which inflict their deepest wounds, not on the segregator, but on the segregated.

On 13 May 1937, Coulter moved an amendment to place 'on record a proviso which will make it clear that no native shall be removed on account of his political or religious beliefs'.

Hofmeyr announced that he would vote against clause 21. He said he could not accept a clause 'which implies the acceptance of the principle that the native is necessarily not merely inferior but subservient to the white man, that he is to be viewed as serving the white man's requirements. This clause implies the denial of the principle that the Native shares with the White man a common humanity. That denial I am not prepared to subscribe to.'

Hofmeyr then said he was in general support of the Bill.

In the end Coulter lost his amendment to protect people from being thrown out of town for their political or religious beliefs, only three others voting for it. C. M. van Coller of Cathcart, who had moved the deletion of clause 21, lost his motion by 49 to 17, Hofmeyr voting with the minority.

At the third reading Coulter returned doggedly to the attack, and used Hofmeyr's Fort Hare speech, with its emphasis on the recognition of a common humanity, as his final weapon. Coulter said it was time to abandon the traditions which had come down from the Voortrekkers. He went on, 'May I add that the conditions of trusteeship we are attempting to frame should likewise be abandoned if we are to act consistently with the underlying principles of this statement by the Minister of Mines.'

Again eleven members voted against a Bill in the final division. But this time Hofmeyr was not one of them. He and the champion of racial indifference were two of the sixty-three who helped to carry the Bill, in spite of its clause 21. Hofmeyr would certainly not have voted for a Bill affecting Indians if it had contained such a clause.

In the session of 1937, Hofmeyr set a standard for ministerial bril-

1. *J. H. (Onze Jan) Hofmeyr.*

2. *Camp in Natal. Hofmeyr (top right) and the author (in blazer).*

3. *Balliol Boys' Club Camp at Radcot, 1915. Hofmeyr seated in right center.*

4. *Albert "Babu" King in 1948 with shield presented to him as founder of the Federation of Mutual Improvement Classes.*

5. *Hofmeyr with his mother, on the steps of the Senate, Cape Town.*

6. *General Smuts, Mrs. Hertzog, Mrs. Smuts, General Hertzog.*

7. *Dr. and Mrs. D. F. Malan. 1939.*

8. *Hofmeyr and Smuts (center) with Senator E. A. Conroy, J. W. Mushet,* M. P., *F. C. Sturrock,* M. P.

9. *Hofmeyr, visiting an army installation in the Middle East.*

10. *Cricketer Hofmeyr at the scoring table.*

11. *At the crease (at bat).*

12. *Among the generals in October 1945 at Oxford, where the honorary degree of D. C. L. was conferred on Hofmeyr. To his right are generals Mark Clark and Dwight Eisenhower; to his left Field Marshals Lord Alanbrooke and Sir Bernard Montgomery.*

13. A Hofmeyr family photo showing the marked resemblance of the two brothers.

14. Mrs. Hofmeyr on her 84th birthday.

15. *Hofmeyr, as Minister of Finance.*

16. *General Smuts at funeral of Hofmeyr.*

liance that has never been equalled. He was Minister of Education and Social Welfare, Labour, and Mines. When Stuttaford went off sick, he took over the Interior, and Public Health. On one busy day in the House he was the only Minister in action. When presenting the Immigration Amendment Bill, he was able to make one of his favourite jokes. He said, 'As Acting Minister of the Interior I am presenting this Bill at the request of the Minister of Mines, but I would not ask for its adoption unless I were assured that it had the approval of the Acting Minister of Public Health.'

This was received with great laughter, which was his reward for a gruelling day.

This prodigious work went on throughout the session, interrupted by his thirty minutes of tenniquoits played with a medicine ball just before dinner. The burden on him was increased when Hertzog and three other Ministers went to the Coronation. Smuts acted as Prime Minister, and deputed Hofmeyr to arrange the order paper. Hofmeyr started a daily consultation with the Party Whips and, according to Kilpin, the Clerk of the House, the whole atmosphere of the House improved, and its work went forward in a spirit of co-operation and a maximum of efficiency. During this period Kilpin developed a warm admiration for Hofmeyr, and regarded him as one of the greatest Parliamentarians that South Africa had known, in his profound respect for Parliament's traditions, his knowledge of its procedures, and his own brilliance as administrator, legislator, debater.

One should not close an account of this session without referring to the Bill which was to become the famous Children's Act, one of the most enlightened measures of its kind in the world; it regarded child offenders as in need of care, not of punishment, it greatly expanded the ages of protection, it softened court procedures, it substituted standard periods of institutional treatment and supervision for individual sentences, it abolished the word detention in favour of retention, and it increased the responsibilities of parents. Three years before, all reformatory institutions for young offenders had been transferred from the Department of Prisons to the Department of Education; now administratively, by the appointment of new personnel, the emphasis on reformatory treatment was to be turned from punishment to education, from the discipline of physical confinement to that of freedom and responsibility, and it was made clear that punishment, if punishment it was, was to be inflicted by the courts, and was no concern of the reformatory institution. While these great changes were taking place in the institutions, the Social Welfare Department was also expanded, to allow, in theory at least, for the care of every child who showed signs of getting into trouble, and the care of every child released from reformatory institutions.

The Children's Bill was the joint work of a distinguished committee led by Maynard Page, the Chief Magistrate of Johannesburg, but it was recognised by friend and foe alike, that if any Minister was qualified to administer such an Act, it was Hofmeyr. Parliament, which had been so torn by Mixed Marriages and Land Tenure, voted the Children's Bill into law without one dissentient. Those who were prepared to discriminate against Jews, Indians, and Africans were unanimously prepared to discriminate in favour of children, and what is more, children of any race or colour. Not one clause in the Bill contained a word of that vocabulary that seemed essential to every other piece of legislation. That was something, but there was something far more important. The Act, which was inevitably called the Children's Charter, could have been applied to white children, and could have been allowed to go by default in respect of others. This did not happen, because Hofmeyr was the Minister and M. C. Botha was the Secretary. It was true that salary scales, diets, clothing, and buildings for African institutions were inferior to those of others; but the basic change, namely that the institutions were now places of education and not punishment, applied to all. One of the sourest observers of this impartiality was Hendrik Verwoerd, the new editor of *Die Transvaler*. He described Diepkloof Reformatory, the institution for African boys, as a place for pampering rather than education, as the place, indeed, where one said please and thank you to the black misters. When he came to power he closed down Diepkloof Reformatory, and replaced it by rural institutions supplying labour to white farmers, although 90 per cent of its boys came from the towns and cities, and would return to them. Administratively Hofmeyr made of the Children's Act a just instrument worthy of a multi-racial country; administratively Verwoerd changed its whole character in respect of African child offenders.

There was one other matter which came under the notice of Hofmeyr as Minister of Labour. The Prime Minister's son, Albert Hertzog, believed that if Christian civilisation were to be saved, Afrikaners must control the trade unions, and oust from positions of authority all Jews, Communists, and negrophilists. Albert was a fanatical Afrikaner, the joy of cartoonists, who elongated his long face, sharpened his pointed beard, and exaggerated whatever light it was that shone through his spectacles.

He had neither the strength nor the ability of his father, but he had the same tenacity, and non-Afrikaners were often angered and frightened by his speeches, with their basic and consistent assumption that life in South Africa was a war, and that the Afrikaner must be eternally vigilant against all others. Albert, having failed to capture the Mineworkers' Union in Johannesburg, had launched the Mynwerkersbond, a purely Afrikaner organisation. At Stellenbosch University, the debating society rejected a motion that Afrikaans-speaking workers should be organised into separate trade unions. More than a hundred men went on strike at the Simmer and Jack mine as a protest against miners' joining Albert Hertzog's union, and the Chamber of Mines agreed to regard the existing Mineworkers' Union as a closed shop. The final step was taken by the Government, when Hofmeyr as Minister of Labour announced that under existing conditions there was little likelihood that the Mynwerkers-bond would be registered as a trade union.

So a hard session came to an end. On its closing day the Rev. C. W. M. du Toit of Colesberg protested that not one of the three Bills dealing with white-Asian relations had come to anything, in spite of the assurance given by the Minister of Railways, Mr. Pirow, that by the end of the session, no white girl would be left in the employ of Asians. With this final thrust, which had also the nature of a jibe, Malan brought his parliamentary offensive to an end.

Hofmeyr and his mother arrived home in time for their annual dinner with the Chemical, Metallurgical, and Mining Society. This was Hofmeyr's first appearance before the society as Minister of Mines, and his jokes kept his audience convulsed with laughter. Then he grew serious, and on the one hand rejoiced in the prosperity of the mines, and on the other referred to the unhealthy state of the 'native reserves', with one-third of the male population away on the Witwatersrand. This was not in accord with the country's policy of encouraging 'the Natives to develop on their own lines in their own territories'; therefore the mines must try to economise in the use of such labour. After this short and inconclusive speech, Hofmeyr brought down the house with the story of the nervous young country curate, who found himself preaching a sermon before the Prime Minister of Great Britain, George Canning. After the service, the young man said, 'Sir, it has been a great honour for me to preach before so distinguished a statesman.' At this, Canning bowed, and the curate, persisting, said, 'I think, sir, I succeeded in being brief.' Canning bowed again, and the curate, unable to leave off, said, 'Sir, I hope that I was not altogether tedious,' to which Canning, determined to bring it to an end, replied, 'Sir, you were both brief and tedious.'

He wrote modestly to Underhill about the session.

'The net result as far as I personally am concerned is that it is generally realised in this country that I do stand for something definite in our political life. As for the future, it seems to me that the role I am most likely to play is that of a mouthpiece of liberal opinion without much political power but with a certain amount of influence in Parliament and outside. But of course it is also possible that the tide of liberalism may rise, and that causes which seem almost lost today may yet prevail.'

That he was recognised as standing for something was very true. The Greyshirts' unpleasant periodical, *Die Waarheid*, referred to the 'Jew-King Smuts' and the 'Communist Hofmeyr'; it warned that the Muslims and the Jews were in conspiracy, and called Hofmeyr a tool of Jewish capitalists and Jewish Communists. Malan, touring the Free State, said that steps would have to be taken to limit Jewish activities in certain directions, and called Hofmeyr their self-appointed champion.

Hofmeyr himself aroused a totally unexpected reaction by repeating in Johannesburg what he had said at Fort Hare.

'It is a conception which ultimately has its foundations in the realisation that all of us, whatever the colour of our skins, are equally God's children and equally have the right to all that participation in the family of God implies.

'Of course, if you are going to follow out that conception it is going to take a good deal of faith, and to my mind the real fight in regard to Native policy in this country is just the issue between faith and fear. People ask me sometimes: what will be the outcome if you follow this policy? Can you be sure that this country will be safe for European civilisation? No, I am not sure. It might not be. But if you follow a policy of fear, in the long run there is going to be a blow-up. I am quite sure that policy is not a safe policy and I am sure we cannot follow a policy in this country which purports to make the country safe for European civilisation and at the same time surrenders those things which make European civilisation worth-while.'

This speech gave new life to the rumour that Hofmeyr would launch a Liberal Party, but he denied this at a United Party meeting at Springs. He told his hearers that he found he could work within the United Party for all that seemed practical and essential in the ideals which he cherished, and he asked those who cherished similar ideals to retain their ideals but to stand by the United Party. At the Natal congress of the United Party Smuts denied that the Government would split because of differences between Hofmeyr and Pirow. He said, 'You will find that both Pirow and Hofmeyr as patriotic men will continue to work together, and just as our opponents' hopes of dissension between General Hertzog and myself have been dashed, so their hopes in regard to Pirow and Hofmeyr will be dashed.'

What Hofmeyr called the cause of liberalism suffered a sharp setback in September. At Vereeniging location, on 19 September, one African and two white policemen were killed by an African mob. Such news flares across the front pages of the morning papers, rousing many emotions, of anger and hate in some, of satisfaction in others, and causing in yet others, lovers of peace and seekers after harmony, a dull gnawing pain in the guts, a feeling of despair about people and country and the righteous cause; and it is common for one such to say to another, 'This sets back the cause for another twenty years.' There were angry White protest meetings in Vereeniging and other parts of the Transvaal, demanding drastic action, air demonstrations above the location, and the dropping of tear bombs till the guilty surrendered. The Malanites called for a ban on communism, and on 'the liberalist doctrine of equality between black and white'. The attorney defending some of those accused of the murder asked for the protection of the court. Hertzog said there was a deep-rooted hostility, perhaps organised, of black towards white, and Smuts suggested that misguided friends of the black put grievances into their heads. However, a commission of inquiry found otherwise, namely that the municipal administration was defective, and the police methods harsh. It is a weakness of South Africa's white politicians that they suppose black men's grievances to be invented by agitators, and spend their energies in trying to silence the second rather than in trying to redress the first.

The election of 1938 was drawing near and Malan was exploiting to the full the Black menace, the Jewish menace, the Indian menace, and the Communist menace. However, he declined to enter into an election pact with the Greyshirts; Malan's anti-Semitism was wicked, but that of the Greyshirts and their paper *Die Waarheid* bordered on the obscene. At last Smuts had made quiet, industrious, and learned Philip Millin a judge, and *Die Waarheid* asked whether the descendants of proud Aryan-European forefathers were prepared to stand trial before Asiatic Jews.

Hofmeyr, speaking at the first annual general meeting of the newly formed Society of Jews and Christians, warned that anti-Semitism was a precursor of dictatorship.

It is impossible to recapture fully the content of those days. Hitler was shaking the world, and many, growing frightened of opposing him, began to look for his virtues. Hitler scorned democracy, so perhaps there was something wrong with democracy after all. Pirow, who was torn between his admiration for Hitler and his devotion to Afrikanerdom, found himself saying at one meeting that democracy was inefficient and could not continue indefinitely, and at another that democracy was safe in South Africa, as no man in his sober senses had any intention of introducing anything else.

In these days of shifting foundations, Hofmeyr's voice was like a clarion. At this same meeting he said:

'I am not blind to the weakness of a democracy. No one who has to play his part in running a democratic Government can be blind to its weaknesses. I know its futilities, its inefficiency, its indiscipline. I appreciate all this, but it still remains the safest and best form of Government that we can possibly have. We dare not trifle with those alternative forms of government which are so foreign to our tradition and outlook. Surely we in South Africa can have no truck with dictatorship in any form, whether it is that dictatorship of the proletariat which is Communism, or that dictatorship of the individual or group, which is Fascism.'

He concluded with the words: 'It is not by showing hostility to a certain section of the people, but only by welcoming the contributions which all sections of the community can bring, that a nation is built. It is only in this way that we can hope to build a great South Africa.'

Hofmeyr did not mention Malan's name at this meeting, but outside he accused him again of being the high priest of anti-Semitism. If indeed there were any further need of proof, if indeed some still believed that the Nationalists were merely opposing Jewish immigration, all doubts should have been removed, when in October of 1937 both the Transvaal and the Free State congresses of the Party decided to exclude Jews from membership.

So another bad year ended, yet with Hofmeyr the hope of many, especially now that Smuts seemed to have fallen so silent. For South African Jews in 1937, Hofmeyr was an honoured name. So was it honoured amongst Indians.

Chapter 9

A Minister Resigns

1938 WAS the year of the general election, and Parliament assembled on 11 February for a short pre-election session. There were seven newcomers, the three Natives' Representatives in the Lower House, and the four in the Senate. They did not ally themselves with any party, but they introduced a new and vigorous and independent note into Parliament. The two notable newcomers to the Lower House were Margaret Ballinger and Donald Molteno, and the two notable Senators were J. D. Rheinallt Jones and Edgar Brookes. When Margaret Ballinger made her maiden speech she pressed for an increase of the miserably low wages paid to non-white employees on the railways, and used an argument new to the House, but one which she was to make well known, namely that non-white people helped to create the wealth of the nation, and should have a just share in it. When she sat down, the House cheered her.

The impression that Hertzog, while as autocratic as ever, was depending more and more on Pirow, was gaining ground. At the opening of Parliament, without consulting Smuts, he arranged—or approved the arrangement—that the Afrikaans patriotic song, 'Die Stem van Suid-Afrika' ['The Voice of South Africa'] was to be played after 'God Save the King', the British national anthem, which had been played at the opening since 1910. Questioned by Stallard in the House, the Prime Minister precipitated a crisis by declaring that 'God Save the King' was not the national anthem of South Africa, but that 'Die Stem' might become so. Smuts immediately left the House and did not return for the subsequent questions which the Prime Minister freely allowed and answered. When Blackwell went to see Smuts, he found him white and shaken; Blackwell wanted Smuts to protest, but Smuts said, 'My position with the Prime Minister is much too delicate. Go and see him yourself.' Blackwell and his deputation warned Hertzog that his statement would stampede English-speaking voters from the United Party, and said that he himself had always considered 'God Save the King' to be the national anthem; he and

217

his colleagues however had no objection to accepting 'Die Stem' as a co-equal anthem. Hertzog refused to admit that 'God Save the King' was the national anthem of South Africa, but he said that whatever its status, he did not wish to supplant it; 'Die Stem' would be supplementary to it.

Satisfied, Blackwell and his friends went away, but Hertzog's statement to the press revived their misgivings. After they had spent hours on yet another statement, Smuts sent for Blackwell and showed him a statement prepared by Hofmeyr, which proved satisfactory to Blackwell, and was finally passed by the Prime Minister.

So the crisis passed, but it revealed again the deep internal strains to which this fusion between English- and Afrikaans-speaking people was being subjected. It revealed something else too, the fact that Smuts, although second to the Prime Minister and acknowledged leader of the stronger section of the United Party, was no longer a member of the inner Cabinet. Hertzog said he had consulted colleagues, but Smuts was not one of them. The truth seems to be that Smuts was willing to endure almost anything to avoid a break in the party.

The big opposition assault was launched by Malan. During the debate on the Part Appropriation Bill he moved an important amendment. Its third clause set out in essence the policy of the Purified Nationalist Party. It demanded separate residential areas for whites and non-whites in urban areas, separate spheres of employment as far as possible, limitation of certain occupations to whites, separate representation of coloured voters, and legislation against mixed marriages and employment of whites by non-whites.

Malan said he wanted 'a clear indication to all who can read that South Africa does not want to have the mixture of all races'.

It was J. J. van Rensburg who opened Malan's cupboard, in a way that most members of the House would have found devastating, but which left Malan unmoved. Van Rensburg reminded the House that Malan, in 1931, speaking on the Franchise Bill, had said about the Coloured people, 'the same political rights as we give the Europeans must also be granted to them in principle'. In December 1923 he had sent a Christmas greeting to the leader of the Cape Malays. 'You as well as the Coloured people will receive a raised status, which will secure the giving of equal rights, economic as well as political, which you wished for.' In 1925, continued van Rensburg, *Die Burger* reported Malan as saying to the Malay Congress, 'The Government will always try to give the Malays . . . equal rights with the White man.' Finally, said van Rensburg, Malan had said in 1928, in that very House, 'I would like to give the franchise to the Coloured women.'

What had caused Malan to change? Was it political expediency? Or was he really beginning to believe that Afrikaner security depended on the segregation of *all* races? We may note that his political autobiography, *Afrikaner Unity and My Experiences on the Road Thereto*, was concerned almost solely with the constitutional rather than with the racial root of Afrikaner politics. His chapter headings dealt with the Commonwealth, the Crown, the Flag struggle, *hereniging* or *vereniging*, rather than with the colour policies he was now advocating. As for his sustained anti-Semitic campaign of the thirties, one finds no mention of it in his book; and of the struggle, fierce and sustained, between himself and Hofmeyr, no word at all. Were these experiences irrelevant to Afrikaner unity, or did he, in the days of his retirement when he was held in veneration, not wish to remember them? That may well be so. After Hofmeyr's death, he informed the writer that he had nothing to say about him, nothing to add, after eighteen years, to the formal words of eulogy that he had spoken in the House.

Racial separation is claimed by its supporters to be a beautiful thing, offering peace to the land and justice to its people. Nationalists grow angry with those who will not believe it, but history will record that racial separation was in those days justified by the basest of arguments. Malan's amendment was strongly supported.

Malan told the United Party that they were too divided to put relations between white and black on a proper basis. He said, 'It is only the Nationalist Party which can affirm to the world that we intend to keep this a white man's country.' According to one observer, Malan was giving notice that his party intended to make all possible capital out of the presence of Hofmeyr and a small liberal group within the United Party.

The great United Party was not really in danger. It had 117 seats out of 153 in the Lower House, and of the 36 members in opposition, 16 were hostile to Malan. In the elections it lost 6 seats, and returned to Parliament 111 strong. The Dominionites lost Stallard and Coulter, but went from 5 to 8, sweeping the city of Durban, whose citizens had been angered by Hertzog's statements on 'God Save the King'. Malan went from 20 to 27, and gave Hertzog a great shaking in his own constituency. Hertzog had won this by 1,301 votes in 1929, and had been unopposed in 1933; but now in 1938 he beat his Malanite opponent by only 526, although the enfranchisement of women had doubled the number of votes.

Hertzog's Minister of Commerce and Industries, A. P. J. Fourie, was defeated by the Malanites at Gordonia. The success of the United Party was in large measure to be ascribed to Smuts and the English-speaking members of the Party; they reminded their nervous voters that Hertzog had said that 'God Save the King' was not to be superseded but to be supplemented. Smuts assured tremendous meetings in East London, Durban, and Johannesburg, that 'God Save the King' would remain a national anthem for ever, for which he was tumultuously applauded. And of course his task was made easier by the Austrian Anschluss and Hitler's claim to the former colonies; whom could one trust better than Smuts?

For Hofmeyr the campaign was arduous. He had 'a desperately busy time', so he wrote to Underhill, he won Johannesburg North by 4,721 votes to his opponent's 1,389. The United Party won all sixteen Johannesburg seats, and lost only two on the entire Witwatersrand. Hofmeyr was not only pleased with this, he was pleased that Malan's appeal to colour prejudice and his attacks on Hofmeyr the liberal had failed to bring much result. Writing to Underhill, he deduced that white South Africa was making progress. In fact the Nationalist vote had increased considerably. Malan had secured only 24 per cent of Hertzog's number of seats, but he had secured 58 per cent of Hertzog's number of votes. In Hertzog's own province of the Orange Free State Malan had won another two seats. It is one of the remarkable facts of South African history, that while it is commonly accepted that today we are ruled by the ideology of the North rather than of the South, of the Transvaal rather than of the Cape, it was in the Cape that modern Afrikaner Nationalism was born and nurtured.

Hardly had the United Party won its great victory when Hertzog, abetted by Pirow, or Pirow, abetted by Hertzog, perpetrated another unbelievable blunder. It was the custom to hold on Union Day, the anniversary of 31 May 1910 when the four provinces came together, military parades throughout the country. 'God Save the King' was not played at these parades unless a direct representative of the King, such as the Governor-General, was present. Pirow, as Minister of Defence, chose this occasion to introduce 'Die Stem van Suid-Afrika' as a slow march. It is hard to imagine a greater stupidity. Stuttaford, Hofmeyr's successor in the Interior, promptly resigned, and Hertzog, without consulting Smuts, called Harry Lawrence of the Cape at once to Pretoria. Hertzog showed his pugnacity by telling his secretary to put all protests in the wastepaper-basket, and then showed his reasonableness by agreeing that if one tune was played on any formal occasion, the other would be played also. The

Government also confirmed Hertzog's view that the Union had no official anthem. Stuttaford withdrew his resignation, and Hertzog gave Lawrence the portfolio that had belonged to Fourie, the defeated Minister.

Hofmeyr meanwhile was keeping out of trouble. When trouble flared up between Smuts men and Hertzog men on matters such as flags and anthems he found himself always ready to accept any reasonable compromise. He thought Pirow had acted stupidly, but he was prepared to accept, unlike many others, that Pirow's decision to use 'Die Stem' as a slow march had no ulterior motive. Hofmeyr had no real interest in these matters, and could even watch them with amusement, especially when Hertzog in caucus, having returned to his pugnacious self, soundly rebuked those English-speaking members who had protested against the Union Day incidents. There were those like Blackwell who thought that the United Party was on the point of breaking up over these repeated anthem troubles, but Hofmeyr was not one of them.

What was going on? Was Hertzog smarting under the losses of two more Free State seats, and the loss of Fourie at Gordonia? Was he smarting under the knowledge that his English-speaking support had increased, and his Afrikaans-speaking support grown less, that he was more dependent on Smuts's support than he had been? Had the old dislike for Smuts, the jealousy of Smuts, returned? Pirow wrote quite frankly that Hertzog and he were almost inseparable, and that if the matter were important, Havenga was called in, 'and thereafter General Smuts joined us to complete the Inner Cabinet'. At this point Hertzog seemed indifferent to the crises he provoked whether by action or by intemperate words. He would plunge the Party into a crisis, and Smuts, without appearing to be too important, would have to get it out again.

Hertzog was now determined to bring back Fourie into the Cabinet. Fourie had stood by him in the experiment of fusion, and now he would stand by Fourie. The obvious way to get him back was for some United Party M.P. to resign his seat, but no one was willing.

Hertzog now decided to get Fourie back as a senator. There were 44 senators in the Upper House, of whom 36 were elected. The remaining 8 were nominated by the Governor-General-in-Council, and 4 of these were nominated because of their 'thorough acquaintance with the reasonable wants and wishes of the Coloured races'. One of these now resigned.

It was now well known in the United Party, or at least in the Smuts wing of it, that Hofmeyr would resign if Fourie were appointed as a person 'thoroughly acquainted'. He told Smuts so, and Blackwell records

that Smuts and Hofmeyr persuaded de Wet of Caledon to offer his seat to
Fourie. However, Fourie would not accept. He had already been humili-
ated, and he could not face another election, where he would probably
have polled fewer votes than de Wet. Hofmeyr then went to the Prime
Minister, and said that he could not agree to the appointment of Fourie as
a senator 'thoroughly acquainted'. Hertzog's response was to create
Fourie a senator at a meeting of the Cabinet on the morning of Friday, 9
September. Neither Smuts nor Sturrock was present at the meeting.

Shortly afterwards Hofmeyr sent in his resignation. The House was
crowded in the afternoon. Smuts had been addressing a meeting of the
Botanical Society at Kirstenbosch in the morning, and did not return to
the House. It was reported that he would support the Prime Minister in
the Fourie affair, so that fusion could be saved. It was also known that
Sturrock, who was away for the day cruising, would follow Hofmeyr's
example; and it was believed that if Hofmeyr were forced out of the
Party, some ten or twelve ordinary members would follow him. The
atmosphere of the House was electric; there was always the possibility
that the great experiment of fusion would end, that Hertzog would be
reunited with Malan, that the Dominionites would return to Smuts and
that Afrikaner Nationalism would gain new strength and momentum.
Such a prospect exhilarated the Purified Nationalists, but it was dreaded
by most English-speaking South Africans, who felt that Hertzog, whatever his shortcomings, stood between them and the implacable Afrikanerdom of Malan.

Hofmeyr told the House that he could not lay his hand on his heart
and say that Mr Fourie was being appointed because of his 'thorough
acquaintance'. He said:

'I consider it as nothing less than a prostitution of the Constitution that
that provision should be used to assist the Government out of a temporary political difficulty . . . but this issue is not merely a constitutional
issue . . . it touches the whole question of the relations between the
European and the non-European peoples in South Africa . . . and this
issue is simply this . . . are we going to allow the non-Europeans to be
made pawns in the white man's political game? That is what this thing
means. One constitutional safeguard goes today, the next will go tomorrow. I for my part cannot accept that.'

Hofmeyr went on: 'I am not prepared to share responsibility for a
breach of the Constitution, and I propose to go. I realise of course that my

action will be criticised. I have already been told that this issue is not big enough for resignation. Of course for those whose primary concern is political expediency, no issue is ever big enough.'

Hofmeyr then dealt with the perennial rumour that he would start a new party:

'I am told also that I am breaking up the United Party and that I am proposing to start a new party of my own . . . I intend to do nothing of the kind. I believe in the United Party and what it stands for. I helped to create the United Party. I have done my share to make the achievement of the United Party and the Government possible.'

Hofmeyr concluded, 'Mr Speaker, may I in all modesty express the hope that this action of mine will be a clarion call to the younger generation of South Africa to set principle above expediency in the approach to public affairs.'

Hofmeyr's speech was described in the English-language press as magnificent, moving, dramatic. There were unusual scenes in the galleries and public bays while he was speaking. Ushers had to eject people who shouted 'hear, hear', and those who clapped at the end of the speech. Hertzog's reply was poor by comparison, and the quorum bells had to be rung on several occasions while he was speaking, owing to the numbers of members who wanted to get to the lobbies to discuss Hofmeyr's speech and the general situation.

The Prime Minister denied Hofmeyr's charge that Fourie was not competent to represent the coloured races. He said, 'Mr Fourie was born in their midst, he grew up in their midst, he had to do with them all his life, just as much as with the Europeans.' What is more, said Hertzog, Fourie had been the Administrator of the Cape, and had to deal not only with the coloured races, but with the 'natives as well', and to look after their needs and interests. That surely was one of the chief things with which an Administrator was entrusted.

Hertzog declared that it was not necessary for Hofmeyr to go out of the Cabinet. '. . . he could have remained in it—but owing to his own obstinacy, or because of his deep respect for principles—which I am prepared to assume in this case, he wants to say that I and the whole Cabinet should have yielded to him. I just want to say that the whole question was considered; my honourable friend could have remained in the Cabinet if he had wanted to. It was at his own wish and desire that he has left the Cabinet.'

So Hofmeyr left the Cabinet, followed three days later by Sturrock.

Frederick Claud Sturrock was a Scot with an agreeable accent, engineer turned business man and financial authority, and respected for both his ability and his integrity. When he resigned he told the House that he did so partly out of loyalty to Hofmeyr, but mainly because of his duty to what he conceived to be right. Sturrock was a conservative rather than a liberal, but he agreed wholeheartedly with Hofmeyr that the appointment of four special senators was part of the pact of Union, and he would be no party to its abrogation.

Hertzog's real grievances against Hofmeyr were first that he had done nothing to help Fourie back to Parliament, second that he had expected the Cabinet to bow to his will. In a strange inexplicable way, he was prepare to bear with Hofmeyr; he could stand it when Hofmeyr opposed parts of the grand segregation programme, but he could not stand it when Hofmeyr opposed him personally.

Paul Ribbink, librarian of Parliament, related that he asked Smuts, 'General, what do you think of it all?' And Smuts put his hand on Ribbink's and replied, 'Paul, don't you think that many a time I wanted to resign myself, crossings of my will, unwise policies, I thought I couldn't stand them. But I never felt free to take an easy way out.' Clearly Smuts did not think the issue big enough, and he was by no means alone in this. John Martin was filled with dismay that Hofmeyr should consider Fourie a greater issue than Hitler.

Now the letters and the telegrams poured in, from judges, teachers, ministers of religion, students and professors, big men in mining houses, old campers, all sorts and conditions of people. Marie Hansen wrote that he must have a party of his own; 'during the day I work as a shorthand typist, but in the evenings I could, along with others, work for your party'. A. L. Gavshon of the *Daily Express* wrote to congratulate him on his speech: 'It all sounds very hopeless but the call you sounded to youth made me feel as though I would like to follow you to the end of the earth.' And Hannah le Roux wrote from Nyasaland, 'West Africa has given us an Aggrey. May not South Africa give us a Hofmeyr of Africa.' Of these hundreds of letters and telegrams most were informed by this love of justice; most of the writers were white South Africans, who, ill at ease with their country's racial policies, found in Hofmeyr their champion.

There was still a third class of critics besides those who blamed Hofmeyr for causing a crisis and those who blamed him for not causing a bigger one. There were those who agreed that if he had been going to resign on a matter of principle, he should have done it in 1936, over the

Representation of Natives Bill, not on a small matter like Fourie's appointment. That was a highly debatable argument. The first action was certainly bigger and more spectacular than the second, but both were examples of white supremacy at work, regarding all national affairs as white men's affairs. In a way argument is irrelevant. What Hofmeyr could not do in 1936, he could do in 1938. The break that Hofmeyr could not make in 1936, he could make in 1938. He was two years older, two years wiser, two years more advanced in his emancipation from the bonds of custom and tradition that hold white South Africa in thrall. He had two years more understanding of his responsibilities, not only to the voiceless people of South Africa, but to hundreds of thousands—no, say one hundred thousand, including men, women and children, including the young woman who would work nights for him and the young men who would have liked to follow him to the ends of the earth—one hundred thousand white South Africans, who faced by the dragon of fear and hate, their own as well as others, looked to Hofmeyr as to a new Saint George.

As for Hofmeyr himself, for a while his diffidence left him. No doubt the support of many exhilarated him, he who did not go in much for exhilaration. Could he hear Sarah Millin's voice speaking, 'The future is yours if you will take it'? Could he hear her saying, 'I hope you come out on the high side'? And could he hear himself replying, 'One must choose one's ground carefully; no, it's not just caution, nor just timidity, but one must choose one's ground carefully'? And she replying, 'If not today, then tomorrow the people will want the just man'? Hofmeyr of Africa? Was that God's plan for him?

But now for a while he is not questioning. He is not asking questions and hearing questions. For a while certitude possesses him. Sarah Millin congratulates him on his resignation. He writes to her: 'From the personal point of view, I feel I have been given a stature in the country such as I never had before. Moreover I am much more conscious than before of what might be called a sense of vocation in our political life. At last I really think I am going to be Prime Minister!'

He closes his sentence with an exclamation mark, but there is no irony in it, just that faintest suggestion of self-deprecation that he should be discussing such things. Is this not exhilaration, housed for a while by an unlikely temperament? And why exhilaration, at this very moment when he is moving, not towards power, but away from it? And why exhilaration from the man who two years before had said, 'I know I am speaking against the feeling of the great mass of the people of this country'? Of course he had meant *white* people, but were the great mass of the white people any different from what they had been then? Like many good men, Hofmeyr is now uplifted, not only by the knowledge that he has done what he thought right, not only by the knowledge that many others think he has done right, but also because they look to him to lead them in their just cause.

For a while youth is restored to him, after the kidney trouble and the constant attacks and the physical weariness of his superhuman labours; now he can see again the holy city, where there shall be no more death, neither sorrow, nor crying, nor any more pain. For a while he is again that young Administrator who, exalted above all earthly strife, can make the young men see visions and the old men dream dreams. For who but the young Administrator would have said in the Lower House of the Parliament of South Africa that he hoped his action would be a clarion call to the younger generation of the country to set principle above expediency in their public life?

In this mood he continued his letter to Sarah Millin:

'I am sorry for Smuts. He has been sorely humiliated. To a large extent it is his own fault. He is really no match for the Prime Minister in simple directness and in straightforwardness of purpose. He is now Hertzog's prisoner in the Cabinet. He must do whatever he is told to do. His only possible escape is through the outbreak of war and the almost inevitable Cabinet split which will result. At the moment our relations are somewhat strained, mainly, I think, because, knowing he has let me down badly, he is sensitive about the whole business . . . I know that he would like to find a way of getting me back into the Cabinet, but how can he possibly expect Hertzog to agree to what must inevitably be my terms?'

To Underhill he wrote that if Smuts had taken a stronger line, the Prime Minister would have abandoned his intention to nominate Fourie as a senator 'thoroughly acquainted'; but when it became clear that Smuts would not resign, Hertzog grasped the chance to get rid of two troublesome Ministers.

Hofmeyr's version was therefore not quite the same as Hertzog's. Hofmeyr thought Hertzog wanted him out because of his liberalism, Hertzog said Hofmeyr was going out because of his obstinacy. Probably there was little difference between the two explanations.

But was Hofmeyr right about Smuts? Was he Hertzog's prisoner? Was it true that if Smuts had been firm Hertzog would have climbed down about Fourie? There was Malan saying that Hertzog was captive to Smuts. There was Crafford the biographer writing that it was Smuts and his genius that held the United Party together. There was Pirow agreeing with Crafford that it was the Commonwealth that mattered to Smuts, and not the political rights of Africans. There seems good reason to reject Hofmeyr's description of Smuts as a prisoner, even though we accept that he had to suffer humiliations.

As was his rule, Hofmeyr did not criticise Smuts in public. On the contrary he expressed the opinion that in his context Smuts was right. Nothing could more clearly show the difference between the two men. Smuts was prepared to countenance present wrong for the sake of future good, but for Hofmeyr the only time to do right was the present.

Was Smuts really 'sensitive about the whole business'? Was that because he knew he had let Hofmeyr down? Whatever the answers may be, there was certainly a constraint between them. The idol of the British people, the man for whom the elite of England stood up as if for royalty, found it uncomfortable to meet the unsmiling gaze of Deborah Hofmeyr, who judged him and found him wanting. She might know little about politics, but she knew that four special senators were appointed from amongst men who had special knowledge of the problems and aspirations of non-white people, and she knew that Fourie was not one. What more was there to say? Smuts felt that some explanation was due to her, but he was afraid to face her, so he sent Mrs Smuts, who was given the worst hour she had ever had. Hofmeyr and his mother had been frequent visitors to Doornkloof, most often on a Sunday for dinner. But now the two families were estranged and the estrangement lasted until the outbreak of the Second World War.

The Hofmeyr home now became the Mecca of his admirers, and they would gather round the celebrated tea-table. No one said anything about Smuts, but Mrs Hofmeyr would say, speaking of Fourie, 'Who knew that Attie had such sp-special knowledge?' It was one of her questions that was answered by her very asking. It was one of those topics not really meant for popular discussion. She would close it herself by saying, 'Now again we are p-poor relations.'

So Hofmeyr went to Pirow at Hertzog's command, and handed over all his portfolios. Perhaps they remembered the day in 1937 when they had saved the nation. It was one of the few things they had in common. In a way it was a relief to get rid of the work that threatened to eat up his life. There was one pity though, and that was to leave the Woolsack and the peace and the trees. And not to be able to go back to the big spacious house at 743 Schoeman Street. They moved into a smaller house, 735 Pretorius Street. He retained his title of Honourable, which any person who has been a member of the Governor-General's Executive Council keeps for life.

With the return of freedom, some of Hofmeyr's youthfulness also returned. He frequently made the joke that he was one of the unemployed, and that he 'rejoiced' in it, and in the freedom from unpleasantness. He was in fact living in the best of two worlds; he was both a potential Prime Minister and an actual John Bright. He wrote, 'I am enjoying a period of relative inactivity, making up arrears of reading, doing some writing, and resuming my study of the Law, so that I can qualify as a barrister at the end of next year unless something happens in the meantime.'

Something might have happened. Soon after his resignation the Chamber of Mines wrote to him offering him the post of general manager at a salary that was the highest in the country, except for the Governor-Generalship. It was reserved only for administrators of supreme quality. However, Hofmeyr did not accept; had he not written to Sarah Millin that he now had a sense of vocation? And had he not in the House expressed the hope that his action would be a clarion call? To change his course had now become impossible.

There were many unpaid jobs awaiting him. He had already resumed his law studies, and on 17 October 1938, the new weekly independent review, the *Forum*, announced that he would now write regularly for it.

The first appearance of the *Forum* on 4 April 1938 was an exciting event. It was a challenge to the whole Malanite creed, with its isolationism and its racial exclusiveness, not by British jingoism, but by a broader kind of South Africanism. The very cover was exciting—three fluted pillars through which could be seen the semicircular amphitheatre of the Union Buildings, all against a bold sky, in one issue blue, in another green, in another flaming red. There was a selection of the week's best cartoons from home and abroad, and an intelligent treatment of the news from overseas. The first editor was R. J. Kingston Russell, who had shortly before retired from the *Natal Mercury;* he had been a strong critic of Hofmeyr the dilly-dallier of 1929, and a stout supporter of Hofmeyr the liberal of 1936. The managing editor was John Cope, just returned from a job as war correspondent in China, and also a Hofmeyr man. Editor-directors were Theo Haarhoff and S. H. Frankel, two of Hofmeyr's collaborators in *Coming of Age*. These four made up the editorial council.

The language of the *Forum* was to be English, but the paper was to support full bilingualism, and to recognise all that was valuable in the Afrikaans cultural movement. It stood for freedom of thought and speech, and 'the fearless expression of opinions by others', with denial of hospitality only to 'the intolerant and ill-mannered'. There was to be one loyalty, namely 'South Africa undivided'.

On 26 September 1938, the *Forum* published an article by Hofmeyr after his resignation, entitled 'Faith, Fear and Politics', which was as clear an exposition of liberal philosophy as could have been had in those times, partly because it did not translate philosophy into policy. He wrote that the problem 'which we are pleased to call the Native problem' revealed sharply the issue between the realist and the much-abused liberal, which is really an issue between fear and faith.

'The realist faces the facts—and the only fact he sees is that of the numerical preponderance of our Native population. Logically enough therefore, he resorts to a policy of repression which is based on fear. He fails to see the further facts, that fear engenders hatred . . . that you cannot go on indefinitely sitting on the safety valve.

'The liberal also faces the facts. He does take account of the numerical aspect of the matter—but he faces other facts as well. He certainly does not lose sight of the facts of diversity between white man and black. His policy is therefore not one of assimilation. But while facing the facts he refuses to abandon the firm ground of principle.

'In particular he asserts the essential value of human personality as something independent of race or colour.'

When Hofmeyr resigned from the Cabinet, it became clear that the *Forum* would openly espouse the cause of Hofmeyrian liberalism. Hofmeyr's first article as a regular contributor was 'My Conception of Liberalism'. He made it clear that liberalism was in his opinion a philosophy, not a policy. In the South African racial context it meant three things: the recognition of an essential value in man as man; the belief that all sections have a contribution to make, and should have opportunity to make it; the determination that the less privileged should have this opportunity. He declared that liberalism did not mean equality; it meant the provision of reasonable opportunities. Liberalism utterly rejected authoritarianism;

there were spiritual values of justice, freedom and tolerance that were higher than the ideals of discipline and efficiency.

Hofmeyr's close association with the *Forum* restarted the rumours that he would found and lead a separate party whose policies would be based on the philosophy of liberalism. As far back as August 1936, a rumour had come out of the country town of Wolmaransstad in the Transvaal, from a resident 'with inside information', that Hofmeyr would form his own party and take twenty United Party M.P.s with him. Hofmeyr's speech at Grahamstown and his address to the Bantu Studies Society at the University of the Witwatersrand were quoted to support this prediction. The editor of the *Natal Witness* wrote to Hofmeyr immediately, asking for confirmation and offering the paper's support. On the same day Hofmeyr denied the rumour and, speaking in Johannesburg, said that the place of a liberal was in the United Party and that the creation of a Liberal Party would be futile from the point of view of the nation's welfare.

When Hofmeyr returned from India at the end of 1936, he was the guest of honour of the Transvaal Indian Congress, and chose that occasion to make an appeal for liberalism. He was indeed bold to go on calling liberalism by its proper name, for the word was anathema to all Calvinists, and therefore to most Afrikaner churchmen. It was identified with looseness, not only of religious belief and thought, but also frequently of living. No one knew this better than Hofmeyr, for in his life of Onze Jan he had told of 'the great battle of the Dutch Reformed Church against the forces of Liberalism', and how his hero Onze Jan had put them to flight. Yet knowing this, he chose to identify his highest beliefs and convictions by the name of liberalism.

A month later, speaking at Yeoville, Johannesburg, he again denied that a Liberal Party was needed. He said that the real danger to the country was the Malanites, and the only way to fight them was through the United Party; he appealed to all liberals to join that party. It was brave stuff, because at least half of the United Party certainly did not want liberals to join it. Heaton Nicholls must have ground his teeth when Hofmeyr visited Natal and told the Natal University College Past Students Union, 'There is room in our universities for Dutch and British, Christian and Jew, rich and poor men's sons, communist and fascist—all have something to contribute.'

The *Natal Mercury* published with approval an interview with him on liberalism. Meanwhile *Die Volk*, the pro-Malan newspaper, declared

that 'under the influence of the friends of natives and coloureds', Mr
Hofmeyr preached a philosophy of cosmopolitanism which would lay the
foundations for communism in South Africa. So Hofmeyr went his way,
preaching in many places his gospel of the beauty of liberalism and the
satisfactoriness of the United Party. The South African correspondent of
the *Manchester Guardian* thought a Liberal Party would get considerable
support, but was inclined to agree that it would be a bad idea, because it
would push Hertzog's right wing nearer to Malan. On the other hand
there were others who thought that if liberals stayed in the United Party,
that would have exactly the same effect.

Early in 1938 the *Daily Express* reported that politicians on the Witwatersrand were busy with plans to launch a Liberal Party. What one
might call liberal and progressive opinion was deeply disturbed by the
paralysing effect which the Malanites appeared to have on the United
Party. The emergence of the *Forum* was in itself a proof of this disquiet.
The United Party would not condone anti-Semitism, yet Smuts hesitated
to appoint any Jewish lawyer to the Bench. The United Party would not
condone a racial injustice, yet it would do little to interfere with existing
racial injustices. The influence of the small determined Malan party on the
giant United Party was out of all proportion to its size.

This liberal and progressive minority was a mixed bunch. There were
the distinguished leaders of the Institute of Race Relations, the two
Hoernlés, the two Rheinallt Joneses, Edgar Brookes, Leo Marquard.
There were the two Natives' Representatives, Margaret Ballinger and
Donald Molteno. There were religious leaders, prominent among them
being the Anglican bishops. There were the socialists and the communists, on the whole contemptuous of liberal, do-good institutes, and religions, though always glad to get a bishop on to a platform. There was a
generation of younger professional men as well as some outstanding newspaper men in the group.

Afrikaners with negligible exceptions did not belong to this minority.
When Afrikaners turned away from the dream of perpetual white supremacy or *baasskap*, they turned usually to the dream of 'total territorial
separation', or the dream of perpetual benevolent 'white leadership', fundamental to all of which was the concept of segregation, later to be called
apartheid, still later 'separate self-development', and today 'separate development'. Even when white South Africans turned to the concept of a
common society, as Hofmeyr had done, apartheid provided many parts of
the new structure; the *Forum*, for example, was revolted by miscegena-

tion and advocated residential and social segregation throughout its distinguished career as an exponent of Hofmeyrian liberalism.

Although the minority was a mixed bunch, all of them, except for the diehard Leftists, looked to Hofmeyr as the leader of such a minority. Some, such as the Hoernlés and the Ballingers, thought it a disagreeable necessity, but where else was there to look? The more militant wanted a new party, and brought pressure to bear on their only possible leader.

Down in Durban a vigorous group of young men was active in the Parliamentary Debating Society, which was run on the parliamentary model. The young men formed a Liberal Party within the society. Advocate Leslie Rubin was Prime Minister, and as he was visiting Johannesburg in June of 1938 it was decided that he should call on Hofmeyr in Pretoria, and express the strong desire of his group that the liberal forces of South Africa should be organised in a new political party, and that Hofmeyr should lead it. This was done in spite of the fact that only two months earlier Hofmeyr had castigated small parties in three successive speeches, but it was generally assumed that he was referring to Stallard's Dominion Party.

This was Rubin's first encounter with Hofmeyr, and he was chilled by Hofmeyr's unemotional, almost phlegmatic, approach to this burning crusade. Rubin and his friends wanted a leader round whom to build their movement. Hofmeyr clearly wanted to see a movement first. The great orator with the ringing words which could make a young man want to follow him to the ends of the earth, was, at his office desk, hard to move. Yet he kept a record of the interview. He did not tell Rubin that a Liberal Party was not necessary, he told him the time was not ripe for it, nor for any organisation bearing the name; rather he favoured the launching of a non-party league which would attract men of liberal ideals from all parties, and which would encourage them to further liberal ideals within their own parties. The league should study, but should be more than a study group; 'it should be prepared to take a definite line in regard to the questions of the day'. The first thing to do was to prepare a statement of objects and ideals; let the Durban group get on with that. When the statement was agreed upon, let the league be launched simultaneously in Johannesburg, Cape Town, and Durban.

Rubin had to be satisfied with that. He had wanted a leader, but the leader had wanted a movement. Hofmeyr was in the same position as he had been as Administrator, when people wanted him to come out and lead a middle party disowning Hertzog and Smuts. He was in the same position as he had been when old Chris Hofmeyr wanted permission to go to Hertzog and say with authority, 'Young Hofmeyr is Nationalist,' and Hofmeyr had replied to him, 'I have so far found that such things as come my way, come without seeking—and in future, things will apparently happen in the same way.'

After his resignation from the Cabinet over the Fourie affair, Hofmeyr wrote to Underhill that he thought it 'not improbable' that there would be a new alignment of parties, 'a more or less liberal predominantly urban party on the one side and a rural conservative party on the other. My future will be with the first of these, and it will almost certainly be the stronger ultimately.'

In November of 1938 a great honour came to him, the chancellorship of the University of the Witwatersrand, in succession to His Royal Highness, Prince Arthur of Connaught. He would never take an honorary degree, because it came in the first instance from the Senate; but the honour of the chancellorship came from Convocation, and he accepted it with pride.

One of Hofmeyr's first duties as Chancellor was to be the conferring of an honorary degree on Advocate E. G. Jansen, Speaker of the House of Assembly. Jansen was the chairman of the committee organising the centenary celebrations of the Great Trek of 1838, that extraordinary migration of the Cape Boers to the north, one of the most notable causes of which was the determination to escape the new equalitarian ideas, that all men were somehow equal in the eyes of God and the law.

The committee had conceived the imaginative idea of sending ox-wagons from various points in South Africa to Pretoria, where on Dingaan's Day, 16 December, the foundation stone would be laid of Moerdyk's massive monument, which was to stand on a commanding ridge just to the south of the city.

These symbolic wagon treks evoked indescribable emotion. There was an upwelling of Afrikaner pride and sentiment such as South Africa had never known. 'Die Stem van Suid-Afrika' became familiar to tens of thousands of people who had never heard it before. The wagons were met in every village and town and city by men and women in Voortrekker dress. Prayers were said, meat and *boerewors*— South African sausages—were cooked over the fires, nostalgic Afrikaner *liedjies* were sung. Old men and women would weep, and touch the tent of the wagon, its wooden frame and its wheels. Speeches were made of dedication and burning love, and history being what it was, many of these told of past British sins. Relief cuts of the symbolic wagon began to take pride of place in thousands of homes. Small monuments, sometimes cairns of stones, rose all over South Africa to mark the passing of the wagons, but when one spoke of the Monument, it could mean only the massive tower that was to be built outside Pretoria.

A respected minister of the Gereformeerde Kerk, Dominee Kestell, called on the people to perform a *reddingsdaad,* an act of salvation, and so was formed the Reddingsdaadbond, which was to help the Afrikaner to take his rightful place in the economic and business life of the country. Another minister, Dominee Christian Kotze, founded the Ossewabrandwag, the Ox-wagon Watch, to cherish 'the spirit of the ox-wagon'. It was called the O.B., and was a secret and semi-military organisation, much more the product of the Germany of 1938 than of Afrikanerdom. Yet so emotional were the times that any new and unusual thing could claim to have hitherto been hidden in old Afrikaner traditions, and even Malan did not recognise the O.B. for what it was until 1942.

It was perhaps inevitable that the Malanites should have played a disproportionate part in the centenary. Afrikaner feelings were intense, and the Malanites were the most intense Afrikaners. Hertzog could not rival this patriotic fervour. To a large extent his own battle was won, but to the Malanites there could be no victory until South Africa was independent of the British Crown.

The Malanites opposed the proposal that Hertzog should lay the stone. Finally three Afrikaner women, descendants of Voortrekker leaders, were chosen for the honour. Nevertheless Malan remained the guest of honour and speaker at the second most important ceremony, the unveiling of the memorial at Blood River, where on 16 December 1838 the Voortrekkers had broken the armies of Dingaan the Zulu king.

The gathering at the site of the new Monument on 16 December was immense, and next to its fervour, its notable characteristic was its exclusiveness. The theme of every meeting was Afrikanerdom, its glory, its struggles, its griefs, its achievements. At one remarkable meeting the voice of Mr E. W. Douglass, K.C., descendant of the 1820 Settlers who had given Jacobus Uys a Bible when he set out on the Trek, and who was bringing a message of goodwill in English, was drowned by the singing of 'Die Stem van Suid-Afrika'. After the singing, a man in Voortrekker costume took over the microphone, and began to recite a patriotic verse. There was tumultuous applause. By this time it was clear that the crowd was in no mood to listen to any English, and Jansen announced that Douglass would say a few words in Afrikaans. This gesture was acclaimed, and Douglass said his few words, which were loudly applauded.

They were lonely and terrible occasions for any English-speaking South African who had gone there to rejoice in this Afrikaner festival, and they were embarrassing for any Afrikaners who had asked English-speaking friends to accompany them. Many Afrikaners could not forget that the very founder of Afrikanerdom was not there, but stayed proud and rejected on his farm. Yet the great Smuts was there, austere and distinguished. What did he make of it all, builder and defender of the Commonwealth of Nations, as he walked through the tremendous crowds, to many of whom he was a traitor?

Hofmeyr was not there. He was at Bloemfontein saying that the Almighty had ordained that Boer and Briton must live side by side as citizens of one State. He told the gathering, 'We should refuse to think in terms of a small South Africa. We have to think in terms of a great South Africa which will become greater.'

Down in Natal Malan spoke:

'Afrikanerdom has found itself again in this year of commemoration. Risen out of the dust of humiliation and self-contempt it now demands full recognition of itself, for its noble ancestry, and their descendants.

'As a sign of your new national pride you are naming your streets after Voortrekker heroes and demanding that "Die Stem van Suid-Afrika" should be recognised as your national anthem. Have you the patriotism and sufficient power in this year of celebrations to use this God-given opportunity also to demand something infinitely more important— the assurance that White civilisation will be assured . . .

'Afrikanerdom is calling again.'

Who could deny Malan's authority to speak for Afrikanerdom? Could Hertzog or Smuts speak like that? While the Free State general stayed on his farm, and the Transvaal general walked through the great crowds urbane and aloof, the real generalship of Afrikanerdom was passing into the hands of the Cape predikant. Those fiery young patriots who were looking for a leader found him in the Afrikaner Malan, not in the bi-racial Hertzog or the international Smuts. Shortly after Centenary Day young Albert Hertzog wrote to his father, on behalf of 'influential Afrikaans societies and leading people', urging him to seek co-operation with Malan in the interests of Afrikanerdom.

Hertzog's reply to his son became famous. He wrote that the basis of his son's contention was that 'the Afrikaans-speaking section of the population would be the only section that would count as *die volk*, and that the English-speaking section of Afrikanerdom would not count as part of *die Afrikanervolk*'.

Hertzog rejected the contention out of hand. He wrote, 'Under no circumstances will I . . . ever lend my support in politics to people who are not prepared . . . to recognise and adopt the principle of complete equality . . . between our Afrikaans- and English-speaking sections.' Hertzog concluded, 'Allow me . . . in all sincerity and with no other purpose than to be of service to Afrikanerdom, to warn you and your young Afrikaner friends that along the road which you are walking only national destruction is to be found.'

So the great centenary celebrations came to an end with Afrikanerdom hopelessly divided. One might guess that one-third of it followed Malan, one-third Hertzog and one-third Smuts. Even Stallard's Dominion Party could raise an odd Afrikaner here and there to preach old-fashioned loyalty to Crown and Commonwealth. Yet underneath the turbulent waters a new tide was flowing. The Afrikanerdom of Hertzog, with its two streams, its scrupulous recognition of English-speaking rights, its tenderness (in spite of its indiscretions) for English susceptibilities, was ebbing, and the Afrikanerdom of Malan was coming in.

The Afrikaner universities were turning out, not Smuts men and women, or Hertzog men and women, but Malan men and women. The Afrikaner schools were turning out Malan boys and girls. The Afrikaner scout movements and the cultural movements were not excited about the Commonwealth of Nations or the bi-racial policy, but about being Afrikaners, about the day when Afrikaners would govern, about the time when all the wickedness and looseness and liberal sentimentality of the last hundred years would come to an end, and all the people of South Africa would be ruled firmly and resolutely by the Afrikaner people, whom God had sent into Africa for a purpose, nothing less than to bring Christianity and civilisation to a barbaric continent. Those who were sensitive about their chauvinism spoke earnestly about their mission, but it was not the mission or the Christianity or the civilisation that could bring that burning light into the eyes, it was being Afrikaner, it was belonging to a people who after years of struggle and suffering were drawing nearer to the Promised Land. Who could doubt the truth of that, especially if he had been one of the throng that gathered on the ridge where the Monument was to arise? Had a general election been held early in 1939, Malan would have taken yet more seats from the United Party, and Smuts would have had to rush round the country, reassuring those English-speaking people whose indignation hid the fear that this stupendous pageant of Afrikaner passion had aroused.

Hofmeyr himself while quite ready to condemn the intolerance that disfigured the celebrations did not like to discuss their deeper significance. This was one of the rare occasions on which he deliberately avoided a topic. To him the celebrations had given a revelation of an intensity of emotion from which he shrank. He had changed a great deal since his early Johannesburg days, when he had spoken of the superior Englishman who had treated the Afrikaner 'if not like a piece of dirt, then as a being in some grade between his exalted self and his native boy'. His mother's teaching, and the Bible, and Balliol, and then the Scots and the Welsh and the Jews and the Greeks and the Indians, had worked deeply in Hofmeyr's heart. And not only these, but also the deep respect that was accorded to him by English-speaking people, so that all resentment was severed at the very root. Was that why he shrank from the intensity of Afrikaner feeling that the centenary revealed? Or did the intolerance of so many of his own people hurt him? Or was there something else, was there a fear of the power of Afrikaner nationalism, a fear for the future of South Africa, a fear for the future of all he believed in? And was this one of the rare occasions when he did not like to look at something because he feared it, and because reason, in which he so deeply believed, was powerless against it? There are grounds for thinking so.

Though Hofmeyr shrank from facing the truth about the celebrations, that does not mean that he banned the thought of them from his mind. His fellow-Afrikaner J. P. Duminy, his cricketing companion, influenced too no doubt by the revelation of Afrikaner intensity and worried by Afrikanerdom's increasing drift to isolation, had written to Hofmeyr wondering whether it was not possible to reach some kind of accommodation with it. Hofmeyr's reply was emphatic.

'In the old days, while the Afrikaner was in a position of inferiority, no true South Africanism was possible. It is right that all traces of inequality should be wiped away. But the trouble about your 100 per cent Afrikaner is that he is out to create new inequalities. He can't conceive of a broadly national culture based on equal contributions. His idea of a South African nation is an Afrikaner *bloc* which may perhaps graciously absorb a few English-speaking South Africans leaving the rest as an unassimilable minority group. On the basis of that conception there can of course never be peace and real progress in South Africa.'

Hofmeyr continued gravely:

'What is one to do about it? Of course one must go on fighting against this narrowness. But will it persist and be intensified, or is it just a passing phase? I would like to think the latter, but I can't convince myself that it is so. That being so, I am not too happy about the future. Still, I suppose in these and other matters, one must be content sometimes to carry on the fight in faith, following the light as one sees it.'

At the height of the celebrations the Libertas Bond emerged in Johannesburg, supported by another young and vigorous group of men and women. In Durban, Rubin and his friends formed a Libertas League of Action, and its aim was 'the peaceful co-operation in the service of South Africa of all sections of its population'.

The two groups met in a private convention in Johannesburg in October of 1938, but could not agree on a basis of action. They sent John Gray, Margaret Ballinger, and Fenhalls to ask Hofmeyr to associate himself with a Liberal Party; but the group came back with a firm No. Without Hofmeyr's leadership, each group decided to go its own way, the Johannesburgers wanting direct political action, and the Durban group deciding to exert non-party pressure.

After the convention the Durban group travelled to Pretoria to see Hofmeyr. He wanted the front broadened and strengthened, especially by forming a group in Cape Town. He told them to go out and gain more support, and promised to visit Durban to address a non-party meeting. This he did in November, when he was entertained by the University Club at a banquet given at the Durban Country Club. The *élite* of Durban was there, some five or six hundred of them. Hofmeyr did not refer to the League, which was a disappointment to some, but he opened his speech with remarks which again encouraged some to believe that a new party was on the way. He said:

'The time is opportune for the expression of a new determination and the breaking of new ground for building up the future of South Africa. I don't think we can close our eyes to the fact that our national leaders and the political parties they represent are ageing although South Africa appreciates their services.'

Then all the striving came to an abrupt end. Early in 1939 Hitler marched into Czechoslovakia, and Britain guaranteed the integrity of

Poland. The uncomfortable question that fusion had never answered, namely, what would South Africa do in the event of war, suddenly loomed up as the only question white South Africans would think about; these events belong to the story of the following chapter.

Meanwhile Hofmeyr moved into yet another crisis in the relations between himself and his Prime Minister and the United Party. Stuttaford, his successor in the portfolio of the Interior, introduced an Asiatics Bill which would restrict Indians from buying land except in the defined Indian areas. Hofmeyr at first decided to support the Bill as an interim measure, but a few days later, not having been given the assurances he sought from Stuttaford, he decided that it went too far. He pointed out that the Bill had not only a 'pegging' effect [i.e., to prevent residential and other expansion] but would also prevent change of personnel, change of ownership or partnership or management, all those inhuman restrictions which white South Africa has all too often imposed on Indian traders. Hofmeyr asked the Minister to take account of natural increase in the Asian population. He also asked the Minister to grant exemptions in the spirit of the two Round Table Agreements of 1927 and 1932, but Stuttaford refused categorically to do so, causing Hofmeyr to protest that members of the United Party were not robots. Hofmeyr's amendment on the point was defeated, he securing the classic eleven votes.

Malan had decided to support the Bill, so that the burden of opposition fell almost entirely on Hofmeyr and Blackwell. Blackwell wrote, 'Throughout one stormy session we fought Mr Stuttaford's proposals clause by clause, and did not hesitate to divide the House upon them, although we were in a hopeless minority.'

This was too much for Hertzog. He had had enough of Hofmeyr and his obstructive ways, and he had had enough of Blackwell on other occasions, usually to do with the sentiments and susceptibilities of English-speaking people. They were summoned the next day to appear before the caucus, and the Prime Minister demanded, as an alternative to his own resignation, a vote of censure on two members who understood neither discipline nor loyalty. The two members refused to recant, and said that if the vote was passed they would resign from the caucus. Smuts tried to keep the peace and moved that the caucus express dissent not censure, but the Prime Minister would have none of it.

Blackwell wrote of Hertzog, 'At one tense moment of that fateful sitting it looked as if he and General Smuts might come to an open breach, but the latter, consistent with his policy throughout several years of grave difficulty and stress, avoided a rupture.'

The discussion was postponed till the next day. Hertzog was adamant, and the caucus, some abstaining, six opposing, gave him his vote of censure. Hofmeyr and Blackwell left immediately, and at the next meeting of the caucus, their tendered resignations were 'noted'; according to the Chief Whip that meant they were accepted. Hofmeyr and Blackwell became, in Hofmeyr's own words, 'independent United Party supporters'.

Their joint statement to the press was a model of lucidity. They pointed out that Dr Malan had virtually abdicated his functions during the debate on the Bill, and they had therefore assumed them, all the more willingly because they were representing a voteless community. They pointed out that in 1937 similar legislation had been opposed by members of the Party 'for diametrically opposite reasons', and nothing had happened to them; on the contrary the Government had bowed to them. The essence of the matter, said Hofmeyr and Blackwell, was that their exercise of freedom of speech and action was distasteful to the Prime Minister; he impugned their loyalty and therefore they had no choice but to resign.

The second part of the joint statement was logically impregnable. Hofmeyr and Blackwell pointed out that prior to the election, Louis Esselen, the general secretary of the United Party, issued an official statement saying that, as the party would be returned by a large majority, it 'would have to adopt a policy of self-criticism to ensure efficiency in Government, and to make up for the lack of an effective Opposition'. Many voted for the United Party, believing it would give the country a kind of national government, and accepted assurances that there would be room for honest differences of opinion. The validity of these assurances had never been destroyed. The United Party caucus had given the lie to Esselen.

The case was logically unanswerable but Hertzog was not disposed to consider it logically. There can be no doubt that he now actively disliked Hofmeyr. Within his ideology and its basic assumptions, Hertzog was a man of integrity, but now Hofmeyr was always tearing the ideology and the assumptions to pieces.

Hofmeyr was also critical of Smuts. Writing in that clear incisive English he used when he was not preaching, he reminded readers of the *Forum* that at the 1917 Imperial Conference Smuts had said, 'I feel sure, I have always felt sure, that once the White community in South Africa were rid of the fear that they were going to be flooded by unlimited immigration from India, all the other questions would be considered subsidiary and become easily and perfectly soluble.'

Hofmeyr wrote, almost as though he could also see far into the future: 'How often have we not been told in South Africa that if we shall but agree to this or that particularly discriminatory proposal as a concession to race or colour prejudice, it would have as effect that the section of the community discriminated against would be very much better treated in all other respects since the cause of friction will have been removed? And how often have the facts not belied these predictions?'

He gave examples to prove his contention: 'The settlement of the question of Asiatic immigration has not made the average European any better disposed to Asiatics. The adoption of the Native segregation policy has not removed or even reduced anti-Native prejudice. The virtual stoppage of Jewish immigration has been followed by attempts to enact discriminatory legislation against Jews already in the country. Today we are being told that when once Coloured segregation has been adopted, a Golden Age will commence for the Coloured community. . . . We must face the hard fact that race and colour prejudice is something which, like jealousy, "grows from what it feeds on".'

Not even Smuts could have answered that case. There was no logical way to answer Hofmeyr. There was only a psychological way, to say to him, 'How you hate your own people, don't you? How you hate to be white, don't you? Why don't you go and live with your coolies and your kaffirs and your hottentots?' And that is indeed what many said to him. But they were wrong. Hofmeyr did not want to live with Indians and Africans and coloured people; he was one of those whites who accepted that one did not. But he wanted Indians and Africans and coloured people to live human lives, free from the inhuman laws that white South Africa had imposed upon them. Hofmeyr was a white South African, with white South African fears and prejudices and irrationalities; but he knew them for what they were and was feeling his way out of the bog into which he had been born. He believed in the brotherhood of man, just as Smuts did, but he suffered for his belief in a way that Smuts, to speak the truth, never suffered in all his distinguished years.

Two days after his resignation, Hofmeyr attacked the Asiatics Bill at its third reading, in a speech that was a masterpiece of oratory. He thrust at both Hertzog and Smuts without being offensive, and the House listened to him in spellbound silence. He demanded that humane provision be made for natural increase.

He went on to say:

'In speaking as I have done I know that I am exposing myself to the jibe that I am the spokesman of the Indian in South Africa. It is a cheap jibe. Since I became a member of this House I have never been dependent on any other than European votes. Yet I have always regarded myself as not merely the representative of those who sent me, but also as a trustee of the interests of the voteless section of the community. It will be a sorry day for South Africa if no honourable members are prepared to take up that line.'

What Hofmeyr was saying was that a member representing Europeans had a duty to uphold not merely their material interests but also their spiritual and ethical beliefs. It was true that when he upheld Christian justice, many said he was a mouthpiece of Indians. It was true that many jibed at him. The Malanites had a simpler solution than justice, and that was to pack off every Indian back to India.

Hofmeyr warned the House that the Indian people of South Africa, instead of seeking justice fruitlessly, would join forces with other non-white people against white South Africa, that their political movements would get into the hands of extreme politicians, and that white South Africa might face a campaign of civil disobedience and passive resistance. He warned the House against the danger of antagonising the people of India, whose country was advancing fast towards independence. 'Let us be wise in the shaping of our policies in relation to this people before perhaps it is too late.'

Even before the caucus censure, Hofmeyr had felt that his days in the United Party were drawing to a close. He was always conscious of the Prime Minister's dislike for him, but he was determined not to be forced out of the Party on any minor issue. He wrote about Hertzog: 'If he remains in office much longer it is almost certain that he will do something reactionary of such a nature that I will have every reason for breaking away. Meanwhile I am content to bide my time, and strengthen my position in the country.'

Six months later, after the caucus censure, Hofmeyr had thought further. He wrote to Babu King to tell him that he had resigned from the caucus though not from the Party. 'But it looks as if in time I shall have to start a party of my own.'

There may have been a reason for this. Hofmeyr may have thought that Smuts was finished. It is unlikely that he would ever have contemplated a new party otherwise. He wrote at the end of 1938 that Smuts had lost 'much of his moral force'. It seems more likely that he contemplated the more or less early retirement of both Smuts and Hertzog, and that the political struggle would be between what Pirow and what he represented, or even between what Malan and what he represented. One thing, however, he never lost sight of, the possibility of war; if war came, it would be a different situation.

Hofmeyr's position was not weakened by his resignation from the caucus. On the contrary his action was overwhelmingly approved by the Witwatersrand general council of the United Party, and by his own committee at Johannesburg North. His appointment as Chancellor of the University had further added to his prestige. He thought his political position was strong, and he was right; it was strong not because of his membership of the United Party, but because of his sturdy independence. When he told people that unqualified caucus rule was dangerous to democracy, they believed him. All over the country believers in democracy were looking to him. The English-language press was divided.

Hofmeyr had a touch of the histrionic that grated on some people, perhaps more so because of the touch of judgement. But on the occasion of his resignation from the caucus and of his later speech in the House, there were no histrionics. Hofmeyr thought that the rights of voiceless people had to be defended, and if no one else would defend them, he would do so himself. It was as simple as that.

When Hofmeyr returned to Johannesburg he was the guest at a dinner of yet another group of young English-speaking South Africans who wished to issue a constructive challenge to exclusive Afrikaner Nationalism. Hugh Dalrymple, son of William Dalrymple of the days of Hofmeyr's principalship, had tried to organise a non-political group to uphold the principles of democracy and liberty. The group, called the South African Group for Good Government, was seeking ways for meeting the deep frustration felt by so many English-speaking men and women in the latter years of the fusion government. At the dinner were several talented young men.

It was a fascinating situation, of groups seeking a leader, and of the leader asking first for more support. Hofmeyr encouraged them all, but he would not take the step so many of them wanted him to take. When Professor Cecil S. Richards, of the University of the Witwatersrand, launched a Democratic League, Hofmeyr wrote him an unsolicited letter of congratulations. He also encouraged the trade unions in their concern about the Nationalist threat to civil liberties.

It was only a month later that the Western world was plunged into war, and South Africa with it. The white electorate was divided into two, those who wanted to fight and those who did not. Liberal explorations came to an end. Hofmeyr threw in his weight behind Smuts, and there was no more talk of a new party.

It was by no means an inconsiderable body of young men who would have followed Hofmeyr into a new party in the late 1930s. Hitler had made men distrust the old order, but they recoiled from his new one; therefore they sought a new order of their own, where a man would no longer be judged by his race, where a man's colour would not condemn him to a life of poverty and frustration. Most of these young men were English-speaking, but that could hardly be held against them; most of their Afrikaans-speaking contemporaries were occupied by other matters. Yet the legend arose, and was believed on the one side by many of the Left, on the other by many Afrikaner Nationalists, that the mainspring of South African liberalism was hatred of the Afrikaner. This belief pleased the Left, who told themselves they had sounder motives, and it pleased the Right, who when they are opposed like to believe it is because they are hated.

Many of the younger men and women who would have followed Hofmeyr, and others too, of the Institute of Race Relations and the churches and the universities, were later to judge Hofmeyr because he did not come out in 1936 or '37 or '38 or '39. They agreed that if he had come out then, liberal opinion would have clarified and consolidated, liberal philosophy would have issued in liberal policy, and liberalism and progressivism would not have been left to emerge when white fear was at its greatest, when events in Kenya and the Congo and the Central African Federation were driving white South Africa to look, not for high adventure, but for security.

Why could Hofmeyr not have come out? He did not enjoy the confidence of his Party leader, he was estranged from the Party's second-in-command, and from all his parliamentary leaders. He had been censured by his caucus. How could he possibly say that the place for the liberal was in the United Party, when his own liberalism had forced him, first to resign from the Cabinet and then to resign from the caucus?

Would he have consolidated liberal opinion? There can be no doubt about it. Such opinion was looking for a lead and a leader. Furthermore Hofmeyr would have been able to control that individualism and that highmindedness which characterise liberalism, that belief that what is absolutely right is immediately expedient. His authority in this direction would have gone unchallenged, because his own integrity would never have been in question.

It is well known that many white South African soldiers came back from the war with a new knowledge of non-white men, and a new view of race relations. Their eyes had been opened and they had seen visions. The intensity of their desire to change their country's laws and customs was something quite new in white South African history. Had Hofmeyr been the leader of a new party, these newly awakened men would have been behind him to a man. But there was neither leader nor party. In three years some of these men had forgotten the needs and wrongs of others, and had gone back to contemplation of their own.

When Malan came to power and embarked on his racial legislation, he was opposed by a party revealing the whole spectrum of opposition, from those who opposed all racial legislation to those who in their hearts approved of it, and thought in their foolishness that it was clever to let Malan make the laws and incur the odium. Such a party could oppose this and that, and ask that this law be softened and that one be postponed, but it could not oppose the fundamental assumption that it was both right and expedient to legislate primarily for white security. A Hofmeyr party could have done it, but there was no such party there.

Why did Hofmeyr not do it? For one thing, he saw the future as fluid. He was expecting the Dominion–Labour–United Party pattern to break up, and a roughly liberal–conservative pattern to emerge. He had written on 16 December of 1938, 'Before long our politics will be thrown into solution, and it seems almost inevitable that I shall have to take a hand in mobilising the resistance to the forces of repression and reaction.' From this it is not clear whether he saw himself playing the leading rôle or not. In Durban he had hinted that Smuts and Hertzog were finished. He had written that Smuts had lost his moral force, that Smuts was Hertzog's prisoner, and by that he surely meant something stronger than that Smuts was biding his time. Yet if he were to play a junior rôle, to whom could he be junior but to Smuts?

Then after the resignation from the caucus his views became more independent. As we have seen, he wrote that it looked 'as if in time' he would have to form a party of his own. He wrote on 18 June 1939, 'I am being pressed from many quarters to start a new Liberal or Democratic Party. But one must be sure of one's issue and one's time before taking such a step.' He added, 'And one is naturally hesitant about any such new venture when the shadow of recurrent European crises is over us. But one never knows how rapidly the course of events may lead one into action.'

So while Smuts was reluctant to leave Hertzog, so was Hofmeyr reluctant to leave Smuts, and for the same reason.

Was that the only reason? Of course it was not. Was loyalty to Smuts a reason? It was said time and time again that Hofmeyr would not leave the United Party in the late 'thirties because of loyalty to Smuts. There is absolutely no evidence of that. It is improbable to the point of being impossible that Hofmeyr would have put loyalty to Smuts before loyalty to his own principles. This is not merely to say that Hofmeyr was a man of integrity; it is also to say that it was in loyalty to principles, not to men, that he found his security.

Were there other reasons perhaps, reasons grounded in Hofmeyr himself, in the kind of man he was? Surely that must be so. He was still the same man who had written to old Chris Hofmeyr that such things as came his way came without seeking, and that it would apparently always be so. It is possible that what had once been a belief was now an expression of his nature, that he would wait for things to come to him because he could not go to them. That was what Pirow called 'lack of aggressiveness'. Had he not once revealed his self-doubt to Sarah Millin:

'Your letter has caused me a good deal of searching of the heart. Am I uncertain and timid? Or are you overestimating my powers? It may be that I have a gift of speech, but is it not of the kind that appeals only to intellectuals, and does not really stir the masses? I wish I could see myself leading people away from the Devil—but when I realise the strength of the forces arrayed against whosoever essays that task, I can, at best, only foresee a more or less splendid failure.'

Had he not written: 'If the other thing were really possible, if there were a chance of leading South Africa from the Devil, I would readily spend myself in the process, but is it? Or is it possibly that there is something lacking in my make-up?'

What did he mean, something lacking in his make-up? Was it a defect? And who was to blame for it? himself? or his mother? or even God maybe? That small boy, who learned to read with no one knowing, who was a woman's solace for all her deprivations, who was at school a child with boys, and at college a boy with men, was he to blame for it, that he could not see himself out there in front like a general?

Is it a defect to be like that? Or can one achieve an integrity of one's own even if one is like that? Was Hofmeyr to blame that he could not or he would not? One halts before so grave a question, which is really the ultimate question of human responsibility, the question that is answered so differently by conscience and by love. We must be satisfied to say that the forces of right and justice could have been marshalled in the late thirties, if Hofmeyr had felt called upon to do it, but that he did not feel called upon. If God was calling him, he did not hear.

There was another factor too, the great Smuts. Though Hofmeyr had called him a captive, others did not. Pirow and Crafford saw him as patiently waiting. The Nationalist cartoonists delighted in depicting Hertzog as an old man being continually duped and deceived by a diabolically clever colleague. Blackwell, much as he respected Hofmeyr, venerated Smuts. Sturrock, a man of 56 when he resigned in 1938, declared that, if it were ever necessary, he would die for Smuts, and Deneys Reitz would have died for him too.

Could Hofmeyr have broken away from Smuts? And led a party that would of its very nature have had to be anti-Smuts? Could he have led a party that would openly have condemned Smuts as a white supremacist and a maker of unjust laws? It was almost impossible. It would have been possible perhaps if Hofmeyr could have led a big break-away, not a small one. But for Hofmeyr to have led a small break-away was almost impossible. It would only have been possible if Smuts had confronted him with a clear-cut choice between good and evil, and Smuts was not likely to do that.

So Rubin and Dalrymple, Margaret Ballinger and Fenhalls, and all the other keen and impatient young men and women were asking, if they had only known it, for the impossible. The exhilaration of 1938 had passed, and the self-doubt had returned.

Chapter 10

War and the Return to Power

NOT only had Hofmeyr's self-doubt returned. War was coming, and it was no time to form new parties. The urgent question was not what policies to follow in South Africa, but what Hitler would do in Czechoslovakia.

What would happen if Britain went to war with Germany? What would South Africa do then?

When Hertzog and Smuts went into coalition, and later into fusion, they left grave constitutional problems unanswered. Could South Africa stay neutral when the King went to war? Did neutrality in war mean secession from the Commonwealth?

In 1934 Hertzog and Smuts had hoped that the questions would never need to be answered, that time would answer them. They had hoped that a generation of racial peace would find English-speaking and Afrikaans-speaking South Africans thinking more and more alike.

Hertzog now drew up a statement of policy in the event of war between Britain and Germany. South Africa would be neutral, but she would abide by the agreement which allowed Britain to maintain a naval base at Simonstown on False Bay. Although Smuts was startled, and asked time to consider the statement, he announced the following day that he and his colleagues would accept it. The quarterly review, *Round Table*, which would probably not have expressed such an opinion without consulting Hofmeyr, said that if war had come then, Hertzog, Smuts, Havenga and Pirow would have been for neutrality. On 28 September 1938 the whole Cabinet agreed to Hertzog's statement.

Hofmeyr wrote to Underhill:

'. . . According to the Prime Minister's view, which General Smuts now accepts, South Africa would not have been automatically at war if Great Britain went to war—it would have remained neutral while our Parliament met and decided whether we would declare war or not. Whether in such circumstances our Government would have advised

Parliament to decide on war is not clear—in all probability it would have been acutely divided.'

The Cabinet decision was astonishing. Eight years, six years, five years earlier, English-speaking support for such a neutrality decision would have been impossible to obtain. Hertzog was entitled to look upon it as the crowning achievement of his lifetime. At last English-speaking South Africa was beginning to understand that independence meant independence, whether one belonged to a Commonwealth or not.

So Parliament assembled in February 1939 in the shadow of grave unanswered questions. Malan on the one side and Stallard on the other were unequivocal. It was the United Party that was uneasy and uncertain. Its English-speaking members were restless for two reasons. They were afraid Hertzog would keep South Africa neutral, but they were also afraid of opposing him, because he was their only bulwark against Malan. Malan, aided by the great wave of Afrikaner feeling during the Voortrekker celebrations, was challenging Hertzog for the leadership of Afrikanerdom. Powerless as Malan appeared to be, he could strike fear into non-Afrikaner hearts.

Hofmeyr was now on the mere periphery of events. He was out of the caucus and out of the Cabinet. There were many who would tell him what happened in the caucus, but since his estrangement from Smuts, there was no one to tell him what went on in the Cabinet, least of all in that inner circle where Smuts consorted oddly with Hertzog, Havenga and Pirow. The country's attention had shifted from its own internal affairs to the crisis in Europe, from the particular issues of mixed marriages and separate areas to the universal issue of human freedom. Yet who could speak better on the universal issue than Hofmeyr, who had always tried to relate it to the particular? He chose a great occasion on which to do it, his installation as Chancellor of the University of the Witwatersrand.

Hofmeyr delivered a great address, as he always did when he deliberately avoided the props of memory. He told the congregation that the chancellorship was to him the 'crowning glory', which was true, and that he had left the University in 1924 feeling that he was leaving a large part of himself behind, which was not. He did not take long to reveal his theme. 'Undoubtedly the greatest conflict in the world today is the conflict between the spirit of democracy and the spirit of authoritarianism. In that conflict no University worthy of its great tradition can fail to range itself on the side of democracy.' Hofmeyr acknowledged, as he had frequently done, the weaknesses of democracy, but he told his hearers, 'The great advances of humanity have not come from discipline—they have come from the operation of the free human spirit.' He declared that freedom to criticise was the first essential element in democratic freedom, and he condemned the tendency to rule through an inner Cabinet, without consulting those who should be consulted.

Of whom was he speaking when he said:

'There are those who, in the absolute assurance of their own rectitude, resent the fact that anyone should hold an opinion different from their own. When that does happen, they ascribe it not to intellectual conviction, but to some form of moral turpitude.

'So they become impatient of the free expression of opinion—they want to put restraints on opposition and criticism—they desire to see created in support of their views and policies, that servile, standardised mass-mentality which is one of the instruments of dictatorship.

'. . . It is doubtless that tendency which expresses itself in attacks on the freedom of the press even in democratic lands.'

The second great freedom, declared Hofmeyr, was the freedom to develop, and he declared that the upholders of trusteeship, which white South Africa had declared to be its national policy towards its non-white peoples, must not fear the day when the wards grew up; otherwise their trusteeship was unchristian.

He reserved his final words for the students themselves:

'To you . . . I am speaking today for the first time as your Chancellor. I have spoken to you of freedom and the modern world's menace to it. It needs, as never before, defenders, stern and resolute, but withal lavish of the best that is in them. I want to enrol you for that fight. There is no fairer cause to fight for than the cause of freedom. Six hundred years ago the Nobles and Commons of Scotland at Arbroath made that historic declaration:

' "We fight not for glory, nor for wealth, nor for honour, but for that freedom which no good man will surrender but with his life."

' "That freedom which no good man will surrender but with his life." That is the good fight I ask you to fight. And may you quit yourselves like men, men at once conscript and consecrated of your own free will, in the warfare that lies ahead.'

Hofmeyr received tumultuous applause, especially from the young. But others were grateful too, those anxious about the future, anxious about Hitler, anxious about the way that white South Africa exercised her trusteeship, under a Government that allowed its private members to bring forward private Bills that seemed designed, not for the exercise of trusteeship but for the strengthening of privilege. To listen to Hofmeyr gave them courage. His speech came at a time when believers in freedom, who were on the whole inclined to like the gay, chivalrous Deneys Reitz, were shocked when he said at Bethal that he favoured press control. The *Forum* called it a 'first-class blunder', and that of course was what it was. Reitz must, in a moment of aberration, have gone off the rails. His blunder was all the more worrying because Hertzog, thought now by many to resent any kind of political criticism, was planning, not for the first time in his career, a Bill to control the press.

Before Hofmeyr left for Cape Town, many of his old students of twenty years before gave him a dinner at the Carlton Hotel. Hofmeyr was now 45 years of age, and many of his old students were more or less that age. Fortified by wine and the passing of years, they openly called him Hoffie, and subjected him to a barrage of affectionate ragging. It was the kind of atmosphere in which Hofmeyr, without the aid of alcohol, could more than hold his own. The bolder spirits brought out the skeletons from his cupboard, but it was like playing chess with a master, for he knew all their names and their years and their skeletons also.

Students laughed and cheered, and Hofmeyr smiled and giggled, especially when the thrusts went home. Some remembered a night at the old Empire, where a travelling revue company added local jokes for a largely university audience. 'Who do you think you are, anyway?' asked one comedian of another, 'The Principal Boy?' 'No,' replied the other with immense dignity, 'I'm the Boy Principal!' Then the joking was over, and the ex-Principal-become-Chancellor turned from the gay to the serious, and for the space of twenty minutes held these gay roisterers in the hollow of his hand.

The day after Hofmeyr spoke in Johannesburg, Hitler marched into Czechoslovakia, six months after he had assured Chamberlain that once the Czechs cleared out of the Sudetenland, he would have no further territorial claims to make in Europe. If Hofmeyr had ever had doubts about South Africa's duty in time of war, he had them no longer. Nazism he had always hated, but now he was prepared to resist it by force.

The Czechoslovakian crisis cast a heavy shadow over Parliament. It was not only the disaster that faced Europe, but that which might face South Africa, that was in all minds. And of course the crisis which faced the United Party. The anxiety of United Party members was in no degree lessened when on 18 April they lost the parliamentary seat of Paarl to the Purified Nationalists. The Malanites were jubilant; to them Czechoslovakia was a faraway country, and would certainly cause no crisis in their own party. But if it led to war, it would rend the United Party from top to bottom.

It was Hofmeyr in the Budget debate who shattered the false silence. Press-men said that he held the House spellbound. After declaring that South Africa had rightly supported Mr Chamberlain, he said:

'Today the policy of appeasement lies a shattered wreck. It was launched on the tide of credulity, it has foundered on the rocks of a base betrayal of solemn assurances.

'Peace by appeasement today is a policy of futility—a policy of negation. I believe that the peace of the world can still be secured, but it can be secured only if the democratic nations band themselves together to resist, by whatever means may be necessary, the onslaught of authoritarianism.'

It had so far been the Government's policy to declare that if there were war, South Africa would not automatically be involved in it; Parliament would decide. But now Hofmeyr was saying that the issue was clear and that the Government ought to decide now. He was highlighting the age-old dilemma of the peaceful, who in the interests of peace will not prepare, even though the warlike are taking up their arms.

When Hofmeyr had finished speaking, he was greeted by a burst of cheers, from the Stallardites and the Smuts wing of the United Party. Of the Hertzog wing some were troubled; they understood the danger of Hitler, but they understood also the danger of going to war at the side of Britain, for the second time in only twenty-five years. And there was now a new danger, for Britain and France had guaranteed the integrity of Poland. As for the rest of the Hertzogites, and the Malanites, their view was simple; Poland had nothing to do with them.

Hofmeyr wrote interestingly to Underhill about the position of Hertzog himself:

'If war had come last September he would undoubtedly have insisted on South Africa remaining neutral, at least for a time. But since then his eyes have been opened . . . to the aggressive nature of Hitler's designs. Today he would certainly not want to remain neutral *in any event*—his attitude would depend on the nature of the circumstances which brought the war about—but he has made it quite clear during this last week that if South West Africa is involved, he will be in the war, boots and all.'

Hofmeyr was writing about Hertzog as though the Prime Minister were facing a practical problem in a rational way. Hofmeyr, on this occasion at least, was not aware of the deep passions that moved the Prime Minister, especially that deep passion for independence, which meant more to him than all the problems of Europe and the Commonwealth.

While in university circles Hofmeyr was calling for a defence of democracy, and in political circles was saying that all democratic nations must stand together, he was saying in religious circles that man himself must be renewed, or his society would fall to pieces. The example of Hitler, who was inspiring millions of Germans with fanatical love of their fatherland, and filling them with a sense of purpose, made many believers in democracy feel ashamed, not of democracy, but of themselves. Things that democrats talked about, but which never got done, began to weigh upon democratic consciences—the miserable wages of Africans, the tensions between Afrikaans- and English-speaking people, the terrible slums of Johannesburg.

He spoke too a great deal about other things, the danger of war, and the challenge of Hitler to all that constituted Christian civilisation, and the moves being made outside Parliament, notably by some professors at Stellenbosch, to bring all Afrikaners together, and to achieve that *hereniging* of true souls that had eluded Afrikanerdom in 1933, when Hertzog, misguidedly they said, had embarked on that disastrous *vereniging* with Smuts and his imperialist followers. There was emotional support for such an appeal, for Afrikaner soul was calling to Afrikaner soul after the Voortrekker celebrations. Hofmeyr wrote that the Nationalist Party was a present danger.

'The danger is not so much in the future. As a matter of electoral responsibilities the chances of the Nationalist Party as such ever having a majority of seats in Parliament are infinitesimal . . .

'The real danger is in the present—it is in the cries the Nationalist Party is raising, the doctrines it is preaching, the spirit it is engendering. Those are the things that should be contested by all who have at heart the peace, the stability, and the ultimate welfare of South Africa.'

In the middle of 1939 the new Ossewabrandwag, the Ox-wagon Watch, caused further anxiety. It found alarming support from Afrikaners who hated Smuts, despised Hertzog, and watched Malan critically. It spread to the Transvaal, and then became, in the words of Eric Walker, the eminent historian, 'the most influential Afrikaner popular movement since the Great Trek itself'.

Times were indeed calamitous. No one had any hope that war could be averted. France and Britain, in spite of their guarantees, had accepted Hitler's seizure of Bohemia and Moravia, so who could expect that Hitler would take seriously their guarantee to Poland? British and French attempts to make a pact with Russia came to nothing.

Times were not good in South Africa either. If Hitler invaded Poland, and it were Britain and France who first declared war, then Hertzog would be firm in his neutrality. If Smuts opposed him, the United Party would be torn in two, and the great experiment of fusion would come to an end. But worse than that, white South Africa would be torn in two also, and all the old hatred between Boer and Briton would be reborn, and all the work of Botha, Smuts, and Hertzog be undone.

On 22 August 1939 Stalin loosed his bombshell on the world. He had signed a non-aggression pact with Hitler. Chamberlain wrote immediately to Hitler warning him that Britain would stand by her pledge to Poland.

In South Africa, owing to an extraordinary oversight, Parliament had to be re-summoned to extend for a short while the life of the Senate, which would otherwise have ended on 5 September. On 1 September, while members were travelling from all parts of the Union to Cape Town, Hitler marched into Poland. On Saturday, 2 September, the Prime Minister, on a demand of Dr Malan, promised the House to make a statement on the situation on Monday, 4 September.

No sooner had the House adjourned than Pirow went to the Prime Minister and told him that Smuts would depart from the neutrality agreement of 1938, and, what was more serious, that Louis Esselen had already organised a majority for war. Hertzog immediately called a Cabinet meeting for the Saturday afternoon at Groote Schuur. He said to Pirow, '*Amice*, it will now become clear whether our unity is sham or real.' Pirow wrote, 'I pressed his hand and left his office.'

Just as the Cabinet meeting was about to begin, Hertzog received from Dr Malan a letter pledging the support of the Nationalist Party for any neutrality motion. Hertzog announced to the Cabinet his decision for neutrality, and said, 'I take it we stand by the policy of neutrality so clearly laid down a year ago.' Smuts announced that, although he had supported the agreement of 1938, he was now convinced that Hitler threatened the peace and liberty of the world; therefore he would oppose any neutrality motion. The Cabinet then adjourned to await the fateful news that Sunday would bring when the Franco-British ultimatum expired; English-speaking South Africa waited for the morrow, tense and anxious, for the decision that would take their young men to war, and begin the grim struggle to prevent Hitler from conquering the world. No English-speaking South Africans were more tense and anxious than the Jews, whose future on the earth depended on the outcome of such a struggle. But Afrikaners were tense too, knowing that for the second time in twenty-five years Afrikaners would be asked to fight for the country that had conquered their two republics; some were willing, some were unequivocally opposed, some dreaded the *broedertwis* [strife between brothers]. Hardly concerned at all were the great majority of the population, the Indians, the Coloured people, the Africans, who watched with astonishment the tribal ferocity of the white rulers of the world, who in a few years could kill more people than all the wars of Africa had ever done.

On Sunday at 11 a.m. Britain declared war on Germany. That afternoon the Cabinet met again at Groote Schuur. According to Pirow, Hertzog began by reading a cable from Chamberlain saying, 'You can adopt one of three alternatives: you can declare war on Germany, you can break off diplomatic relations with her or you can remain neutral. I beg of you not to follow the third course.' But Hertzog was adamant on following the third course. It was clear that the Cabinet was irrevocably split, seven for Smuts and six for Hertzog.

Pirow added grave words: 'That Sunday afternoon's Cabinet meeting not only killed fusion; it also made it a certainty that when the political pendulum swung back again, as it was bound to do, Malan's extremists would take over and the English-speaking South Africans would become *bywoners* [tenant farmers] in their own country.'

Hertzog's biographer, in a compassionate passage, wrote that after the meeting there was in his hero almost a feeling of despair:

'He had hoped, with the zeal of a missionary, that the English-speaking people would now give a conclusive answer to the charge that they had a divided heart and put England's interests above those of their own country. He had now expected that gesture, as an answer . . . to Afrikaner doubters. It would have given racialism the death-blow . . . Had it been worth it, his hard struggle to convert the people? If General Smuts had only helped him! But it was all in vain, and with a feeling of many things in ruin about him, the grey-headed statesman stood at the end of a long road, full of sombre thoughts.'

The House was silent when Hertzog stood up to speak on the morning of 4 September. Europe had its drama, but there was drama enough here, at one of the decisive moments in South African history. Hertzog moved that South Africa remain neutral, except for Simonstown. His throat was troubling him and members leaned forward and cupped their hands behind their ears in order to hear.

He announced immediately that there was an unbridgeable division in the Cabinet, which in his opinion was beyond repair. His own views on neutrality were known; he had often made them known to the people. Not looking at Smuts at his side, Hertzog said, 'If there were those who differed from me, then I would have thought it was their duty, while there was time, while the people could still have been informed, to have spoken and to have stated their view.' He did not deserve to be left in the lurch at such a critical time, he said. If South Africa took part in this war, would any occasion ever arise when she would not need to join England in war? Why had England declared war on Germany? Because she had certain obligations towards Poland. But South Africa had no such obligations. Why had England not declared war on Russia, who had also marched into Poland?

He declared that the issue was greater than one of declaring war or protecting property or persons; it was an issue of a national independence that ought to be maintained and exercised in comprehensible ways. No one would reproach England for declaring war without consultation; South Africa was in the same position, it could act without consultation, and it was its duty to do so.

There were observers, Blackwell and Reitz amongst them, who thought that Hertzog might have won the day if he had confined himself to pleading for neutrality stemming from independence, or if he had pleaded for the continuance of fusion, which in his eyes meant more for the peace of South Africa than any righteous anger about Poland. But he did not. He embarked on a defence of Hitler and his invasions and blamed it all on the Treaty of Versailles. He said he could understand the humiliation and the feeling of the German people. 'I know, for I have been through the same mill . . . I know what it is to be driven by humiliation to a point where one says, "Let happen what will, let everything be subject to the removal of that humiliation which is inflicted on my people day after day. I will not endure it, I shall rather die than let it continue." ' If South Africa took part in the war, he declared, that would be the end of her membership of the Commonwealth of Nations.

Smuts rose to follow Hertzog, and declared that whatever could have been said for Hitler, could be said no more after his rape of Czechoslovakia. It was not a problem of Poland. Hitler would next demand South West Africa. He was out for one thing and one thing only, the domination of the world. He moved that South Africa sever relations with Germany.

About nine o'clock that evening the debate came to an end. All were aware of the grave cleavage in the House, those supporting Hertzog being overwhelmingly Afrikaans-speaking, and those supporting Smuts about two-thirds English-speaking. When the count was taken, Smuts had triumphed by 80 votes to 67.

Hertzog then went to Sir Patrick Duncan and asked that Parliament should be dissolved and the issue be put at a general election. Duncan had considered well the dangers both of agreeing and of refusing. He refused, and Hertzog resigned as Prime Minister. Duncan then called on Smuts to form a new Ministry.

Anti-war Afrikanerdom was dumbfounded. The man who had led them for fifteen years was gone, and in his place was the Imperialist Smuts, who on 6 September severed relations with Germany. Smuts formed a new Cabinet. Heavy tasks lay ahead. Smuts himself would be here, there, and everywhere, Britain, France, America, North Africa and the Middle East. And who would look after things at home, and look after them well, and work without ceasing? Smuts sent for Hofmeyr.

And Hofmeyr, as it were, came running.

He came running, not to war, but to the man from whom he had been separated, who now amidst the anger and hatred of many, the Nationalists and the Hertzogites, the Blackshirts and the Greyshirts, the secret Broederbond, and the openly defiant Ossewabrandwag, moved swiftly and confidently to take all affairs into his hands. Six and a half years of acquiescence had fallen away, revealing Smuts at the age of 69 a man keen and vital as he had ever been. Great events were about him and he marched with them as with his equals. He wasted no time on speculation and anxieties about what outraged Afrikanerdom would do, and whether it would win the next elections and make a separate peace. He went ahead with his plans.

His name was on all men's lips, even those who hated him. Even some of his bitterest enemies felt some odd perverse pride that he was an Afrikaner, and famous throughout the world. One could hate a man and say that he counted for nothing, but one did not say that of Smuts. Not even his other most bitter opponents, the communists, ever underrated him.

At first it seemed that Smuts might have to face serious internal disorders. On 4 and 5 September rioting pro-war crowds, seeking to damage buildings owned and occupied by Germans, were batoned and tear-gassed by the police, many of whom were pro-Hertzog and pro-Malan. A rumour swept the country that all white men would be conscripted, and many an Afrikaner announced openly that he would rather be shot than fight. It was necessary for Smuts to deny the rumour, and the impression grew that South Africa, though she had declared war, would in fact adopt what was called a 'passive belligerency'. The Ossewabrandwag grew stronger and stronger. There were reports of night drilling and no one doubted that the Brandwag was meant to be Afrikanerdom's counter to Smuts's armies. The gravity of the situation was made clearer, and the blood of many a person made to run cold, when insurance companies advised insurers that their policies did not cover the contingency of civil war.

Hertzog had a triumphal journey home from Parliament. At every station and wayside halt, by day and night, 'true Afrikaners' waited to pay him homage. He and Malan had become the heroes of 'true Afrikanerdom.' The *vereniging* of parties was done with, the *hereniging* of souls was there. On 9 September a great crowd of people, inflamed with South Africa's second kind of patriotic emotion, gathered in Pretoria to give Hertzog their support, on the site of the Monument beginning to rise above the ridge. On 12 September the head committee of the United Party of the Transvaal gave Hertzog their support by 26 votes to 16. Both Hertzog and Malan called on Smuts to resign, and to ask for a mandate from the country.

In the midst of it all Smuts laid plans for waging a war, at least on the continent of Africa. Others might think of 'passive belligerency', but not he. He took the dangerous step of calling in all arms, on the grounds that the army needed them; it was expected that the farmers would refuse, for the Boer and his rifle are inseparables, but they obeyed. He received surprising support from rural districts in the Transvaal, and his majority climbed from 13 to 18; he also found good support for his policy among the senior officers of the Union Defence Force.

For a short while there was a painful wrangle between the old Prime Minister and the new. Hertzog declared that Smuts had deceived him by concealing his change of attitude over neutrality, and Smuts declared that Hertzog had Malan's promise of support in his pocket and had concealed that also. Walker the historian wrote that the sufficient cause of the breakdown was an honest difference of opinion in a time of acute crisis between men who had never been easy partners, and with this judgement we may rest content.

So Smuts moved with certitude through these many dangers. In those days the whole of English-speaking South Africa, and probably a third of Afrikanerdom, were under his spell. And among these Afrikaners was Hofmeyr, who had once escaped from it, but at the age of 45, had fallen under it again. Yet in spite of that, because of electoral underloading and overloading agreed to in 1909, he could have lost a general election, even with a majority of votes.

It was only ten months earlier that Hofmeyr had told a public meeting in Durban that the national leaders were ageing. Yet after Smuts's victory when the writer said to him, 'Now Smuts will be able to write the great last chapter,' he had replied with something close to anger, 'Why the last chapter? Why not many chapters?' When white South Africa, to the surprise of many, swung nearer to Smuts as the war proceeded, Hofmeyr wrote, 'Smuts has certainly handled the situation so far with great skill and moderation—and his inspiration has been felt not only in South Africa but outside.'

A year later he wrote at great length to an Oxford friend: 'You wrote about the hour bringing forth the man, with reference to Churchill. Much the same might be said with reference to Smuts. This year has seen him at his very best—all his old qualities have again been in evidence, but with a mellow sagacity and tolerance which was sometimes lacking in the past.'

The breach of 1938 was healed. Mrs Hofmeyr, who believed that Smuts had left her son in the lurch over Fourie's appointment, and who had given Mrs Smuts a terrible hour, now forgave them, and she and her son resumed their almost weekly visits to Doornkloof. Hofmeyr forgot his opinion that Smuts had lost his moral force, and was fascinated by the wisdom and innocence of those clear blue eyes. After family gossip, he and the General would go into Smuts's library, and there they would discuss the war.

In those early days, when Hitler seemed always to have the initiative and the advantage, it was an inspiration to be near Smuts. When the outside world seemed so perilous, what comfort it was to have such a giant at home! His vitality was infectious, and Hofmeyr was infected by it. But there was something else in it too, something of the return of the son to his father. If 1939 proved anything about Hofmeyr, it proved this, that for him to break with Smuts, except on a clear and unambiguous matter of principle, was psychologically impossible. Hofmeyr flowered in 1939, not only because Smuts's vitality infected him, but because he was again working with, and working for, the man whose approval meant more than most other things in the world.

Smuts had a name as a philosopher, but he was really a lover of action. He had little time to ponder, in 1939 at least, over the nature of man and society. But Hofmeyr, who was now, as Smuts's lieutenant, a doer of work rather than an initiator of action, had time for thinking. After war was declared he spoke frequently, but his subject was peace rather than war. He told his audiences that without spiritual revolution, civilisation would perish, that men must find a moral equivalent for war that would harness the energy of people for the building of a worthy society. Like many others, Hofmeyr took seriously the threat of Nazism to human freedom; he spoke gravely of the consequences for South Africa if Hitler should win the war. At all costs Hitler must be defeated, but men and women must also examine themselves to find the causes of war.

Parliament met on 19 January 1940. For the first opening in sixteen years, Hertzog was not in the Prime Minister's seat. Smuts was there, and Hertzog faced him from the seat where Malan had sat for the last seven years. Hertzog was now the leader of the new group, which was still a coalition, not a fusion, and Malan sat next to him.

To Hertzog was given the honour of moving that the war with Germany should be brought to an end. Again he detailed the grievances that had tormented Germany into war, embarrassing some of his own colleagues. He declared that she had been ravaged and tortured since 1914 as no other people had ever been ravaged and tortured by Western civilisation, and she had taken over the Rhineland, Austria, Sudetenland, Czechoslovakia, and finally Poland, 'to repair the atrocities of Versailles'. But in fact Hertzog's lament was not for Hitler, but for himself and his life's work, and for the independence of his country, which a declaration of neutrality would in his eyes have established for ever.

Hofmeyr, with greater psychological insight than he usually showed, dealt with Hertzog's preoccupation with Versailles, and declared that when he thought of Versailles, he thought really of Vereeniging; when he spoke of Germany's humiliation, he was thinking of the humiliation of the republics. Hofmeyr said that was understandable, but no basis for a national policy. Then he deserted the psychological and returned to the logical. He said, 'Versailles no longer exists, Vereeniging no longer exists —those things have been effaced.'

The vote was taken in the small hours of 26 January. Smuts's amendment of Hertzog's motion to end the war was carried by 81 votes to 59, a majority of 22. It seemed as though Smuts had turned the corner. He addressed himself with even greater resolution to the successful prosecution of the war. His constraint had either vanished with political victory, or he was now able to overcome it, for on Hertzog's birthday he crossed the floor and sat for a while chatting to the former Prime Minister.

Hofmeyr took over the Ministry of Finance with a mixture of elation and trepidation. It was one of the few departments he had never controlled, and Havenga, having been there for fifteen years, had become an elder statesman, held in respect by all. Yet to use his own words, he had dreamed of taking it over.

His first big financial transaction was to put through with complete success a large conversion loan, converting £14,000,000 of 1940/50 stock at 5 per cent into a loan at 3¾ per cent, thus declaring his intention of keeping down interest rates, and safeguarding previous investments. But of course his biggest transaction was his budget, which he presented to the House on 28 February 1940. Since he had become Minister of Finance his dress had noticeably improved, almost as though he thought that Finance demanded more of him than Education. Photographs of him at this time, especially when compared with those of his administratorship, showed him as quietly and neatly dressed, and the *Forum* began to print a head-and-shoulders picture of a Minister who was clearly wearing white tie and tails. It was custom for the Minister of Finance to wear morning coat, striped trousers, and a white flower when presenting the budget. It was not only the morning coat and the striped trousers at which Hofmeyr boggled, but also the top hat. However, he decided to conform—after all, Havenga had done so—and to dodge the top hat by bringing the morning coat and trousers to the House in a suitcase, and changing there. He thought the morning coat undemocratic, but nevertheless did not like to break the tradition. Then so arrayed, he walked in to present his first budget, and had anyone laughed or gibed, he might have given his snort, showing that he was on guard, but no one did.

Hofmeyr's first budget was an outstanding success. He charmed all but the sourest by saying that his problems were made easier by the soundness of Havenga's policies. He startled a House used to an overall budget of some £40,000,000, by proposing to spend £79,000,000, of which £14,000,000 would go to a new War Expenses Account. He abolished the 30 per cent income tax rebate given by Havenga in good days. He instituted an Excess Profits Duty which commerce and industry were to hold against him throughout the war. Declaring that the gold-mining industry was still the keystone to South Africa's economic structure, he nevertheless changed the basis of mining taxation. When sterling had declined in relation to the dollar, the price of gold had risen, but Havenga had fixed the price to the producer and had taken the balance. Now Hofmeyr proposed to give the full price to the industry, so that it could continue to operate declining mines, and be able to meet the rising costs of mining. He reckoned that this relief would bring in an extra £3,500,000 to the Treasury; but in addition he proposed an additional tax, which he called 'the complement of the Excess Profits Duty'. This would bring in another £3,500,000.

Critics may not have liked Hofmeyr's budget proposals, they may have declared that he had no understanding of money, but it must be recorded that no critic in the House ever matched the Minister. It must be recorded that Hofmeyr's replies to the budget debates were amongst the most lucid, in some cases amongst the most devastating of all his speeches.

Havenga was essentially moderate in his criticism of the budget. To use Hofmeyrian language, he was possibly not entirely uninfluenced by Hofmeyr's praise. He certainly did not accuse Hofmeyr of parsimony; instead, discussing Hofmeyr's additional £250,000 for social services, he said, 'It will be interesting to note how the part of an enthusiastic social reformer is going to go hand in hand with that of Minister of Finance.' Havenga thought Hofmeyr had come down too lightly on the mines; he actually congratulated Hofmeyr on the country's financial position, but he wanted to know how long it would stand up to 'this mad war'.

Hofmeyr's reply to the debate was witty and confident. He pointed out that for the first time in ten years there had been no Opposition amendment to a budget. 'The budget therefore I would claim, stands unshaken and unshakable . . . there are two hypotheses which can be advanced for the failure of the Opposition. The one is the unassailability of the budget and the other is the incapacity of the Opposition. It would be unbecoming of me to choose between these two hypotheses. I prefer to leave the choice to my friends opposite.'

Was Hofmeyr parsimonious? He had just given a personal donation of £500 to the Bantu Welfare Trust. Botha had just got £30,000 from him for the University of Pretoria, and had offered to give Raikes tips on how to get money out of the Minister. E. G. Malherbe, who later became Principal of the University of Natal, was to declare after the war that Hofmeyr starved the Information Services. Raikes complained that the University of the Witwatersrand had no sooner begun to recover from Hofmeyr's principalship than he became Minister of Education; and when fortunately he had resigned from that, he unfortunately had become Minister of both Education and Finance twelve months afterwards.

Of course much of this acrimony had to do with other things besides Hofmeyr's frugality, but it was real acrimony nevertheless. Just as Hofmeyr was to many the champion of righteousness, so to others he was the apotheosis of meanness and pettiness. This has to be remembered lest a writer, honouring him for his virtues and inclined perhaps to minimise his faults, should neglect to record that a large number of men and women of substance regarded the faults as the man, and actively disliked him; only by straining their eyesight could they see any virtue in him at all. The writer must record also that Douglas Smit, the Secretary of Native Affairs from 1934 to 1945, declared that Hofmeyr was a very tower of strength in all matters to do with African development, both as Minister of Finance and as Minister of Education. It was Hofmeyr who each year increased the grants for African education, who quietly extended benefits to the African and Coloured and Indian blind, who encouraged the admission of the first African students to all-white medical schools, who found it intolerable that any social welfare scheme should apply to white people only. His critics argued that such benefits were always extended on a racially discriminatory scale, his supporters argued that otherwise there would have been no benefits at all. His critics argued that it was Hofmeyr who made it difficult in the war years to buy more land for African settlement under the 1936 settlement; even Edgar Brookes and Margaret Ballinger were amongst them. But it was argued that so many of the technical staff of the Native

Affairs Department were in the armed forces that it would have been impossible to arrange more than a very limited number of purchases.

Some of those who criticised him for demanding the impossible in politics went away angry because he would not give them the impossible in social welfare. Some went away angrier still because he dissected their arguments and showed them the flaws. Members of a medical deputation fell to arguing in his office as to whether they wanted a full six-year medical course for Africans or a shorter course for so-called medical aids. With something like anger he brought the interview to an end, thus dividing the deputation into two, those who thought he had been right, and those who thought he had been arrogantly rude. Some of these later would find the memory of their rebuff as vivid as ever after twenty years, and would remember with clarity the dirtiness of his clothes, the sanctimoniousness of his religion, the triviality of his resignations, the manufactured oratory of his addresses.

Hofmeyr did not suffer fools gladly during the early years of war. It would be no exaggeration to say that he was the brain and power behind the South African war machine, in all aspects except the military. Smuts did not hesitate to load him with work and he did not hesitate to accept it. Though Hofmeyr himself complained about the complacency and selfishness of white South Africans in those days, tens of thousands of them were working harder than they had ever worked in their lives. Yet it would have been hard to find one of them who demanded as much of himself as Hofmeyr. He tried however to play cricket regularly. He gave up the terrible game with the medicine ball, and took up squash. In 1940 he attained his highest cricketing honour. He was unanimously elected captain of the Parliamentary Cricket Team, and scored 38 runs against a side from the *HMS Shropshire*. It seemed to be his forte to lead teams of eleven.

After Parliament had risen, Hofmeyr attended a great banquet in the Johannesburg City Hall on Empire Day, 24 May, which was Smuts's seventieth birthday. Smuts wore the general's uniform that he had worn when he visited the Western Front in the war of 1914–18. He received an indescribable ovation, and made a fighting speech, attacking the fifth columnists who did not mind being tools of the Nazis. 'They dream of a republic and would welcome it even from the hands of Hitler, not stopping to think that he would betray them just as he had betrayed all other small countries who took his assurances and promises seriously.'

He reminded them of the determination of the allied peoples in Europe. 'Shall we their offspring in South Africa not prove worthy of the rock whence we are hewn? I have no fear, and in that faith as to the issue we shall push on with all our resources and perseverance to the end. For weal or woe, South Africa will be in this struggle to the full and to the end.'

Smuts's speech was given another tremendous ovation. Women wept and strong men felt like weeping. The thought in every mind was, 'Where would we be without Smuts!' Smuts liked ovations, he was neither embarrassed nor made constrained by them. He looked about him smiling, nodding at people whom he did not know, acknowledging their homage, looking the very picture of health and confidence.

Two days later Hofmeyr addressed a great crowd of 30,000 people in a solemn service at the Wanderers Ground, Johannesburg. He told them what was now always uppermost in his mind, of his concern that out of this cataclysm there should come something good for mankind. He said: 'Out of the present travail it is inevitable that a new world order will be born. We are starting on a great divide in human affairs. The issue is one between a great advance and a great setback for humanity.'

The situation in Europe could hardly have been worse at the time when Smuts and Hofmeyr were speaking. On 28 May the Belgian army surrendered, and the British armies were saved only by the miracle of Dunkirk. On 11 June Mussolini, reading the signs, declared war on Britain and France, and Paris fell on 14 June. The aged Marshal Pétain came to power, and sought an armistice. On 3 July the British, failing to get guarantees, sank the French fleet at Oran. So Britain stood all alone, with her armies virtually unarmed. On 19 July Hitler offered peace to Britain, but the offer was ignored. He then prepared to invade the island country, and to bring the war to a speedy and shattering end.

In South Africa the Opposition was now convinced that Afrikanerdom would win salvation through a Nazi victory. Hertzog demanded that Smuts sue for peace, and Malan urged the establishment of a republic and withdrawal from the Commonwealth as the only hope for Afrikanerdom. It was not uncommon for gentler Hertzogites to say that they did not want Britain to lose, but they wanted her to suffer even as Afrikanerdom had suffered. A Nationalist M.P. said in Parliament that he thought it right that the people of London should have their homes burned so that they could realise what Afrikaners suffered in the South African War. Many Malanites, however, wanted nothing less than Britain's total and humiliating defeat, even though it meant defeat of their own country.

In June 1940 when the Allied fortunes were low, a peace procession of white women, most of them wearing Voortrekker dress, marched from Church Square to the Union Buildings to present a petition bearing signatures to the Prime Minister. Smuts passed the job on to Hofmeyr, who received the leaders gallantly, offered them refreshments, and was thanked by them for the excellent police arrangements.

The Ossewabrandwag now claimed to be 200,000, even 400,000 strong, considerably more than Smuts had in the armed forces. As the fortunes of Britain waned, so did the Ossewabrandwag wax in numbers and courage, under a leadership which expressed the greatest contempt for democracy and party politics, was strongly influenced by Hitler, and believed in the authoritarian State. There seems little doubt that had Britain's fortunes still further declined, the Ossewabrandwag would have tried to seize power by violence; and police raids at their headquarters revealed evidence of widespread subversive activity.

Even the new Hertzog-Malan group had to consider the Ossewabrandwag as a serious rival. Therefore Nationalist politicians made intemperate speeches of the kind that today would be regarded as treasonable, and unhindered by Smuts held stop-the-war meetings throughout the country.

Through all these days Smuts moved with confidence. He called Parliament together for the second time in the year, so that Hofmeyr could present a supplementary budget, asking for another £33,000,000 for carrying on the war. That meant a total of nearly £128,000,000 for the year, of which £74,000,000 was expenditure on war. Hofmeyr increased taxation by £9,000,000, and raised the rest on loan account. He added a 20 per cent surcharge to income tax, and increased duties on petrol and tyres. He increased company tax, and taxes on alcohol and tobacco. The tax on gold mines he increased by another million pounds.

Being a Finance Minister in time of war was certainly a new kind of experience for Hofmeyr. He was now collecting and spending money on the grand scale. Five months after his supplementary budget he asked for an additional £14,000,000 on loan account, bringing expenditure under that head to £39,500,000 for the budgeting year, only £5,000,000 less than the entire war expenditure for 1914-18. Two months later, in his main budget, he asked for another £72,000,000 for Defence. There were two reasons for his recklessness. One was that he understood clearly what Hitler's victory would mean for the world. The other was that it was

Smuts who wanted the money, and when Smuts wanted money, he expected to get it. More than once during the war Hofmeyr was to have the experience of refusing money to some supplicant, and being later told by Smuts that the money was to be given.

On 29 August, with the Battle of Britain fiercely raging, Hertzog again moved that South Africa should immediately make peace with Germany and Italy. He declared that Britain had lost the war, and his speech hinted at rebellion. 'I warn this House . . . that if this sort of thing is allowed to go on much longer, if the abuse of the rights and liberties of the Afrikaner Nation is persisted in with impunity any longer, no force, no power, no authority from wherever it may be will be able to prevent the people of South Africa setting an example to those who are misgoverning her; that through all times it will reverberate throughout the history of Afrikanerdom.' He told the House that it was no longer England or France but Germany to which the nations of Europe looked and to whom they attached their hopes for the future.

Smuts's reply set his followers cheering. He said: 'We are not deserters, we are not "hands-uppers". We are not going, in the hour of danger when things are going against us, to turn about and run away . . . I ask my honourable friend to throw his memory back to the history of forty years ago when the same arguments were used as those which he is using today. Those arguments did not induce him or me to surrender. We carried on.'

Smuts's mastery was complete. Some of his followers urged him to take action against those whose speeches were calculated to goad and wound. They wanted him to declare martial law and suppress all opposition without mercy. But he would not. When asked why he took no steps, he said that his enemies were taking steps for him. That was true. The Malanites and the Hertzogites were both watching the Ossewabrandwag with apprehension. What is more, it was rumoured that the Malanites, after their joyous reunion with the Hertzogites, now planned to jettison the old Prime Minister. Towards the end of 1940, Pirow further complicated the political scene by launching his 'New Order', which he claimed to be based on the National Socialism of Portugal's Salazar. So Pirow made his final break with democracy.

Smuts now had 137,000 men under arms, most of them willing to go anywhere. More and more young Afrikaners decided to join the forces, tempering thus the anti-war passions of parents and sweethearts. Afrikanerdom was torn in two. There were cases of young Afrikaners in uniform being asked to keep away from churches, lest they affront the worshippers. For this, the dreaded *broedertwis*, Smuts got the blame.

At the outbreak of war, the cause for anxiety had been, not the loyalty of the Union Defence Force, but the loyalty of the South African police. In 1940, Smuts felt strong enough to forbid any policeman to belong to the Ossewabrandwag. Civil servants were forbidden to wear the Ossewabrandwag badge, and in defiance took to wearing the tops of mineral-water bottles. Angry and frustrated, the Nationalists began to announce the inevitable coming of a new republic, and threatened that it would deal drastically with those who had dragged South Africa into yet another European war, and who were prepared to pour out Afrikaner blood for the sake of a foreign country. Though Smuts was firmly in power, many listened to these threats with apprehension, not least the Jews, who were to be excluded from the enjoyment of civic rights. Because of their anger, Nationalists also uttered threats against the English language, which could be removed from the status of an official language by a two-thirds majority of both Houses sitting together.

Hertzog, despite his bitter disappointment in English-speaking South Africa, said publicly that he would have nothing to do with any campaign to diminish English rights. However ambiguously Hertzog had appeared to use the word 'Afrikanerdom' in 1912, there can be no doubt that in 1940 he meant by Afrikanerdom all white South Africans who gave their first loyalty to South Africa.

To the extreme anti-war factions Hertzog's tolerance seemed the greatest foolishness. They held public meetings demanding a republic with Afrikaans as the sole official language, and citizenship only for Afrikaans-speaking people. They rejected altogether Hertzog's long-established principle that a republic would be established only on 'the broad will of the people', pointing out that Smuts had declared war with a majority of 13.

The tragic end of Hertzog's leadership came on 6 November 1940, at the Free State Congress of the Volksparty at Bloemfontein. The Federal Council presented a Programme of Principles for the new Party, but Hertzog presented an alternative programme which stated specifically that English-speaking South Africans would enjoy political, language, and cultural equality. When his programme was rejected by an overwhelming majority, he walked out of the hall, followed by Havenga and other faithful friends. Hertzog's tragedy was not that he was rejected for defending the rights of the English-speaking. His tragedy was that Afrikanerdom was finished with him.

Hertzog's faithful followers formed the Afrikaner Party, of which Hertzog became honorary leader, but in fact his politcal career was finished. What he had done in 1912, full of fire and vigour, he could not do again in 1940. He retired to his farm, and on 11 December he and Havenga resigned from Parliament. A final blow was dealt them when Malan captured both their seats, defeating the candidates of the Afrikaner Party. After his resignation Hertzog emerged only fitfully and pathetically from obscurity. In October of 1941, strongly under the influence of Pirow, who visited him in his loneliness, he delared that National Socialism was the political doctrine for South Africa. On the twenty-first day of November 1942, he died just after he had said to the nurse, 'Sister, all will come right.'

So the leadership of Afrikanerdom passed finally into the hands of Daniel François Malan at the age of 68 years. By his side were Charles Robberts Swart who became M.P. for Winburg after N. J. van der Merwe's death, Theophilus Ebenhaezer Dönges who captured Fauresmith after Havenga's resignation, François Christian Erasmus who had stood by Malan at the time of fusion, Eric Louw the expert on foreign affairs, J. J. Fouche who captured the historic seat of Smithfield after Hertzog's resignation, and Johannes Gerhardus Strijdom the leader of the Transvaal. It was a powerful team, with one overriding purpose, and that was to see that the cause of Afrikaner Nationalism was triumphant, for thus only could Afrikanerdom itself survive.

Hofmeyr saw Hertzog go without showing anything but the most formal regret. Was that because Hertzog had disliked him, even to the point of wanting him expelled by the caucus? Perhaps so. But there was something else also, that quality which was a defect of which H. P. Cruse had written to him in his Oxford days, that he was too much inclined to reason and too little to feel. Hofmeyr was indeed unable to feel the tragedy of Hertzog's fall and loneliness. It was the tough Pirow who felt it more, but of course he was bound to Hertzog by filial affection. In Hofmeyr's younger days, when he had been so fond of lecturing on Rhodes, Kruger, and Onze Jan, he had declared that Rhodes was a tragic figure, who had used ignoble means to reach a majestic end, and had thereby been broken. That was no doubt true, but for one person who was moved by the tragedy of Rhodes there would have been a thousand to feel the downfall of Hertzog, the man who had built Afrikanerdom and had now been rejected by a new and tougher breed. For all Hertzog's headstrongness and petulance and hatred of being crossed, his tragedy was that of the downfall of generosity, not of power. Politically he committed a cardinal error; he allowed from time to time ideals such as magnanimity and tolerance to challenge the ideal of Afrikaner supremacy. That was the unforgivable sin.

Van der Brugge had said that Hofmeyr lacked *mousike*, that in a person which responds to music or poetry or painting or drama. It went further. He could not respond to the tragedy of another, whether Lear or Macbeth or Hertzog; that final identification he could not achieve. No one had ever seen him at a concert or a play lost and absorbed in what he was seeing and hearing. Was it that he had no feeling? Or was there some censor that would not allow any feeling of that kind to cross the threshold?

One is dealing here surely with a consequence of the strange childhood, with the consequence of being a small boy who talked to almost nobody but his mother, who blossomed late in the camps and clubs and in the presence of a few Balliol men, who first grappled with life at the university and was worsted in the encounter, who by great fortune was lifted up to a higher and safer eminence where he displayed genius in management and great skill in communicating by public address, and then finally took up a career which allowed him to go on managing superbly and communicating brilliantly by public address. His personal communications were rare, except with his mother, and those were domestic. His letters to his friends, except the earlier ones to Sarah Millin, were personal only in the most moderate sense; if they told any secrets about him, then they told them unintentionally. Thus, if he revealed himself, anyone who sought to know him would treasure these communications. The earlier letters to Sarah Millin were such, revealing the diffidence guessed at by some, unknown to most. When he said, 'If my mother died, I should like to marry,' that was such a communication. When he discussed a woman's figure with Dames, that was another. Equally informative was his remark —though it was made deliberately—'Smuts looked after the sheep but I looked after the pigs.'

The writer must record one of these communications, which when heard seemed unbelievable. In May of 1940 the first of Smuts's troops left for Kenya to drive the Italians out of Africa. Smuts made them one of his own inimitable speeches, addressing them as a father would address his sons. On the platform with him was his indispensable lieutenant, the Minister of Finance. Hofmeyr related the account of this solemn and exciting occasion to the writer, for it made a deep impression on him.

Then he added the unbelievable remark, 'You know Smuts isn't much taller than I am.'

Of anything in his whole life which could be called personal, it was his relationships with his mother and with Smuts that were the most important, although his mother would never agree that that was so. She reacted angrily to the suggestion that she and Smuts were the two dominant figures in her son's life. In spite of the reconciliation beween the two families, she continued to resent Smuts's sovereignty over so much of her son's loyalty and time and energy. If one questioned Hofmeyr about Reitz, Fourie, or any other of his associates, he would answer with the greatest dispassionateness. If questioned about Hertzog and Duncan he might find it difficult to be generous, but he would show no great emotion. To listen to him was like watching a man pulling out the appropriate drawers of his filing cabinet and reading out dispassionate dossiers. But when the name of Smuts was mentioned, though he preserved his outward impassivity, Hofmeyr was like a man on guard. He was no longer standing in front of a pigeon-hole, but in front of the door of his own house, which if opened would reveal, not Smuts's secrets, but his own. There was no other person in the world, except his mother, whose life was so much entangled with his own. There was no other name in the world, except perhaps one of those of the Stibbe episode, the sound of which would bring the whole man to attention. And though his mother denied it vehemently, it was true, so true that Hofmeyr was conscious of the man standing by him taking the salute of his men going 'up north', and was conscious, after having known the man for twenty years, that he was taller than himself, but not so much.

Before the session opened, there were ugly incidents in Johannesburg. Soldiers who volunteered for service anywhere in Africa now wore distinguishing orange flashes on their shoulders. The police authorities, with doubtful wisdom, introduced orange flashes into the police force, and one could now tell at once which policemen were for Smuts and which were not. Furthermore, if a civilian wore a beard, it could be assumed that he was almost certainly an anti-war Afrikaner. On 31 January of 1941 soldiers and civilians fought for two hours outside the Johannesburg City Hall because it was believed that a sailor in uniform had been refused admission to a concert organised by the Afrikaans Language and Culture Society. Naturally the police intervened, and this mixed force, some wearing the orange tabs and some not, had to go through the ordeal of keeping pro-Smuts soldiers and anti-Smuts civilians away from one another. The police used batons and tear gas, but before order was restored 20 men, mostly soldiers, had to be taken to hospital.

On the next evening soldiers tried to wreck the gymnasium of a general in the Ossewabrandwag. They were again held back by the police, and they jeered at those not wearing the orange tabs. Later the buildings of the anti-war newspapers, *Die Transvaler* and *Die Vaderland*, were damaged. Military police tried to calm the soldiers by calling on them not to let General Smuts down. The police again used batons and tear gas, and 140 men, mainly soldiers, were taken to hospital. Down in Cape Town Smuts promised an inquiry, after denying that this conduct was typical of his soldiers. Nevertheless he shortly after issued a National Security Code, which prescribed severe penalties against those possessing explosives, assaulting policemen, interfering violently with lawful gatherings, circulating inflammatory pamphlets and taking part in unauthorised drilling and military exercises.

Malan now returned to his seat as Leader of the Opposition, and moved a vote of no confidence in Smuts and the Government. He was at a psychological disadvantage, for not long before E. A. Conroy and nine other M.P.s had left him to form the Afrikaner Party. Malan was also having trouble in the Transvaal, where Pirow, although still a member of the Nationalist Party, felt it necessary to propagate his views through the New Order, and was enjoying considerable support. That was no doubt why Malan used the Ossewabrandwag as a weapon with which to frighten Smuts; it had a discipline, he declared, far superior to that of Smuts's army. 'I say you must leave the Ossewabrandwag alone. The fact that the Ossewabrandwag has a membership between 300,000 and 400,000 shows the place it has in the hearts of the people.' But Smuts showed no fear of this Ox-Wagon Watch. On the contrary he declared that it was Malan who needed to fear it. As for Malan's motion of no confidence, he ridiculed it; what alternative could Malan offer to the present Government?

Hofmeyr moved an amendment proposing full confidence. His speech was full of vigour. He challenged Malan to disown Pirow and his National Socialism. Pirow had declared in the House that if Afrikanerdom ever got the reins of power in its hands, it would never relinquish them. Hofmeyr said, amidst uproar, that these words were a declaration of war on the parliamentary system. He pointed out the irony that Pirow was using democratic freedom to fight democracy, while the Government was fighting to maintain the very system which gave him freedom to attack it. Hofmeyr warned the House that some of Malan's followers were already preaching 'one flag, one language, one people'.

Hofmeyr was at this time enjoying unusual popularity. After Smuts, no one could demolish the Opposition as he could, and make the fighting speeches that people wanted to hear. Racial legislation had receded into the background, and Hofmeyr found himself in the van of a popular cause. Reitz was in fact the second man of the Cabinet, but no one took him seriously as an administrator. Colin Steyn was considered a possible successor, but at no time did he ever set himself up as a rival to Hofmeyr.

Hofmeyr was working hard, preparing for his budget. He wrote, 'I live strenuous and laborious days, but keep very fit and seem to come through my troubles successfully.' Almost as he wrote these words, they ceased to be true. In February he was troubled by severe headaches, and fainted once for a short time, a kind of black-out. His blood pressure was found to be high, with a systolic index of 210 and a diastolic index of 120. His pulse rate was high at 120. His doctor ordered him treatment and a special diet; of the diet, Hofmeyr said to him, 'You will have to tell my mother about that.' Otherwise his mother was to be told nothing, only that he was not as well as he should be.

He seemed to be at the very height of his powers, but in fact he was not. Before the end of the session he experienced more black-outs. At a Rotary luncheon in Cape Town he had an unusual, perhaps unprecedented, experience. He was in the full flow of his speech, when he stopped to make a quotation and then could not remember it. Those who knew well his prodigious powers of memory, sat disturbed and silent while he tried to recall the quotation. He then gave it up and proceeded with his speech, but now his hearers, who had so often admired his effortlessness, felt that he was feeling his way forward, like a veteran acrobat who had nearly made his first mistake on the flying trapeze. Towards the end of the session the long hours of Parliament became a burden to him, and he returned with relief to Pretoria, where as a rule he could finish his work within normal office hours.

To King, his old friend of the Oxford days, he wrote, 'I am none the worse for a strenuous year.'

But of course it was not true.

Chapter 11

War-time Minister 1

THE internal position was growing more favourable for Smuts when Parliament assembled on 12 January 1942. The relations between Pirow and Malan, and especially between Pirow and Malan's lieutenants, including Dr Verwoerd, editor of *Die Transvaler,* had reached breaking point. Even the small Afrikaner Party was made to look foolish when Havenga had to repudiate Hertzog's statement that National Socialism was close to 'the spiritual and religious outlook of the Afrikaner nation'. One of the Party's members announced that he would in future support the Government on the war issue. But most favourable of all for Smuts was the fact that the two most powerful Afrikaner organisations, Malan's Nationalist Party and van Rensburg's Ossewabrandwag, were now completely estranged. If Smuts had needed encouragement to be firm with the Ossewabrandwag, he would have found it in Malan's declaration that it was an 'unnational organisation'. Smuts announced the death penalty for saboteurs, purged the police force, and interned more of his opponents. The Opposition was weakened further when 16 members of Parliament followed Pirow out of the Nationalist Party into the New Order Party, which soon received the support of van Rensburg and the Ossewabrandwag. Pirow made it clear that the New Order Group, though in Parliament, was not of Parliament. Anti-war Afrikanerdom was in chaos, and Smuts faced the 1942 session with confidence.

Malan, instead of moving a vote of no confidence, moved that South Africa become a republic, separate from British Crown and Empire, independent of any foreign power, established in accordance with its own national character, free of the defects of British liberal democracy, Christian-national in deed and character, guaranteeing equal language and cultural rights for both sections of the white population, designed to preserve white civilisation, offering protection against capitalist exploitation and hostile and unnational elements.

Smuts was in fighting mood, and stoutly championed the cause of the

Commonwealth. He taunted Eric Louw, the foreign affairs expert of the Malanites, because he had predicted that America would not enter the war. America had tried to remain neutral and the result was Pearl Harbor. He moved that South Africa declare war on Japan, Rumania, and Finland. His motion also condemned the raising of fundamental constitutional issues at such a time.

Hofmeyr seconded Smuts's amendment. He declared that by talking of a Christian republic and at the same time preaching doctrines of racial intolerance and colour prejudice and anti-Semitism, the Nationalists were guilty of 'rank hypocrisy'. He invited the House to look at the Opposition. 'Think of them two years ago, how proud and confident they were . . . And today they sit like all Gaul—divided into three parts.' Hofmeyr concluded by declaring there would have to be a new world organisation, less embracing but more cohesive than the League of Nations, having a closer organic unity, which could be achieved only by 'the pooling to some extent of sovereignty as a means of protection against the common danger of aggression'.

J. G. Strijdom, leader of the Transvaal Nationalists, was given the task of replying to Hofmeyr. He did so with vigour. Hofmeyr was to him one of the greatest threats to Afrikanerdom, because of his lack of devotion to Afrikaner things, his 'English' mind, his espousal of dangerous ideals of racial equality that if realised would destroy white civilisation in Africa. At the end of his speech, if Strijdom had shut his eyes, he could have imagined Hofmeyr was 'speaking from the pulpit of some Wesleyan church'. There he stood with his arms around Satan's neck—Satan being represented by Josef Stalin—there he joined hands with the only Godless and God-renouncing nation in the world, the Communists of Russia. Hofmeyr, the lay preacher, the fighter for Christianity! Talk of hypocrisy! Strijdom wanted to know whether Hofmeyr would give the same franchise as he himself enjoyed to the coloured people and the Indians? He wanted to know whether, if Britain had been conquered by Germany and given dominion status, she would have been proud of it.

Strijdom quoted passages from Hofmeyr's address to the Eclectic Club in 1917, which were the basis of N.K.R.'s article on the Republican Movement, in which article the annexation of the diamond fields was called a robbery, the annexation of the Transvaal was condemned, in which the reader was reminded that 26,000 women and children had died in the concentration camps, and was advised to go and contemplate the sombre Vrouemonument in Bloemfontein, which commemorated the grief of a whole nation. He said, 'The author of this article is nobody but Jan Hofmeyr, the present Minister of Finance.' Strijdom then quoted the sentence, 'It is only through Republicanism that you can hope to abolish racialism and create a united nation.' Strijdom omitted to state, as others had omitted before him, that Hofmeyr was here quoting from H. H. Moll, the man who, like Strijdom, had begun by admiring Hofmeyr and ended by despising him. Strijdom concluded his speech by saying, 'England's end is approaching, and as surely as England's end is approaching, so surely will the Republic of South Africa arise.'

Walter Madeley defended Hofmeyr. He said that Strijdom took no account of Hofmeyr's progress in the direction of a broader conception of a human relationship. It seems certain that Madeley must have consulted Hofmeyr before stating that his view had changed for the better. If that were so, then Hofmeyr had finally buried the ghost of N.K.R. It seems reasonable to believe that in later years his republican article embarrassed him and this was not so much because of its republican views, but because it revealed a resentment that should not reside in anyone who aspired to be noble.

Malan's motion was defeated by 90 votes to 48. Pirow would not stay in the House to vote for it. Malan suffered another reverse when Professor L. J. du Plessis, personal friend of both Malan and Verwoerd, gave his support to the Pirow–van Rensburg alliance. The fortunes of 'true Afrikanerdom' were at a low ebb. Nationalist parents of Smuts's soldiers, sick and tired of bickering, and solicitous for their sons, began to give more support to the war effort. Many people began to think—the *Forum* amongst them—that the Smuts propaganda machine should cease ranting against Malan, and turn its attention to the Pirow–van Rensburg axis, to which Pirow was now seeking a third recruit, the failing Hertzog, whose grasp on reality was fast loosening.

So strong was Smuts's position, and so strong was South Africa's economy, that Hofmeyr budgeted for a new record total expenditure of £139,000,000, and a new record expenditure on Defence of £80,000,000.

Hofmeyr's 1942 budget was delivered in the prevailing atmosphere of idealism. In August of 1941 Roosevelt and Churchill had signed the famous Atlantic Charter, which promised the world freedom from war, want, tyranny, and fear. Smuts himself had declared that there must be a new world order, and that in South Africa itself there must be no more poor-whiteism, no more unemployment, no more waste of human and material resources. He had set up the Social and Economic Council to plan for a national economy offering security and well-being for all. He was immensely proud of the camaraderie that had developed in the Army up north, between English- and Afrikaans-speaking soldiers, and between white and non-white soldiers. Smuts declared that there must be a dropping of the old racial ideas, 'which had brought nothing but bitterness and strife'. When Malan justified Japan's search for *lebensraum,* Smuts declared that if she sought it in South Africa, he would 'see to it that every native and coloured man, who can be armed, will be armed'. These were strong words, for although there were precedents for the arming of black men, there was an intense fear of it as well, especially on the platteland. Malan declared, 'If this is the price South Africa must pay to the Empire . . . then rather let the Empire fall.'

Smuts publicised his views by declaring to a public meeting in the Cape Town City Hall that segregation had fallen on evil days. 'How can it be otherwise? The whole trend both in this country and the African continent has been in the opposite direction, towards closer contacts between the various sections. Isolation has gone. The old isolations of South Africa have gone, and gone for ever.'

Over against segregation Smuts set the policy of trusteeship, which existed for the benefit, not of the trustee, but of the ward. This was one of the few occasions on which Smuts was obviously indebted to Hofmeyr in his thinking. But here also was revealed a striking difference between the two men, for while Smuts would paint trusteeship in glowing colours, emphasising both its moral beauty and its indeterminate duration, Hofmeyr always asked the difficult question, 'What happens when the ward grows up?'

Smuts spoke of the neglect of African housing and the lowness of African wages. 'We . . . ought to give more attention to these matters and extend help and sympathy far more than we do. Even if we don't do that in the interests of the native we shall have to do it in our own interests, because if we don't, there will be something to pay.' He declared that there was 'the best feeling between white and black in the new big army we have in the north'. Men must give up old controversies, and build a new South Africa to a new pattern, 'a pattern unlike the pattern of any other continent but something worth having; a pattern which might be a lesson to the rest of the world'.

Smuts sat down amidst prolonged applause, pleased as always when people liked what he said. It was a great speech, even if not quite real.

Strangely enough, or perhaps not so strangely, Hofmeyr was critical of the current idealism, not because of the things it believed in, but because it did not consider seriously enough the question of ways and means. This was a duty he as Minister of Finance could not evade. And the idealists, the educators, social reformers, new-worlders, were just as critical of him. Instead of showing enthusiasm, he would ask, where is the money?

Therefore he moved cautiously, confirming in their opinion those who thought that caution and parsimony were amongst his most striking characteristics. However, he pleased many by increasing the pensions vote by £229,000. This was largely for the dependants of killed or disabled soldiers, who were treated with a generosity unknown in 1914–18, though still on the racially discriminatory scale which is a part of white South African tradition, and is justified, by those who think in racial categories, on the grounds that white people, African people, coloured people, Indian people, all have different standards of living. He also revised the maintenance grants under the Children's Act known as mothers' pensions, these improvements to be applied to non-white as well as white persons. As has been said before, Hofmeyr never altered the discriminatory basis of such grants and pensions; what he did do was to narrow the gap between the highest and the lowest, and to make all such provisions applicable to all people.

He did something else. He was weighed down by the poverty of African school buildings, the low scales for African teachers, the miserably low grant made for each African pupil, and the great numbers (over 50 per cent) of African children who were not in school at all. In 1940 he had increased the percentage of general tax paid to the provinces for African education from 60 to 66⅔ per cent. Now in 1942 he increased it to 83⅓ per cent, which meant an increase of £232,000. The whole grant of £1,361,000 was still a miserable one when compared with the amount spent on white education, £9,000,000, but Hofmeyr was of the opinion—and it is hard to know who could have judged better than he—that it was all he could dare to do. Smuts might call for new ideas, but even he had to bow to the general fear among white people, of too much education for African children.

On 21 June 1942, the South African army suffered an almost irreparable loss, when two out of the three brigade groups of its 2nd Division, and two battalions and four batteries of the 1st Division, were lost in the fall of Tobruk. Smuts immediately set himself to replace the losses and set Hofmeyr to find the money. The Allies suffered a severe defeat in Libya, and the Battle of the Atlantic was going badly. Nor was the home front free from anxiety. The Nationalists were elated by the fall of Tobruk, and did well in several provincial by-elections. Malan was slowly re-establishing himself as the leader of 'true Afrikanerdom'. If Hitler succeeded in capturing Stalingrad, it would be another victory for the Nationalists. It was under these circumstances that Reitz said angrily that the Government would not resign even if it lost the 1943 election. Walker the historian wrote that as a result of this indiscretion Reitz had to see Hofmeyr, his junior, become Acting Prime Minister and Minister of External Affairs, on the next occasion that Smuts flew to London.

The great responsibility now lay upon Hofmeyr for the peace and safety of his country. It was sometimes said, most often by his mother, that Smuts used her son as one uses a tool, and had no real appreciation of his generosity and loyalty. This is a statement that must later again be considered, but meanwhile one can note what Smuts wrote to him from Cairo. After giving Hofmeyr good news from North Africa, and a cheering account of the Russian situation, he turned to topics of home. 'I was so sorry to hear that Conroy is also on the sick list, and for the same reason as Deneys. I hope you will pull through even with this decimated team. It is all bad luck with three Ministers out of action, and so much to do. It may mean that I shall have to do my best to return as soon as I can.' Smuts concluded his letter, 'My love to you and Borrie, and my best wishes for you in your heavy burdens.'

Hofmeyr's burdens were indeed heavy. In mid-November of that year 1942, he suffered 'a touch of kidney trouble'. He passed a stone, and went through a week of considerable pain. Even a month later he wrote that he found his work 'still much of a burden'. But he was cheered by Rommel's defeat at El Alamein in November, by the capture of 9,000 prisoners, and the certainty that Africa would soon be freed of German and Italian troops. The Russians were beginning a massive counter-offensive, and demonstrating military genius second to that of none. Nevertheless Hofmeyr was glad to see Smuts return, and to be relieved of some of his work. No sooner had he been relieved than he went on a week of travel, to Standerton, Pietermaritzburg, and Durban, at each of which places he was the guest of honour at important functions. He looked forward to a quiet Christmas before leaving for Cape Town early in the New Year. To sit on the *stoep* and rest was now his greatest joy.

His friends did not know the true state of his health. Hofmeyr was not one to talk about it. When he was in pain he concealed it, so that often it was only his mother and his private secretary who knew it. Inquiries as to his health he answered, not rudely, but with a brevity that indicated clearly that he did not wish to discuss the matter. So it was that his friends, used to his reservedness, were conscious of a further withdrawal, which was to continue throughout the years of the war. To some of his associates this was reprehensible. He was clearly marked out as Smuts's successor, and yet here he was shutting himself off from people, satisfied with the company of the cats and his mother and the inner circle of his mother's tea-table. Passers-by in Schoeman Street, who saw the Minister sitting quietly on his *stoep,* might have supposed that he was thinking great and deep thoughts, whereas he was in fact doing nothing of the sort. He was resting. He was a desperately busy man, who would the following day have to work without ceasing; and now, if Smuts were away, this work would be not mere routine, but would involve the making of important decisions. When Smuts was away, not even Sunday was safe. Always somewhat withdrawn by nature, he withdrew yet more, in order to resist further inroads on his dwindling stock of time and privacy, which he could use for talking to his mother, playing with the cats, listening to the radio and accompanying the hymns, and writing to his friends about South African politics, the war, and the glories of an English river; and, of course, if he were lucky—and he tried to court such luck—a game of cricket on a Saturday afternoon with simple honest friends who knew that the Minister did not come to cricket for heavy conversations.

There seemed little doubt but that Smuts would strengthen his position still further at a general election. The Allies were beginning to win the Battle of the Atlantic, and the Russians, having captured 300,000 Germans around Stalingrad, were continuing their massive offensive, causing many to wonder whether they would reach Germany before the Allies. The Japanese attack on Pearl Harbour was now seen as a colossal error of judgement. At home, though the Opposition was still in a chaotic state, Malan was strengthening his position. The seats of the Afrikaner Party would no doubt fall into his lap, and Pirow, by professing contempt for elections, had caused consternation amongst his followers, who were faced with the choice of retiring from politics or returning shamefacedly to Malan. Yet the fortunes of the Nationalist Party were at a low ebb, for its parliamentarians one and all had made fools of themselves in their prophecies as to the outcome of the war. There was only one thing to do politically, and that was to exploit this new idealism that was sweeping the country, this new demand that there should be a brave new world.

Malan on 19 January 1943 moved a social security motion of a far-reaching nature in Parliament. It called for nothing less than a 'speedy and radical reconstruction' of the existing system, and 'social security for every individual'. It asserted that the State should as its first duty take human values and human needs into consideration. It called for a 'more equitable distribution of the wealth of the country', and the 'elimination of all parasitic activities from our economic life'. And finally it declared, as it hardly could have omitted to do, that the State should maintain, in the social and economic sphere, the position of the white race and of white civilisation, 'in accordance with the principle of trusteeship'.

Hofmeyr said Malan had been a Minister for nine years, and asked what he had done in that time to carry out all the great plans embodied in his motion. Hofmeyr's statistics of national progress under Smuts were formidable. Before the war the external debt had been £103,000,000; under the present policy of repatriation, it would soon be £7,000,000. The Land Bank instead of increasing its capital had the previous year begun to reduce it. Farmers had paid back £1,680,000 to the State Advances Recoveries Office, and in 1943 would pay back more. The Post Office Savings Bank funds had increased by £7,500,000 the previous year, and Union Loan Certificates by £6,000,000.

In the current financial year the Government had made available £750,000 to the Industrial Development Corporation and nearly £4,500,-000 to the Iron and Steel Corporation. In 1939 there was £13,000,000 available for sub-economic housing and now there was £17,000,000. Expenditure on public health and public welfare had both risen considerably.

Hofmeyr declared that South Africa would not return to the status quo. It would become a more democratic country. There would be a greater measure of equality and justice. There would be more freedom, both political and economic. There would be no return to pre-war taxation. After the war, taxation would be used to redistribute income. But that was not enough. The public income must be raised, and all sections of the population would have to be better fitted for making the best use of natural resources. Hofmeyr moved an amendment praising the Government, and this was carried by 59 votes to 39.

At the same time that pressure was put on Hofmeyr to raise more money for the brave new world, a strong attack was launched against his Excess Profits Duty, which in the current financial year had brought in an amount of £7,500,000. Hofmeyr was criticised because he allowed an 8 per cent industrial dividend, took two-thirds of the profits over that amount, and still taxed the remaining one-third. Thus, it was argued, industrialists preferred to squander money rather than lose it in taxes, and young expanding industries had to borrow from the banks because Hofmeyr had taken all their profits.

Another strong attack came from J. G. N. Strauss, a vigorous young M.P., whose exciting electoral victory in 1932 had paved the way for the reunion of Hertzog and Smuts. Strauss was of course a Smuts man, and his criticism of the tax indicated the growing unpopularity of Hofmeyr's taxation measures within the ranks of Smuts supporters. He quoted that remarkable man Dr H. J. van der Bijl, the creator of the South African steel industry, in his annual report to the Industrial Development Corporation, which report also maintained that excessive taxation was preventing that development of industry which alone could raise the standard of living of the poorer sections of the population. Smuts had virtually entrusted to van der Bijl the entire industrial and manufacturing side of the war effort. Van der Bijl had also inspired a memorandum from the Federation of Iron and Steel Industries to the Minister of Finance, declaring that so long as the Minister took so much of their profits, they could not expand their industries, and therefore they would be unable to assist the Government in its task of post-war reconstruction.

No matter from where the criticism came, it was consistent, namely that heavy taxation of profits meant careless administration, extravagant spending, discouragement of new industrial ventures and entrenchment of old monopolies; furthermore the public would not invest their money in young industries. That was what some people meant when they said that Hofmeyr 'had no feel for money', or when they said he was merely a tax-gatherer. They said he was killing the goose that laid the golden eggs, that he wanted money and that he strangled the industries that could give him money, that his moralistic view of excess profits prevented him from comprehending their vital role in development.

Hofmeyr's reply to his critics was jaunty, and roused anger in some who felt they were being treated like children. He said that this doleful recital reminded him of the remark made by an Irish Minister of Finance, that 'there is more joy in the Book of Lamentations than there is in any budget'. He said that Strauss had objected to the tax, but he also wanted a successful prosecution of the war; then the onus was on Strauss to say how he would make good the £7,500,000 raised by the tax, and he had not discharged the onus. Hofmeyr reminded the House that only the day before it had voted more money to van der Bijl's Industrial Corporation, and that the Corporation was interesting itself in the salt industry, plastics, animal feeds, heavy engineering, paper, cotton, and wool. He quoted figures to show that the share values on the Stock Exchange had gone up in spite of the Excess Profits Tax. He said, 'I do not find much ruination in these figures.'

Hofmeyr then said he had no intention of abolishing the Excess Profits Duty, because neither the country nor the House would stand for it.

The motion on the Excess Profits Duty was never put. The debate was adjourned and never resumed. But the effect on Hofmeyr was not noticeable. In his 1943 budget he increased the excess profits tax from 13s. 4d. to 15s. in the pound. He increased the tax on the gold mines by a million, on the personal taxpayer by nearly a million, and on dividends to foreign shareholders by half a million; he discouraged travelling by train by levying 15 per cent on all first- and second-class fares to bring in another half-million. It was another record budget. Of the total expenditure of £164,000,000, one-third was raised by loan. Of a war expenditure of £96,000,000, half came out of revenue. Taxation was increased by nearly £10,000,000. Hofmeyr himself said that it would not be unfair to describe the budget as drastic. But he did not apologise for it. 'In a time like the present a nation does not expect to be let down lightly and to be led through green pastures—it prefers to be led through dangers and privations and over rough courses until its aim is achieved.'

South Africa's 1943 budget was not really drastic compared with the war budgets of some other countries. Nevertheless Hofmeyr was going as far as he could. He was taxing a nation far from united in a determination to win the war. In proposing expenditure on buildings, airports, and the expansion of industry, he had often to show, not that they were essential for the present, but that they could be advantageous for the future. The social reformers wanted him to tax more heavily, but political observers reckoned that he had gone as far as he could. Others anxious to see South Africa contribute more heavily to the war effort wanted rationing and purchase taxes, but Hofmeyr considered these unfeasible in a country whose officialdom was recruited from one-fifth of the population. The

Nationalists wanted Hofmeyr to tax the mines more heavily, but Hofmeyr himself thought that he had taxed them to the limit. It was said by the Nationalists that Hofmeyr, like all the members of the United Party and its predecessor the South African Party, was 'in the pocket of the Chamber of Mines', but leading members of the mining industry thought Hofmeyr had an active antipathy to the industry. If they could have read his private letters, they would not have thought so; time after time he wrote to his friends that South Africa could have contributed little to the war had it not been for the gold mines.

The truth was that Hofmeyr, after having discussed the year's finances with Smuts, and to a lesser degree with the Cabinet, having studied all the departmental estimates, having summoned the heads of departments collecting revenue, having consulted Frankel his friend and adviser, having finally formulated with Holloway his departmental chief the proposals for the year, was thereafter almost unshakeable. His attitude to the gold-mining industry, apart from his gratitude for such a national asset, was far from antipathetic; it was in fact as cool and calculating as it could have been. The possibility that he would have allowed some antipathy to affect his taxing demands is not worth considering.

He was determined to exact from the mines every penny that he could without doing any harm to the industry. There is no proof whatsoever that Hofmeyr inflicted permanent damage on the gold-mining industry or on industry in general even though this allegation was often made by eminent critics. One cannot escape the conclusion that much of the hostility to the Minister of Finance was hostility to Hofmeyr the man, and that was caused by his probity and his obstinacy, but still more by his manner.

Kilpin, Clerk of the House, was of the opinion that 1943 saw the beginning of the decline of Hofmeyr's popularity within the Party. His heavy taxation of profits, his logical replies to what were in fact emotional questions, his growing aloofness were responsible. Then in March he made a serious error of judgement.

On Saturday, 20 March, a detachment of Coloured soldiers left Cape Town for the north by train. Some of these soldiers had drunk a good deal of liquor, and some had been smoking the plant called dagga, which is related to the American marijuana, and gives the smoker illusory ideas of his powers. At Huguenot there were signs of coming disorder, and at Worcester the windows of an empty train were smashed and a freight train carrying fruit was raided. The white officers were unable to control the men, and stones were thrown at officers who attempted to do so. The situation was now completely out of hand. At Kleinstraat, through threats of molestation, the station foreman had to flee his house with his wife and children. At Laingsburg the police and a number of National Volunteer reservists were waiting. The rioters stormed out of the train, and some reservists opened fire, wounding three soldiers, one of whom later died. Farther on, at a station in the Orange Free State, soldiers smashed windows of the southbound train, which was carrying a large number of white passengers, some of them women and children, who were naturally terrified by a phenomenon so seldom seen yet so deeply feared by white South Africans. By now the fury was spent, and the train completed with little further delay its discreditable journey.

It was Malan who raised the matter in Parliament, calling for an adjournment on a matter of urgent public importance. He declared that this was not a partisan matter, but one which affected them all. He hoped the discussion would be 'in that spirit'. Of the attack on the southbound Cape train he said, 'We can well understand what a situation that caused on the train, in which there were probably a considerable number of women and children who were exposed to attacks on the train and we can understand the fright and the anxiety which those people endured.'

Although Malan had called for a non-partisan discussion, he said that a new spirit had risen amongst the Coloured people, for which he blamed the policy of arming Coloured persons, the calling in of the Coloured man to be the arbiter between white man and white man, and the incitement of the Communists. He had warned of these dangers before. 'I said that the result of everything would be that ultimately blood would be shed between white and non-white in South Africa. The bloodshed, although on a small scale, has already begun . . .' Malan concluded by saying that he did not believe that anyone could be against drastic action.

Eric Louw in seconding, said that a contributory cause was putting Coloured soldiers to guard white prisoners-of-war. He himself gave examples of the disgraceful behaviour of Coloured soldiers. They had attacked an African constable at Beaufort West, and had torn the clothes off Coloured women. A white shopgirl who told Coloured customers that cigarettes were not for sale at her counter was 'abused in a frightful manner'.

Hofmeyr was in a most unpleasant situation. Smuts was in Pretoria, and Hofmeyr would have to deal with the matter himself. He had received the news of the rioting, but it was not until he walked into the House on the Tuesday morning that he knew that Malan would move the adjournment. Nothing more easily creates a state of righteous indignation amongst white people than a non-white riot. Feelings run high, of anger, disgust, and anxiety. A rift develops between those white people who want drastic summary action, such as was no doubt taken in Voortrekker days, and those who want calm and deliberate action. The initiative, in the heat of the crisis at least, lies with the first group, not the second.

There was nothing in Hofmeyr's experience that would have specially qualified him to deal with a riot by coloured soldiers. He was not a soldier, nor had he ever worked with the police. He was essentially a civilian. He was a profound believer in law and order but never in his whole life had he had anything to do with maintaining them. What was more, he was intensely suspicious of Malan, and believed that he was using the riots to further the cause of the Nationalist Party. This was clear as soon as he opened his mouth to reply.

HOFMEYR: . . . I want however to ask the House not to form its opinion on the basis of a one-sided statement in connection with this matter. We have heard the case from one side. We have only heard here an incomplete statement by the Honourable Member for Piquetberg and he said very clearly and I thank him, that he bases his speech on newspaper reports, and he urged that a statement be made on the part of the Government. He asked therefore for a statement on the part of the Government, apparently realising that there were two sides.

MALAN: I hope the Government is not out to take up the case of the other side.

HOFMEYR: The Hon. Member presented his side and asked what our side is, but before he had heard our side he drew certain conclusions. He talked of communism and the arming of non-European soldiers, and he drew the conclusions. He asked to hear the other side, but before he has heard the other side he draws conclusions. Then he blandly said that this is not a party matter.

SERFONTEIN: Why do you accuse us if you know nothing of the matter?

HOFMEYR: Of course I regret the incident where people were killed and wounded. The Hon. Leader of the Opposition said that he did not envisage party political advantage, but in spite of that when he presented his side of the case he asked that we should also put our side, but nevertheless he drew conclusions before he heard our side. I believe that the House and the public will consider it fair and right that no judgement be made in the matter before all sides of the case have been heard.

Louw: What of the facts?

HOFMEYR: They have not been investigated and established.

Louw: I have information from eye-witnesses.

HOFMEYR: The description of an eye-witness is not necessarily a correct picture of what happened. There must first be an inquiry. It is certainly not right that on the ground of certain reports in the newspaper a general accusation should be made against all the non-European troops that we have in the service today.

MALAN: It happened on Saturday and it is now Tuesday and still the Government apparently knows nothing about the matter.

HOFMEYR: . . . I can only say . . . that an order was given for a full inquiry and that was to have been carried out as soon as the train arrived at its destination.

SWART: Then they had the chance to smash up things again on the way.

HOFMEYR: . . . the inquiry is taking place. In the meantime it is clear that there was indeed hooliganism, but only the inquiry can determine how far it went . . . it is clear that the incident was to a great extent the result of the abuse of liquor . . .

ERASMUS: They were still drunk next morning.

HOFMEYR: It is clear that many of them were under the influence of liquor . . . it is also clear that . . . damage was done to property. Only the inquiry can determine . . . It is also clear that the trouble reached a peak at Laingsburg Station and that action was taken there not by the Police but by the N.V.R. and that an order was given by the officer in command to shoot with the result that three persons were wounded and one died afterwards. Those are the facts.

ERASMUS: What is not clear then?

HOFMEYR: It is right that members should know the further circumstances and what gave rise to the trouble. It is not right on the ground of such reports to make a general accusation against the troops as a whole, especially the non-European section of the army. It is not right to make a general accusation and in this connection also to raise matters like communism and the arming of coloured people.

E. R. STRAUSS: They are possible causes.

HOFMEYR: . . . I can say nothing further. The inquiry will go through and the necessary steps will be taken to prevent a repetition of a similar incident in future.

Hofmeyr was clearly irritated that Malan should try to exploit the situation for his own profit. What he chose to ignore was that Malan was playing on the feelings of anger and anxiety that such riots arouse, and that it would have been politically wise to allay them rather than to show irritation. The Nationalists played their game with great skill. Sauer described Hofmeyr's speech as definitely one of the most peculiar speeches he had ever listened to.

SAUER: The only deduction that we can make from the words of the Minister is that they are going to act as protectors of the soldiers.

HON. MEMBER: He is the Counsel for the Defence.

Sauer put the Nationalist case in a nutshell when he said that the people did not want an inquiry, but a protection against disorder. Erasmus taunted the Government for being lost without Smuts. 'One has hardly ever been more impressed today by the lost feeling of the Government when the Prime Minister is not present. They are like a lot of lost sheep. If the Prime Minister had been here he would also have performed an egg dance, but he would have been more skilful than the Minister of Finance.'

Smuts arrived that afternoon from Pretoria to hear a Nationalist M.P. attacking Hofmeyr for expressing no disapproval of what had happened. Smuts apologised for entering the debate so late. He said: 'I take the matter up seriously. Here is a portion of our troops in the country who got beyond themselves and who did things that are deplored by everyone and by nobody more than me . . . I was proud of the fact that we have brought into being an army that was fairly well disciplined; and now I am being put to shame.' Smuts promised that every possible step would be taken to prevent any recurrence. He promised the strongest possible military inquiry, and also a civil inquiry. He said the troops had been on embarkation leave and had entrained full of drink.

SMUTS: I know the difficulties with which we have to cope in the Cape Province. The purchase of liquor is free to coloureds and I can comprehend that these people went to the train full of liquor and also with liquor in their pockets.

ERASMUS: The train should have been stopped.

SMUTS: No. The sooner they got away from the station the better . . . do not let us fight about the matter here blindly, seek all sorts of motives and use all sorts of arguments to try to give an explanation of a matter about which we do not know enough . . . We know there was bad discipline; there was drunkenness and things happened that are a disgrace to the army and to the country . . . I promise the House that the inquiry will be thorough and factual.

Louw: Will the result be made public?

Smuts: Yes, it will be made public, and if it is necessary it can be discussed in this House. It is not something that should be kept covered.

Malan said that the Prime Minister had 'made good to a very large extent the wrong done by the Minister sitting next to him . . . he tried to hide behind the Commission of Enquiry . . . the Prime Minister does not take up that attitude. He admits in the main at least that the facts are correct, that the position is serious and that a stop must be put to it, and he goes further and says he guarantees it will be done.' Malan said he was glad that the Prime Minister also recognised there was more than drunkenness to the matter. He said in conclusion, 'the other Minister resented our referring to it'.

Smuts's Court of Enquiry found that there was no organisation behind the riots. They were caused by indiscipline, liquor, and perhaps dagga. The firing took place without orders, and was totally unnecessary. After a while the fuss died own.

For Hofmeyr it had been an unpleasant experience. His prestige had suffered while that of Smuts had been enhanced. Hofmeyr had given the House the impression that he looked on a grave matter as just another subject for debate, in which he would take one side because Malan had taken the other. On the other hand Smuts had appeared as a statesman, not only quick to realise the gravity of the matter, but equally quick to sense the mood of the House. Smuts told Henry Tucker, one of his leading Transvaal supporters, that Hofmeyr's line was 'too academic'.

Yet Smuts was largely responsible. That morning Hofmeyr had communicated with Smuts in Pretoria, and Smuts had told him not to commit the Government until he himself returned to Cape Town in the afternoon. Smuts had certainly not told him to take the line that the Government fully recognised the seriousness of the riots, and would take immediate and drastic steps. Then when he arrived, he himself took that line, and made Hofmeyr look inefficient and foolish.

This was one of the occasions on which Hofmeyr made his grievance known to his friends. He felt that Smuts had put him in a weak position, and having found it weak, had left him to bear the humiliation. In the years that followed he did not speak again of the train rioting. It was an experience he did not care to remember.

In any case he was entering a new crisis in regard to the eternal question of Indian trading and residence. In 1941 Parliament appointed Mr Justice Broome to investigate the purchase of land and houses in 'white' areas by Indians; meanwhile it passed a Pegging Act, which would peg the position till 1943. The Broome Commission reported that the position in the Transvaal was as congested as ever, and that Indians in desperation used every stratagem to increase living space. It reported that in Durban Indian penetration was not serious.

The report did not in the least satisfy the white people of Natal. The Natal Municipal Association called for legislation to deal with 'a very serious menace'. The Dominion Party, which was strongly supported in Durban, was now calling for the repatriation of every Indian. Smuts therefore reappointed the Broome Commission, which reported in April 1943 that while most Indians in Durban had abided by the 'gentlemen's agreement' of 1927, a small minority was buying as much property as it could in the 'white areas'. Since October 1940, Indians had bought 326 properties at a cost of over £600,000.

Smuts's response was to introduce the Trading and Occupation of Land Bill, which would peg the position till 1946. Hofmeyr decided that he would have no alternative but to oppose the Bill and he offered his resignation to the Prime Minister at the Cabinet meeting of 6 April. His grounds of opposition were not that he objected to separate residential areas; he was in fact in favour of them, and continued to be so till his death. He accepted the proposals in regard to Durban, because the evidence justified them, and because the restrictions applied to White and Indian alike. He objected to the proposals in regard to the Transvaal, because they applied to Indians only.

Smuts asked Hofmeyr not to press his resignation; surely it was important to maintain the united front. Hofmeyr agreed, but wrote to the Prime Minister on 7 April:

'I have therefore agreed to remain a member of the Cabinet, it being understood that I do not accept responsibility for the proposal referred to and that I retain my freedom of action in regard thereto.

'I propose to exercise that freedom by stating my position in the second reading of the Bill, but shall thereafter abstain from any speaking or voting in connection therewith.'

Smuts was not happy with Hofmeyr's decision. He wrote asking Hofmeyr merely to keep silence and to abstain from all the proceedings, so as to cause less pain to his friends. He concluded, 'I must of course leave the final decision to you.' Hofmeyr replied that silence was impracticable; his constituents had a right to know his views, and what better place to make them known than in the House? There he said:

'I believe that every time the facts are brushed aside and a surrender is made to racial and colour prejudice, impairing the human rights of a part of our people, every time that happens we are sapping the moral foundation of leadership which the European people in South Africa enjoy today. Regretfully I have to say that in this case I can only regard this proposal for the unjustified prolongation of an unjustified piece of discriminating legislation as such a surrender, and with that surrender I must decline to be associated.'

As Hofmeyr sat down B. J. Schoeman called out, 'But you have surrendered.' When he got the chance to speak, he said that Hofmeyr reminded him of a tight-rope walker. 'He walks nervously and creates the impression . . . that he is undertaking a grave risk, but at the same time he knows he has a net under him, and that when he falls he will land in the net without being hurt.' Schoeman added that when Hofmeyr had resigned from the caucus on a similar matter, he had had ten supporters; now he had only two. He suggested that Hofmeyr should join the Natives' Representatives where he could apply his principles 'more loyally than he is doing today'.

Marwick the Dominionite, whose party was a member of the Smuts coalition, was more scathing. He said Hofmeyr's 'almost lighthearted tendering of his resignation really bordered on the ridiculous'. He was reminded of the hero in *Iolanthe* who told of his narrow escape from death, but could not get his audience to cry. Instead the chorus replied, 'But rather let us pipe our eye, because our Strephon did not die.'

So that was how Hofmeyr now appeared to Marwick, who had been one of the famous eleven who had voted against Hertzog's Representation of Natives Bill in 1936. And that was how the 'Indian question' now appeared to the Dominion Party, which was the self-appointed champion of the British Empire and Commonwealth, and found even Smuts's championship too lukewarm. Hofmeyr spoke of the Dominionites with a snort, not quite of contempt, rather of derision. Strange it was that the championship of what are called British ideals should have been left to an Afrikaner.

The 'Indian Bill' caused the session to end, so Hofmeyr wrote, 'on a none too pleasant note'. Some of his colleagues thought his action ridiculous; there was too much parading of his exquisite conscience. There was not one member of the Cabinet who congratulated him. His constant supporter, Leslie Blackwell, had gone, having lost all hope of ever getting a seat in the Cabinet; when Smuts offered him a judgeship, he left politics. Hofmeyr and his like-thinking colleagues in the United Party refrained from voting on the Bill. The Dominion Party voted solidly in its favour. It was left to the Natives' Representatives, Margaret Ballinger, Molteno, and Hemming, to vote against it.

About this time Underhill wrote to him, expressing the hope, as all of his friends did from time to time, that he would succeed Smuts. He replied: 'The fact that I am not in line with the dominant sentiment in this country on colour questions militates against that. It may be that despite that I may some day have to be accepted as a *pis aller*. For my part, I view it with a somewhat detached interest.' He could have added that another handicap was the Excess Profits Duty, which now had to be paid by complaining farmers who earned more than £1,500 a year.

Was Hofmeyr really so detached? In the past he had often written and spoken of detachment, but he had not been without emotion. Now there seemed no doubt that his personal ambition was dying down. He faced two insuperable obstacles, his adherence to principle, which so inhibited political adroitness, and his health, which even when it was not bad, was certainly not good. If he was called upon to lead the party, he would do it. That was duty, a thing he understood well. When duty called, he was still able to summon up energy that ambition was no longer able to muster. Dutifully he turned himself to the big task of the year, the 1943 general election.

Malan had by this time renewed his hold on anti-war Afrikanerdom. His campaign was uncompromising, and by the standards of his successors would undoubtedly be regarded as treasonable. He promised to withdraw South Africa from the war, and he said that it would be a hundred times better for England and America to lose the war than to win it, because, if they won, communism would be forced on the world. On 24 May, Empire Day and Smuts's birthday, Malan, with a theatricality foreign to him, appeared at a meeting in Pretoria draped in the Vierkleur [the flag of the former South African Republic].

Malan prophesied bad days for Smuts. He gave Hofmeyr's offer of resignation as proof of rifts within the Party. *Die Burger* said there was a race between Hofmeyr and Steyn for the succession, which was enough to give many a Smuts man the cold shivers. It said that Hofmeyr was a liberalist without following in his party, and Steyn was a protector of communists; neither had a single attribute of leadership. To these provocations both Hofmeyr and Steyn responded suitably. Hofmeyr said nothing, and Steyn said he was not a rival to Hofmeyr.

In May, Dr H. F. Verwoerd, champion of the Transvaal Nationalist leader Strijdom, and the editor of *Die Transvaler*, brought action against the *Star* for saying that he falsified the news in support of Nazi propaganda. The judge, Philip Millin, said of Verwoerd in his judgement:

'His legal right to publish what he did is not in question. The question is, whether when he exercises his legal right in the way he does, he is entitled to complain if it is said of him that what he writes supports Nazi propaganda and makes his paper a tool of the Nazis. On the evidence he is not entitled to complain. He did support Nazi propaganda, he did make his paper a tool of the Nazis in South Africa, and he knew it.'

No Nationalist likes it to be said that he supported the propaganda of a foreign power against his own country. There was however a way out, and that was to retort that Judge Millin was a Jew, and that was the way that was taken. On the whole the judgement did the Nationalists little political harm in the general election. It was the other opposition parties that were destroyed by the 1943 election. Pirow boycotted it, and he and his New Order began to fade away. The Ossewabrandwag and the Afrikaner Party were soon to learn that anti-war Nationalism preferred Malan to both Hitler and the ghost of Hertzog.

Smuts was full of confidence. He made a generous pact with the Labour Party, allowing it to keep its four seats, and to fight five others without opposition from the United Party. He made another pact with the Dominion Party not to oppose it in its eight seats. He promised the country, not only a Ministry of Reconstruction, but also a Cabinet of Reconstruction. He told his audiences that it would be a starving world after the war. Was South Africa not able to feed its own people properly, and to send its surpluses abroad? No one gave him the answer, which was, that whatever South Africa was theoretically able to do, she would in fact go on exporting surpluses at lower prices because the great majority of her people could not afford to pay the higher prices that were asked at home.

It was an amazingly free election. Quite a number of independents offered themselves. Pirow, that practical man, and all his followers in the New Order, would not stand at all, because they thought parliamentary government was breathing its last. Havenga, hoping to return to it all, stood at Frankfort in the Orange Free State, one of eight Afrikaner Party candidates. A few communists offered themselves as candidates. It was not only an amazingly free election, it was also remarkable in other respects. Considering the bitter issues involved, the campaign was peaceful, and was relatively free of hooliganism and ill-feeling. One of the hardest workers in it was Hofmeyr. Even though the fire of political ambition burned low, he carried out his duties to his Party, his country, his constituents, and his helpers.

Unfortunately, he was hampered by a bad right arm. It was a swollen vein, and according to Hofmeyr, the doctor had said it might happen to anybody. The arm was swathed in 'Elastoplast', and had to be carried in a sling. He was allowed to shave and write, but not to drive a car. In fact a blood vessel in the right arm had clotted, and Dr Loveday took quite a serious view of it. The pulse was 110, and Hofmeyr's shortness of breath showed that there was some congestion of the lungs. He had to give up strenuous exercise for several months, and this in itself was a worry to him, because he clung to the belief that strenuous exercise was essential for his well-being.

Smuts himself restarted speculation about his successor by saying on 16 June that this old horse was running in its last race. It was not clear to many whether Smuts meant that this was his last election, or that he would soon retire. His actual words were: 'I want this fight to be final. I have carried on a long fight in this country. I have not spared myself. And this old horse will run in its last race.'

He certainly frightened many of his supporters. There were hundreds of thousands of Smuts voters who regarded Hofmeyr and Steyn as quite unsuitable for the prime-ministership. They wanted Smuts to live for ever. They said he was indispensable, although they knew he was 73 and sooner or later must retire. Smuts felt he must reassure them, and he did so promptly; he said he had no intention of retiring in the near future, and that he regarded it as his personal 'duty and honour' to see that his soldiers were securely re-established in civil life. The fuss died down, but certainly no aspirant leader would have been encouraged by it.

Smuts's victory was spectacular. He had 72 seats at dissolution and 89 after the election. Pirow's New Order, by self-immolation, had gone from 16 to nothing. The Afrikaner Party was wiped out; Havenga, trying to make a comeback at Frankfort, was defeated by a Malanite. The Dominion Party dropped from 8 to 7, and Labour rose from 4 to 9. Malan, who had 42 seats at the dissolution, now had 43. Smuts and his allies controlled 107 seats in the Lower House as against Malan's 43. The voters cast 528,000 votes in favour of continuing the war, and 338,000 against continuing.

One thing was clear however—Malan had suffered no loss of strength. In his autobiography, he wrote that he could see rays of the long-awaited dawn. Amidst the jubilation the more apprehensive noted that the United Party had polled 427,000 votes and the Nationalists 313,000. It was the largest vote that the Nationalist Party had ever known. The Nazi radio-station at Zeesen must have been pleased, because it had advised South Africans to vote Nationalist, saying, 'We have always liked Afrikaners more than Bolshevists and Jews.'

Hofmeyr himself was pleased with the results. He wrote 'I was particularly pleased, because I had a larger majority than any of my Cabinet colleagues.' Whatever they thought of him in the Party and in the Cabinet, the people of Johannesburg North knew that they had a treasure.

Hofmeyr's arm did not recover quickly. He could not play tennis; fortunately for him it was not the season for cricket. He made light of his disability; it was annoying, but apart from that it had 'no other significance'. His sense of humour did not suffer. He was invited to a formal lunch at the Monastery in Pretoria, to meet Archbishop Spellman, who had been forced by war conditions to return from Rome to New York via South Africa. There was no question as to who should be one of the speakers; Hofmeyr welcomed Spellman to South Africa, but said he had a grudge against him because candidates were not allowed to canvass the nuns during the election. Spellman replied that there was a very good reason for it; how could the nuns be expected to record an unbiased vote once they had seen Mr Hofmeyr? It was one of those jokes that could get past Hofmeyr's defences and render him quite helpless. There was another version of it; if it was true, then Spellman used his wit, not to launch a sally against the Minister's personal appearance, but to pay him a high compliment. He is said to have replied that the nuns did Hofmeyr a much greater service than merely to vote for him; they prayed that justice would triumph.

Smuts would soon be going overseas again, so Hofmeyr took his holiday for 1943, and spent five days with Reg Pearse. Pearse was a mountain lover, and spent most of his leisure in the Drakensberg. Not far from Estcourt the escarpment reaches ten and eleven thousand feet; it falls precipitously to the Little Berg, a shelf about 7,000 feet high. Pearse took

Hofmeyr there for 'a splendid day', but they could not risk any climbing. The hills and valleys there are virgin, and one has the fancy that so the earth looked in the early days of the Creation. Hofmeyr thought he had never seen mountain country so beautiful.

Rested, he returned to Pretoria and trouble. Labour was restless, both in commerce and in the mines. What was more, he was preoccupied with the budget of 1944. People wanted a new earth, and indeed Smuts had almost encouraged them to expect it. But Smuts also wanted yet more money for the war. It was burdensome to be both Minister of Education and Minister of Finance, both to want a new world and to know that a ruling class would never die and suffer for a new world as they would die and suffer for an old. Luckily the provincial elections in October went well for the Government, but he ended the year tired.

On 1 December Hofmeyr opened the seventh session of the Natives Representative Council. To the disgust of the Nationalists the Council met at the Pretoria City Hall, in a smaller hall named after the great Voortrekker Pretorius, and councillors were free to make use of the washroom and other facilities, and to have lunch in the basement. Mrs Hofmeyr was there, sitting on the platform behind her illustrious son. In the chair was the Secretary for Native Affairs, supported by the Chief Native Commissioners of the Transkei, Witwatersrand, and Northern Transvaal. Down below were the councillors, among them Chief Victor Poto from the Transkei, A. W. G. Champion from Natal, Dr J. S. Moroka, the veteran R. V. Selope Thema, the youth Paul Mosaka, and the scholar Z. K. Matthews, who could mix diplomacy and bluntness with the greatest urbanity.

Hofmeyr's speech was based largely on material given to him but his conclusion was his own:

'I have never accepted the policy of the development of the African "on his own lines", in so far as that was merely a cloak for keeping him in what is regarded as being his place, a place for stagnation and servility. But I have also never believed that the African should develop simply as an inferior type of European. There is, as I have said, too much of value in his tradition and heritage for that. And that is true also in relation to education. There should be something distinctive also about the aim and methods of education for the African, especially the rural African, but it is to the African himself that we must chiefly look to determine what that distinctive element should be; he must decide what features of his indigenous culture should be preserved.'

Hofmeyr was touching a sore point. What he said was what many continental African leaders were already saying. But Africans in the south have always been sensitive about being warned of dangers by white people. Matthews was riled, but in proposing the vote of thanks he spoke as though his only concern was to set Hofmeyr's mind at rest about the danger of Africans becoming 'imitation Europeans'.

'I feel that the Europeans should leave this question of reminding us of this danger, a danger which I can assure you we do not run at all. There is no risk of our forgetting the traditions of the African people. The danger which I see, a danger which we are running, is that of going off into this blind alley of African civilisation and not marching together with the rest of the peoples of the world towards a world civilisation.'

Thus Matthews expressed one of the deepest African fears, namely that the white authorities would devise a special African education which would have for its prime objective the maintenance of the status quo. But to Hofmeyr himself he paid a great compliment, saying that History would remember him and his work for race relations, and calling Mrs Hofmeyr 'the great mother of a distinguished son'.

Moroka, seconding Matthews's vote of thanks, said to the Acting Prime Minister: 'In your speech you say that we must love our land . . . We love it and we shall always do so. We only hope that it will be made possible by the rulers of this country that we may have some land to love.' Moroka said that Hofmeyr had given them hope, and that without hope they would be nowhere. He concluded, '. . . we hope that a new spirit will come about in South Africa, and that that new spirit will bring about a condition so that Europeans and Africans can live together happily in this land of ours, and can co-operate for the welfare and happiness of this land.'

Hofmeyr was very pleased with his visit to the Council, and his mother left the hall beaming. Hofmeyr said to the writer that he thought his visit had been 'very useful'. He was pleased too that the year's duties were done, and that Smuts would soon be back. There was hope of a quiet Christmas after all, and that was what he seemed to want most nowadays, to be quiet. Of course there would be one more great event before the year ended. On 5 December his mother would be 80. There was to be an extra-fine party at 743 Schoeman Street, and all of white Pretoria that mattered would be there.

Chapter 12

War-time Minister II

HOFMEYR entered 1944, as he had entered every year of the war, expectant of victory before December. Few people outside Germany now thought Hitler would win. Smuts had uttered what he called 'explosive thoughts' to the Empire Parliamentary Association in London. After saying that any new world organisation must provide not only for freedom and democracy, but also for leadership and power, he declared that this could be done only by giving due and proper place to the United States, Russia, and Great Britain with the Commonwealth; Germany would never emerge again in the old form. Smuts also asked whether Britain would not strengthen her position by working closely together with the smaller democracies of Europe. Smuts still had his blind spot; he wanted the African colonies regrouped into great regional dominions. He was unable to foresee what would soon be happening in Africa. Yet he said it would not be wise to look only to an Anglo-American Union as a solution for the future; 'we shall have to stick to the Trinity'.

Hofmeyr was more or less in agreement with these views. He had known for a long time how Smuts was thinking, and had inevitably been influenced by him. It was consistent with the Smuts-Hofmeyr pattern that Hofmeyr never publicly, and to the writer's knowledge never privately, differed from Smuts on international affairs.

1944 was a great parliamentary year for Hofmeyr. He put through nineteen of the fifty-one Bills passed during the session. He scored 32 against the Royal Navy cricket team at Fernwood for the parliamentary eleven, and was very proud of it. On 20 March he attained the age of 50, and Sarah Millin was among the many who congratulated him, writing on 16 March that he was runner-up for the highest at 50. By now their friendship had lost its fervour, and she was losing hope. She was disturbed about the future of South Africa, and had said to Rayner Ellis of the *Rand Daily Mail*, 'Help Jan Hofmeyr, he's our only future hope.' She was even more disturbed by anti-Semitism, and asked Hofmeyr why he did not make a solemn speech in Parliament about it. In the second half of the thirties she had been the gadfly, but more than that, the believer in him; she had stung, praised, challenged, and loved him. Her thoughts had been for him, but now in her melancholy they were more often for herself. She did not know—she was not able to see—the great change that had come over him since 1938, when even he felt for a while that the great last door might open after all. They did not talk about such things any more.

Another big event of the session was the celebration on 17 March of the 200th anniversary of the arrival of the first Jan Hendrik Hofmeyr in South Africa. About 150 members of the family gathered at the Wool-sack, and there would have been more if one of the living Jan Hendrik Hofmeyrs had not made travelling so expensive, and his colleague, the Minister of Railways, had not made it so difficult. Mrs Hofmeyr and her son received the guests on the wide lawns under the oaks, the eldest an 81-year-old Jan Hendrik Hofmeyr, the youngest a 15-month-old Jan Hendrik Hofmeyr. And of course the most illustrious Hofmeyr made a speech. He told the family that the first Jan Hendrik had arrived 200 years before in Table Bay as a soldier of the Dutch East India Company in the warship *De Standvastigheid* ('Determination'). He became super-intendent of the company's estate, *De Groote Schuur* ('The Big Barn'), after which Rhodes had named his famous house, and on which this beautiful house, the Woolsack, was later built. The superintendent had had to collect the tithes, and therefore, said Hofmeyr amidst laughter, he was the first Jan Taks. Hofmeyr said, after recalling the contributions of many Hofmeyrs: 'The Hofmeyr family has distinguished itself by readi-ness to be of service to the country and its people. To us has been handed the torch of readiness to serve, and it is our duty to see that that torch is not extinguished.'

Hofmeyr, though no lover of privilege and title, had a strong sense of family. He was proud of the Hofmeyrs and proud to be one of them. He identified himself completely with the country to which the first Jan Hendrik had come. He had been a great lover of the Cape and of the city under the mountain; now he was as great a lover of the highveld, and of its two cities, the restless, feverish Johannesburg and the quieter, more decorous Pretoria. No man was ever a truer South African. But the elect denied him the name of Afrikaner because of all the accidents of upbring-ing and circumstance, which themselves were as South African as any accidents could be: the bilingual home, the English school, the Rhodes

Scholarship, the years at Oxford. He pooh-poohed this nationalism, but it could wound him nonetheless.

This is well illustrated by an exchange with Strijdom in a parliamentary debate on the issue of 'dual-medium' education which involved the proper use in the schools of the two languages, Afrikaans and English. Strijdom had said that he was glad Hofmeyr had not contended that Afrikaans was his home language.

CONRADIE: That is rather cheap.

STRIJDOM: It is neither cheap nor common. He admits that English is his language.

HOFMEYR: I did not admit that.

STRIJDOM: I am thankful for that.

HOFMEYR: I did not admit it.

STRIJDOM: Then I want to tell him now that English is his language.

HOFMEYR: That is not so.

These exchanges are obscure, but part of their obscurity is removed when we remember that Strijdom fiercely claimed Afrikaans as his own language, whereas Hofmeyr would have claimed both languages. Hofmeyr did not like these exchanges; he did not like this probing into his private life, into what language he spoke at home, and what language he thought in. The facts will bear repeating, that the domestic language of the Hofmeyr home was Afrikaans, frequently punctuated by English, always switched to English if the visitor knew no Afrikaans. The language of study and of conceptual thought was English. Therefore, outside the domestic situation, Hofmeyr's English was more idiomatic than his Afrikaans, which was correct and stilted. He was no doubt sensitive about that, but he regarded open discussion of it, and especially in Parliament, as an impertinence.

It was lucky he was able to enjoy so full a year. His health was better, he could play cricket again, and he wrote that though busy he was not so burdened as in previous years. So active was Hofmeyr, so magnificent in debate, that again the stories went round that his succession to the leadership was inevitable.

Dr R. H. W. Shepherd, principal of the famous Lovedale Missionary Institution, wrote that 'we believe that the day will come when South Africa will turn to him, from a sheer sense that its supreme need is for a leader who will be true to himself, without regard to passing popularity —a leader who will strive to bring it into a condition of racial peace through a policy of fair dealing'. Hofmeyr replied to him, 'If I have to make any comment, it would merely be that if there are people whose wish it is that I should be the next Prime Minister, I myself am not one of them.'

Yet Hofmeyr made no such public declaration. It would have been inappropriate, if not improper, for him to do so. Smuts, beyond designating him as Acting Prime Minister, said nothing about the future. Hofmeyr's private utterances to people like Shepherd and Underhill did not reach the public ear. Thus there was a considerable body of opinion in South Africa that believed, not only that Hofmeyr would succeed Smuts as leader of the United Party, but also that he wanted to do so.

A few days before his budget, that redoubtable man Hendrik van der Bijl, Director-General of War Supplies, delivered a direct attack on Hofmeyr's taxation policy. It was true the Government was a big employer but it taxed other people to create the work. The gold mines could not go on paying heavier taxation and providing large-scale employment. The present system of taxation was stifling enterprise, and gave no incentive to the entrepreneur. Any major improvement in agriculture would be useless without industrial expansion.

Hofmeyr hit back in Parliament two days later. He was cheered when he said van der Bijl had a right to express his views in the press, but that this was more conducive to publicity than helpfulness. He asked, why could van der Bijl not have consulted him before going into print? It would be interesting to know if van der Bijl had gone to Smuts before criticising Hofmeyr, and if Smuts had told him there was no harm in speaking out. Smuts was neither financier nor industrialist. He wanted money, and Hofmeyr gave it to him. He wanted equipment, and van der Bijl gave it to him. And here was van der Bijl saying that Hofmeyr was killing industry. In fact all three men were struggling with the same problem, how to reconcile the claims of the present and the claims of the future. All three of them had different solutions, but two of them, Smuts and Hofmeyr, were deeply influenced by the resolution of the British, who seemed to be risking their whole future in their struggle to save the present.

It would be quite foolish to suppose that Hofmeyr simply did not understand van der Bijl's criticism. He understood it very well. His reply was lengthy. He dealt particularly with the criticisms of the Excess Profits Duty. In the year ended 31 March 1941, the tax had brought in £2,600,000. In 1942 it had brought in £7,500,000, in 1943, £11,900,000, in 1944, £13,600,000. 'The figures therefore do not show a falling off in productivity,' he said. Hofmeyr clearly thought that the country was expanding fast enough, and his critics thought that it should be expanding faster. They thought Hofmeyr should be raising money by other means, but they never were helpful in telling him what these were. Between Hofmeyr and them there was little hope of reconciliation, and they thought him arrogantly stubborn.

The inward truth did not come out. Hofmeyr was growing sick and tired of budgeting, he was sick and tired of being Minister of Finance. No man could hide from himself that some of these criticisms of his policies contained personal barbs. He had stood up for what he thought was right, and people suggested he was unctuous. He was physically tired too. In April Smuts went off to London again, and Hofmeyr again became the Acting Prime Minister.

In the heady air of London Smuts hatched a startling idea. He cabled to Hofmeyr:

'In view of our manpower position and prospect of very heavy fighting in Italy where our 6th Division has gone, I have in principle agreed to Coloured fighting brigade being formed from our Coloured battalions in Middle East. That will largely solve our manpower problem in case war is unduly prolonged. Matter being examined by Defence Department and I hope my colleagues will give sympathetic political consideration.'

It is highly improbable that Smuts would ever have thought in South Africa of such a plan. In the sober air of Cape Town his colleagues turned down the idea unanimously. Hofmeyr drafted a note to Smuts in his own hand. He wrote:

'It is considered that we are bound by assurances given in Parliament not to arm non-Europeans save in last resort of direct threat to Union itself. Political repercussions of going back on that would be serious and it would probably be necessary to secure approval of Parliament for change of policy. Apart from that we feel that long-range consequences of Coloured men being asked to do fighting job for which we have been unable to find white men would be considerable. Any good done by making 5,000 more fighting men available would be out of proportion to ultimate harm . . .'

What did the Cabinet fear? They feared exactly what Malan feared, that if you let non-white men fight for the country, you would soon have to give them greater rights. And they feared something else too, that if a United Party Government armed Coloured soldiers, Malan would get more votes. Again one can see clearly the dilemma of both Hofmeyr and Smuts.

The war news was exhilarating. On 16 June, Allied forces landed in Normandy; an attempt was made by Germans to assassinate Hitler. It looked certain that the Germans would soon be expelled from Italy, and the Japanese from the Philippines. These events were a tonic to Hofmeyr. Smuts wrote optimistically from London, confident that the war would end before the year was out. He also wrote sympathetically:

'Your session has lasted far beyond my worst anticipation as the opposition looked tired when I left. They must have got their second wind thereafter, and I felt sorry for you and my other colleagues who had to bear the brunt of this long session. However you got through all that lengthy programme of important measures and I cannot tell you how grateful I am for your patient endurance. I hope you will have a bit of a rest before plunging into the arrears of office work at Pretoria.'

Strong words those—'I cannot tell you how grateful I am for your patient endurance.' Yet they also had an ambiguity not intended by Smuts, like the testimonial written by a professor for a mediocre student, 'I cannot speak too highly of Mr X.' Perhaps it was Smuts's weakness that he could not tell how grateful he was. Mrs Hofmeyr, watching her son closely, thought Smuts was ungrateful. One thing she was thankful for—her son was much fitter than he had ever been in 1943.

It was in the year 1944 that many of Hofmeyr's friends noted a change in him, in that he appeared to grow more humble and approachable. Kilpin noted that he was not now so easily offended if people went to Smuts when they should first have come to him, or if Smuts saw people alone when Hofmeyr considered he should have been there also. It was almost as though, now that he had decided that he would not lift a finger to become Prime Minister, he found no further need for manoeuvring. He seemed to be less inclined to jump on mistakes in that deflating way of his, not brutal, but definitely chilling.

Smuts's talk of a break for Hofmeyr proved not to be empty. When he returned from England he suggested that Hofmeyr should fly to Egypt and Italy to visit the South African troops, 'and incidentally get a bit of a break from the pressure of things here'. There is no record of Smuts's reasons. Undoubtedly he wanted Hofmeyr to have a break. He probably thought that Hofmeyr ought to see something of the war effort for which he had worked so unceasingly. Some thought he wanted Hofmeyr to see something of the world, so that his 'academic approach' could be enlivened by the spice of war, masculinity, and a few oaths. It is unlikely that Smuts could have entertained so naïve a hope; at times no doubt Hofmeyr irritated him, but no one knew better than Smuts his qualities of tenacity, courage, and integrity, and his sheer administrative brilliance. It was said—with no evidence but hearsay—that the Army wanted to make Hofmeyr a Brigadier-General for a fortnight, and that Hofmeyr snorted at the suggestion. He wanted to go North as what he was, a plain civilian, but the Army insisted that he should wear a khaki bush-shirt and long khaki trousers. For a man so indifferent to dress, Hofmeyr was remarkably upset about it. He was especially angry about his cap, which had a flap to protect the back of the head and neck. He kept flipping at it petulantly and saying, 'It makes me look like a monkey.' While up North he took good care not to be photographed wearing it.

Hofmeyr wrote to Underhill on 19 November: 'I spent 4 or 5 days in Egypt, Cairo, Alexandria, and the Suez Canal, touching at Nairobi and Khartoum on the way up. Then I had 5 or 6 days in Italy, touching down at Malta on the way across, and incidentally, enjoying a splendid view of Syracuse from the air, which awakened memories of Thucydides VI and VII. I met a lot of interesting people, Nahas Pasha and some of his Ministers in Egypt, also Lord Moyne, now unhappily no more, Prince Umberto, and one or two leading Italian officials in Rome, Harold Macmillan (with whom I spent a night in Naples—you remember him at Balliol, no doubt), L.S. Amery, Oliver Lyttelton, General Maitland Wilson, and General Alexander. In some ways I felt that Alexander was the greatest of them all—a man with a fine spirit and attitude of mind, and a great deal of strength in reserve.'

Hofmeyr was paying an extraordinary tribute to Alexander. He seldom spoke in such a way about any person. The writer does not remember anyone about whom Hofmeyr spoke so unqualifiedly. Nor was he usually so ready to pass judgement after so short an acquaintance. Nor was he usually so good an observer of persons. The fact was that Alexander had the qualities that Hofmeyr could most easily recognise, because they were the qualities that he knew best; they were in fact the same that Smuts saw in Hofmeyr, tenacity, courage, and integrity. But Alexander had one other quality that Hofmeyr did not possess, a massive self-confidence, devoid of arrogance, some deep certitude of self that is mysterious, but certainly has something to do with childhood. One was not jealous of it, nor was one angered by it, because it had no element of aggressiveness; but when Hofmeyr spoke of it, he was almost wistful.

Hofmeyr visited the Vatican, and could have been received by the Pope had he wished to; but this most tolerant of Protestants decided against it. Instead he went to see the Mayor. Wherever he could he visited the Union Defence Force Institutes, and saw their recreation huts, their houses, and their travelling canteens. He visited the 6th Division and the South African Air Force. For pleasure he visited Pompeii and Herculaneum, known to him from boyhood. He returned home on 23 September, having been away sixteen days, the longest holiday he had had since his trip to India in 1936. He had travelled 13,000 miles. He wrote that it was strenuous, with not much sleep, but that he was all the better for the change. He would like to have flown another six hours, and visited England, but he could not have returned immediately. It would have added another four days to his holiday, and this man who had hardly had a holiday in eight years, and who had carried burdens as heavy as any other of his countrymen, decided that he must go back to his duties. He returned to find his mother fit and well; he wrote on 30 September, 'She is very remarkable at almost 81.'

So ended a strange adventure. It was proof of a noble man's humility. Hofmeyr was not a soldier though there may have been times when he had wished he was one. He was perhaps the next Prime Minister, and if he were, he would follow three men who had all been generals. On his trip to the North he was surrounded by generals, whom he treated with respect; they in their turn treated him with respect, as indeed they should have done. The common soldiers did not cheer him, as they would have done to Smuts; but they knew he was coming, and they treated him with respect too. If they had cheered him, it would have been an experience without parallel in his life. What would he have done? Would he have taken it impassively, inwardly elated, or appalled? Or would the ovation have broken down the barriers of a lifetime, and released the flood of emotions of which men had only caught glimpses? Might it not have reduced him to uncontrollable tears? How fascinating and how useless to ask such questions! Yet some there were among those common soldiers who greeted him, whose hearts warmed to him. They were those to whom this war was only part of an unending struggle, to whom this short, heavy man in the khaki bush-shirt and the long trousers was the bravest general of them all.

The end of the war was now clearly in sight. When the Nationalists referred to it, they no longer praised Hitler; they condemned rather the folly of America and Britain in destroying Germany. The danger of Russia was now the theme of any important Nationalist speech, and history will be able to say better than we why Afrikaner Nationalism reacted so violently to Communism and so indifferently to Nazism, why it was revolted by Russia's godlessness and unmoved by Hitler's.

A profitable new line of attack now offered itself to the Nationalist Party. The Union's note issue had doubled in four years but there was less to buy. The price of food had risen by at least one-third, and not all the efforts of the Price Controller could keep it down. Food had to be imported at higher prices than it could have been produced for at home, and this was because the war effort had drawn labour away from food production. Then Allied ships purchased great quantities of food at the ports, so that the South African civilians had to put up with occasional meatless days and the banning of white bread, and only the rich could afford to drink their troubles away. It seemed a trifle, this lack of white bread, but the Nationalists were to make it an election cry.

There was great public dissatisfaction with the efficiency of those Government officials who were controlling food and prices. It was now widely said that the Cabinet, except for Hofmeyr and of course Smuts, was inefficient, and Strauss, the new Minister of Agriculture, was blamed for much of the food and production muddle. Louis Esselen's health was declining, and Smuts thus lost the services of his life-long adviser.

There was a growing belief that Smuts, for all his genius, was useless at picking men. Even within the United Party, there was dissatisfaction with taxation, food shortages, and incompetence. Within the coalition were also rifts. The Dominion Party, the upholder of the Empire, wanted sterner action against Indians. The Labour Party, the upholder of the working man, refused to agree to the training of non-white artisans to build houses for non-white people at lower wages, thus in effect preventing their training altogether.

In spite of these difficulties, Smuts's party was still, even without allies, extremely powerful. But the Nationalists were militant in the closing days of the war. For the second time in their history they took from Smuts the Transvaal seat of Wakkerstroom. What is more they were angered when Smuts proclaimed the Broederbond to be a subversive organisation, to which a man could not be loyal, and at the same time be loyal to the country. He ordered public servants to resign from the Bond, or from the

Public Service. Malan declared that the Broederbond had done no more than serve the Afrikaner people as the Sons of England had served the English-speaking South Africans, and the Jewish Board of Deputies had served the Jews. Yet this was not true. Neither of these societies had ever set out to become the ruler of South Africa.

Founded in 1918 as a cultural organisation, the Broederbond, with Malan as an early member, soon thereafter set itself the aim of ruling South Africa. It took its first tremendous political step in 1934, a gamble that meant all or nothing, when it decided to reject the coalition of Hertzog and Smuts. Its membership was secret, and it met in secret; no notice or resolution was ever sent through the mails. Though small, its membership was powerful, containing almost every Afrikaner of note who was a 'true Afrikaner' in the Malanite sense. The Bond dominated the cultural *Federasie van Afrikaanse Kultuurbewegings*, the economic *Reddingsdaadbond*, the political *Herenigde Nasionale Party*. No matter what the electorate might decide, the Bond resisted uncompromisingly any dual-medium education. Its influence over the symbolic Trek of 1938 was immense; during that time the great United Party, especially its English-speaking members, felt their powerlessness. It was the Bond that decided that Malan must first praise the Ossewabrandwag, and then turn against it. The Ox-Wagon Watch was a people's emotional movement that would flame up today and burn out tomorrow, while the Broederbond was a movement of a couple of thousand picked men, whose emotions were indissolubly wedded to their wills. It was the people who brought Hertzog and Malan together in the great reunion at Monument Koppie on 9 September 1939; it was the Broederbond that threw Hertzog out when the popular emotion had subsided. It was only Smuts who ever successfully resisted the Bond, partly because of his own great gifts, partly because the war had loosed a passion and a fury and created a resolve that for a time overshadowed the passion and fury and resolve of the 'true Afrikaner heart'.

What was the Broederbond? A clique seeking power? Agitators playing on grievances? Afrikaner zealots with one overriding and patriotic purpose? Undoubtedly it was all these. Whatever else it may have been, it drew much of its power from the resentments of the 'Century of Wrong'. Its relation to Afrikaner Nationalism was vital yet obscure. Not every member of the Nationalist Party was a member of the Broederbond, and some Nationalists, among them General Hertzog, condemned it, root and branch. Of course both the Broederbond and the Nationalist

Party kept wounds open and played on grievances of the past, but who can doubt that the grievances were there? And what artists to play on them! Malan himself, the old veterans Swart, Strijdom, Erasmus, Eric Louw; and the newcomers, the smooth-tongued Dönges, and Hertzog's fanatical son Albert with the little pointed beard, and the up-and-coming editor Verwoerd, the former professor who was now learning the art of applying psychology to a nation.

Smuts's banning of public servants from the Broederbond had little effect except to make Malan more than ever the champion of oppressed Afrikanerdom, and the unquestioned leader of any opposition. He called for a vote of censure on the Government for its laxity and incompetence in the distribution of food. The Nationalists exploited the position well. Swart painted a picture of the food shortages which would have convinced every poor white voter that the Nationalists were the real champions of the people.

Smuts admitted that there were grumbles, but he denied that South Africa was exporting a great portion of her food. He said that the Minister of Agriculture was preparing a rationing system, but he must have known that rationing without a system of personal identification would prove impossible. He said the food difficulties were the result of the amazing increase in consumption caused by the plentifulness of money. His answers did not satisfy his critics. A contemptuous Strijdom, becoming better and better known for his implacable opposition, said that Smuts was a man of high intellect who did not have the time to deal with the daily affairs of the people.

What Strijdom said about Smuts and daily affairs contained much truth. This was February 1945 and in a few weeks he would be leaving again to spend nearly four months in Europe. He had such a tonic effect on Churchill and his Ministers that whenever he went to England they did not want to let him go back to South Africa. His enemies accused him of regarding South African affairs as small potatoes; his mind was full of the Great Bear and the American Eagle, and he was thought to understand their affairs with special insight.

Geoffrey Clayton, the great Bishop of Johannesburg, gravely concerned over the squalor and misery in which so many of the city's African workers were living, and supported by his entire synod, went to see Smuts. Clayton was an Englishman whose reserve hid deep and strong feelings, and the thought of a brave people living in physical misery with the rain flooding in through roofs of tin and sacking, in unlit streets stinking of sour mud, waking at four in the morning so that they could appear punctually before employers who expected them to rise out of the filth and shine, weighed down on him continuously. Clayton had been to the Johannesburg municipality, whose officials had explained to him that they could not accept the whole responsibility and bear the whole burden of re-housing; the Government must help. Clayton then went to Smuts, and with justified hope, because Smuts had said publicly that something must be done about African housing; but Smuts explained to him that the Government could not accept as much of the responsibility and the burden as the municipality thought it should. Smuts did not even promise to have the position sympathetically investigated, and Clayton came away shocked by his apparent indifference to the suffering of people. He said afterwards of Smuts and the municipality, 'They put *things* before people,' which for him was the severest of judgements.

It would have been wonderful if, with Smuts as the international leader, Hofmeyr could have been the national one, planning the new world at home, the kind of world that men and women had been talking about during the years of war. It would have been the kind of world in which men and women would have had food enough for themselves and their children, and in which the grosser disparities of wealth and privilege would have been wiped out. Among helpers, whom better could Hofmeyr have had than Frankel, eager to be used, eager to study the problems of the brave new world, and to advise Hofmeyr how to build it. It was a task Frankel would have given a lot for. He was ambitious but not vulgarly; it would have satisfied his ambition to have had a position of high responsibility under Hofmeyr. He had never forgotten Hofmeyr's kindness to him when he had been a poor but aspiring student. To put it plainly, he loved him.

Frankel loved Hofmeyr. Did Hofmeyr love him? Who would know? The writer never heard Hofmeyr use the verb in that way. 'Fell in love?' Yes, of others. 'Love of neighbour?' 'Love of country?' Yes. But never, 'I loved.' Frankel not only loved him, he wanted to serve South Africa through him, with him, under him. During these years of the Finance Ministry, Hofmeyr could have called on Frankel any hour of the day or night.

Hofmeyr adopted by no means all of Frankel's suggestions. In the late thirties, when Hofmeyer was free of the Cabinet, Frankel was one of those who wanted him to come out as a liberal. It was only later he learned he was asking for something that for Hofmeyr was temperamen-

tally impossible. When in the early forties, scents of the new world were
in the air, Frankel was one of those intoxicated by them. Surely there was
a job for him in such an age, something more than teaching economics or
advising on a budget? But councils and committees were created to plan
for the new age; the initiative which in Frankel's eyes should have come
from Hofmeyr, who surely of all South Africans understood best what
the new world should be like, was passed to others. Smuts set up the
Economic and Social Planning Council with another as chairman, while
Hofmeyr examined its blueprints with a cold and judicial mind, apparently never thinking to get Frankel put on it. Then Oxford offered
Frankel a professorship. At once he let Hofmeyr know, hoping with all
his heart that Hofmeyr would say, 'Don't go, there's a job for you here,
I've work for you here.' He wanted him to say, 'Smuts will be going
soon, and I'll need you, Frankel.'

When Hofmeyr made no response, Frankel accepted the Oxford
offer. He went over to Pretoria to break the news. Hofmeyr was pensive,
said Frankel, and then he said, 'I don't blame you.' To Frankel it was both
a shock and a revelation; it was his first insight into the relationship
between Hofmeyr and Smuts. Frankel never quite recovered from the
words, 'I don't blame you.' It explained to him much of the events of the
late thirties and the early forties. He remembered the excitement of
those earlier days, when they had been writing *Coming of Age*, when he
as a young man had been admitted into the select company of Hofmeyr,
Haarhoff, Brookes, Schreiner, Ramsbottom, and Currey. He said to the
writer, with a mixture of sadness and pain, 'Damn it, Paton, what has it all
come to?'

Frankel's experience was painful but not unique. Others would have
come running had Hofmeyr called them, but he did not call. Some
thought it should have been easy for Hofmeyr to call them, because he
was so near to Smuts. But Hofmeyr was never to Smuts what Smuts had
been to Botha, or what Havenga had been to Hertzog. And the reasons
for that were plain. In the first place, the difference in age had proved for
Hofmeyr insurmountable. In the second, Hofmeyr was weighed down by
sheer hard work, and it must be concluded that the lack of creative
leadership and the burden of administrative labour were closely connected with each other; there is here a deep secret of temperament and
nature that defies easy analysis. Had Hofmeyr in 1945 enjoyed the health
and self-confidence of the period of his administratorship, had Hofmeyr
from the beginning enjoyed a more independent relationship with Smuts,

with weaker elements of submissiveness and stronger elements of asser-
tiveness, then perhaps he could have undertaken the national leadership
while Smuts roved abroad. But there was yet another reason why Hofmeyr proved disappointing to the would-be builders of the new South
Africa; for him the first priority was still the winning of the war.

The Nationalists were perturbed by features of Hofmeyr's last war
budget. The Government had already extended benefits and pensions to
the blind, invalid, and aged of all races. Hofmeyr had already said that
every child at school would receive a daily free meal. Now he had gone
further. He had created a new vote to be called Native Education, and
had swept away the old makeshift of relating the revenue from African
taxation to the expenditure on African education. Furthermore he proposed to increase the expenditure by a further £255,000.

Malan wanted to know direct from the Prime Minister where South
Africa was going? What was the future of the white race? Malan said the
communists were preaching the end of all colour bars, and coloured
people and natives sat next to whites in the buses and trams. There were
about 100 non-white students at the University of Cape Town, others at
the University of the Witwatersrand and 134 at the Natal University
College. The Fort Hare Native College was being forgotten. Formerly
Smuts had supported separation; now he said segregation had failed; he
said that South Africa's days of isolation were past, and that relations
between white and non-white should now be considered not from South
Africa's point of view alone. Malan said that the Prime Minister had a
habit of not looking at matters from a South African point of view.

Malan, if he was genuinely worried, need not have been. There were
two Smutses, the one Smuts who wanted to deal actively with the problems of the world and was a war leader in a thousand, the other Smuts
who shirked the problems of his own country, and yielded, first to Hertzog on the grand scale, second to Hofmeyr on the petty scale, little
niggardly concessions. Smuts might say that segregation had failed, but he
did nothing, and there is no evidence that he ever intended to do anything, to put something in its place; he might coin as he did as far back as
1937, the magnificent phrase, 'racial indifference', but it was only playing
with words.

Now Smuts was yielding to Stallard, whose party controlled the city
of Durban. The Natal Provincial Council had passed a housing ordinance
which created a housing board with powers to buy properties 'in danger

of passing from one race to another'. The ordinance had been declared *ultra vires,* and now Smuts promised national legislation. He said there were certain things on which all South Africans were agreed; it was fixed policy to maintain white supremacy. He said that South Africans had kept their race pure for 300 years, and were determined to maintain it so. He did not want residential separation 'to be forced unnecessarily'. It could be done by providing separate housing areas. In regard to Africans, his idea was to develop them in their own areas 'in harmony with native life and traditions'. Smuts did not favour preventing rural Africans from coming to look for work in the cities; because a man had a black skin there was no reason to prevent him from seeking work.

There was Smuts's practicalism in a nutshell. White supremacy, race purity, residential separation but not by unnecessary force, economic integration, freedom to seek work, development of the reserves. Surely Smuts was the very prototype of white South Africa, pursuing the supreme goal of self-preservation, sometimes brutally, sometimes with noble affirmations, which in their turn were sometimes true, sometimes false, but most often a compound of true and false, so blended by time, so familiar through use, so learned from infancy, that one no longer knew which was which. One could be cynical about it, but Smuts would close with a disarming peroration, which would show that separation did not exclude togetherness, and that the pursuit of a supreme monoracial goal did not exclude co-operation in the inter-racial goals. He concluded that only by a policy of co-operation between all classes and colours of the community could South Africa find her future.

On this occasion Hofmeyr said nothing. He had already expressed himself in favour of some control in Durban, on the grounds that it would apply equally to white and Indian. His paper the *Forum* was unequivocally in favour of residential segregation, though not of economic segregation. Surely he too was a prototype, of another kind of white South Africa, moving with painful slowness, for some too painful, for others too slow, away from the cruelties of a colour-bar society. Yet slow though Hofmeyr's evolution might be, it was too fast for the great majority of his fellow M.P.s.

On 29 March Hofmeyr saw Smuts off at the Cape airport on his way to London for the Prime Ministers' Conference, and then to San Francisco to lay the foundations of the United Nations Organisation. Three days later he moved the second reading of the Native Education Finance Bill, the projected law that made the education of African children a charge on general revenue, and while leaving such education in the hands of the provinces, established a Union Advisory Board of Native Education, with the Secretary for Native Affairs as chairman, and with Hofmeyr's own Union Education Department providing the secretariat. Out of consideration for provincial feelings, and with regard no doubt for provincial voting, Hofmeyr left control with the provinces. If he had thought central control necessary, he would have vested it in his own Union Department of Education. There was one thing he would not have done; he would not have vested it in the Department of Native Affairs. It was the fear of missionaries, African teachers and parents, liberal educators, and indeed all who belonged to what Strijdom called 'the liberalistic clique', that African education would pass out of the hands of educationists into those of administrators and officials, many of whom upheld the ideal of 'development of the native along his own lines'.

While the bill met with Nationalist opposition, it was welcomed by G. K. Hemming and Margaret Ballinger, two of the Natives' Representatives, but the most remarkable speech of all was made by Arthur Barlow. He said there were two distinct 'Native policies' in South Africa, Hofmeyr's, and the policy of van der Byl, the Minister for Native Affairs. 'I back Mr Hofmeyr's policy because it is the policy of Christ. It is the policy that the man on top must take the man who is down below by the hand and guide him along. White South Africa is doomed if it rejects that policy.'

Hofmeyr's Bill was passed, and so for the first time in South African history, the education of African children was financed out of general revenue. There was the hope, though there was no guarantee, that the disproportion between the amounts spent on white and black education would progressively be made less shocking, for at that time the amount spent on each white pupil was approximately seven times the amount spent on each African pupil. General Kemp's threat that the Act would be repealed was partly realised; in 1955 the Nationalist Government pegged the contribution from general revenue at £6,500,000 plus four-fifths of the African general tax.

On 12 April 1945, the people of the Allied world were shocked to learn that the great Roosevelt was dead. Parliament met in a state of tension, not only because of the news, but because it was known that Malan refused to co-operate with the Government in a vote of condolence. He had told Hofmeyr it would be a precedent, and that one day the House would be asked to mourn for Stalin. Reluctantly Hofmeyr decided to drop the matter and told Malan so. But many members of his party were rebellious. The debate was little short of disgraceful. Van Nierop the Nationalist from Mossel Bay put the matter well. He said, 'I want to ask honourable members if anyone should come into this Chamber and hear us talking about the death of a great man, sitting here and laughing and shouting at each other—could such a person think it possible in these circumstances to express our condolences on the death of this great man?' Ultimately Hofmeyr moved the adjournment as a mark of respect and deep regret on the occasion of the death of the President, and the motion was then allowed to go through unopposed.

Hofmeyr was certainly embarrassed by this unpleasant episode. It was not only Nationalists who criticised him. Barlow for one decided that Hofmeyr was not the leader he had thought him to be. Hofmeyr had been caught between his passion for order and precedent, and the strong emotions aroused by Roosevelt's death. Rather than disturb order and precedent, he would deny the House release for its emotions. Perhaps Malan smiled to himself, for though in him emotion was disciplined, he knew exactly what could be done with it, and when it should not be ignored. But Hofmeyr would ignore the emotions rather than the precedents. On this occasion the sticklers for order in his own party supported him, but there were others who thought he should have moved a vote of condolence and let the Nationalists disgrace themselves if they wished.

With Smuts away, the burden on Hofmeyr was heavy. This was the fourth time that he had acted as Prime Minister. It was the end of the summer, 'an occasional hot day, and sometimes a fair amount of wind, but on the whole a good climate, and much beauty all around one'. He was feeling better in health and more cheerful in mind than he had felt for some time; he wrote to Underhill that he was grateful to have been able to carry the burden so long with virtually no holidays, and 'without any apparent physical impairment'. He wrote, 'If only one could look forward to something in the way of a real break ahead.' Then the dry Cape summer ended, and the rains began, bringing with them cold and damp. The Woolsack, so beautiful in summer, was cheerless in the winter, and he was a little worried about his mother's health. He wrote again to Underhill, 'It is always a difficult problem for me when she is not well. We have only native (men) servants, and she won't have another woman about the house.'

There were exceptions. Sometimes Mrs Hofmeyr's sister would come to stay. One of the stepdaughters, Hester, would also come.

Although she was a woman in her sixties, she always came with apprehension. Her visits were a kind of duty, and she would live like a mouse in the house till the duty was done, and she could return to the warmth and freedom of her son's home at Conway, a tiny station on the line from Port Elizabeth to Johannesburg. All the stepdaughters were proud of their young stepbrother, and who prouder than Hester when the train made a special stop at Conway so that the Minister of Finance could get down for a moment to talk to his stepsister. One of the stepdaughters never visited at all, and that was Susie, who more than fifty years before, when she had qualified as a schoolteacher, had run away from home, and brought disgrace on her home. That was why Mrs Hofmeyr always said she had three stepdaughters, partly because the one was not worth mentioning, partly because it was painful to mention her. Hofmeyr's own brother A.B., the attorney, would come visiting the Pretoria home with his wife; but the two women disliked each other so much that the visits were fewer than they might have been. A.B. and his wife never slept there. Her dislike was increased by the way Mrs Hofmeyr spoke to her elder son, as though he were 16 and not nearly 60, and the way she compared him with the model, industrious, younger brother. A.B. had a cheerful, happy-go-lucky manner, but sometimes his resentment would pour out of him like a flood, so that he lost control of it, and he told things he would have liked later not to have told at all. He had been in financial difficulties more than once, and his younger brother had come to the rescue, another thing Mrs Hofmeyr would not forget and would not let him forget.

Between the two brothers there was a strange companionship; A.B. was proud of his younger brother, and Hofmeyr in his turn enjoyed the quite fabulous wealth of gossip that A.B. could retail, about the private lives and infidelities and defalcations and intrigues of Nationalists and mine magnates and editors and business men and professional men and professors and ministers of religion. A.B. could even tell him things about his own Cabinet colleagues and their wives and sons and daughters that Hofmeyr had never heard. In a strange way also Hofmeyr would give A.B. great credit for a kind of popular political *nous*, and would ask him how things were going here and there, and what the feeling was here and there, and what they were saying in Johannesburg and Vereeniging and Potchefstroom and Heidelberg.

These family comings and goings were not many. Just as the elder son and the stepdaughters had felt themselves excluded in the little house in

Rheede Street fifty years before, so they still knew that the relationship between Mrs Hofmeyr and her son Jan Hendrik was a thing apart. Not that they wished to be included; they were always uncomfortable in their mother's house. They never saw the charm that so many of Mrs Hofmeyr's friends saw in her. They felt only the strength of her imperious will, which in its eighty-second year was as terrifying as ever.

Chapter 13

'Hofmeyr Must Be Destroyed'

MEANWHILE in San Francisco Smuts was witnessing and assisting in the birth of a new world. To Hofmeyr he revealed his anxiety that the San Francisco Conference would drag on, until events in Europe would call every European statesman of any importance back to duty, to attend to the new problems created by the lightning advance of the Russians into Germany. Smuts kept urging the conference to hurry, and he himself was preparing the preamble to the Charter, with its noble emphasis on fundamental human rights, the sanctity of personality, the equal rights of men and women, and of nations large and small.

The Charter gave Britain, the United States, Russia, China, and France permanent seats on the Security Council. Provision was made to convert League of Nations mandates into United Nations trusteeships, falling under a Trusteeship Council. Smuts formally reserved South Africa's rights in regard to her mandate over South West Africa. Smuts was not the figure in San Francisco that he had always been in London. The two giants of the world were America and Russia, and the first knew little and the second nothing of the veteran soldier so held in honour by the Commonwealth. Smuts had prophesied that the world would be ruled by the Trinity, but it was already clear that it would be ruled by the Big Two. Already the Commonwealth to which he had devoted so much of his life was beginning to decline in power. While he was working on the Charter, which was to enshrine all the freedoms longed for by men, people of the new nations were framing for Smuts the question, and would soon be asking it, 'What happens there in your own country?' He wrote to Hofmeyr:

'As regards the Conference I find not only power politics well to the fore, but also a strong humanitarian tendency, finding expression in provisions for equal rights all round, and other embarrassing proposals so far as we are concerned. The Conference has to be carefully and even anxiously watched, and I am doing my best in that respect.'

On 7 May, the day after Smuts wrote his letter, Hofmeyr received the secret cable that the German forces in Europe had surrendered to the Allies and the Soviet High Command. The next afternoon Hofmeyr announced in Parliament that the war was won.

On the evening of 8 May, Hofmeyr made a victory broadcast to the nation. He said, 'We have made a much larger contribution to the cause to which we pledged ourselves than at first we dared hope we would be able to make. This has been a great period in our history. Viewed aright, it could become a mighty force for the building up of a great, a truly united South African nation.'

This broadcast brought a telegram from Smuts in San Francisco to the Secretary for External Affairs: 'I have read with deep emotion Mr Hofmeyr's beautiful victory broadcast to the nation this week. I congratulate him on a message which must have been as moving to our people as it has been to myself. It is all true and I trust its hopes and prayers will also come true. Thank him for it.'

It was regrettable, one might almost say tragic, that though Smuts had throughout the war remembered to mention Hofmeyr's 'burdens', that though he sent a special telegram from San Francisco to congratulate Hofmeyr on his 'beautiful victory broadcast', yet Mrs Hofmeyr openly stated that Smuts was ungrateful, and Hofmeyr did not contradict her. Mrs Hofmeyr no doubt meant that whatever statements Smuts may have made, none of them gave either mother or son a feeling of satisfaction. What was the truth? Mrs Smuts knew that Mrs Hofmeyr had this grievance, and she could only shrug her shoulders as if to say, 'Well, it's a pity, but there it is.' There seems little doubt that one is dealing here, not so much with Smuts's ingratitude, but with his insensitivity. Smuts did not know what his praise would mean to Hofmeyr. Perhaps if he had praised him publicly, explicitly, and generously, he might have put Hofmeyr under the spell again. But he did not. One feels readier to conclude that Smuts was insensitive rather than ungrateful, but that does not remove the tragic element, that the relationship between this brilliant leader and this most brilliant and selfless servant was marred by Smuts's ignorance of what his praise might mean. Yet he was not alone in that; Hofmeyr had the same insensitivity.

Smuts returned to South Africa on 16 July. Ten days later while he was still responding to calls from all parts of the country, from people who wanted to see him and hear him and cheer him, Winston Churchill was swept from power, the Labour Party having defeated his party by almost 200 seats.

On 2 August the United Party caucus met in Pretoria to discuss the eternal 'Indian question'. In particular they discussed the master zoning plan envisaged by the Natal provincial authorities, a plan which would create separate residential areas, and move tens of thousands of Indian citizens from the land and houses they occupied; some of them had owned their land for almost a century.

On 6 August the United States of America dropped an atomic bomb on Hiroshima, Japan, killing 78,000 people and wounding 59,000 more, of whom a great number later died.

On 15 August, at 1 a.m., Japan surrendered. The Second World War was over.

The next day the Natives Representative Council passed a motion of appreciation for Smuts. Dr Moroka, the chairman, commended his courage in entering the war with the white population divided, but they reminded him that the African people had been unanimous. Councillor S. Thema said:

'The Natives participated in this war because they felt they must be on the side of democracy. I hope now that General Smuts . . . will address this Council so that we can convey to our people how they stand as far as the San Francisco decisions are concerned . . . Recently the Prime Minister said that there is room enough for both races in South Africa. We want to know in what way there is room for us both.'

Another distinguished member of the Council, Professor Z. K. Matthews, asked that Africans should be drawn more and more into the ordinary life of the nation.

The Council a few days later criticised the Government for passing the Native (Urban Areas) Consolidation Act without putting it before the Council. The chairman, W. J. G. Mears, a white official versed in what were called 'Native affairs', a man known for his courtesy and humanity, could not understand the resentment against a mere consolidating measure. But the laws that were being consolidated were always restrictive, often humiliating, and sometimes quite cruel and inhuman. The council demanded a complete overhaul of all laws governing the movement and residence of Africans in urban areas.

Up North the new world spirit still brooded over the Army. South African soldiers in Rome decided to launch a great national fund to found clinics throughout the reserves and all areas of dense African population.

Down South the National Union of South African Students (NUSAS) made history by admitting by 11 votes to 3 the Fort Hare

Native College. J. P. G. Eksteen, Afrikaans-speaking Vice-President of the Students' Representative Council of the University of Cape Town, said NUSAS was offering the Afrikaans Universities affiliation with one hand, and hurling Fort Hare in their faces with the other. Arnold Klopper, Afrikaans-speaking Vice-President of the Students' Representative Council of the University of the Witwatersrand, said his students were interested only in a 'fighting policy'. The following day the University College of the Orange Free State announced that it had broken away from NUSAS.

In Durban on 24 August, a tremendous crowd, greater even than those which had celebrated V-E Day and V-J Day, gathered at the City Hall to see Smuts arrive to accept the freedom of the City. The *Natal Mercury* photographed the Prime Minister talking to Mr A. Mtimkulu and Chief Albert Luthuli. Smuts did not mention the Indians, and he demonstrated again his dangerous gift of affirming great principles and keeping silent about their infringements. Smuts owed a great deal of his popularity to this gift, and Hofmeyr a great deal of his unpopularity to his lack of it.

On 7 September Smuts experienced a tremendous defeat in the parliamentary constituency of Kimberley, where the Nationalists won by a majority of 244 a seat which the United Party had held by a majority of 511, a great change in a constituency of 8000 voters. Hofmeyr's taxation policy received the lion's share of blame for this.

This then was post-war South Africa, Smuts acclaimed, Kimberley lost, Nazism defeated, Indians to be restricted, the Natives Representative Council generous and moderate, many soldiers still earnest about the things for which they had fought, the National Union of Students reaching out across the colour line, and the Free State students withdrawing. Already there were signs that the new South Africa would not be born. Many of the returned soldiers, especially those of the Springbok Legion, were already being accused of being too far left. Strongly anti-Nationalist, and contemptuous of Smuts and Hofmeyr, they were demanding far-reaching reforms in South Africa, especially in matters of race. When the Nationalists attending the Party congress, held a 'victory' procession in Johannesburg to celebrate the capture of Kimberley, the police charged ex-soldiers with batons and drove them off. Malan said, 'This Congress has a motto, to save South Africa from Communism.' After the meeting Malan was spirited away by the police.

So in the months immediately after the victory over Nazism, the

Nationalists laid down the pattern for their campaign. The goal was—as ever—the preservation of white supremacy. The dangers were communism, the new United Nations with its licentious Declaration of Human Rights, liberalism, and as always, the 'Black flood'. Liberalism was in some ways the most dangerous, because—wittingly or unwittingly—it opened the way for communism; in the striking language of a later Nationalist Minister of Justice, 'Communism kills, but Liberalism leads one into ambush in order to kill.' And if liberalism was ever embodied in a man, that man was Hofmeyr. Wittingly or unwittingly, he was leading South Africa into ambush. Strijdom said, 'Hofmeyr must be destroyed.'

The anti-communism of the Nationalists had many elements. It could call on the Churches, because communism was godless. It could call on big business, because communism would destroy big business. It could call on Afrikaner workers and persuade them they were Afrikaners before they were workers. It could call on all conservatives, and seduce many who should have known better, because communism meant revolution and change. But fundamentally the anti-communism of the Nationalists was not religious or capitalistic. There was one change, one revolution, which the Nationalists feared more than they feared God or poverty, and that was the easing of the colour bar. Malan was beginning to drop the word segregation, and was beginning to use the word separation, which in Afrikaans is *apartheid*, the word which was to find its way into the languages of many countries. Strijdom was more outspoken; he used the word *baasskap*, which means the condition of being boss, and that meant white supremacy. The anti-communism of the Nationalists was primarily and fundamentally based on the determination to maintain the colour bar. Therefore Hofmeyr, though anti-communist himself, though also religious and conservative, was accused of assisting the advance of communism.

It is easy with hindsight to see that within a few months of the end of the war, it was almost as though the war had never been. It is easy to see with hindsight that the old struggles were being renewed with a new intensity. Some people saw it even then. The apostles of social security had to learn the bitter lesson that people, the great bulk of people, wanted taxation to be eased so that they could have more money for themselves. Earnest soldiers returned from the North to find that nothing had changed. There was an exciting theme for a story—used more than once —of the white soldier who had met a black soldier up North, and perhaps the one had saved the life of the other, and they had vowed when they went back home to ignore the evil colour bar that kept one man from another. But when they got back home, the colour bar was too much for them; the white civilian was embarrassed, the black one was disillusioned.

Hofmeyr was disquieted about South Africa too. He knew well—as well as anyone in South Africa knew—that the defeat of Smuts would be an event far more portentous than the defeat of Churchill.

Yet he himself was cheerful. And he had reason to be, for he had been offered an honour which for him was the greatest in the world. Oxford University had offered him the honorary degree of Doctor of Civil Laws, the D.C.L., in recognition of his services during the War. He wrote to Underhill, 'That satisfies my only ambition.' When he spoke of the coming honour, a little smile of pleasure could be seen on his face. He did not talk excitedly, nor did his eyes shine; there was just this small smile of pleasure to indicate that something had happened to him, to him personally, the like of which had not happened, say, since 1924, when the great Smuts had made him Administrator. He was excited in the same fashion over the thought that he would visit England, be honoured in Oxford, see Secretan, Murray, Underhill, King, Jacks, look in at his old rooms at Balliol, and inspect the buildings of the Balliol Boys' Club.

[In the fall of 1945 Hofmeyr visited England where he was widely feted and honoured, and in addition to receiving the degree at Oxford, he was appointed a Privy Councillor and thus became the Rt. Hon. J. H. Hofmeyr.]

The question of the succession was always uppermost. Smuts was nearly 76. Both the Labour Party and the Dominion Party now left his coalition. He could still count on a majority of 25 in a House of 153, but there was a feeling of political restlessness abroad. There was excitement when both Havenga and te Water attended debates in the House in January 1946. What were they doing there? They would not say.

There was talk that influential Johannesburgers wanted Havenga to form a new middle party, as Hertzog had done in 1934. He could discard Malan on the right and Hofmeyr on the left. The political correspondent of the *Natal Mercury* reported that these backers had promised Havenga an initial sum of £25,000. The important thing was to get rid of Hofmeyr and his restrictive financial policy.

In 1940 Hofmeyr had paid a handsome tribute to Havenga. But when Havenga, after his eclipse, flirted with Pirow's New Order and van

Rensburg's Ossewabrandwag, Hofmeyr would have nothing more to do with him. In such matters his judgements were severe. Whatever Havenga's motives may have been, whatever his disagreement with Smuts, it was his duty in Hofmeyr's view to have no truck with anything that smelt of dictatorship; and if he once did so, that revealed something about him that should never again be forgotten.

Malan, in the traditional 'no confidence' debate, launched a strong attack on the Government's racial policies. He declared that the colour problem had to be solved then or never. It had been aggravated by the war and the growth of communism. Relations between white and non-white worsened daily. The Natives Representative Council was little more than a communist body. In Cape Town and Johannesburg non-white students were infiltrating the universities.

Malan revealed again the ruthless aspect of his politics. He congratulated Smuts on his intention to control land ownership and occupation by Indians. But why not the coloured people also? Were they immune because they had the vote? Thus Malan gave notice to the coloured population that not even they would be immune from the impact of the new doctrine, 'Apartheid'. A few days later Hofmeyr was attacked for setting aside £200,000 for African school feeding on the Additional Appropriation Estimates. Kemp said it would bring Africans streaming from the reserves to the towns.

A few days after Hofmeyr had delivered his budget speech, there was another ominous swing away from Smuts. This was in Caledon, the place where in childhood Hofmeyr had looked after the pigs. Smuts had held Caledon by 1,112 votes in 1943. Three years later his majority had dropped to 446, a big shift in a constituency of 8,000 voters. Hofmeyr knew the Caledon district well, and he knew that the swing was ominous. It was all the more ominous because the budget had just provided generous assistance for farmers and agriculture. He was depressed by the result, which for him had one clear meaning, that now the war was over, many voters were turning or returning to Malan.

He was not only depressed, he was ill again. He hid the fact that on Budget Day he was in pain, with another acute infection of the kidneys. On 7 March he took to his bed, and left it to Sturrock to handle the budget debate. He was restless and impatient. He followed the debate with the greatest concentration, but he had another worry. In January, Smuts, under the pressure of the Dominionites and the Durban city council, froze all property transactions between Indians and other races, and promised the country another Asiatic Bill to replace the Pegging Act of 1943, which had frozen the position for only three years. This new Bill would create white areas and Indian areas, and no white person might buy property in an Indian area, nor any Indian person in a white area. In addition there were exempted areas, where any person might buy. The new Bill contained one entirely new feature—it gave Indian citizens representation in Parliament, and in the Natal and Transvaal provincial councils.

Smuts was in an extremely difficult position. Nehru had suggested another round-table conference, but white South African opinion was hardening against what it called interference in domestic matters. Meanwhile the Natal Indian Congress had decided to oppose the Bill completely, to send one delegation to India and another to the United Nations, and to invite a delegation from India. Smuts must have winced when he heard that these delegations would 'draw attention to the Fascist tendencies of the South African Government'. The meeting decided also to explore the possibility of establishing a world organisation of colonial and oppressed peoples. Smuts was right. He must anxiously and carefully watch. The new world organisation that he had done so much to bring into being was being used against him and by some of the people of his own country. On 7 February, in a fog of unreality, Parliament ratified his acceptance of the United Nations Charter. On 8 February, A. Ismail, president of the South African Indian Congress, said to the Congress *in absentia*, 'This is a crisis for the Prime Minister, the greatest test of his career.' A. I. Kajee, who led a Congress delegation to the Prime Minister, said that General Smuts might gain the support of British people in Natal, but would lose 'his international soul'!

Ismail and Kajee spoke nothing less than the truth. What they did not understand was that no one could be Prime Minister of white South Africa and keep his international soul. They were asking Smuts to do something that no leading white politician could do, unless, of course, he was prepared to cease to be a leading white politician. They were asking Smuts to do what Hofmeyr had, in part, already done.

Hofmeyr was more sympathetic towards Smuts's dilemma than he had been in 1936 and 1938. He himself had a hard choice to make. He was against the property clauses of the Bill, which he regarded as a 'surrender to European prejudice' in Natal. He was against the electoral provisions also, because Smuts had finally agreed that the Indian representatives in Lower House and Senate and Natal Provincial Council should be white persons. Hofmeyr wrote to Smuts from his bed in his room at the Wool-sack:

'In sticking to the colour bar as far as concerns Indian representation in Assembly and Senate, we shall be making a further surrender. To impose in respect of the Natal Provincial Council a colour bar which does not exist today is yet one more surrender. I regard it as the last straw breaking the camel's back and I cannot be a party to it.'

No one was more censorious of a compromise on principle than Hofmeyr. Yet his very being in the Government and the Cabinet was a compromise, and once that was accepted, other compromises would follow. Therefore he wrote:

'If the pressure from Natal is going to be too strong on this point, I suggest that you abandon the communal franchise proposal and go back to the Browne Scheme of a loaded franchise on a common roll. That would be a substantial concession to the Indian point of view, and I think one could in that event justify the colour bar as far as representation is concerned.'

Why should a colour bar on the common roll be justifiable, but not a colour bar on a separate roll? It would be hard to say. In any event Hofmeyr wrestled with the matter on what he called his 'bed of pain', and finally decided to accept the compromise to which he had told Smuts he could not be a party. What was more, he was now prepared to describe what he had once called a surrender, as a 'restoration of rights'.

A few days later on 16 March he flew up to Johannesburg to speak as Chancellor at the University of the Witwatersrand graduation. He was far from well and should not have gone at all, but he wanted to speak on the one theme that now was always on his mind; would the evil that South Africa had helped to defeat in Europe, now conquer her at home? And what was the danger? The belief that any nation, any race, was a *herrenvolk*, and had a right to determine the destinies of others.

Hofmeyr's 1946 address as Chancellor became known as the Herren-volk speech and ranked with the best addresses of his career. His theme was old, that is true, the eternal problem of the reconciliation of freedom and order; but he gave it a modern urgency. He first declared himself to be in favour of a world government as the expression of the principle of order; otherwise the atomic bomb would bring civilisation to an end. But lover of order as Hofmeyr was, he was more a lover of freedom.

To the four freedoms we must add a fifth, he said, 'the freedom from prejudice'.

'Surely it is a mockery for us to talk of ourselves as free people, or acclaim ourselves as the inheritors of a tradition of freedom, while we are as a nation to so large an extent the slaves of prejudice, while we allow our sense of dislike of the colour of some of our fellow South Africans to stand in the way of dealing with them, while we let ourselves become victims of the anti-Semitic doctrines which were a most important part of the Nazi ideology that we have fought to destroy. By way of illustration of what prejudice means in South Africa I cannot do better than refer to the growing tendency to describe as a Communist—and therefore one who should be condemned by bell, book, and candle—anyone who asks for fair play for all races, or who suggests that non-Europeans really should be treated as equals of Europeans before the law.

'The plain truth, whether we like it or not, is that the dominant mentality in South Africa is a *Herrenvolk* mentality—the essential feature of our race problems is to be found in that fact. The true solution of these problems must be found in the changing of that mentality. Ten years ago it was announced with a great flourish of trumpets that we had found a solution of our Native problem—but there was no change of our *Herrenvolk* mentality. I said then in an address delivered at this University, that it was futile to make such a claim. Today there are few people who would not agree that I was right. At this time when we are dealing with the Indian problem, though we may be able to settle certain aspects of it, it would be just as futile to claim that we can solve it, while in relation to it also that mentality continues to prevail to so great an extent as is obviously the case today.'

Hofmeyr concluded:

'Freedom from Prejudice—that is not least of the freedoms for which we must fight. We are paying a heavy price for our subservience to it today. Part of that price is material—undoubtedly we are the poorer as a nation because of our unwillingness to make full use of all our human resources. Part of it is being paid in the form of loss of international esteem and goodwill. We cannot hide our prejudices away in a cupboard from inspection by others. More and more South Africa is suffering because its policies and dominant attitudes of mind do not measure up to what are coming to be accepted internationally as standards of values. But our chief loss is a moral loss. As long as we continue to apply a dual standard in South Africa, to determine our attitudes towards, and our relationships with, European and Non-European on different ethical bases, to assign to Christian doctrine a significance which varies with the colour of men's skins, we shall suffer as a nation from what Plato would have called the lie in the soul—and the curse of the Iscariot may yet be our fate for our betrayal of the Christian doctrine which we profess.

'To you then as members of this University, as such playing today and likely to play in future, a great part in determining the intellectual and moral outlook of our nation, I commend this fifth freedom—freedom from prejudice—as worthy that you should fight for it. I shall put it more strongly than that. May you be prepared to say with Thomas Jefferson, "I have sworn upon the altar of God eternal hostility against every form of tyranny over the mind of man"—and here in South Africa the greatest evil of all is the tyranny of prejudice.'

Hofmeyr's address was greeted with thunderous applause. People crowded round him with shining eyes to thank him, and to thank God for him, and he, as always, replied to them formally, more constrained than they by the presence within him of this prophetic spirit. It was a great day for him and for the University, and for the first two African students to graduate from the medical school; they too were received with thunderous applause. Yet many of those who went with shining eyes left him with anxious ones, when they saw that the hope of their country looked like a man sick unto death.

Nothing showed more clearly than this speech that Hofmeyr had finally passed from optimism to resolution, from the affirmation 'the good will triumph' to the adjuration 'fight for the good'. Yet it showed something else too; it showed the clear-eyed vision of a man who could speak so stirringly about the toils in which he himself was caught. For was he not going back to Cape Town to vote for the Asiatic Bill that must be, and could not help being, the forerunner of a Group Areas Act that would cut up all South Africa into separate racial areas, into which members of other races could enter only for certain defined purposes? One could put forward the argument that the law would apply to all races; that was true. But would it apply equally to all races? Especially when it was made by a Parliament with not one representative of the Indian community. Should not one therefore welcome the Bill because it gave representation to the Indian community? This indeed became the ground on which Hofmeyr decided to support the Bill.

Yet he had to retreat several times. He wanted Transvaal Indians also to be represented on the Provincial Council, but his fellow Transvaal M.P.s declared that they would never be able to face the electors in their

38 constituencies, which included Hofmeyr's own. He also had to retreat before the caucus, which declared that it would be suicide to ask for Indians to represent Indians in Parliament.

Smuts was certainly having a tough time. Douglas Mitchell, Administrator of Natal, was in Cape Town to advise the Prime Minister that the Natal Provincial Council, which under Mitchell's leadership might have swallowed two Indian provincial councillors, was angry now to hear that the Transvaal Provincial Council would not have to swallow any. Charles Clarkson the Minister of the Interior, who had earlier caused a sensation by advocating municipal franchise for Indians, was under fierce attack from the municipalities, which could swallow Indian M.P.s and Indian provincial councillors but not Indian municipal councillors. Then there was R. M. Deshmukh, High Commissioner for India, who having failed to get a round-table conference, had to tell Smuts that the Government of India took the gravest possible view of the situation.

What could have been tougher? If Smuts made more concessions to India, he would lose voters in Durban. One thing could have been tougher, and that would have been if Hofmeyr had decided to oppose him; but luckily Hofmeyr had agreed to support him, on the condition that he could say just how and why.

Finally, after endless discussions, Smuts decided to proceed with a Bill which would contain segregation clauses, and would at the same time give Indians representation in Assembly and Senate and in the Provincial Council by persons of their own choice, provided such persons were white. On the afternoon of 12 March Smuts was informed that the Government of India gave notice of its intention to break off trade relations. It is hard not to reflect ironically on Smuts's situation. He was the first man to cause such a rift inside the British Commonwealth. It was under his prime-ministership that South Africa began her steady drift towards international isolation. It was his Asiatic Bill that provoked the United Nations into its first attack.

Hofmeyr returned from Johannesburg to join in the debate. He said he welcomed the Bill because it stopped the process of depriving the Indian community of their rights, and because it started the process of restoration. But he accepted the Bill as a second best. He would choose a communal franchise rather than no franchise, and hoped that the Indian community would see in it a recognition of their citizenship. However, he would not accept communal franchise for the coloured people, just as he had once resisted it for Africans. He had resisted because rights were being taken away, but here rights were being given. He quoted Onze Jan to support his dislike of the colour bar in parliamentary representation and by that he meant the colour bar which prevented Indians with a communal franchise from electing an Indian to represent them.

Hofmeyr then made the remark that gave the Nationalists a stick with which to beat him on the platteland. 'I take my stand for the ultimate removal of that colour bar from our constitution.'

When this was greeted with a buzz and murmur from the Nationalists, he continued defiantly: 'If my honourable friends want to use it to make political capital against me, they are free to do so. So far their attempts to undermine my position by misrepresentation of my attitude in these matters have yielded them very poor results.'

Then he repeated the truth that he had told white South Africa so many times before:

'If we act under the tyranny of prejudice and fear, we shall not save our white civilisation in South Africa. We in fact then abandon those principles which make European civilisation worth while. It is only to the extent that we can see in this Bill a means also to the upliftment of the at present still unrepresented Indian community, that we are justified in supporting it.'

Strijdom rose immediately to attack. He said that Hofmeyr had gained a 'glorious victory'; he had got his way, and the Afrikaners in his Party had been defeated.

'I want to say to the Minister of Finance that the white man will shed his last drop of blood to remain the master in South Africa . . . if the white man's rule in South Africa must come to an end—and it is clear that the Minister of Finance desires it—then I want members on the other side of the House and every white man in South Africa to review the future which awaits South Africa.'

Strijdom challenged Hofmeyr to endorse the maxim that the white man must be master. Hofmeyr interjected that there could be no lasting relationship on that basis. That was all Strijdom wanted. He did not want to argue with Hofmeyr, he merely wanted him to refrain from endorsing white supremacy, *baasskap*, so that white South Africa could see him as a betrayer.

Thus Hofmeyr's stand to remove the parliamentary colour bar became Hofmeyr's threat to remove all colour bars. Some of his own United Party men shook their heads over it, and thought that for a clever man he could be abysmally stupid. They were angered by the satisfied looks on the faces of the opposition; Hofmeyr had given them a priceless weapon, an accusation that would be hurled at the United Party from a thousand platforms, the accusation that Smuts's successor stood for racial equality.

Barlow made the most extraordinary speech in Hofmeyr's defence. He declared that the speech was one of the most remarkable ever made in the House. He said to the younger members of the House:

'Forget about the leaders of the parties. Go into the world and talk to the young black man and the young native and the young Indian and get him to come and sit down and reason with you to see if you cannot save this country for western civilisation. We old men have probably lost it for you.'

The great debate drew to a wearisome end. Stallard, the defender of all things British, supported the Nationalist amendments to defer the Bill and widen its scope and sharpen its teeth. Madeley, champion of the working man, declared that Indian representation in Parliament would endanger European civilisation. The Labour Party was split hopelessly, most following John Christie of Johannesburg in supporting the Bill; but Madeley voted consistently with the Nationalists, and van den Berg resigned from the Labour Party and joined them. He told his constituents that Hofmeyr's actions were diabolical, and that it was time for both English- and Afrikaans-speaking people who believed in a white South Africa to unite and fight Hofmeyr. The slogan for the next election must be 'Hofmeyr must be destroyed'. Such was the death of the Labour Party in South Africa.

The tension of the debate was eased when the lights failed during Smuts's speech on the second reading, and E. R. Strauss, the Nationalist M.P., called out, 'You see it is already dark, General,' to which Smuts replied, 'The light will come.' When the light came, Malan was speaking, and the Nationalists cheered and cried, 'Now there is light,' at which Malan smiled, and Smuts laughed heartily. Such was the jesting that preceded the passing of the Asiatic Land Tenure and Indian Representation Bill by 78 votes to 50. Smuts had really little to laugh about, for his local victory meant his international defeat, and the end of the great Smuts legend. A few days after the Bill was passed, he flew to London for the Commonwealth Prime Ministers' Conference. There his sun shone as brightly as ever and few knew that it was setting.

Smuts's absence meant that Hofmeyr had to assume the duties of the Prime Minister for the fifth time. He was in no state to do it. After a quick but false recovery, kidney trouble returned in June, and he was often in pain. As usual he replied curtly to inquiries about his health, but on some days one did not need to inquire, so shocking was his appearance. The last colour left his always sallow cheeks, leaving him not pale but dark. Sometimes he would stop in conversation, and tense himself, so that one knew he was in pain. He worked as hard as ever, but his extraordinary powers of concentration, memory, analysis, co-ordination, failed him for a while. Those who loved him watched him with distress.

Hofmeyr found it difficult to admit that he should be concerned. He wrote to Underhil:

'Since coming back here, I have had myself thoroughly overhauled by the doctors, who have now given a very satisfactory report, indicating that there is nothing to worry about, but insisting on the need for a holiday, with which I agree, so that my mother and I will be going down to the Natal Coast in a week's time. I shall not be able to be away from office for more than three weeks in all, if only because the Prime Minister may be going away again early in August but that should be enough. It is certainly more of a holiday than I have been able to allow myself for many years.'

For ten years in fact, since the trip to India!

He was again as excited as a schoolboy. Smuts had offered them the use of Botha House, the Prime Minister's residence at Umdoni Park. It was a beautiful house, white and gabled, standing in a great expanse of lawn. Not far away was a swimming bath built in the rocks, a placid pool at low tide, but at high tide full of the commotion of the sea.

Who was going? Mother and son, of course. And who else? She asked him that, because it was his holiday. He said that he would like Peter R., a 15-year-old boy who lived near them in Pretoria. Mrs Hofmeyr demurred, because in that case Mrs R. would have to be asked also; and Mrs R. was an attractive woman and a widow. Hofmeyr's reply was devil-may-care and nonchalant; if that was the case, then let Mrs R. come too. One could see from his manner that most of his mind was on his holiday, and a little on having Peter there as a companion, and none at all on having Peter's mother. Perhaps the old lady was clever too. She invited Sampie de Wet, the unmarried daughter of the former Chief Justice, because she thought Sampie needed a holiday; but Sampie thought she was being asked to provide the safety of numbers.

Sampie de Wet had a real affection for Hofmeyr, but now she saw him in a new light. It was not often when one visited Schoeman Street that one saw him as he was now, divested of his gravity. *Gravitas* indeed was laid aside, and *dignitas* also, leaving *simplicitas* in charge. And what a simplicity! He dressed in his camping clothes, his old floppy hat, his incredible long shorts, his dirty sandshoes. He shouted about the house, and if he could waylay Peter in the garden, he would trip him up by fair means or foul, and the two would wrestle on the lawn, to the accompaniment of Hofmeyr's giggles. They spent a great deal of time at the swimming pool, and took their first dip before breakfast. For a day or two Mrs Hofmeyr went with them, but after that she left the chaperoning to Sampie. Hofmeyr, in spite of the fright he had received at Aliwal North, thought it safe to duck Peter in the pool. There was more horseplay than swimming, and Hofmeyr managed, when splashing water over Peter, to see that Mrs R. was splashed also. Mrs R. was both a nice and a wise woman. She understood well the meaning of the splashing. She had been married and had had children of her own and she understood very well that Hofmeyr was interested in her as a woman; she understood also that in some things Hofmeyr was a boy who had never become a man. On one occasion Hofmeyr left the pool before she did, and sat across one of the steps so that she could not pass him. When she asked him to let her pass, he laughed at her. But when she continued to look at him, he became self-conscious and drew his legs up and let her pass. Her son Peter said to her, 'Hoffie likes you,' and she pretended it was news to her, news that interested her, but not profoundly.

After lunch the old lady ordered a siesta until four o'clock. Peter would go to the beach, and Mrs R. would go into the garden with a book. If the siesta was compulsory for anyone, it was for Hofmeyr, for what was the holiday for but to restore his health? But after a while he would come down the stairs in his socks, and take a chair and sit by Mrs R. in the garden, where they chatted together of many things. When it grew nearer to four o'clock Hofmeyr would take up his chair and leave her, and go back up the stairs to his room, from which he would emerge soon after, giving his impersonation of a man who had slept well.

For a short time he was transformed. It was what Sampie called 'a holiday out of this world'. He was with people he loved, and who loved him. They played 'Snap' and 'Donkey' and 'Ricketty Ann', which he called the de Wet game. He played with zest. He was out to win, and gloated over his victories and explained away his defeats. He made a great deal of noise, and his mother would reprove him, but with no intention of stopping him. When it was time to swim, he rounded up the others with admonitions and shouts. He was amused to find that one of Smuts's grandchildren had written on the wall of the writing-room abusive words about another, 'Sybella is a cow.' He would talk to Sampie about the books she had written, and compare the numbers sold with those of his own. Sometimes they would talk of something more serious, some public question, and the boy would drop away from him, so that he stood revealed for what he also was, a man of gravity and responsibility. She was touched by one of his attentions; the party had left Mrs Hofmeyr at the house, and walked to Sezela, but Sampie was tired and came back by train. He was at the station to meet her, courteous and solicitous, as became her host. She remembered his anger when some man came uninvited from Port Shepstone, to talk to him about some difficulty in regard to a township. He was astonished and said more than once, 'How dare he come here and worry me?'

Two weeks, and all too short. No cares of office, the sun and the sea, surrounded by lovers, eating and swimming and playing and sleeping, and a little flirtation. He had taken three weeks, but they could not stay longer, because Smuts wanted the use of the house. For Mrs Hofmeyr, it was another proof of Smuts's insensitivity. Did he not know that this was the first holiday for ten years? Did he not know that her son had worn himself out in the service of his Prime Minister and his country? Yet for the mercy of that happiness, that shouting about the house, let thanks be given.

Chapter 14

A Turning Point in South African History

On 16 August Smuts flew to the Peace Conference at Paris and the United Nations meeting at Lake Success, N.Y., leaving Hofmeyr to act as Prime Minister for the sixth time. Things were not easy at home. The president of the Natal Indian Congress, Dr G. M. Naicker, had called on 13 June for a Gandhian campaign of passive resistance, which would continue till the offensive Asiatic Land Tenure and Indian Representation Act was repealed. The Mahatma and Mr Nehru had sent special messages to a meeting of Indians in Johannesburg. It was announced that when Smuts arrived at Lake Success, the Government of India would attack him for his Land Tenure Act. All over the world it was known that people were willingly going to prison in protest against Smuts's law.

Smuts had another setback before he left.

On Monday, 12 August, 50,000 African miners went on strike, demanding 10s. per shift. Because they could not negotiate, some of the strikers marched through the streets towards the Johannesburg City Hall, but were driven back to the mines with the loss of four lives. At West Springs 4,000 miners, reported by the *Rand Daily Mail* to be armed with axes and iron bars, tried to march to Johannesburg, and police had to be summoned from all over the Witwatersrand to turn them back. At several mines the police had to drive miners underground and then drive them up again. Not until some had been killed did the strike come to an end. Smuts spoke to the Transvaal head committee of the United Party just before his departure, and said that the strike was not the result of real grievances but was the work of agitators.

Hofmeyr as Acting Prime Minister had to be fully prepared to crush disturbances by force, when he would rather have tried to remedy their causes. He had to turn down the plea of the Anglican synod of Johannesburg, under its great bishop Clayton, that the African Mine Workers' Union should be recognised and negotiated with. At a Circle Conference of the United Party in Pretoria, he had to declare that the Indian problem was not a matter for the United Nations, and that the Prime Minister would 'put the matter in its right perspective' at Lake Success. Like many white South Africans, he was torn in two between his loyalty to his country and his criticism of her policies, all the more so because he was both an eminent critic of the Government and an eminent member of it. At the same time that he was objecting to interference by the United Nations, he was declaring at the Johannesburg branch of the United Nations Association that in the last resort there would have to be some form of international government.

Meanwhile in Durban a mass meeting of between two and three thousand people, the overwhelming majority Indians, declared that they would enter the second phase of their passive resistance, namely to occupy property in controlled areas. The statistics of passive resistance were by no means negligible. On 4 October the *Natal Mercury* reported that since 13 June, 809 people had gone to gaol, 106 of them women. The resisters were drawn from all classes of the community, from the humblest to the most fortunate. Hofmeyr never underestimated them, in fact he did not like to speak about them. He was spiritually akin to them, but he was also their ruler; therefore they must obey a law that neither they nor he believed in.

On Wednesday, 14 August, while 4,000 African miners were attempting to march on Johannesburg, the Natives Representative Council was holding its annual sitting in Pretoria. Chief Victor Poto, Chief S. Moshesh, Professor Z. K. Matthews, Messrs A. W. G. Champion, R. H. Godlo, Selope Thema, Dr J. S. Moroka, they were all there, men highly respected in their communities, men who were as fit as any in the country to share in the work of government. A welcome was given to a new member, Chief Albert Luthuli from Natal.

A young Under-Secretary, Fred Rodseth, took the chair and made a speech containing no reference to the crisis. The youngest councillor, Mr Mosaka, promptly asked for a full statement, and the chairman said he would have to refer the inquiry to the Minister. Matthews expressed his distress, and Moroka said the Government was treating them like children. Thema said that 50,000 men do not leave their work because of agitation. Mosaka called the shooting 'wanton'. He said that the real cause of the trouble was the Native policy of South Africa; he said to the Government, 'You can do what you like, you can shoot us, arrest us, imprison us, but you are not going to break our spirit.' Councillors asked to go to Johannesburg and the Witwatersrand to see for themselves what was happening, but their request was refused.

The Council stood revealed in all its impotence. They represented 8,000,000 people, but they had less power than this young Under-Secretary for Native Affairs. They were advisers to the Government, but they could not even visit the scenes of these grave events. The Minister of Native Affairs seldom visited them, and the Prime Minister had not been near them since 1937. For ten years they had passed resolutions, but no one listened. Mosaka called the Council a 'toy telephone'. Thema said bitterly that it was not Hitler who had invented Nazism, but white South Africa.

On the second day of session Moroka put an urgent resolution which the official chairman, now in attendance, accepted, whether inadvertently or not, no one can say. Moroka moved:

'This Council, having since its inception brought to the notice of the Government the reactionary character of the Union Native Policy of seg-regation in all its ramifications, deprecates the Government's post-war con-tinuation of a policy of Facism which is the antithesis and negation of the letter and the spirit of the Atlantic Charter and the United Nations Charter.

'The Council therefore, in protest against this breach of faith towards the African people in particular and the cause of world freedom in gen-eral, resolves to adjourn this session, and calls upon the Government forthwith to abolish all discriminatory legislation affecting Non-Europeans in this country.'

The chairman would have liked to refuse the motion, but the twelve elected councillors persisted, and it was carried unanimously; even the three Government-appointed chiefs voted for it. It was history being made. No African political organisation would thereafter ask for less. The Council was virtually asking for the repeal of half of the important laws made by Parliament in the preceding thirty-six years. It was asking for the repeal of the Mines and Works Act, the Native Trust and Land Act, the Urban Areas Act, the Industrial Conciliation and Wage Acts, the Representation of Natives Act (in which Hofmeyr had voted in the famous minority of 11), the Hertzog Lands Act, the Native Laws Amendment Act, the Immorality Act, the Apprenticeship Act, the var-ious Asiatic and Land Tenure and Pegging Acts,—the whole array of segregation legislation which buttressed white supremacy and white privi-lege. The Council's action was proof of the saying, 'He who asks little and gets nothing will sooner or later ask everything.' Its resolution was sent to the Minister of Native Affairs and through him to the Acting Prime Minister.

So, in the eyes of an overwhelming majority of whites, the Council became extremists. It was proof, was it not, that if you gave a black man your finger, he took your hand? It was proof, was it not, of his ingratitude? It was proof, was it not, of the folly of the white liberals who thought that there could be a common society?

Soon after these events were over Hofmeyr was involved in yet another situation which highlighted the insolubility of his dilemma of being the acting chief executive of the all-white Parliament, and at the same time a believer, 'certainly in some respects', in the rejection of the colour bar. On 21 September the police raided the offices of the Communist Party, the Congresses, the Trade Unions, the newspaper *The Guardian*, and the Springbok Legion. The Minister of Justice declared that the raids were not anti-Red; they were made necessary by the violence of the miners' strike. Hofmeyr stated that the raids had taken him by surprise. The Communist Party, the Springbok Legion, and the Trade Unions protested to the Acting Prime Minister that the Government had never acted in this way against the New Order, the Ossewabrandwag, or the Greyshirts, but their protest bore no fruit.

Marquard wrote to Hofmeyr expressing his deep anxiety about these raids. Marquard declared himself to be one of those who regarded any interference with civil liberty as dangerous; he deprecated any attack on the Left simply because it was the Left, and he feared for white-African relations. Marquard pointed to the grave lack of support for liberalism within the United Party, which had the effect of alienating all liberals. Why didn't Hofmeyr come out and lead a Liberal Party? He wrote, 'This is the only hope I see of defending liberal ideals in this country.' Hofmeyr replied that the matter of the raids was *sub judice*, and therefore he could not discuss them; in regard to the establishment of a Liberal Party, they should get together for a talk, it being unwise to comment in writing.

Hofmeyr was far indeed from the happy position of Onze Jan or John Bright. He had less influence on the making of laws, and greater responsibility in the carrying out of them than either of them had ever had. He had taken high office and from that moment his dream had become unattainable. Yet while he pondered over his own future he had duties to perform. He wrote to Smuts and reported that the African miners were working well, but nothing had really been settled. He wrote, 'We shall undoubtedly have to set up machinery for the consideration of disputes affecting them.' More serious, wrote Hofmeyr, was the attitude of the Natives Representative Council.

'It seems that the (hitherto) moderate intellectuals of the Professor Matthews type are now committed to an extreme line against colour discrimination, and have carried the Chiefs with them. We can't afford to allow them to be swept into the extremist camp, but I don't see what we can do to satisfy them, which would be tolerated by European public opinion. The Native Representative Council was, however, a vital part of the 1936 legislation, and if it cannot be made to function, far-reaching questions will arise.'

A few days later Smuts replied to tell Hofmeyr of his own troubles:

'There is a growing widespread opinion adverse to us. South Africans are getting into ill odour, owing to colour bar and wrong native publicity, and perhaps also owing to our prosperous condition in an impoverished world. I fear our going will not be too good . . . I sense a worsening atmosphere in many directions. Mostly of course the trouble is due to South African attitudes on native political rights and the difficult structure of our social racial system. Our difficulties in this "one world" are increasing, and I don't see clearly what can be done about it. On top of all this came the matters you mention, the difficulty with the Native Representative Council and the question of Native Trade Unions and the right to strike.'

In due course Hofmeyr received a memorandum from the Natives Representative Council. He drafted a letter saying that he understood the reasons for their impatience and admitting that there were disciminatory laws. But to ask for their repeal forthwith was to ask for the impossible; while working for their repeal one had to live with the laws and, of course, obey them. This draft he sent to Smuts, and wrote to him also:

'You should know that Professor Matthews came to see me a week or two ago. He was at great pains to emphasise that they did not want the Council to be abolished, and hoped that we would be conciliatory. I told him that having regard to their resolution, and the speeches that led up to it, we could not do anything that would be interpreted as a surrender, and suggested that they should reconsider the question from that angle. He said he would take steps to consult his colleagues. As a result there may be something in the nature of a climb-down, in which event I shall of course let you know. It is clear that some of them at least are now frightened of the possible consequences of their action.'

Hofmeyr was quite wrong. While he was writing, the African National Congress was holding an emergency conference with no less than eight councillors on the platform, and adopted by an overwhelming majority a motion which supported the adjournment of the Natives Representative Council, said that the Representation of Natives Act of 1936 was a fraud, and called for a boycott of all elections in future.

Smuts left for America, to face an attack in the General Assembly on the Union's treatment of Indians, and its administration of South West Africa. He wrote to Hofmeyr that he would resist United Nations inquiry on the spot, but he would not ask for annexation, for that would only lead to a defeat, to be avoided at all costs. He had, already, in April of the same year, given an undertaking that the territory would continue to be administered scrupulously in accordance with the obligations of the mandate.

Smuts's letters to Hofmeyr reveal that he went to Lake Success with trepidation. It was not only the *Observer* and the *Manchester Guardian* he had to contend with. Back at home the passive resisters staged a special demonstration to coincide with the meeting of the General Assembly. On 23 October no less than 358 resisters were arrested.

At the Assembly Smuts declared that the United Nations would fail if it started to interfere in the domestic concerns of member countries. He told them what the Government did for its non-white peoples. He told them that hundreds of thousands would be only too glad to escape from India to South Africa. But no one would listen to him. His old power and prestige had gone. No illustrious gatherings rose to their feet as he came in. He was no longer one of the chief ambassadors of a great family of nations. He was only the leader of a small white aristocracy seeking to cling to its privilege in a changing world. In the old days, when mankind went on the march one could imagine Smuts marching at the head of it. Now men were on the march again, but Smuts could no longer march with them. At Lake Success they demanded that South Africa treat her Indian citizens in conformity with past agreement. No one gave him a word of praise for giving parliamentary representation to Indians. The Assembly rejected the suggestion that South West Africa be incorporated in the Union, and demanded that the mandate be converted into a United Nations trusteeship.

While Smuts was battling at Lake Success, Hofmeyr was declaring to the United Party congress in Natal that the relations of white South

Africans with their fellow-citizens of other races were part of a world-wide clash of colour. Hofmeyr said:

'Time was when the relationship between Europeans and non-Europeans was a matter for ourselves alone. We still like to regard it as such. We resent anything in the way of external interference. But in this shrinking world the position in this regard has changed considerably.'

In Pretoria on 20 November, Hofmeyr opened the resumed session of the Natives Representative Council. It may have been partly, or even wholly, due to Brookes that Hofmeyr opened the resumed session. Brookes knew the meeting was critical, and he urged Hofmeyr as Acting Prime Minister to show the Council a recognition that they had not received before. Brookes's affection and regard for Hofmeyr had never wavered, and it was Hofmeyr's doing that Brookes was now on the Native Affairs Commission.

Yet Brookes was disappointed and humiliated to hear Hofmeyr's reply to the Council's demand made in August for the removal of all discriminatory legislation. Hofmeyr first reported the regret and surprise felt by the Government at the 'violent and exaggerated statements' made in support of the demand. He then said that the removal of all discriminatory legislation was not practicable, and would not be in the best interests of the African people themselves; he gave as an example the Native Trust and Land Act, which preserved for Africans land which they would lose under conditions of free competition. He said much had been done to improve the lot of Africans, and told how expenditure on education which in 1926/7 was £543,000 had increased to £986,000 in 1939/40, and to £3,400,000 in 1946/7. Hofmeyr also dealt with health, and with the scheme of the committee on technical training, which was training African builders for African areas. He told the Council that considerable work had been done towards recognising African Trade Unions, but that the Government did not propose to recognise miners' unions. Finally Hofmeyr reported further purchases of land under Hertzog's Native Trust and Land Act of 1936. All the benefits, he contended, proved good will, and were 'an answer to the resolution passed by the Council'.

Hofmeyr received a unanimous vote of thanks, but both mover and seconder made it clear that they were thanking him for his courtesy, and that they would later consider his address. One thing was already clear to them, that the Government could think only in terms of lubricating the existing paternalistic machinery, not in terms of delegating power or responsibility, especially power. Brookes felt he had made a great mistake in urging Hofmeyr to come. If such a speech had to be made, then better for all if someone else had made it.

There was another thing that left a bad taste in the mouth. Four days before the Acting Prime Minister replied to the Council, the Chamber of Mines placed enormous advertisements in the newspapers, declaring that its policy was one of trusteeship. The advertisement declared, 'A Trade Union Organisation would not only be useless, but detrimental to the ordinary mine native in his present stage of development.'

Z. K. Matthews was Hofmeyr's most trenchant critic. Here was another man whom fate was forcing into a mould for which his temperament did not fit him. He was physically a big impressive man, but by nature he was deliberate and gentle, with none of the tricks of the demagogue. If the white people of South Africa had been willing to embark on a steady process of evolutionary change, they would have found no better man than Matthews to plan it with. Although he did not possess Hofmeyr's more startling gifts, he was his intellectual equal, and the best equipped of all the councillors to reply to the Acting Prime Minister. This he did five days later in the Council when he moved that, pending a reply from the Government more reassuring than the speech of the acting Prime Minister, the proceedings of the Council should be suspended, and that the councillors should remain in Pretoria to await such a reply. He said that to the Council Hofmeyr's statement 'seemed merely an apologia for the status quo, apparently oblivious of the progressive forces not only in the world in general but in South Africa itself'.

'The statement makes no attempt to deal with some of the burning questions of the day such as the pass laws, the colour-bar in industry, the political rights of the non-European in the Union; and in effect it raises no hope for the future as far as the African people are concerned . . .

'In his statement the Acting Prime Minister virtually denies that the Native Policy of the Union is in need of revision and proceeds to justify the policy of segregation and discrimination on the grounds of its supposedly protective character.'

A. W. G. Champion seconded Matthews's motion, gave the long list of discriminatory laws, and declared that the more advanced, the more urbanised, the more westernised an African became, the more harshly these laws operated against him. Without further discussion the motion was carried unanimously, and a copy was taken immediately to the Acting Prime Minister.

When the Council reassembled at 11 a.m. on 26 November, all knew that it was a fateful occasion. Although the Council was a body of responsible men treated like children, yet it was the only link between white and black South Africa, the only means whereby black South Africans could speak to their white fellow-countrymen, and tell them their hopes and sorrows. All present on that morning of 26 November were grave; if the Natives Representative Council refused to meet, then, to use Hofmeyr's own words to Smuts, 'far-reaching questions would arise'. It was certain that white South Africa would never return to the common franchise. Then the only alternative would be to accept Malan's contention that no black man could have any say whatsoever in the government of that part of the country known as white South Africa; if he wanted to rule, he must go back to his own territory.

Hofmeyr's reply to the Council's resolution had already arrived, and without delay the chairman, after prayers, read it out to the members. It was brief. The Government found itself unable to vary its decision. But it hoped that the Council would continue to play its part in the promotion of the further advancement of 'the Native peoples'.

The chairman appealed to the Council to consider earnestly before taking any drastic step. The Council then adjourned until 2.30 in the afternoon to consider the reply from the Acting Prime Minister. The councillors wanted to determine, Matthews told the chairman, whether the reply 'makes possible the co-operation which you have asked for, and which we are very willing to give—provided we can give it on conditions of dignity and self-respect'.

When the Council resumed at 2.30, it found itself unable to co-operate further with the Government. Matthews moved a resolution to adjourn, so that the councillors could go to the country 'to make fully known to the African people the nature and contents of the Acting Prime Minister's statement'.

Thema, in seconding the resolution, put a question to white South Africa, 'Do you want us to join those forces that are outside, those forces which are out to destroy? If you drive us to that we shall know what to do; but we don't want to do that. That is my answer. I second the motion.'

Moroka said that the true reason for the Government's refusal to agree to the Council's resolution was that it was afraid of the Nationalists, who were preparing to fight the next election on the colour issue. He asked how Smuts, who had been partly responsible for the Atlantic Charter, could allow the colour bar.

'I just cannot understand it. I cannot get into his heart, and find out how after all he has done in the world, the big work he has done for humanity, he can now return to his own country and say that freedom cannot be given to the black people because they will murder the Europeans, and will want to marry Europeans.'

Matthews's resolution was passed unanimously.

26 November 1946 was a turning-point in South African history. After that the demand of non-white people was for equality, not alleviation or improvement. And Hofmeyr, in the eyes of many non-white people, ceased to be the spokesman of freedom and became the spokesman for white supremacy. He knew it, and found it painful.

26 November was also virtually the end of the Natives Representative Council. It did not meet again until January 1949, when the chairman, still Dr W. G. Mears, who one assumes spoke with considerable pain, told the Council that it had hardly been missed, that it was doubtful whether it 'ever presented the real needs of the natives', that it had turned its mind to politics, especially the politics of equality, and that the Government had it in mind to take the necessary steps to abolish the Council. This address came in fact from Dr E. G. Jansen, Malan's own Minister of Native Affairs who had voted for the establishment of the Council in 1936. As a result of this address, the Council resolved that it was unable to proceed. In 1951 it was abolished altogether. The machinery created by Hertzog's famous Bill of 1936, the passing of which was greeted by an unprecedented storm of cheering in the House, had fallen to pieces. White South Africa had resolutely turned its back on the concept of a common society.

Five days after the Council's adjournment, Hofmeyr said to the Caledonians at their dinner in Johannesburg, 'We must decide tonight whether we will accept Robbie Burns's dictum that "a man's a man for a' that", and if we do, then we must go on to unity with whole-hearted acceptance of that spirit of mutual trust which alone can make for true prosperity.' The Left sneered at him for speaking brotherhood to Caledonians and white supremacy to the Natives Representative Council.

Only Hofmeyr himself, and those who supported him, and those who were sufficiently remote from politics to see things clearly, understood the inwardness of the situation. How could one be simultaneously both governor and crusader? Hofmeyr had begun to question the view that he himself had held so strongly, that the best way to change the United

Party was from within; he had begun to believe that it might embarrass both the Party and himself.

No one understood the United Party position better than the Nationalists. Out in the countryside they were attacking Hofmeyr, and saying that the next election would be a Hofmeyr election. Strijdom was using with deadly effect Hofmeyr's declaration that he stood for the abolition of that colour bar in Parliament which prevented coloured people, Africans and Indians, from being represented by their own people. Hofmeyr had challenged the Nationalists to use it against him, and now they were doing it. If a man wanted coloured people and Africans and Indians in Parliament, where would he stop? The Nationalists were declaring that the answer was simple: Hofmeyr was in favour of abolishing the colour bar altogether. What logic was there in having all races in Parliament, and not in schools, cinemas, hotels and restaurants?

In January 1947 the United Party lost the Cape constituency of Hottentots Holland to the Nationalists. Sir de Villiers Graaff was the popular United Party candidate, but he could not prevent the conversion of a United Party majority of 1,228 into a Nationalist majority of 637. It was a spectacular defeat.

On the eve of the election Graaff held a meeting, and invited Hofmeyr to speak. Of this meeting Graaff said, 'Hofmeyr came with great delight to help me; he had known me as a child and was always most gracious to me.' At about 11 p.m., when everyone was wanting to go home, a Nationalist asked Hofmeyr a question on the franchise, and Hofmeyr repeated his parliamentary statement of 1946, 'Natives will eventually be represented in Parliament by Natives and Indians by Indians.'

Was it this statement that lost the election? Graaff said it did not, that the election was already going against him, and that the statement might have lost him fifty votes. Graaff's opinion was supported by a meeting of the United Party M.P.s and provincial councillors, who at a post-mortem decided that the threat of food-rationing, the multiplicity of control boards, the fear of immigration and immigrants, the housing shortage, and the shabby treatment of pensioners, were the cause of defeat. Hofmeyr's racial views were not cited, but the meeting declared that the Fixed Property Tax and the Excess Profits Duty were affecting Party funds.

Others held a contrary opinion. When the victor of Hottentots Holland was escorted into the House, a Nationalist called out, 'Hofmeyr should bring him in.' The *Sunday Times* of Johannesburg said that Hofmeyr had made 'a gift of the seat to the Nationalists,' and that he must not race ahead of public opinion. Hofmeyr himself did quite a courageous thing; on the Saturday following the election he visited United Party supporters in the Hottentots Holland, and reported to Graaff that some of the old stalwarts had said to him, 'Well, we don't think you were politically wise, but you didn't lose the election.'

Parliament resumed on 18 January without ceremony, for this was merely a continuation of the adjourned session of 1946. The new session would be opened by King George VI on 21 February. The Nationalists decided in 1947 to launch a full-scale campaign against Smuts and Hofmeyr. They attacked Smuts because he was involving South Africa in an unwanted, futile, even hostile internationalism. They attacked Hofmeyr because his franchise policy would lead to the downfall of 'white civilisation'. The first Nationalist attack was mounted by Malan on 21 January, and it gave every evidence of having been thoroughly prepared.

Malan moved that the Union should reject the right of the United Nations to concern itself with South West Africa or South African Indians, that it should give South West Africa the status of a province, and that it should repeal those provisions of the law which gave Indians parliamentary and provincial representation. Malan also moved the appointment of a joint committee of both Houses, to devise a comprehensive policy based on racial separation, politically, residentially, and as far as practicable, industrially; such a policy would be 'constructive and equitable in respect of the specific interests of each separate population group'. Malan quoted Hofmeyr's reply at Hottentots Holland and declared that once Indians and Africans were allowed in Parliament, all barriers would go.

When Smuts spoke, Swart confronted him with Hofmeyr's election statement, to which Smuts replied that he did not know what the views of the next generation would be. Strijdom pressed him about Hofmeyr, and Smuts declared all men had their own views. He himself had views that were not part of the policy of the party or the policy of the country. He said, 'Perhaps that applies also to the Minister of Finance.'

Nothing could have shown more clearly than this debate the fierce hostility of the Nationalists to any kind of internationalism that would come poking into their affairs and telling them how to run their country. Nationalists seldom look for strength outside, they look for it within, and they had found it in their victory at Hottentots Holland. Hofmeyr and Hottentots Holland, these were the two names with which the Opposition taunted the Government.

The fierce debates of the 'thirties had caused painful stresses in Hertzog's United Party; so now did this debate tear the heart-strings of Smuts's more conservative Afrikaners. J. B. Wolmarans said in his bewilderment: 'I have sat and listened to the charge . . . that we are engaged in removing the dividing line between white and black. There is nothing . . . in that allegation.'

SAUER: Ask Hofmeyr.

WOLMARANS: The United Party does not stand for that. The Hon. Member for Krugersdorp . . . requested that the Prime Minister should stand up and say: My Party and I stand for white South Africa.

MEMBER: And he cannot say it.

WOLMARANS: I say this: Yes, the United Party stands for white South Africa, and the best proof that I can offer of that is this: should the day break when the United Party no longer stands for a white South Africa, you will no longer find John Wolmarans in their ranks.

MEMBER: It will then be too late.

F. E. Mentz, M.P. for Westene, Johannesburg, made in brief compass as honest a confession of white South African fear as anyone could have done. He said:

'The Minister of Finance is now seeking a solution—a middle course between separation and equality. There is no such thing as a compromise. On the one hand we can have separation and, failing that, we must have total equality. There is no middle course. If we endeavour to effect a compromise between the two, it will only mean that we are digging the grave of separation in South Africa, and at the same time we are digging a grave for European South Africa. We cannot have a compromise.'

On the third day of the debate, Strijdom, the Lion of the North, roared to the attack. He declared that Smuts's policy and Hofmeyr's were one and the same. But Hofmeyr stated his policy clearly, and Smuts put his vaguely so that he could satisfy now one side, now the other. Strijdom declared again that Hofmeyr stood for 'the removal of the colour bar in the political sphere'. Strijdom read Hofmeyr's words from *Hansard*, 'I am in favour of the ultimate removal of that colour bar from the Constitution.'

Strijdom went on to argue that that meant the swamping of Parliament by non-white representatives and the downfall of 'white civilisation'. Yet only racial separation could save the country from bloodshed.

When Hofmeyr had made his famous remark in Parliament in 1946, he had challenged the Nationalists to use it against him. And they had done so, with Strijdom leading the attack. For a Nationalist any breach in the colour bar was the breach in the dyke that would let in the sea, the innocent cup of tea that led to other forms of intercourse. But for Hofmeyr, the Nationalist accusations were distortions. He had been speaking about communal franchise, but the Nationalists declared that his remarks must apply to all franchises, and to many other things also. Had Hofmeyr not refused to forbid mixed marriages? Had he not refused to forbid the 'white' universities to admit non-white students? Who thought for a moment that he stood only for the removal of one, specific, parliamentary colour bar?

When Hofmeyr rose to reply to Strijdom, he was angry in a way that no one had seen him angry before. Seasoned reporters, such as Tom Macdonald and Scott Haigh, thought it was his finest hour. Why was Hofmeyr so angry? Did Malan's thrust go home, that if you removed this one colour bar, then the social colour bar—which Hofmeyr approved—would begin to yield? Was there not pain too in Hofmeyr's anger? Never before had his position in the Party appeared so impossible. Every Opposition speaker had turned on him. Could he go to Wolmarans's rural constituency of Losberg and tell them that he could not stand for a white South Africa? Who would appeal more to that community, he or Strijdom, especially when Strijdom reminded them that the constitution of the old Transvaal Republic laid it down, 'no equality in Church or State'?

Hofmeyr was not a man to base a speech on pain or anger. He was not a man to reveal pain at all. But now he was fighting for those values which, whatever his faults, were his very life, and therefore, he was fighting for his life too. His strong clear voice rang out over the chamber, asking the members to get away from Strijdom's 'supercharge of emotion', and to return to calmer waters. Yet he himself was in the grip of emotion. He spoke of Strijdom's 'career of distortion', and reproved by the Speaker, said he would not repeat the phrase, and finally withdrew it. He and Strijdom entered into a heated exchange, he saying that he was referring to one specific colour bar, Strijdom saying that he referred to the general colour bar. Four times Hofmeyr struck the volume of *Hansard* from which he quoted, with Strijdom, van den Berg, Sauer,

Serfontein, all interrupting. Hofmeyr challenged them to bring a single proof that he had ever lifted a finger to get the succession. He said emphatically that he did not aspire to that position. His passion was now subsiding, the interruptions died down, and the House fell under the spell that he could cast when he spoke without the aid of memory.

If Malan believed, said Hofmeyr, that Indian representation spelled the end of white civilisation, then he must demand the abolition of 'native representation', the abolition of the coloured vote on the common roll, the abolition of the coloured representation altogether. Malan disapproved also of the Natives Representative Council, and called its members agitators; therefore they must go too, but what would he put in their place? Was South Africa to go back to the United Nations, and tell them that neither Indians nor Africans would be represented in the House? Malan wanted racial policy to be definite, but his own policy was political separation, residential separation, and industrial separation 'as far as practicable'. Therefore Malan acknowledged their common interests, but in regard to these common interests only white people would decide. Malan wanted a great non-white university, but what would he do with the Matthewses and Morokas that the university would produce, people whom he branded as agitators?

Hofmeyr declared that Malan had no logic on his side, but some of his followers had. Strijdom was logical because he said openly that the policy of racial separation was to preserve, not justice, but white domination. Logic was on the side of those Nationalists who had opposed bigger grants for Native Education.

In conclusion Hofmeyr suggested the proper attitude towards the United Nations:

'The right policy for us is that of standing firm where we have right on our side, and for the rest being conciliatory and acting with a view to strengthening our own position within UNO itself. The policy of defiance without the basis of moral principle which this resolution or most of it proposes, would mean the acceptance of the very gravest risks for our future. It is not along those lines that the preservation of the things which we hold dear in South Africa can be secured.'

After Hofmeyr's speech the storm died away in a postlude of flashes and rumblings. But the thunder rolled again when Swart attacked Hofmeyr's paper, the *Forum*, for its equivocal race policies. Dönges challenged Hofmeyr to state whether he would extend the municipal franchise to non-whites in the Transvaal and the Free State. Malan in his concluding speech said that Hofmeyr endeavoured 'to disguise his real attitude and policy by making an attack on the principle of separation'.

Not in the whole history of the Union Parliament from 1910 to 1947 had any member suffered such a sustained attack, always fierce, sometimes virulent, sometimes contemptuous. Was it true that Hofmeyr tried to disguise his real attitude? The truth was that as second Minister in Smuts's cabinet he could not answer the questions that were being put to him. If he had answered them, in some private capacity that he no longer possessed, he would have caused a crisis of the first magnitude in the United Party. But that was not his only difficulty. His other difficulty, just as great, was that he also was a white politician, dependent on white support, and would have had to resort to the same compromises as René de Villiers had advocated in the *Forum*, a social colour bar by common consent, a colour bar in schools but not universities, a communal roll for Africans but the common roll for Indians, yet with higher qualifications for Indians than would be needed by whites. It is quite meaningless to say that Hofmeyr never compromised. He was a Christian moralist and a Minister of the Crown, in a society where power had reached almost no mutual accommodation with justice, and he could do nothing else but compromise. Here one remembers John Gray's remark that Hofmeyr was born to be a Charles James Fox, but that he wanted to be a Pitt.

No one understood his predicament better than the Nationalists. They turned to Hofmeyr the politician and said to him, 'Come to the Free State and tell us about your colour bars.' Therefore when one writes that 23 January was one of Hofmeyr's finest hours, one must write also that it was one of the most terrible. Only thus can one understand the anger that possessed him, and made him strike a book four times with his hand. It became clearer than ever—except to those who would not give up hoping—that Hofmeyr would not be Smuts's successor. Yet who else was there?

But now was the time to put these problems away for a while, and to enjoy the excitement of the royal visit. Parliament sent a message of welcome to the King and Queen and the two Princesses, and Malan did not oppose it. The royal group, with the King in the white uniform of an Admiral of the Fleet, was met at the Cape Town docks on 17 February by the Governor-General and the Prime Minister. Guns boomed and bands played. The royal route up Adderley Street to Government House was all flags and bunting and illuminations, and was lined by the densest crowd ever seen in Cape Town, cheering their heads off. At Government House the King received a joint address of welcome from South Africa's legislators. Only eleven Nationalist M.P.s were present; Malan and the provincial leaders of the Party did not attend. After the address had been presented, the King invested Smuts with the Order of Merit. That night there was a State banquet, and Smuts spoke of the great opportunity given to all the people in South Africa of showing 'their loyal affection'. The King replied, paying tribute to South Africa's soldiers, to Botha and to Smuts, of whom he said, 'The whole Commonwealth is indebted to you.' That evening the orchestra, correctly as it transpired, at one point played only 'Die Stem van Suid-Afrika'; but Stallard disapproved of this, and began singing 'God Save the King', and was joined by both crowd and orchestra.

On Wednesday the royal family visited the parliamentary sports-ground at Fernwood, and were photographed with a smiling Hofmeyr, dressed in immaculate white. The Queen tried her hand at the game of *jukskei*. On Thursday, Mrs Hofmeyr, at the Prime Minister's special request, accompanied him to Stellenbosch, where 15,000 people gathered to give the royal family a decorous welcome.

On Friday, 21 February, with Malan and all the Nationalist M.P.s attending, the King and Queen drove to Parliament. As the royal pair sat down in the House of Assembly, the band played 'God Save the King'. The King, after a brief and formal speech, declared the fourth session of the ninth Parliament to be opened, first in English and then in Afrikaans, and thereafter the band played 'Die Stem van Suid-Afrika'.

Then the royal family set out in the White Train on their strenuous 9,000-mile tour of the Union, a journey marked by no unpleasantness. It is true that the Transvaal Nationalist daily, *Die Transvaler*, under its editor Verwoerd, ignored the tour altogether, but that did not prevent Nationalists in all centres from 'going to have a look at the English King and Queen'. The King won many hearts by calling on President Steyn's widow in Bloemfontein, and by restoring President Kruger's Bible to his heirs. African and coloured people turned out in hundreds of thousands to see the great-grandson of Queen Victoria, and the Indians of Durban and Pietermaritzburg joined in heartily.

Smuts was in his element. He was thoroughly at home with the royal family, and they with him. Hofmeyr's latent republicanism was brought out, not by the presence of the royal family, but by the ubiquity of the Prime Minister. Smuts was there in Cape Town, at Government House, at the House of Assembly, at the Ball, on the top of Table Mountain. He was there at Stellenbosch and Paarl. On their way north, he met the royal party at Harrismith, escorted them to Ladysmith, and accompanied them to the Mont-aux-Sources National Park in Natal. Then he took them to Pietermaritzburg, and having seen their Natal tour well launched, he flew back to Parliament. He was there at Standerton to welcome them to the Transvaal, and accompanied them to Pretoria and Johannesburg. Mrs Smuts was not well, and the King and Queen paid a special visit to see her at Doornkloof. Smuts was photographed with the party in a dozen places, wearing well-cut suits, white tie and tails, and climbing kit, always smiling in a way that managed to be both loyal and benign.

Hofmeyr, always so circumspect in relation to his chief, thought it was going a bit far. He who had been declared by Oxford University to be the 'strength and stay of the British Commonwealth' thought that Smuts need not have been so openly royalist. He was a little peeved too, because he thought that Johannesburg should have been left to him. He wrote that the royal visit had proved strenuous for him 'when the PM and half my colleagues were away from Cape Town in attendance on the Royal Party, and I was left to mind the Parliamentary baby'. Mrs Hofmeyr was of course more forthright. She would say of Smuts with that look in her eye that did not invite further comment, 'At his age he ought to know b-better.' She also had reason to be peeved. Owing to Mrs Smuts's illness, Smuts asked Mrs Hofmeyr to accompany him to the State banquet in Pretoria, but when the banquet was over, he forgot all about her, and friends had to take her home. She was however not humiliated by this, but told the story with gusto, adding in her own inimitable fashion, 'Of c-course I am not Royalty.'

There seems little doubt that Smuts was attracted by royalty and by the institution of royalty, with its pomp and proprieties and protocol. When the royal family of Greece had to leave their country in 1941, the Crown Prince Paul and his wife Princess Frederika made their temporary home in South Africa. Princess Frederika was a striking-looking woman, and Smuts was certainly attracted to her, and she to him. When the Crown Prince returned to Europe and the Middle East, the Princess stayed in South Africa, and saw a great deal of the Smuts family. In Cape Town she and her children stayed in a wing of the Governor-General's residence, and when it was destroyed by fire, they were taken in by General and Mrs Smuts at Groote Schuur, the Prime Minister's residence. When Parliament rose and the administration moved to

Pretoria, the Princess would often visit Doornkloof, and walk with Smuts over the farm, learning about grasses and flowers. When Parliament resumed, she found a large pleasant house in Cape Town, and there her third child was born, Smuts standing as godfather. When duty recalled Prince Paul to Cairo, she insisted on going back with him, and did so. However, when Rommel threatened Egypt, she returned to Cape Town, and took to rock-climbing as a pastime.

It was natural that the Princess should try to use Smuts's enormous influence to secure the return of the royal family to Greece, for there were strong forces in Athens seeking to overthrow the monarchy. After the return had been effected, Smuts formed the habit of dropping in at Athens on his journeys to and from Europe. With the true nature of the attachment this book has nothing to do, but there was a certain amount of amused talk about it, though not in very wide circles. For a collector of Mrs Hofmeyr's rank, it was the find of a lifetime. She would survey her guest with that famous look in her eye, and say, 'General Smuts has g-gone to Greece again.' If the company was very select, someone might add something. But in one company not so select, no one said anything at all, until she spoke again, as though she were adding an inconsequential afterthought, 'He's having a r-royal time.' Then the company knew that the subject was closed; it was as though a witch had lifted the lid off her brew, and allowed one to smell it, and had put the lid on again, all on condition that no one said a word. In more select company she was scathing about the attachment, and used both ridicule and censure. Hofmeyr himself was more temperate in judgement, but he too thoroughly disapproved of the whole business, and thought it did neither Smuts nor his causes any good.

Behind the brilliant façade of the royal tour of South Africa, politics proceeded as usual. About this time there were persistent rumours of disaffection and dissatisfaction in the ranks of the United Party. While the food planners reported progress, the newspapers reported shortages of meat, sugar, butter. The Nationalists were, as always, trying to split off the conservative members of the United Party, but now they hoped for more. The political correspondent of the *Natal Mercury* reported that there was criticism within the caucus, not only of the incompetence of Ministers, but of the Party leadership itself. There was no doubt truth in the report, yet when Smuts returned to Cape Town during the royal tour, he was cheered when he walked into the United Party caucus. He offered to hand over the leadership if the caucus was dissatisfied; after that the criticism died.

To whom indeed could the caucus entrust leadership? Sarel Tighy, the tough United Party member for Johannesburg West, wrote to Smuts and warned him that Nationalists might win the 1948 election on the colour issue. It was urgent to lift the issue out of the political arena. It was urgent, in fact, to do the very thing that Malan had asked for, and to appoint a committee of experts to study the whole question. Tighy wrote that Smuts's rejection of this suggestion had made a powerful weapon for the Nationalists at Wakkerstroom.

It will be remembered that Smuts had rejected Malan's suggestion because Malan had insisted that the basic assumption of such a committee should be racial separation. What was more, Malan knew that that was the basic assumption of many Smuts supporters. The United Party remained in its insoluble predicament. Harry Lawrence, the Minister of Social Welfare and Demobilisation, would not introduce a colour bar into the board controlling welfare bodies, but gave a verbal assurance that he would not appoint a mixed board, 'so long as feeling in the country is as it is at the present'. Erasmus called this a policy of deceit. Haywood of Bloemfontein District declared that Hofmeyr, because he pleaded for absolutely equal political rights, was encouraging agitation and communism. A United Party member interjected that Hofmeyr had done no such thing, and the whole sorry subject was reopened. Piet van der Byl, the Minister of Native Affairs, stated that Hofmeyr had 'absolutely refused to give in' to the demands of the Natives Representative Council.

While the Nationalists, with their eyes on the elections, were asking for the abolition of the Council, Smuts, with his eyes on the outside world, was trying to make it work. Those two illustrious parliamentarians, the Natives' Representatives, Margaret Ballinger and Donald Molteno, urged the Government to end the deadlock. Smuts's two proposals to the Council were that African trade unions (except mining unions) would be recognised, and that the powers of the Council would be increased, especially in respect of the development of the Native reserves. The six councillors asked to be allowed to consult their colleagues. Almost immediately Dr. A. B. Xuma, the chairman of the working committee of the African National Congress, rejected the Smuts proposals. He said, 'We do not accept any proposal that does not provide for direct representation of all sections of the community in all legislative bodies.'

The Nationalists had no sympathy for Smuts in his difficulties. They declared that the Council was impudent and truculent and should be abolished.

Smuts was in a difficult situation. Every concession he made to the Natives Representative Council meant that a few more white voters decided to support Malan; every rebuff by the Council meant a few more still. Smuts's problem was that he was trying to delegate power, and that white South Africa was either determined not to delegate power or was nervous about doing it. It is often said that Smuts failed to use his great influence to get white South Africa to move with the times; people suggested that this was because he was at heart a Boer. If Smuts can be judged, then History may be able to do it. All that one can say now is that his problems were immense. History may well say that far greater than Smuts's power was the intransigence of white South Africa, which was to evolve, under the Nationalists, a new way of dealing with the problem of power. The Nationalist solution was to keep white power intact, and to create new centres of limited black power elsewhere.

But if Smuts was in a difficult position, the United Party was in one yet more difficult. On 24 May Smuts turned 77. He was given a great party in the caucus room, and he said: 'No one at 77 should still need to be in harness and I hope that it will not be necessary for me for very long now either. An old fellow must be spared to have at least some rest at the end of his life.'

It was both a grave and a jolly occasion. At the end of it Senator A. J. de la Rey, who had been with Smuts on commando half a century before, led the assembly in singing, 'Dat's Heeren Segen op u daal' ('God's blessing descend on you').

But would God's blessing descend on the United Party? That was the question. It was almost impossible for two members of the Party to be together long without talking about the succession. Though Hofmeyr had no desire that he should succeed Smuts, it was painful for him to know that so many members of the party shared his desire.

Hofmeyr's dislike of his Finance job grew steadily. His desire to get rid of it had nothing to do with the theory that a future Prime Minister should steer clear of the Treasury, especially when the time for succession draws near. His dislike was no secret. Smuts knew of it, but did not respond to it. Dr Loveday spoke to Smuts more than once of Hofmeyr's health. It may have been Loveday's doing, or the King's, but Hofmeyr was surprised when in May 1947 Smuts suggested to him that he should drop Finance and take over Smuts's own portfolio of External Affairs.

Hofmeyr said he would welcome the change; in any case he felt that his job at the Treasury was finished. After that nothing happened. Two months later Hofmeyr raised the matter again, and Smuts told him that while he could find someone to succeed Hofmeyr at the Treasury, it would be difficult to find a substitute for his successor. Smuts indeed indicated to Hofmeyr that there was no likelihood of any immediate change. Hofmeyr wrote that it was clear to him that Smuts wanted no change before the 1948 election, and that he was not anxious to give up External Affairs, 'in which', Hofmeyr added with his extraordinary honesty, 'he is probably correct'. But one person did not accept the situation so passively, and that was Mrs Hofmeyr. She knew what it cost her son to be Leader of the House, Minister of Finance, Second Minister, and substitute for sick and travelling Ministers. She made no jokes about it, she was unsmiling and silent. But her anger against Smuts mounted.

In 1947 Parliament was prorogued fairly early, on 5 June. At one time it looked as though Smuts might send Hofmeyr to represent South Africa at the wedding of Princess Elizabeth to Prince Philip. But Smuts decided to go himself. Hofmeyr wrote to Underhill: 'I am not entirely sorry since I am loath to leave my mother for any length of time. She is getting old—almost 84 now—though happily not showing any signs of it.'

He was always solicitous for her, but that did not prevent him from thinking what his life might have been had she not been there. Before he left Cape Town, Brookes had gone to see him on some matter of business, in the office of the Minister of Finance. After some twenty-five years of married life, Brookes had asked his mother to leave him and his wife and family, and to make her home somewhere else. It was a step he had wanted to take many times before, but only now had he felt able to take it. When he and Hofmeyr had finished their business, Hofmeyr said to him, 'So your mother's left you.' Then Hofmeyr added, with all gravity, 'How did you manage it?' Brookes, not yet recovered from his painful experience, was embarrassed and constrained, and evaded the question. But afterwards he was remorseful, and felt that he had failed Hofmeyr in some important way. Yet in all probability he had not. Hofmeyr was not asking advice on how to do it, he was probably only fascinated to know that it could be done.

Back in Pretoria Hofmeyr had to take his part in the preparations for the elections of 1948. Usually he had a zest for elections, but this time he had not. He knew it would be a Colour election, and that meant it would be a Hofmeyr election. That was hardly something to look forward to.

The thought of the future hung like a cloud over his life. He wrote:

'In my own mind there is a growing sense of unsettlement. It would be difficult for me, if Smuts were to fall away, to lead the United Party, without either doing violence to my convictions or taking a line which would split the Party.'

He was not only unsettled, he was in a graver situation. He still worked hard, as he had always done, but now the work did not satisfy him. Winning the war, that was something, it was something to have been the Minister of Finance during the war. But now the job seemed to him more and more negative. Then his mind was full of the everlasting and unsettling question, not only of the succession, but of what would happen when Smuts went.

The question was made still more urgent because Arthur Keppel-Jones, Senior Lecturer in History at the University of the Witwatersrand, had just finished a frightening forecast of the future, called *When Smuts Goes*. According to him the United Party would disintegrate, the Nationalists would come to power, and would embark on a programme of racial legislation the like of which the African continent had never seen. English-speaking people would leave the country in great numbers, and finally black and white would meet headlong in a catastrophe of violence and destruction. America and Britain would intervene, with the result that the black nationalists would take over, and those white people who were left would ask earnestly and pathetically of anyone who was prepared to listen to them, 'But what did we do wrong?'

With a mind full of these unsettling thoughts, and a soul seeking confidence and peace, Hofmeyr decided to keep a diary. He opened his diary on Friday, 22 August 1947, with these words, 'I have decided to commence a Diary in the hope that if I am able to keep it up, it may, in future years, be of interest to myself and, possibly, to others.'

In the Hofmeyrian sense, it was.

Chapter 15

The Fall of Smuts

HOFMEYR's opening entry in his diary dealt with one topic that continually troubled his mind—the succession. This problem he took to Cope, during their weekly conference on the *Forum*. Both of them had read *When Smuts Goes*, and this had turned their thoughts to the grave questions of the future. Suppose that Smuts won the election; then, said Hofmeyr to Cope, there might be a disintegration in the Nationalist Party. Then the Keppel-Jones sequence of events would not be started. Then he, Hofmeyr, could take an independent line without danger.

But suppose Smuts fell away *before* the election. Then Hofmeyr's refusal to accept the leadership would probably mean the defeat of the United Party. But would not his acceptance of the leadership also mean the defeat of the United Party? And would not Hofmeyr have compromised his future as a leader of any kind? What then should he do?

Cope was both surprised and excited by Hofmeyr's question. He was one of the younger men who hoped that there might one day be a Hofmeyr party. Now it seemed within reach. When he met Hofmeyr at their next conference, he told him his conclusions. They were that the best thing Hofmeyr could do for South Africa would be to decline the Premiership, hasten whatever political crisis might follow, and above all stick to his principles on the 'Native question'. Cope said that the danger of a Nationalist accession was not so great as to justify compromise; in any case, if the Nationalists were destined to get in, then the sooner the prospect was faced, the better.

Hofmeyr also consulted Edgar Brookes, who thought that a Nationalist accession would be so calamitous that Hofmeyr might have to make a temporary sacrifice of principle to keep the Nationalists out. Such were the contrary opinions of two good men, both devoted to their country.

It was Cope's recollection that Hofmeyr said that he had 'more or less decided' to decline the Premiership and face the consequences. Thus he decided at long last to become an Onze Jan. Yet it was no longer possible.

The last twenty years had completely changed his situation. During the administratorship he had seemed chosen by destiny to bring the two great parties together. He had even helped to do it. But now he stood to the left of them both.

There was another profound difference between Onze Jan's situation and his own. Onze Jan had never accepted—except briefly—a position of power; but Hofmeyr had taken leadership in the Party and high office in the Government. He had thus created fresh loyalties and obligations, and he was the last man in the world to treat them lightly. He was in a trap, but it was a trap he had made for himself in 1933, from which he might have escaped in 1936 but did not, and from which it was harder to escape the longer he delayed. Power was very like a mother; the longer one put off the weaning, the more impossible it became.

Hofmeyr's diary confirmed the change that had come about in him during these years of the war, the change that many of his friends had already noticed in him. The things that had so irritated people were dying out in him, the occasional arrogance, the selfrighteousness, the tendency to be sardonically amused at the misfortunes of others, which made people wonder whether the teasing was not tinctured with cruelty. In the place of these things was a new quietness, almost a humility. The Hofmeyr of the diary was no longer the man who waited for the doors to open for him, no longer the man who used—almost—to boast that God always opened the way to him.

Hofmeyr writes of his 'malaise' more than once. In his younger days he would have felt almost contemptuous of anyone who confessed to a malaise. He knows that the ideal of service should help one to overcome it, but now he has no sense of mission; he adds, because he knows the gravity of what he is saying, 'in relation to the work I am doing'. Yet what other sense of mission has he? He confesses he has 'no political ambition left'. Then what other mission is there? He no longer wishes to be an evangelist, or to go back to the University, and to go crusading through South Africa. He writes something which shows clearly the change in him, 'I do seem to appreciate more and more quiet domestic spells (preferably with no visitors).' The fact that he suffers a malaise disturbs him; he writes: 'So I can but seek to do my duty to the best of my ability, and hope that the way will open for me to get out of it. In the meantime "my times are in Thy hand".'

What can be the matter with him except that he is worn out? Again and again he writes that a Sunday is peaceful, quiet, restful. He is reading more than he has read for years, and he writes down brief comments on the books. He favours history and biography. He finds Trevelyan's *Social History of England* 'a magnificent piece of work'. It is the kind of litera-ture he understands and enjoys. Was his weariness the kind that could be cured by rest, or had it touched his soul too? One thing is certain, he had no premonition of death. Though he had no such premonition, he wrote that he found a recurrence of kidney trouble on 20 September 'a little disturbing'.

But he never cosseted himself. The next day his mother and he went to Johannesburg, and had tea with Sarah and Philip Millin. He found Sarah still embittered against Smuts for his speech in Parliament explaining why South Africa could not admit unlimited numbers of Jews. Smuts had written to her some months before trying to bring about a reconciliation, but she wanted to answer in such strong terms that her husband had dissuaded her; so she had not written at all. Hofmeyr and Sarah Millin no longer wrote the old kind of letters to each other, in which she saw him as the saviour of South Africa, and in which he alternately responded and withdrew, and poured out his soul as he had never done to any other person. Now she wanted to tell him her troubles, and he had enough of his own; he was suffering a malaise, but she a melancholy, which is worse.

If home gave him peace, the cricket field gave him joy. He had given up squash but still played tennis regularly. But on 1 October he recorded his first cricket practice. The practices were held at Government House, and there was always the chance of a bit of gossip with the Governor-General, Brand van Zyl. On 15 October the first match was played on the new turf wicket at Government House. Hofmeyr scored nothing, but was kept in countenance because Alan Melville, the South African cap-tain, scored the same. He was now 53, but was playing as eagerly as ever; and indeed, as badly and as well. Very few, if any, people thought it strange any more that a man should continue to play a game in which he performed so moderately. It was a passion. It was the passion of a man who didn't go in for passions.

On 14 November Smuts flew to London for the wedding of Princess Elizabeth and Prince Philip, leaving Hofmeyr Acting Prime Minister for the seventh time. He was also Acting Minister of External Affairs, of Mines, and of Social Welfare, during the absence of Lawrence at the United Nations. His own ministries were Finance and Education.

On 30 November his kidney trouble returned, but with no pain until 5 December, his mother's eighty-fourth birthday. He wrote to Underhill that his mother retained her vitality, 'something for which one cannot but be very grateful'. It was a greater occasion than ever before, with more guests than ever before, calling continuously morning, afternoon, and evening. Hofmeyr was glad when it was over, and had a bad night. Most men would have spent the next day in bed, but not he. He had a heavy day's work before him, a meeting of the Rhodes Scholarship selection committee in the morning, a prize-giving in Johannesburg in the afternoon, a cocktail party in his constituency. By the end of it he was exhausted. He struggled through the United Party Congress in Pretoria, and on Sunday the 14th, accompanied by his mother, and feeling what he called 'a good deal better', he travelled by train on a series of ministerial rather than political visits.

In Port Elizabeth W. H. Craib, his friend and admirer of the Cape Town student days, was shocked by his appearance. Craib had become Professor of Medicine at the University of the Witwatersrand, and then, dissatisfied with the lack of vision of the authorities, had thrown it all up, and had taken up specialist practice in Port Elizabeth. But his reputation as a heart specialist was national not local. Craib spoke to him about his health, about his weight, about the amount and kind of food that he ate, about his heart and his kidneys, and about the way that he was working. Craib said to him, 'You must go slow, and if you don't go slow, you soon won't be able to go at all.' When Hofmeyr said, 'What do you mean?' Craib said bluntly, 'You'll be dead.' Hofmeyr told him that he saw no chance of taking his advice while he remained Minister of Finance and Leader of the House. Craib asked why he didn't lay down the tasks, and Hofmeyr admitted that he had tried to. It was then that Craib decided that he would write to Smuts himself.

When Hofmeyr returned to Pretoria, he was still far from well. On the day before Christmas, when he was clearing up his office so that he could spend four days at home, Smuts sent for him, and said he had received a letter from Craib. Dr Henry Gluckman, Minister of Health, was there too, and Smuts had no doubt shown him Craib's letter. Smuts said he hoped Hofmeyr would have a holiday before the session commenced, which would not be until 16 January. Hofmeyr recorded in his diary:

'I said there was not much time left but I hoped to be able to take things pretty easily the next two or three weeks. He said that I had had a very heavy burden and wished he could make me a Minister without portfolio (at which Gluckman remarked that in that event everyone would be putting jobs on me)—also that he had thought of relieving me of Finance, but there were difficulties about replacing me. That was all—but I suppose he feels that he has now cleared his conscience about me—and that things will continue as before!'

What was wrong? Why could these two men not reach any final clear-cut decision? Had Smuts, even in spite of Craib's letter, failed to realise that Hofmeyr was tired out? And why did not Hofmeyr speak out, and say he could endure it no longer? Was it implicit in the relationship that Hofmeyr could not speak frankly to Smuts, except on political issues? Eighteen years earlier, in 1929, Hofmeyr had kept Smuts at arm's length. But now he no longer seemed able to do so.

He closed his diary for 1947 with a humble summing up of the year.

'31st December. Again office in morning only. Spent rest of day quietly at home.

'Now that the prospects of our winning the election have improved, I view with apprehension the prospect of a continuance of the labour and the strain of the last eight years. It has occurred to me that I should ask the PM to relieve me of departmental duties until after the elections, and let me remain in the Cabinet merely as Minister without Portfolio and Leader of the House. I must think this out carefully during the next few days. It would give me a measure at least of much needed relief.

'For the rest, although my personal position in politics has been strengthened, I still doubt whether I should accept the leadership of the United Party if anything happened to the PM. It is true that the Party has moved considerably in the direction of what I stand for, but it is not clear to me that I could hold it together while attempting to do what it would be my duty to do if I had the responsibility of being the PM.'

On 5 January he went to Smuts and asked to be Leader of the House and Minister without Portfolio; and, in case that might be asking too much, he asked to be relieved of Finance. He wrote humbly about it. '. . . If the Prime Minister is able to give me the promised relief, I should be able to face the future without any anxiety on the physical score.'

And what would happen if the Prime Minister did not give him relief? Would he go on till he killed himself? It almost seemed so.

The Governor-General sent for him on 13 January, very disturbed by what the Prime Minister had told him about Hofmeyr's wish to be Minister without Portfolio. The Governor-General did not like it. He wanted to see Hofmeyr succeed Smuts, and that was not the way to do it. Then

Hofmeyr told him he was to be Minister of Mines and Education; the Governor-General was immensely relieved.

Hofmeyr did not know with certainty that he was to be relieved until two days later. On 15 January at 10.45 a.m. Hofmeyr was called to the Prime Minister's office. At 11.15 he returned no longer Minister of Finance, but now officially the Deputy Prime Minister.

So at last the intolerable burden was lifted. Nothing revealed more clearly than this episode the enigmatic nature of the relationship, Hofmeyr the Prime Minister's equal in some things, in others, almost a supplicant.

The reshuffling of the Cabinet took a great majority of people by surprise. There was speculation of course. Some thought that Smuts was naming his successor, and that Hofmeyr was dropping Finance because the Premiership was near. Others smelt smoke inside the United Party, as they always smelt it when they wanted to.

On 26 January, Hofmeyr intervened with great clarity and cogency in the debate on Malan's motion to rescind the provision for Indian representation in Parliament, to confine Native representation to the Senate, to abolish the Natives Representative Council and substitute tribal authorities, and to censure the Prime Minister for proposing to increase that Council's powers. Malan declared that Hofmeyr's appointment as Deputy Prime Minister meant only one thing, that the coloured policy of the United Party was to be a Hofmeyr policy. He declared that the Prime Minister's proposed concessions to the Natives Representative Council encouraged more extravagant demands.

In his speech Hofmeyr repeated his statement of 1936 that if racial separation of black and white could be complete, he could say a great deal in favour of it. Separation had become a magic word, and had put ministers of religion and professors under its spell, but they did not understand that it was impossible.

Hofmeyr declared that Afrikaner Nationalism had profound inconsistencies. It was said in one and the same speech that the white people in South Africa would remain the Herrenvolk for as long as they could, but that a policy of trusteeship would be followed.

HOFMEYER: The Hon. Member said that he does realise that it is a wrong thing in the eyes of the Native to break up his family life . . . But he said, from the point of view of the Europeans it cannot be done otherwise. Is that the policy of trusteeship which should be followed?

SAUER: I said that I had to choose between two interests.

HOFMEYR: . . . But trusteeship also means—seeing that good faith is the core of trusteeship—that the trustee must do everything he can to avoid the appearance that he is thinking merely of his own interest and that he is not prepared at all times to treat his ward fairly and justly.

Hofmeyr said that in 1936 he had voted against the Representation of Natives Act, but after that he had accepted the policy of group representation. Now twelve years later, the trustees wanted to take even that away.

Strijdom sneered at Hofmeyr. He thought that Hofmeyr's speech, as usual, consisted of 'moralising high-flown language, honour, and goodness knows what else'. Strijdom had no time for fancy stuff. He declared himself robustly for white supremacy, *baasskap*. He sneered at Hofmeyr's conscience. How could the Minister of Mines sleep while 200,000 women in the 'native areas' were separated from their husbands, and brothers and lovers? Could not Hofmeyr understand that the white man ruled by power, not by merit? Was not Hofmeyr sitting on the ministerial benches because power had put him there? Strijdom sneered at Hofmeyr's soulmates, the liberals, Senator Brookes and Mrs Ballinger, the National Union of Students, Bishop Clayton of Johannesburg. He sneered at those Government members who pretended they could not understand what apartheid really was, what the Nationalists really meant by it.

STRIJDOM: I hope that even the Hon. Member for Middelburg will understand me. I say that in a bus I will not sit alongside a Native. That is apartheid. If we raise our voices and if we urge on the Minister of Transport that there should be apartheid in our public transport . . . do we get the support of the Hon. Members on the other side?

DR EKSTEEN: Yes.

STRIJDOM: . . . they come with this rubbish about not knowing what apartheid means. I hope the Hon. Member will know what it means if it is again his fate to sit alongside a Native woman on the same seat.

DR EKSTEEN: That has never happened to me.

STRIJDOM: . . . Either you are *baas*, the equal, or the inferior, one of the three. If you are not *baas*, you must be a man's equal. . . . It is so clear and logical. If you say that you do not want to dominate the Native it simply means that you stand for a policy of equality.

Hofmeyr was not impressed by the debate. Of his own speech he said it was mostly cold logic, and not easy to put across at 6.15 p.m. Of Strijdom's attack he said nothing. It was strange that he should react so little to Strijdom, who spoke in many ways most contemptuously of him, of his morality and his piety; Strijdom also spoke contemptuously of his intelligence, that a man so clever should understand so little of the political facts of life. He declared, 'We have never heard greater nonsense from a clever man.'

Hofmeyr was right in describing his own speech as cold logic. Logic was in fact the weakness of the United Party attack on apartheid. United Party members asked the Nationalists, 'What does it mean?' But they should have known what it meant. It meant what Strijdom said it meant, not wanting to sit alongside a black man (or a black woman) in the bus. It was no use being logical and asking, 'But why do you let him (or her) bake your bread?' It was a silly question because the vital element was not the propinquity of the black man; the vital element was whether you were near him as an equal or a *baas*.

On the whole, however, the session was easy for Hofmeyr. On 31 January he again wrote of the relief from strain and the improvement in his health; he played cricket at Fernwood against the Navy, and made 18 runs in 75 minutes. However, the entry in his diary did not satisfy him—perhaps it was too staid. Therefore he added in the margin, 'Life has come to wear a different hue.'

So bright was the hue of life that Hofmeyr thought all the debates dull, Malan's motion on the Natives Representative Council, the Gold Loan, Pensions, the Railway Additional Estimates. The debate on Part Appropriation in which he had played the leading role for so many years, he called 'the weary waste'. The Railway Budget debate was 'the abomination of desolation'. These things he kept to himself. One may doubt whether even his mother knew the depth of his malaise. But how did one treat a malaise?

Of course one could not recuperate for ever. On 8 March the Prime Minister announced in the House that the general election would be held late in May or early in June. An unreal parliamentary session drew to its close. Hofmeyr recorded that the Opposition wanted nothing more than to get away from Cape Town, and to begin the campaign which would, they confidently hoped, take a few more seats from Smuts. Their strategy was clear—to exploit post-war dissatisfactions, the dangers of UNO and communism, the breakdown of the Natives Representative Council, the menace of the Indian population and, above all, the colour policy of the United Party, which, now that Hofmeyr had been appointed Deputy Prime Minister, was clearly the colour policy of Hofmeyr.

And according to Strijdom, Malan's chief lieutenant, Hofmeyr stood for nothing less than complete equality. He might think he stood for something less, but he was only deceiving himself. He was leading the white man to the grave. Strijdom was not interested in the session. He was interested in the election. And for him it would be a Hofmeyr election.

As for Hofmeyr, when the time came for him to stand up and fight again, he would do his duty. But not yet could he be enthusiastic.

Parliament rose on 24 March, and that evening Hofmeyr wrote in his diary:

'Now for the election campaign. The indications are good, but one can't be certain. It will be a somewhat hectic two months.

'My position in the House has, I think, strengthened considerably. The party seems to accept me almost unquestioningly as the next leader. I don't feel quite so sure as I did a few months ago as to what I should do if the call came. I still feel that it would be better for me to keep out of the Prime Ministership, but the difficulties likely to arise in the way of my doing so seem to be increasing. But it will be easier to come to decisions after the elections.'

So the question of the succession was still troubling his mind. Cope had said that Hofmeyr was more or less decided about the succession, and that was literally true; sometimes he was more decided, sometimes less. Hofmeyr was no lover of power. But something else was true also. It was power, his assumption of power, that had changed the whole tenor of his life. In a way he was like a Samson who had bound himself with his own seven locks of hair.

When Parliament rose in March 1948 Smuts appeared to be in an invulnerable position. In a House of 153, he held 89 seats. Malan held 49, Labour 6, the Stallardites 3, the Independents 3, and three were held by the Natives' Representatives, Margaret Ballinger, Donald Molteno, and Douglas Buchanan. Thus Smuts on his own commanded an absolute majority, and on most issues could count on the support of the other fifteen non-Nationalists.

Malan and his ally Havenga of the Afrikaner Party would have to win 28 new seats to command a majority. Such a swing would have been unparalleled in Union history. Therefore the United Party began its election fight in good heart. That does not mean to say there was no anxiety. Malan had climbed from 19 seats to 49 in 1948. In 1934 the great issue was Anglo-Afrikaner co-operation, about which Malan was not much concerned. In 1948 the great issue was the future of white South

Africa, of which Malan had made himself the champion. Smuts's Achilles heel was in the Afrikaans-speaking countryside. He had already lost Hottentots Holland, while in 1947 J. B. Wolmarans of Losberg, smarting under the taunts of the Nationalists, went over to them at the end of the session.

In September of 1947 Malan launched a pre-election attack on Hofmeyr, and this was the signal for an anti-Hofmeyr press campaign. Hofmeyr wrote in his diary, 'I can't help feeling that they are overselling their hand and that the result may well be to facilitate, rather than otherwise, the adoption of a more liberal policy.' On Sunday, 12 October, he wrote in his diary, 'such things as political attacks and misrepresentations, which seem to disturb others, leave me quite cold'.

Did these attacks leave him cold? Some of them were so fierce, and so deadly, that others went hurrying to him to tell him of their deadliness. Was Hofmeyr so tough that he was left cold by attacks which were shaking his Party? It is almost impossible to believe.

On 19 November 1947, the Nationalist paper *Die Kruithoring* put fourteen questions to the Deputy Prime Minister. It asked him what he meant by Christian trusteeship; then the electorate would know the exact meaning of his policies. The questions were these:

1. If natives had the ability, should they be trained as skilled workmen, with the same pay and conditions as whites?

2. Should educated natives have the right to supervise the work of white girls?

3. Should native workmen have the right to found their own trade unions?

4. Should natives enjoy the same academic and social rights at white universities as whites?

5. Should a native be allowed to become, for example, Chancellor of the University of South Africa?

6. Should natives enjoy the same conditions of service and pay as whites in the Public Service and the Railways?

7. Should qualified natives, immediately or eventually, enjoy the same voting rights as whites?

8. Should such voting rights be extended to native women?

9. Should the pre-1936 vote be restored?

10. Should such rights be extended to the northern provinces?

11. Should natives be allowed to sit in Parliament?

12. Should these rights apply also to municipal and divisional elections?

13. Should native farm-workers be entitled to wages on the basis of 'equal pay for equal work'?

14. Should the highest posts in agriculture, education, and the professions be open to natives?

To all these questions *Die Kruithoring* answered with a resounding No. But, according to the editor, Hofmeyr answered Yes. Yet the editor wished to allow him to answer for himself. The paper would therefore give him so much time, and if he was too busy to reply, it would assume that his answer was Yes. The editor would not however announce that the Deputy Prime Minister wanted all these changes immediately, merely that he wanted to see them 'within a short or a long time'. The editor concluded, 'We wait, Minister Hofmeyr.'

Hofmeyr refused to answer. He said that questions should be put to a Minister in Parliament or at public meetings. He scribbled a note, 'It is childish for a paper to put a questionnaire to a Minister in its columns and then assume that when he hasn't replied to it he can be assumed to have answered to it what it would like the answers to be.'

The questions put by *Die Kruithoring* were difficult ones to answer. Most of them were moral questions, and there was only one answer that Hofmeyr could give to them. It is both fascinating and terrible to think that to every question to which Hofmeyr would answer Yes, *Die Kruithoring* would answer No, and would not only be proud of it, but would think it morally justified.

Equally fascinating and terrible was Hofmeyr's own situation, for his political answers to these questions and his moral answers would have been hard to reconcile. In fact his answers as Deputy Prime Minister would not have been Yes, they would have been 'Yes, but . . .', which answers are embarrassing to others, and humiliating to oneself.

Hofmeyr's failure to answer was used as ammunition against him. But so were his answers to earlier questions. The National Party Information Office in Cape Town produced a famous pink pamphlet called 'Meet Mr. Hofmeyr'. It quoted his speech in the famous debate of 1936, where he declared that he objected to 'a citizenship which has the marks of inferiority in clause after clause of this Bill'. It quoted his now famous remark in the Hottentots Holland campaign about the representation of 'natives by natives, and Indians by Indians'. When Strijdom had asked him in Parliament in 1946 to endorse white supremacy, he had replied, 'On that basis there can be no lasting relationship between the races.' When Erasmus had asked him in Parliament in 1947 whether he wanted the trade unions to be free to allow all races in one union, the Minister had replied, 'If they wish it so, then very well.' When in 1937 Strijdom had advocated job reservation, Hofmeyr would have none of it. In that same year Hofmeyr had told a meeting at Ceres that he would not be a member of any Government which legislated against mixed marriages.

And this was the future leader of the United Party! The pamphlet declared, 'The road he is following leads to equality, and the downfall of white South Africa!'

Meanwhile Hofmeyr scored a reasonable triumph in a small Transvaal country town. When questioned about *baasskap*, white supremacy, he replied that it would have to give way in time to *leierskap*, leadership, based on white merits. He gave his answers with such force and sincerity that there were cries of 'Bravo' and 'Kolskoot' [bull's-eye]. He wrote that this 'in a typical backveld area, is an encouraging sign of progress'. He repeated this line of argument at Fochville, at an excellent meeting, which resurrected all his hopes and doubts about the succession.

'Fochville has been a bad knock to the Nats and has made my own stock rise. There seems to be a better response to my ideas on colour questions than was believed to be possible. There seems to be just a chance that if Smuts went, I might carry the Party and the country with me—a better chance than has hitherto seemed to be the case—but still only a chance.'

A few days later Strijdom poured scorn on Hofmeyr's idea of *leierskap*. He quoted Hofmeyr as saying, 'We must not dominate, we must lead, I do not doubt that the European will always maintain the leadership on merit.' To this Strijdom replied, 'I never knew that such stupidity could come from such a clever mind—either it is stupidity or political deception.'

The United Party had to counter this anti-Hofmeyr propaganda, that Hofmeyr wanted 'to make South Africa a black man's country, and that he advocated the removal of all colour bars'. It reminded the voters in pamphlets and newsletters of Hofmeyr's declaration to the United Party Congress of November 1946, where he said:

'I am not in favour of a policy of assimilation. I have repeatedly stated that the essential difference between Europeans and non-Europeans must be taken into consideration. The policy of Christian trusteeship I have in mind does not mean suppression, nor does it mean equality. It means the realisation of our responsibility not to ignore the interests of people of whom we are the guardians.'

Before the campaign began in earnest Hofmeyr had a minor tussle with his own Craighall branch in Johannesburg North. His committee members deplored the fact that South Africans sent so much money out of the country to buy lottery tickets in Rhodesia, Malta, and Ireland. They wanted a national lottery established which could make handsome grants to hospitals and charities. However much Hofmeyr had changed from the days of his early upbringing, both in his mother's home and in the Baptist Church, he was adamant on the question of lotteries. His view was that a lottery was immoral, because it catered to the desire to get much for little, and discouraged industry and thrift. He found however that he could not persuade his committee members to accept his view. He was so adamant on the point that instead of allowing himself to be embarrassed by his supporters, he embarrassed them, and did so deliberately. He wrote:

'One has to go on making it clear that I am not prepared to stay in politics at the price of a moral principle. The dilemma then passes to the other side. They must decide whether they want me with my principles or are prepared to see me go.'

The question of lotteries never caused him so much difficulty as the so-called 'Native question'. If Smuts had introduced lotteries, Hofmeyr would have rejected all idea of compromise. He would have resigned forthwith, and what is more, he would have done it even in the most anxious days of the war.

Hofmeyr stood fast on another point. There were members of the Cabinet who wanted to present a popular budget before the Party went to the country in May of 1948. But Hofmeyr dissented. He declared that it would be improper for the Government to present a budget just as it was about to go out of office. Strauss considered that Hofmeyr made an error of judgement. There was a surplus and the Government could have used it to make further tax concessions. Such arguments Hofmeyr dismissed with a loftiness that was intensely irritating to many of his colleagues and friends, but Strauss was prepared to believe that it was his health rather than his conscience that was to blame.

On the very day that Hofmeyr arrived back from Parliament, he went off to Johannesburg North to meet Party leaders, and found their reports encouraging. But to his diary he committed the confession, 'I could be happy with either result.' He wrote enigmatically, 'And while I still think that it would be very unfortunate for the country—especially from the point of view of race relations—if the Nats were to get in, from other points of view the consequences would probably not be so serious as they would have been at one time.'

Whatever he meant, he could not have been more in error. His own indifference to the result, he kept to himself, though there can be little doubt his mother knew of it. In her old age she was growing more and more disillusioned with the world and with mankind. No sooner was Germany conquered, than Russia and America were growling at each other. Man's genius seemed at its most brilliant in inventing tools for his own destruction. And here at home her son, who had lived an honourable, law-abiding, industrious life of service to his country, was the target for the bitter attacks of so many of his own people. She too had once believed that righteousness triumphed, but she found little comfort in the belief that righteousness was its own reward. She would say sombrely, 'But why should I worry? I have no children to bring up.' She had tasted power through her son, but the taste had turned from sweet to sour. Why should her son not withdraw? What thanks had he received for his devotion?

Hofmeyr was able to study closely a statement by Malan, entitled 'Colour Policy of the National Party'. Malan said that the choice was clear, between equality on the one hand, and on the other the separate development of racial groups, each with national pride, self-respect, and respect for others. Malan stated emphatically that the best way to achieve the happiness of all South Africa was to maintain and protect the white race, and that was to be the very root and fundament of Party policy. There would be residential, social, industrial, and political separation. Coloured voters would be placed on a separate roll, and elect white representatives to Parliament. All mixed marriages would be forbidden. 'The Native Reserves would become the fatherland of the native,' and all important services, including education, would be provided there, and not in the towns as at present. 'The native in our urban areas must be regarded as a visitor.' Movement from country to town would be rigidly controlled. 'Native education would be Christian-National,' and the money spent on it must be in proportion to the contribution made to the state income. Natives' Representatives in the Lower House would be abolished, but retained in the Senate. As for Indians, they were aliens. As many as possible would be repatriated, and those that remained would be subject to rigid separation, and would have no representation in Parliament. Family allowances to Indians would be abolished, and drastic steps would be taken against Indians who incited non-white people against white.

That was Malan's programme. Hofmeyr wrote in Afrikaans at the bottom of the statement these words, 'No longer a policy of uplift but one of oppression.'

Hofmeyr had now before him the report of the Fagan Commission, which dealt particularly with the question of migratory labour and the pass laws and made many humane recommendations for reform. Nothing could have contrasted more vividly with Malan's programme than Fagan's report. Malan aimed at achieving the maximum racial separation in every department of life. Fagan aimed at recognizing the fact of interdependence and adapting oneself to it.

The Smuts campaign was subject to one great handicap, namely that Louis Esselen was dead. What the United Party needed was one big and active mind that knew the danger of the Hofmeyr bogy that the Nationalists were creating, and would counter it confidently and aggressively, using the Fagan Report. Instead, the United Party kept on trying to prove that Hofmeyr was not as bad, not as extreme, as he was painted. Another mistake of the Party was to rake up Malan's past, which was a good deal more tolerant than his present. Yet hardly one of the Nationalists supported Malan for his tolerant past. They supported him because of his uncompromising present.

On 10 April it was officially announced that the general election would be held on 26 May, and the campaign began in earnest. The succession was undoubtedly one of the prime issues of the election. If the United Party won, and Smuts retired, Hofmeyr would be Prime Minister, and South Africa, said the Nationalists, would become the home of 'a coffee-coloured race'. Down in Natal, Charles Neate, M.P., one of the remaining Stallardites, declared that if Hofmeyr became Prime Minister, the United Party would be split from top to bottom.

Both Smuts and Hofmeyr thought it necessary, and more than once, to reassure the voters about the succession. Smuts spoke to a United Party rally at Bloemfontein and told them he would carry on as long as he had the strength to do so. He said:

'It has been suggested that I am trying to trick South Africa, that I am trying to get the people to follow me, while actually somebody else was going to take over.

'This was really a war against Hofmeyr, and Hofmeyr is one of the best men we have ever produced in the country. They are trying to wound him in advance. If you want me to carry on I shall go on, but I do hate these attacks on Hofmeyr.'

Speaking a few days later at a small country town in the Transvaal, Hofmeyr said, 'I do not aspire to the Premiership, and General Smuts has told me personally that he will remain Prime Minister as long as his health permits and as long as the people of South Africa want him.'

While the official Nationalist propaganda was aggressively and persistently anti-Hofmeyr, there was also underground propaganda. In and around Johannesburg, in Maraisburg, Westdene, Johannesburg West, and Mayfair, amongst the Afrikaner workers, a story was being circulated by canvassers that Hofmeyr had an African mistress and that was why he resisted all attempts to ensure that marriage, adultery, and prostitution were made segregated activities. There was another story, told in the clubs, that Hofmeyr had got into trouble at a boys' camp, and that only the intervention of Smuts had saved him from public exposure. There was a story about Smuts, too, that in fact he was a Jew, and that one only needed to study his portraits to see that this was true. Both these men, it was said, desired only one thing with all their hearts, and that was 'to plough the Afrikaner under'. If the United Party was returned to power, black men would take away jobs from white men, black men would supervise white girls, black doctors would give orders to white nurses. An election worker in Mayfair, Johannesburg, told the writer that if Hofmeyr ever came to power, black men would importune white girls in the street.

Hofmeyr was not much troubled by such scurrility in Johannesburg North. His constituents had known him so long and so well that the spreading of such stories would have aroused only anger. He held several meetings in his constituency, and his success seemed beyond all doubt.

With twenty-four days left before the election Hofmeyr found time to rest, for white South Africa observes a political truce for ten days from Ascension Day to Whit Sunday, and no political meetings are held. However, one politician did not observe the Whitsun truce. J. L. Brill, the Nationalist candidate for Mayfair, was so outraged by the holding of a mixed meeting in the Kimberley Town Hall that he published a vigorous leaflet. It was headed in inch-high letters

S.A. ENTERS A NEW EPOCH!

and below that in smaller but heavier print

MIN. HOFMEYR'S LIBERALISM TRIUMPHS
AT UNITED PARTY MEETING!
COLOUREDS AND EUROPEANS ON U.P. PLATFORM

Kimberley, Wednesday, 5th May.

The United Party held a mass meeting in the Kimberley Town Hall last night totally ignoring the colour bar. On the platform was Dr H. Gluckman, Minister of Health, together with the candidate of the U.P., Mr Harry Oppenheimer, and numerous Coloureds, Indians, and Malayers.

The audience consisted of Natives, Coloureds, Malayers, Indians, Chinese, and Europeans, and the stage was decorated with banners condemning Nationalism by the Springbok Legion.

The chairman Mr Graham Eden in welcoming the masses eulogised the spectacle as symbolic of the future nation of South Africa. (Loud and prolonged cheers.)

ELECTORS, BEHOLD THE U.P.'S NATION OF TOMORROW

Vote BRILL

for White Dominance.

The Nationalists were conducting their campaign with great thoroughness. They had their own troubles, and these were of course magnified by those newspapers which supported the United Party. It was supposed that Malan and Havenga were having difficulties in working together. It was reported that Dr H. F. Verwoerd, editor of *Die Transvaler* and Nationalist candidate for Alberton, was having trouble with members of the Ossewabrandwag in his constituency; also that the Broederbond was interfering in the nominations.

It seems almost certain that the Nationalists, who naturally showed massive confidence in public, did not think they could win the elections. Barlow travelled with Malan on the plane from Johannesburg to Cape Town, and went and sat with him to talk about the prospects. Barlow reported Malan, who needed 28 seats to win a bare majority, as saying to him, 'Do you agree that we are going to capture 20 seats in the election?'

Barlow replied to Malan that he would not get 20 seats or anything like it; at the most he gave the Nationalists 57 all told, if they were lucky. Barlow was full of praise for the way Hofmeyr was playing his part in the campaign. He wrote:

'The more country audiences are addressed by the Deputy Prime Minister, it now seems, the worse it is going to be for Dr Malan's party. The Minister fills the bill, draws big audiences and is listened to by the country voter with rapt and respectful attention.'

Meanwhile the Nationalists continued to attack Hofmeyr relentlessly. Verwoerd's paper, *Die Transvaler*, attacked him daily in the news, or the cartoons, or the editorials, on some days in all three. The words *liberal, liberalist, liberalistic,* had become words of contumely, and the greatest of the liberals was Hofmeyr. Strijdom declared at Nylstroom that despite all denials, Hofmeyr's policy was equality; had he not in the famous debate of 1936 lamented that 'the most educated native would never get political equality, not even with the least educated white or coloured person'?

Monday, 24 May, with two days to go, was a public holiday, Queen Victoria's birthday, shared by her with General Smuts. Hofmeyr played cricket at Government House, and that evening spoke in Pretoria in the Jewish Memorial Hall to the most hostile audience he had yet encountered. When he predicted that on Wednesday South Africa would give General Smuts a birthday present in the form of the greatest victory he had ever had, students who had packed a large part of the hall greeted his prediction with jeers and songs and cries of 'Vodka', to which he replied, 'Our friends have got themselves around some vodka or something.' He started to speak again, but the students resumed their singing, and after they had finished he said, 'Now that our friends have refreshed themselves with a little singing, I shall continue.' Horak watched him anxiously, realising that this was not the old Hofmeyr who revelled in this kind of encounter, and brought the house down with his repartee. He was pale and sweating, and Horak could see that the fight was taking all his strength.

As for the students, they were at last confronting the arch-enemy of Afrikanerdom and White Civilisation, and they shouted their hatred at him. For more than a month now they had read about Hofmeyr every morning in Dr Verwoerd's *Die Transvaler*. Had not Dr E. G. Jansen, respected ex-Speaker, said that the *swart gevaar*, the 'black danger', was not the black people but the Hofmeyr policy? Had not *Die Transvaler* pictured a beautiful Miss South Africa pleading with Hofmeyr to stop chopping down the colour-bar tree, while a gleeful black man danced and shouted, 'Jo, moi, hy's amper af,' which meant 'Wow, lovely, it's almost down'. Had not Mr Havenga said that Hofmeyr should stop explaining what he said about the parliamentary colour bar, and explain what he meant by South Africa's Herrenvolk mentality? Hadn't the great Malan attacked Hofmeyr at Germiston, and the near-great Strijdom attacked him at Witbank, as the betrayer of white civilisation in Africa? Was it not Hofmeyr's liberalism that brought white, coloured people, Indians and Malays on to the same platform at Kimberley? Had not *Die Transvaler* pictured Hofmeyr as a two-headed jackal, the one head mouthing, 'Away with the Colour Bar,' and the other, 'I am for Christian trusteeship'?

Here was their enemy in the flesh. They shouted out questions to him about mixed marriages and mixed universities and mixed trade unions, and about 'educated natives' supervising white Afrikaner girls, but such was the noise that Hofmeyr could not answer them. Shouting above the din, he challenged them to prove that he had ever advocated equality between white and non-white. On the contrary, he was opposed to the two extremes of oppression and equality. While they were shouting at him, he was shouting at them that the Fagan Commission indicated a third course, namely, that of Christian trusteeship. Horak said to him, 'Mr Hofmeyr, let's close the meeting,' but Hofmeyr said, 'Don't be silly.' He looked exhausted, and Horak was glad when the meeting came to an inconclusive end, and he could get Hofmeyr into the car and drive him home.

On the day before the election Hofmeyr was in his constituency, putting the finishing touches to his organisation. He was confident, and the Party was confident too.

Meanwhile that fighting newspaper *Die Transvaler* showed no signs of pessimism. On 24 May it recorded unprecedented enthusiasm on the Witwatersrand for the Nationalist Party, and said that a big swing was already apparent. Malan sent out a last clarion call from Cape Town that the battle was for nothing less than the future of white South Africa. On 25 May the cartoon of *Die Transvaler* showed the dark and rising flood of Liberalism, Communism, and Equality that threatened to overwhelm South Africa, and urged readers, 'Save Her in time by voting Nationalist.'

Hofmeyr lacked no help on 26 May. He had represented the constituency for eighteen years and he had never suffered a setback. Polling began at 7 a.m. and there were no signs of apathy. Reports from other centres indicated that there would be a record poll all over South Africa. At his own polling stations there was abundant confirmation that he would win handsomely. At 8 p.m. polling closed, and now counting began. At 2.45 a.m. on 27 May, the returning officer announced that J. H. Hofmeyr had beaten F. S. Steyn by 3,281 votes in a poll of over 8,500. His prediction of two and a half to one was close to the mark. The early results, always those in urban seats, were invariably United Party victories, but Hofmeyr was immediately aware of the fact that in these tradition-ally United Party seats, there had been a slight swing to the Nationalist Party, though not enough to disturb the huge U.P. majorities. In the afternoon, as the first rural results came in, it was clear that in the coun-try the swing had become a landslide, especially in the Transvaal, but also, to a lesser degree, in the Cape. It was Smuts's Afrikaner countryside that was deserting him, following J. B. Wolmarans when he left the United Party because it would not stand unequivocally for a white South Africa. The crowning disaster was when Smuts himself was announced defeated by a man whom he had forced to choose between his job and the Broederbond in 1944.

By evening it was clear that Smuts would not be able to command an absolute majority in the House. By the morning of the 28th it was clear that he would have no majority at all. Malan and Havenga between them won 79 seats, and commanded an absolute majority of 5 over all comers, including 3 Natives' Representatives. Between them they had taken 34 seats from the United Party and had driven that Party out of virtually every Afrikaans-speaking constituency in the country. Smuts's total had dropped from 89 to 65.

The disparity between the number of seats Smuts won and the num-ber of votes he polled was remarkable. Malan and Havenga won 79 seats, with a total of votes 100,000 less than the total of votes for Smuts, who won only 65 seats. Smuts polled 50 per cent of the total vote, and Malan and Havenga together polled 40 per cent. This was due to the electoral provision that allowed rural seats to be underloaded 15 per cent and urban seats to be overloaded 15 per cent. Thus Smuts was defeated because of the provision that he himself had agreed to in 1909, and which many had urged him to abolish. Had he listened, he would have won the election of 1948. Another reason for this disparity between number of votes and number of seats was that many urban seats voted overwhelmingly United Party, and presented Smuts with spectacular but otherwise useless majori-ties.

After listening to the news at 7 a.m., Hofmeyr went into his mother's room, and said to her, 'We've just lost it.' They did not speak much.

What could she say who did not know whether to grieve or rejoice? What could he say who had written, 'I could be happy with either result'? What did he feel? According to her, 'He never showed it much.' But she said that he felt it deeply.

How does one feel when an age comes to an end? For it was that and nothing less. Smuts was almost beside himself. J. C. Smuts junior declared that the result shocked his father more gravely than any event he had ever witnessed. After Smuts had resigned on 29 May his son took him down to the farm in the bushveld, but his father's thoughts were far from the trees and the grasses. Hofmeyr wrote, 'It is a great blow to him—and he obviously feels it.' Smuts told Hofmeyr at once that he did not want to carry on, and Hofmeyr, as in the far-off days of 1933, tried to tell him it was his duty. Hofmeyr came away seeing 'little chance' that Smuts would take another seat—'and from the personal point of view I doubt very much whether he can be expected to'. Of himself Hofmeyr wrote:

'My own feeling is one of relief—it will be good to be able to take things more easily for a while. I think too that it will tend to make my political position easier, though it will be difficult in the first instance.'

Hofmeyr wrote also of the profound shock to many in his own circles. What made the shock more painful was the triumph of others, the roaring crowds on Pretoria's Church Square, the jubilations in Potchefstroom, Witbank, Standerton, Bloemfontein, Worcester, Caledon, Stellenbosch, the blowing of the motor horns, the singing of the songs and the anthems, all the prayers and boasts and promises and new dedications of those for whom the dawn was breaking after a night of long despair.

Krüger in his book *The Age of the Generals* later wrote:

'Apartheid overthrew Smuts . . . It was the last desperate attempt of Afrikanerdom to stem the rising tide of colour. The electorate believed that the salvation of the white race in South Africa lay in entrusting the National Party with the defence by every possible means of their White heritage. White South Africa believed that the racial estate it had inherited in 1910 could still be made solvent, disregarding the unfavourable balance sheet. For a century and more Afrikanerdom had managed to preserve its life through heroic action. It now thought to prolong its existence by heroic thought against the whole world. The Age of the Generals was past and done with forever. Afrikanerdom would endeavour to maintain its existence through an age of politicians.'

The first of the 'age of the politicians' was Daniel François Malan, who, once taught by Smuts in Sunday School, had been for almost forty years in political opposition to him. Malan, though he thought ill of Smuts's politics, recognised in him that strange quality of greatness. He recognised also that the general election of 1948 was the tragedy of a great and illustrious life. In a message of thanks to his supporters, Malan said that the United Party had tried to use the prestige of General Smuts during the election to distract attention from the great and urgent problems that cried for solution. He said it was tragic to think that at this stage in his life, Smuts had thrown himself 'into the battle to protect another man, and had thus sacrificed himself'.

It was not only Malan who believed that Hofmeyr had cost Smuts the election. Others were beginning to believe it, not Hofmeyr's enemies, but his allies. Peace had not yet come to the tired man.

Chapter 16

The End of the Road

WHY did Smuts lose the election? His son considered Hofmeyr had lost Smuts the election, because he would not listen to those 'who urged him to keep a diplomatic silence'. But *Round Table* declared there were five reasons. Malan had dropped the Republican campaign, he had dropped anti-Semitism and all talk against English as an official language, he had given an assurance to war veterans that their interests would be cared for, he had offered to fight against Russia if necessary, and he had appealed to colour prejudice.

Bill Horak, organizing secretary for the United Party, came to see Hofmeyr, as faithful as ever. Hofmeyr was very depressed when Horak arrived, and said, 'There's no hope for this country.' He hesitated and added, 'Unless they fight amongst themselves.' Then he said, 'They always do, don't they?'

Sarah Millin telephoned Hofmeyr to tell him that he was being blamed in Johannesburg for the fall of Smuts. Again his thoughts returned to the problem about which he could never finally make up his mind, the problem of the succession. He wrote of Sarah Millin's call:

'This confirms the doubts which I was already feeling as to whether I should accept the leadership of the Opposition if Smuts decides not to come back. It might be better for the party not to have me as Leader unless it had full confidence in me, and from my point of view freedom from responsibility would enable me to take a more independent line and ultimately perhaps work myself into the John Bright position which I have always had in mind. But it is not easy to see what effective alternative the party would have.'

The next day, with Smuts absent, there was a meeting of former Ministers at the Union Buildings, and Senator Andrew Conroy demanded that Hofmeyr should resign as chairman of the central executive of the Party, and that he, Conroy, should take his place. Hofmeyr also gathered from the behaviour of Colin Steyn, who had once declared that he was not a candidate for the succession, that he was now willing to be.

So now the affair was in the open. He had been used as a bogy by the Nationalists, now he had become one to his own party. No one could tell what was going on behind those spectacles. He appeared as impassive as ever, and took his stand on a matter of procedure; Smuts had appointed him to the chairmanship, and only Smuts could remove him. In regard to the leadership he told them that he was not anxious for it, and certainly would not accept it unless he were assured of unanimous support. He also told his colleagues—perhaps for the first time—that he would feel freer and happier without the responsibility of leadership.

Hofmeyr decided to see Smuts soon about what he called the unsatisfactory position of the Party, and to tell him he should make a steadying statement before he left for England for his inauguration as Chancellor of Cambridge University. However, Conroy was there first, and urged and pleaded that Smuts should return to Parliament and to the leadership; otherwise the Party would break up beyond all hope of repair. Conroy was overjoyed when Smuts agreed. Sarah Millin went to see him too, and told him that he could not go away and leave his friends in the lurch, or leave Hofmeyr with an intolerable burden; what is more, he must speak in world affairs as Leader of the Opposition, and not as a nobody. Smuts said to her, 'You are all gold,' and embraced her. When Sarah Millin later told this to Hofmeyr, she told him something else too. He recorded:

'She also told me very confidentially that while she was with Smuts a letter came from van Rensburg's Ossewabrandwag—delivered by one of van Rensburg's children with instructions to hand it over only to someone in personal touch with Smuts—and that Smuts replied to it at once. She indicated that she believed that it conveyed an overture from van Rensburg to Smuts.'

The next day Hofmeyr saw Smuts early. Smuts told Hofmeyr that he would make a statement that day about the leadership, and announce that he would stand for Pretoria East. As a result of this, Hofmeyr recorded, some of his colleagues seemed to be recovering from the jitters, and 'the premature aspirants to the succession . . . have piped down'.

That morning Malan arrived in Pretoria, and was given a tumultuous reception. He was driven through the streets in a car covered with the *Vierkleur*, and Hofmeyr wondered how he felt. It was clear what many others felt, for men and women wept unashamedly in the streets. That afternoon Malan announced his Cabinet, all the heroes of the freedom struggle. Havenga for Finance, Jansen for Native Affairs, the redoubtable Strijdom for Lands, the six-foot-six Swart for Justice. The new Minister of Transport was the genial Paul Sauer, whose father J. W. Sauer had been one of the outstanding Cape liberals of the latter half of the nine-teenth century. Eric Louw succeeded Hofmeyr for Mines, and Dr A. J. Stals succeeded him for Education. The silver-tongued Dönges was for Interior, Ben Schoeman for Labour, F. C. Erasmus, who had backed Malan in his break from Hertzog in 1934, was for Defence.

It was the first Cabinet in the history of the Union without any English-speaking Ministers, and the first Cabinet to have such a command of both official languages. And it goes without saying that it was pledged to two supreme causes, the sovereign and unfettered independence of South Africa, and the preservation of Afrikanerdom and the white race through the instrument known as apartheid.

Smuts had flown to England after sending a sad message to the nation, 'If there is blame for the present failure, let it be mine—as no doubt the heavy punishment will be.' It was left to Hofmeyr to welcome the new Cabinet in the Prime Minister's office. Malan was deeply affected. He had entered Parliament thirty-three years before and now he was about to enter the promised land. Before he went into the room he prayed silently that he might prove worthy of his great office. Again one is moved to honour him, again one is repelled, remembering the laws which he had already planned, so callously indifferent to the sufferings of persons, espe-cially those who were voiceless and powerless. Hofmeyr said a word of welcome and congratulation to him in Afrikaans, to which he made a reply difficult to hear, but Hofmeyr took it to be 'Thank you'. When Hofmeyr left the Prime Minister, he said to him, still in Afrikaans, 'Every best wish,' to which Malan replied, 'We shall do our best—you also tried to do your best'; Hofmeyr agreed, and Malan went on to say, 'You mustn't be too hard on us in Opposition!' Hofmeyr said, 'We shall do our best as an Opposition—you also did your best.'

Later Hofmeyr learned that Malan had refused to be photographed with him, just as Hertzog had refused to be photographed with Smuts in 1924.

On the evening of 5 June Hofmeyr spoke to a meeting of his constit-uents at Ferndale. He was loudly applauded when he said, 'I was the chief villain of the piece in the election and that is significant because the support I got in Johannesburg North establishes that I am not such a villain after all.'

They laughed when he told them that he had been serving a sentence of nine years, but had been given a reduction of three months for good behaviour. They were angry when he told them that a woman voter in the Karoo had signed an affidavit that the Nationalist candidate, when canvassing her vote, had patted her little daughter on the head and said, 'Isn't it a pity that this beautiful child should have to marry a native?' She replied angrily, 'Of course not, why should she?' The candidate then said, 'When Hofmeyr becomes Prime Minister, then all our daughters will have to marry natives.'

He told them that he believed that the main factor in Smuts's defeat was the exploitation of post-war grievances, what he called the 'irritation vote', and before long they would see the irritation vote swinging back in the U.P.'s direction. He said: 'People make a mistake when they think that the election was purely a colour election. The other factor . . . of more importance . . . was the factor of the irritation vote.'

Did Hofmeyr believe what he was saying? He did not. Only six days earlier he had written to Underhill, 'The determining factor in the election has undoubtedly been the appeal to colour prejudice. That it should have succeeded as it has done, puts us in a very bad light in the eyes of the world.'

Hofmeyr concluded his speech by declaring that the Government was in an impossible situation, with a small majority in the Assembly and a large majority against it in the Senate. He said, 'Therefore we may anticipate another election within a year's time, if not sooner.' The Ferndale meeting was an encouragement to him.

He needed encouragement. Although Smuts had now announced that he would stay in politics, the Party had been left leaderless for three catastrophic days, and the question of the succession had become an obsession. Barlow, who had once said in Parliament that Hofmeyr's policy was the policy of Christ, now came out openly and backed Steyn for the succession, declaring that Hofmeyr would destroy the United Party. He went even further; he wanted Smuts to retire, and Steyn to take over the leadership.

The whole United Party was in a turmoil. The landslide of the *platte-land*, the country districts, had created virtually a new political world. The support which in the past had been given so generously to Botha, Smuts, and Hertzog, had overnight been transferred to the man who had been their implacable enemy. Would it ever come back? For if it never came back, the United Party would never come back either. And how

could one get the platteland back? Could one only get it back by appealing to racial fear and colour prejudice? And what was the use of that,
when the Nationalists could do it so many times better? In that case
should one come out boldly with a liberal policy? And did that mean
giving up the platteland for ever? These were the questions that occupied
Hofmeyr's mind.

When he wrote to Egeland giving reasons for the defeat, he again
adduced post-war grievances and colour prejudice, but now he added a
third, namely the advent of a new generation from the Nationalist-
orientated schools, that new generation of young Afrikaners which was
fanatically Afrikaans, and knew all the events of the 'Century of Wrong',
and the crimes of British imperialism. Hofmeyr was correct in adding this
third reason, and he could have added two more, first the 15 per cent
underloading of rural constituencies and 15 per cent overloading of urban
constituencies, and second the enormous and useless majorities that the
United Party piled up in the cities. And he could well have added yet
another, the pressure of world opinion, which, too weak to induce
change, was driving Afrikaners together to resist change.

Was Hofmeyr the cause of Smuts's downfall? Some said he was, and
some denied it hotly. The answer depended on the meaning of the question. The cause of Smuts's downfall was undoubtedly the growing Afrikaner fear of the non-white world, the growing fear of one common
society ruled by one representative Parliament, the determination to ensure Afrikaner survival. The enemies of the Afrikaner were liberalism,
communism, internationalism, multi-racialism, non-racialism. In so far as
these could be identified with a man, that man was Hofmeyr. Therefore
Hofmeyr was the enemy of Afrikanerdom, and he must be destroyed. In
that sense Hofmeyr undoubtedly was the cause of Smuts's downfall.

Yet any other person would have served, though none would have
served as well. Smuts himself might have served, but he was never as
forthright as Hofmeyr, and there was less to pin on him. Had there been
no Hofmeyr, Smuts might have won the election, but he would still have
lost ground. It was Hofmeyr's very courage and honesty that made him
the perfect target. Outdated as some of his ideas might appear to those
who came after him, they were honourable attempts to break out of the
chains in which white South Africa had been confined for centuries. It
was not just the defeat of Hofmeyr, it was the defeat of every South
African of whatever colour or kind who desired to strengthen inter-racial
bonds, to deepen inter-racial knowledge, to teach South Africans not to

judge in terms of race and colour, to teach them to see each other as men and women with a common land and a common destiny, however great the difficulties in the way. It was the defeat of all South Africans who regarded apartheid as a creed of despair, fundamentally a rejection of one's fellowman, a creed convinced of man's wickedness, and profoundly sceptical of his goodness. It was in a way not Smuts who was defeated, but Hofmeyr. In a way Smuts had ceased to matter. What was reactionary in him had been championed by Malan, what was liberal in him had been championed by Hofmeyr. This genius of a man had succeeded all his life in being two things at once; he tried it again in 1948, after Malan and Hofmeyr had made it impossible.

Was Hofmeyr misrepresented? Undoubtedly he was. But even if he had not been, his speeches and actions of the past had provided the Nationalists with target and ammunition enough. He had made a Herrenvolk speech at the University of the Witwatersrand, and that in itself was enough. Strijdom stated openly that he himself believed in a Herrenvolk, and that anyone who did not was a traitor. In his own forthright way, Strijdom would have scorned to misrepresent Hofmeyr; he merely quoted Hofmeyr's statements, he made deductions from them, and if Hofmeyr protested, he declared contemptuously that Hofmeyr must be blind and foolish. It was not the things that Hofmeyr had never said that cost Smuts the election; the things he had said were enough.

Did these attacks on Hofmeyr, first from his enemies and then from his allies, cause him great pain? Or did the attacks from his enemies leave him cold, and attacks from his allies pierce the armour after all? Had ingratitude, as it had Caesar, 'quite vanquish'd him', so that the mighty heart did burst? If his heart was breaking—that means if the pain was too deep to be borne—there was no word of it in his diary; but if his heart had been breaking, then he, being what he was, was not likely to put any word of it in his diary. One thing is certain, if the pain was deep, his mother did not know how deep it was. He and she had always enjoyed news of intrigue, but here was an intrigue he would have liked to keep away from her. It was the Stribbe affair all over again, her son standing for the right, with almost none to defend him. Her deepest resentment was for Smuts, who had gone off to England again, and left the burdens to be carried by her son.

Mother and son now had to leave 743 Schoeman Street. They had found a house in the suburb of Brooklyn, 191 William Street, but they moved there with sad hearts. One thing that distracted Hofmeyr's mind was the plan to start an Afrikaans daily newspaper in Johannesburg to counter Verwoerd's vigorous *Transvaler*, and he travelled frequently to Johannesburg, to discuss plans for the new paper with the United Party general secretary, and some of the big editors. Plans were almost complete for him to become chairman of the *Evening Post* in Port Elizabeth, with the good will of men like the editor, John Sutherland. All these things encouraged him at a time when the hostility to him inside the Party was growing daily.

It was reported that an anti-Hofmeyr group was active in the western Cape, and included ex-Ministers and Members of Parliament, though some important members of the Party were strongly opposed to it. Colin Legum, general secretary of the Labour Party, while regarding Hofmeyr as a 'tragic failure' as Minister of Finance, wrote in the *Forum*:

'To throw Mr Hofmeyr to the Nationalist wolves is to throw the anti-Nationalist soul of the U.P. to Dr Malan. It will feed his rapacious pack, but will not satiate their wolfish appetite. The U.P. would be weakened by the loss of its most outstanding young leader, without any gains being obtained as a result.'

Of one thing Legum was certain, that Smuts with his 'gallant courage' would not throw Hofmeyr to the wolves.

A stout champion of Hofmeyr was the Natives' Representative, Donald Molteno, who wrote glowing words: 'One man, and one alone, tried to teach his Party its real significance in the present phase of South African history . . . That man was Mr J. H. Hofmeyr, the bearer of as honoured a name as South Africa has ever known . . .'

Barlow took another view. He wrote:

'Mr Hofmeyr chose the weapons for the last election. It was a Hofmeyr election, and resulted in a debacle for our party. The Hofmeyr policy led to the defeat of almost all our platteland Afrikaner MP's, including Smuts. Tens of thousands of loyal Afrikaner United Party men, who stood with us in the war, voted against us because of the Hofmeyr policy. I am a liberal but believe that Hofmeyr went too fast and too far.

'How can we fight a new and critical election with Hofmeyr as one of our chief leaders? It will mean the end of the United Party. I do not want to see the Nationalists smashing my party completely, so, as a leader, Hofmeyr must go.'

It was Molteno again who rose to the defence and demolished Barlow with serious purpose and deadly skill. In the *Cape Times* he quoted one of Barlow's speeches:

'I am not afraid of any voters. But let us be truthful about the matter. The black man is not represented in this House except by my honourable friends over there (the Natives' Representatives). But he will be represented by more of that type of member before many years pass away. And the time is coming when there will not be three representatives here; there will be six and nine and twelve. You cannot treat the Native as you treated him before.'

Though Malan had wrought such havoc on the United Party, he now tried to split what remained of it. The Nationalist press exploited the strains in the United Party. *Die Burger* attacked Hofmeyr for blaming the 'irritation vote', and wrote arrogantly in a leading article, 'It is now a question whether South Africa can afford Hofmeyr even as an important Opposition leader.'

Leo Marquard wrote warmly to Hofmeyr. His advice was clear—it would be useless for the U.P. to try to appease the platteland. It must face up to the implications of a liberal policy, and let its waverers go. He urged Hofmeyr to cast personal feelings aside, and not to let anti-Hofmeyrites gain control of the Party. Hofmeyr replied, 'very confidentially of course', that Smuts was still the leader; and he, Hofmeyr, was 'pretty sure' that Smuts would have nothing to do with the witch-hunt, yet would appease the witch-hunters, to keep the Party together and to win back the platteland. Therefore there would be no marked liberal advance. What should he do then? Should he force a showdown and start his own party? Would that not further strengthen the Nationalists, and enable them to carry out the programme that so many feared? Would Marquard give his advice?

Marquard replied with a memorandum which stated that the urgent need was a party other than the Communist Party, to which African, Indian, and coloured opinion could attach itself. Hofmeyr must put a liberal policy to the United Party, and if the Party did not want it, it must force him out. There was another possibility, that the United Party would accept the liberal policy, and thus lose its right wing to the Nationalists. Marquard was prepared to face that; what he wanted was a party with a clear policy and Hofmeyr for leader. Hofmeyr's reply was to arrange to meet Marquard in Johannesburg.

He wrote in his diary: 'It is becoming increasingly clear that there is no future for me in the United Party, a large part of which regards me as an embarrassment. Quite probaby I shall be able to achieve more for the issues I have at heart outside the Party, but I feel that my line should be that the onus is on the Party to force me out or at best to make my position in the Party untenable.'

Vacillation was no more than a trace element in Hofmeyr's character, and when he vacillated, it was almost always in his relationship with Smuts. He had resisted the idea of joining him in 1929, and now he resisted the idea of leaving him. Marquard wanted him to leave Smuts in 1948; Margaret Ballinger thought he should have left him in 1936.

When he met Marquard, he told him that he could not strike out on his own while Smuts was leader of the Party. For one thing, such a course would not lead to much success so long as Smuts was there. For another, he could not do anything 'that might look like a desertion'. This was what many people called 'Hofmeyr's loyalty to Smuts'. Of course loyalty was there, but the whole thing was more complex, and contained at least two other elements, expediency, and an avoidance of the appearance of evil.

After talking to Marquard, Hofmeyr went on to attend a meeting of the Witwatersrand executive of the United Party. It was here that his greatest strength lay, and though Barlow and others attacked what they called the Hofmeyr policy, they were overwhelmed, and retreated in good order, to wait for the meeting of the Transvaal head committee, where there would be many representatives from the lost constituencies of the platteland. Hofmeyr was encouraged when Rayner Ellis, whose tongue had more power to wound him than that of most other men, came out in the *Rand Daily Mail* with a strong attack on the witch-hunters.

Smuts was now back from England, and Hofmeyr went out to Irene to see him, and got the impression that he was reluctant to get back into the political fray. A few days later he went out again, and found him in a different mood. Smuts declared that he did not regard the election result as really decisive, and he refused to take too tragic a view, though the situation was 'damnably difficult', the great difficulty being, of course, to win back the U.P. platteland. Hofmeyr wrote:

'With regard to my own position he made no very definite statement, although it was pretty clear that he was prepared to back me. He seemed to regard the intrigue as mainly a "Barlow stunt". He thoroughly approved of the proposal that I should in my personal capacity take a hand in the proposed Afrikaans daily in Johannesburg.'

It was the same old situation, of two men who had been inseparably associated in the affairs of their Party for almost twenty years, and yet could not speak to each other of the most critical affair of them all. Two days later they met again at the meeting of the head committee of the United Party in the Transvaal. It was a long and gloomy meeting, a protracted post-mortem. The main attack on Hofmeyr came from the Transvaal platteland. It was led by David Jackson, who had lost his country seat of Ermelo to General Hertzog's son, Albert. Jackson was a man in his fifties, a lawyer in Ermelo, pleasant and well liked; he was deputy chairman of committees, and therefore a man of substance in the Party. What was more, he was an authority on the platteland, and knew what won elections there and what lost them. He declared that Hofmeyr was responsible for the Party's defeat, because of the unwise things he had said about the colour bar; so long as Hofmeyr was a leader of the Party, it would never recapture the platteland. He had been fifty years before his time. Jackson was supported by all the plattelanders, some of them, like Ben van Graan, lifelong supporters of Botha and Smuts. There were three factions, the Hofmeyr liberals, the anti-Hofmeyrites, and a large middle section, some of them Hofmeyr admirers, who thought him too heavy to carry and too dangerous to drop. Even these would have liked him to occupy a less prominent place in the Party. Had any formal resolution of censure been put, it might well have been carried, although Hofmeyr was not without defenders.

Hofmeyr said nothing at all. In his own words, 'I lay low and said nuffin, the more so as General Smuts was to reply to the debate.' Smuts did what Hofmeyr had predicted, he did not repudiate Hofmeyr, and he tried to appease the attackers. Friedman said he was weak, and Hofmeyr said he was evasive, saying he would have to meet the other executive committees first. Hofmeyr wrote: 'I appreciate his difficulty—but none the less found his attitude disappointing from the personal point of view. At next week's caucus meeting I shall almost certainly have to speak, and throw the onus where it belongs—on the party and its leader.'

What did Hofmeyr mean by that typically Hofmeyrian expression, 'disappointing from the personal point of view'? He could only have meant one thing, namely that Smuts had wounded him again. What he would have given if only Smuts had come out wholeheartedly in his defence!

Hofmeyr presumably left the meeting before it finished, because on the following day, so he recorded, he was informed that a resolution had been passed unanimously, thanking him for his services and hoping that all would continue to work together in the Party. The next news of an

anti-Hofmeyr move came from Natal. There was a story that Mervyn
Ellis, the editor of the *Natal Mercury*, would start a Natal Party unless
Hofmeyr renounced all office at the meeting of the Party caucus.

Those who thought Hofmeyr altogether too good and too gentle for
the rough game of politics should take note of his behaviour at this time.
A more sensitive man, and especially one who was tired as Hofmeyr was,
might have taken the opportunity to get out of politics, although ad-
mittedly, had he gained a majority of votes equal to Hofmeyr's in Johannesburg North, he would have found it difficult. A more sensitive man
might have winced and recoiled every time his name was mentioned. A
smaller man might have believed that the trouble lay not in his policies,
but because there was some deep and fatal flaw in himself. Whatever
flaws Hofmeyr may have found in himself, he believed that the Party was
facing, not a 'Hofmeyr-crisis', but a spiritual one. Was the United Party
going to become a pale copy of the Nationalist Party, or was it going to
offer a modern solution to the co-existence of so many races in one society?
That was the real question before the caucus, and he intended to throw
the onus of answering it on the Party and on Smuts.

The caucus meeting was held on 6 July. It was not confined to members of Parliament, but was also open to members of the central head
committee. It may have been that the presence of M.P.s from other parts
inhibited the Transvaal anti-Hofmeyr faction. It was a long time before
Jackson of Ermelo stood up and gave his reasons for thinking that Hofmeyr must cease to be a leader of the Party. It was a tense audience that
listened to Hofmeyr's reply. Every man and woman there knew that they
were listening to one who had given more of his time and talents to the
Party than any one of themselves, a man who had been called the 'strength
and stay of the British Commonwealth', a man known for the probity of
his public and private life.

Hofmeyr made no attempt to convince the caucus of the rightness of
his views. He first disarmed them by saying that he himself had given
careful thought as to what was the best course for him to take as far as
the interests of the United Party were concerned. He had decided that it
would be worse for the Party if he left it than if he stayed in it. He had
done nothing that was not in line with Party policy, and whatever he had
said and done, had the full concurrence of the Party. He had the right to
state his own views within the framework of the policy of the Party. He
asked the caucus, 'If you expel me, what reasons would you give?' If he
resigned, he would have to give his reasons for doing so. If they expelled

him, they would have to give their reasons for doing so. In either case, the United Party would be shown up in a bad light.

What could one say to that? What could one reply to a man who cared not so much to defend himself as to consider the effect on the Party if he left it? He did not tell them what a loss he would be; he told them they would be hurting themselves. And what would the outside world say—and their friends in the Commonwealth they so strongly upheld—when it was known that Hofmeyr, who had so loyally supported Smuts all through the long struggle against Nazism, had had to leave the United Party because he said that black men should represent black men in Parliament? Seen in the cold, calm light of Hofmeyr's reasoning, the whole thing was seen to be preposterous. Hofmeyr himself was loudly applauded, and after Smuts had endorsed the arguments, the attack was not resumed. Jackson and others were left with the glum conclusion that Hofmeyr was right and the longer he went on being right the more votes they would lose in the platteland. Strauss gave another reason for the dropping of the attack; he thought it was the first time that many of his attackers realised that Hofmeyr did not want to be a Prime Minister. That night Hofmeyr wrote in his diary, 'I think we have now got to the end of the witch-hunting episode.'

One result of the caucus meeting was that the United Party decided to set out its 'Native policy' in more specific terms. Such a step was essential; in some way or another the deep divisions in the Party must be healed or concealed. The *Natal Mercury* speculated that if Hofmeyr could not agree with the new formulation, he would leave the Party, and twenty M.P.s would go with him.

After the caucus meeting Hofmeyr turned to his own affairs. He was frequently in Johannesburg to have discussions about the Afrikaans daily, and at home he was writing a series of thirteen articles for his friend and supporter, Victor Norton, the editor of the *Cape Times*. These articles called on the United Party to be vigilant in its defence of freedom, which was menaced by the Nationalist philosophy of control, resulting in interference with private rights and impairment of fundamental freedoms. Hofmeyr reaffirmed his thinking of 1936, and rejected what he called the extremes of repression and equality, in favour of a doctrine of development. He also reaffirmed his belief that repression could lead only to disaster; one must go forward in faith not fear.

Though Hofmeyr had borne the witch-hunt stoically, its cessation brought him much relief. After four easy days, he wrote in his diary:

'The position is different from what it was when I was out of the government in 1938. Then I had a sense of grievance—I felt that I had personally been badly treated and that I could not rest until my position had been restored . . . What I am concerned about now is not the personal aspect, but the danger to the country.'

Smuts was now back in politics, having been returned unopposed for Pretoria East. Both he and Hofmeyr had made it quite clear that Hofmeyr's having been Deputy Prime Minister did not make him Deputy Leader of the Party. Speaking in Durban to the Natal head committee, Smuts said that the Nationalists had combined misrepresentation of the U.P.'s 'Native policy' with a personal attack on Hofmeyr, 'on the basis that I am an old and dying man, fighting the election for my successor. It was a downright lie. There is no Deputy Leader of the Party . . . Mr. Hofmeyr is not on any ground entitled to be my successor. That would have to be decided by the Party itself.'

Nevertheless it was widely said that if the United Party fought another election under Smuts, it would first have to name his successor, otherwise many would abstain from voting. A new and sensational rumour began to circulate, namely that Havenga was to be the successor. It was rumoured that Havenga was so appalled by the totalitarian intentions of the Nationalists that he was ready to cross the floor with his Afrikaner Party and make Smuts the Prime Minister. It was rumoured that the Chamber of Mines and the Rand Club wanted to see the end of Hofmeyr, but did not fancy Steyn or Conroy or Strauss as Smuts's successor; there was only one possible man and that was Havenga. Cope had long before brought the story that the Rand Club was waiting expectantly for Havenga to repudiate Malan, and Smuts to repudiate Hofmeyr. Hofmeyr wrote in his diary: 'There are indications of a Colin Steyn–Havenga intrigue to bring about a "new fusion" when Smuts goes. Very interesting.'

Was there any truth in the Havenga rumours? It is doubtful whether History will ever give the answer. The facts are that Havenga was Malan's second-in-command, and that Malan's wish was that Havenga should succeed him on his retirement. Their trust in each other must have been considerable. Therefore, if Havenga ever contemplated leaving him, it is doubtful whether any evidence of it will ever be found. It is also doubtful whether these rumours had at that time any foundation other than the deep anxious wish of so many white South Africans to be rid of a government they so greatly feared. All that one can say is that the rumours were many and persistent. One cannot easily dismiss Sarah Millin's story of the secret letter which Smuts received from van Rensburg of the Ossewabrandwag, which was strongly in support of Havenga.

Hofmeyr's reaction to a coalition with Havenga would at that time have been sharp and final. He would have nothing to do with a man who had had the support of the Ossewabrandwag, and who still had it. So great was the United Party fear of the new Government that many members of the Party would have regarded this as typical of Hofmeyr's rigidity. But if young Smuts's book was to be relied upon, his father would have rejected Havenga also, regarding him as an ambitious opportunist. There it was—Smuts and Hofmeyr regarding Havenga as an opportunist, Malan regarding him as one of the greatest figures in the history of the Afrikaner.

Hofmeyr was looking forward to the parliamentary session almost with detachment. He wrote: 'I am still enjoying my freedom from responsibility. Of course I am quite satisfied that it is a national disaster that our opponents should be running the country, but from the personal point of view I am quite happy.' What a great change had taken place in him! He thought it was a time of national disaster, yet he was quite happy! There was a time when he could not have separated the interests of the nation from his interests as a person. One cannot help concluding that when he wrote 'freedom from responsibility', it meant something even deeper than he intended to reveal. And what was the cause of the change? Was it advancing age? Or was it because half of the white electorate had rejected all he stood for, and the other half was confused and uncertain? Or was it those eight years of incessant and exhausting toil? It was no doubt all three together.

The day before he left for Cape Town he wrote in his diary that he expected the session to be 'interesting'.

'As for myself, no doubt the malaise in the Party with reference to my own position will continue, though it may not come up to the surface. I find myself viewing the situation from a very objective point of view, interested to see how things develop for me personally, but from the purely personal point of view not caring very much. In any case I do not intend to exert myself unduly to play the party game.'

The next day he left for Cape Town, to attend the first session of the tenth Parliament of the Union of South Africa.

What a change in Parliament! Malan, predikant and editor, now sat where Botha, Smuts, Hertzog, and again Smuts had sat for thirty-eight years. He was 74—twenty-five years older than Smuts had been when he first became Prime Minister. As the historian Krüger was to say, the Age of the Generals had passed. Malan's Minister of Defence, F. C. Erasmus, though he had lived through two world wars, had never heard a shot fired in war. What is more, he had angered many by sending South Africa's most experienced soldier, General Evered Poole, to Berlin, just as he was about to succeed to the command of the Union Defence Force.

These were not the only humiliations that Malan inflicted. Swart, his Minister of Justice, released Robey Leibbrandt, who had served in the German army, returned secretly to South Africa to organise sabotage, been condemned to death for treason, and had his sentence commuted to life by Smuts. Now after five and a half years he had been released, and *Die Huisgenoot*, a respectable sort of family weekly, featured his story as heroic drama. Van Blerk, who had tried to blow up a post office and had killed a bystander, was released, and his story was featured in *Dagbreek*, not as one of violence and treason, but as one of Afrikaner patriotism. Another Government action stemming from the same sources of past humiliation and present jubilation was to allow public servants again to belong to the Broederbond and the Ossewabrandwag. This did not affect the Ossewabrandwag, which was virtually dead; nor did it affect the Broederbond, which was very much alive, and whose complex relations with the Nationalist Party were as strong and numerous as ever.

Sitting opposite Malan was Smuts, in the seat which Malan had occupied for fourteen years, and which Smuts himself had occupied for nearly a decade before that. Hofmeyr no longer sat next to Smuts, but a little behind him. This set tongues wagging, but it was Hofmeyr's own arrangement. Behind Smuts sat all the former Ministers, except Clarkson and Conroy, who were in the Senate, and the elegant Piet van der Byl, who had been thrown out of his country seat of Bredasdorp.

Experts prophesied a quiet session, and on the whole it was to be, the Government's main purpose being to present the budget. Malan, taken by surprise, had hardly had time to frame his sweeping succession of racial laws. There were people, but Hofmeyr was not one of them, who thought that apartheid was an election cry rather than a programme, and did not understand that it was intensely both.

But the foretaste of apartheid was there. Schoeman, Minister of Labour, had already put an end to the training of Africans as building artisans, except at Zwelitsha because it was on Native Trust Land. Sauer, Minister of Transport, born and bred in the Cape Province, had ended the 'scandal' of Cape Town suburban trains, where white people had to travel with coloured people and Africans. Dönges, Minister of Posts and Telegraphs, had decided to end the 'scandal' of the Cape post offices, where non-white people 'jostled' white people in the queues. Malan had promised to abolish the representation of Africans in Parliament, but that he could not achieve yet, for he would need a two-thirds majority of both Houses sitting together. There was one thing, however, which could be done immediately, and would be done this very session—the Indian franchise which Smuts had given in 1946, and which had never been used, would be summarily abolished.

For some reason it was Smuts, not Hofmeyr, who rose first to criticise the budget. He made a rambling speech in which he asked what apartheid was, and discussed the report of the Fagan Commission. Malan reproached him for not allowing the financial experts to open the debate, and he also twitted Smuts because Hofmeyr sat behind him, and said that Smuts was trying to create the impression 'that he has no deputy or that he does not want a deputy'.

Malan said he would tell Smuts what apartheid was not. It was not repression; it had its positive side. If it took something away, it gave back something better. It certainly did not mean Indian representation in Parliament nor new power for the Natives Representative Council. It did not mean having non-white students at 'white' universities, but it did not mean withholding higher education. Malan roundly condemned those who misrepresented the Nationalist Government abroad, or even at home. He asked the Opposition the question which showed that the Nationalists were beginning to identify themselves with South Africa. 'You may hate me as a leader of this side, and you may hate us as a Government and party on this side, but I want to ask you why you also hate South Africa.'

Smuts in his rambling speech was in fact trying to set the pattern for the Opposition attack, which was to ask without ceasing, what is apartheid? what does it mean? why has it so many contradictions? It was a wasted campaign, an attempt to pooh-pooh a deep emotion.

Hofmeyr made his real return to form in the debate on the Native Affairs vote. It was a short, concise speech on apartheid, clear and logical,

Six days later the committee found its compromise, which was to move an amendment in the House that Chapter Two be referred to a select committee.

Smuts moved his amendment in due course, that Chapter Two be referred to a select committee, which would also try to get 'international co-operation' for a policy of repatriation. He made one extraordinary revelation. It was he, and he alone, who had offered Indian representation in Parliament, and he had done it deliberately, so that no one could say, 'This is another Hofmeyr action.' Smuts said, 'I kept him out! I never spoke a word to him about it. I had this fear of misrepresentation.'

The debate was notable in that Hofmeyr took no part in it. Yet his name was heard often enough. In particular J. S. Labuschagne of Klip River referred to him, saying that he had never thought that Hofmeyr would allow himself to be silenced. He said the Nationalists had respected Hofmeyr for his courage, but where was his courage now? The Bill was passed by 63 votes to 54, four Durban United Party M.P.s abstaining.

Why did Hofmeyr not speak? It is improbable that the caucus asked him not to, and possible that he himself said he would prefer to abstain. One thing is certain, his heart was not in the session. It seems also certain that his heart was no longer in the Party, and that he was sick and weary of the humiliating compromises he was forced into.

At the end of the debate on the Prime Minister's vote, Malan delivered a powerful attack on the United Party. He said that it was because the United Party had no policy that they kept on asking, what is apartheid? He would tell them what apartheid was. Had they not seen apartheid introduced on the Cape trains? They would soon see it in the universities, in political institutions, in residential areas. The United Party itself stood for residential apartheid, then how could it pretend not to know what apartheid was? Malan said that Hofmeyr had gone to the Natives Representative Council to tell them of all the benefits their people had received, and their reply was, 'We want equality.' There were two movements in the country, one represented by Hofmeyr, the other by the Government, the one moved towards equality, the other towards separation.

According to Hofmeyr, Malan's attack 'obviously embarrassed the Party', but Hofmeyr felt no sympathy. He wrote in his diary, '. . . in view of the attitude so many have taken up that I have been an embarrassment to them on colour questions, I decided not to relieve them of their present embarrassment, and so did not reply.'

In a detached way he enjoyed the session. He certainly took it easily.

and in the opinion of many restored his reputation within the Pa
dealt with the consequences of the Nationalist policy of making
serves the national home of the native peoples. Would not lar
industrial development of the reserves compete unfairly with est
industry? Would not the establishment of ultimately independent
the reserves expose them to foreign ideologies and influences?
reserves were really made more attractive than the towns, would t
attract labourers from the white farms also? Would not a greate
migrant labour mean an increase in crime? Hofmeyr said the Minis
spoken of removing redundant people from the towns, but the
Commission had said, 'There are virtually no superfluous natives
towns.'

Hofmeyr quoted Malan's statement that apartheid had both a n
and a positive side, but said that it was on the negative side t
Government wanted to go forward immediately, such as the fai
raise the pensions of African people, and the threat to remov
franchise. 'The Government is prepared to take away these thing
away, but on the positive side—delay, delay. That is why I have sa
I repeat it, if apartheid is conceived in that manner, it is a cloak for rep
and nothing else.' There is one sure way to anger Nationalists, a
is to suggest that their policy is one of repression.

This challenging continued throughout the session. The Nation
believing that more and more of white South Africa could be swur
way—ceaselessly probed the weak spots of the Opposition, while the
sition uttered their quips about the baffling nature of apartheid.

Then Malan played his trump card, the Bill to repeal Chapter 7
Smuts's Asiatic Act of 1946, the chapter which provided for repr
tion of Indians in Parliament and in the Natal Provincial Council.
August the United Party faced a crisis. Most of the caucus was wi
stand by the Act of 1946, but the Natal members were intransigent
of them had actually undertaken during the election to support the
of Chapter Two. White opinion was doubly hostile because Indian
cal leaders had said that the Indian people would boycott a franc
which they could elect only white representatives.

What would Hofmeyr do? That was the big question. Had he r
that he voted for the Act only because it gave the Indians a fra
Would he agree to any watering down of the Act? Yet he did not
crisis. He agreed to serve on a caucus committee to find a comp

He enjoyed going about on foot instead of in the ministerial car, and was pleased by the number of people who gave him friendly greetings. He flew to Pretoria twice to see his mother, and on the second occasion found her 'cheerful but disturbingly thin'. He first stayed at the Civil Service Club, and later at an hotel, and went out a good deal to see his friends. After lunching with Sir Herbert Stanley, retired Governor of Southern Rhodesia, for whom he had a great regard, he wrote grave words in his diary:

'Stanley voiced the growing "malaise" which he (and some of the rest of us) feel because of the rising tide of Herrenvolkism. One wonders what would have happened if Smuts had given a clearer lead to Liberalism. Perhaps it would merely have precipitated reaction. And where he has failed, how can I hope to succeed?'

There were many—and there are many still—who blamed Smuts for the rise of Herrenvolkism, because he had not given a clearer lead. But here Hofmeyr appears to judge him less harshly. What would have happened if Smuts had come out boldly in his younger days? Would he not have lost the platteland earlier? In fact Smuts began to lose the platteland in 1912, and his decline was masked by two great events, coalition with Hertzog in 1933, and war with Germany in 1939. Was it not true, that whatever faults or weaknesses there were in Smuts and Hofmeyr, they were both defeated by the refusal of white South Africa to share its power? Therefore the story of their lives is also the story of white South Africa.

In his younger days Hofmeyr had been the hope and inspiration of those who longed to see the new South Africa—the inevitable South Africa—come because of what both he and Smuts had called 'a change of heart'. Had Smuts himself not cried, 'What we want is not a change of machinery but a change of heart'? Now Hofmeyr—and especially since the election of 1948—had come face to face with white intransigence. In 1936, at the end of his great speech on the Representation of Natives Bill, he said, 'I believe that there is also a rising tide of liberalism in South Africa.' But after a dinner with his old friend Peter Clouts, at which Advocate A. A. Roberts, Secretary for Education, was present, he wrote, 'Roberts was more hopeful than I am disposed to be, about the growth of a liberal spirit.'

Nevertheless he was given a pleasant surprise by Harry Lawrence during the first day of the debate on the Asiatic Bill. He wrote: 'On Wednesday during the division on the Asiatic Bill Harry Lawrence said to me how much better it would be to be one of a group of say 25 under my leadership which could take a positive line.' To this he added: 'Today Robinson spoke to me on similar lines. He said that all the back-benchers would follow me and probably 50 out of our 65 members. I said that nothing of this kind could be contemplated while Smuts was still there.'

The session was drawing to an end and he did something unprecedented. After persuading the Government on 28 September to appoint a select committee to report on the advisability of continuing some of Smuts's war measures, and after speaking on the Finance vote on Wednesday, 29 September, he left that night for Pretoria on the eight o'clock train, leaving Parliament with three days to go. No one knew that his voice would not be heard again in the Assembly, that he would never again stand up to defend his causes, that no one would ever again ask him where was his courage. Never again would some hard-living, hard-bitten reporter listen with unaccustomed stirring of the blood to this sober and industrious man. Nor would anyone see him again sitting at the scoring table at Fernwood, with that small smile playing on his lips, listening to gossip and to the sound of bat on ball, all cares forgotten. Nor was it likely that Parliament would ever again see such a parliamentarian, such a lover of order and precedent, such a genius in administration, such a master of work in all things but one, that he let it eat away his life, he who was so careful and frugal in his stewardship of other things.

So Hofmeyr left for ever the fairest cape in the whole circumference of the earth, and the great mountain under which he had been born, and the gracious city of whose children he had been the most miraculous, with who knew what shining future before him. He no longer travelled in luxury, but because he had been a Minister, he travelled with a free-for-life gold pass, in a first-class coupé, reading E. M. Forster's *A Passage to India*. He was looking forward to getting back home, to his mother, to the peace and quiet of the house where he could do what he liked, though not altogether. Yet by this time he had got used to the things he could not do. What his mother had done was done. If he had complaints against life, they were not so grievous as to devour what was left of it. He wanted to get home and go into his study and write his chapters on the history of education in South Africa, and more newspaper articles, and play some cricket at Government House and some tennis at Farquharson's, and have some Sundays of rest and peace.

On the day after his return the revised version of the United Party's Native and coloured policy was published. This had been produced in response to Nationalist taunts that there was no policy, and also to prevent too great variations in interpretation of the policy. The main work of draughtsmanship had been given to Strauss, but it was the result of considerable discussion inside the Party.

In what way did the new statement of policy differ from the old? Both emphasised that Christian trusteeship was the Party's Native policy, but the new policy said that the Party stood for European leadership and authority, while the old said it stood for European civilisation. The new policy was based on the 'factual position', namely that there were 'differences between Europeans and natives', and therefore the Party rejected equality, and stood for social and residential separation, avoidance of race intermixture, 'and the development of the native peoples in their own and the country's interests'. The old policy had not specifically rejected equality, and what is more, it had allowed a great deal of liberty to M.P.s in the matter of political representation, 'separate . . . or otherwise'. Such liberty was not mentioned in the new policy; on the contrary the Party declared that it stood by the settlement of 1936. Lastly the policy recognised the permanence of African urban populations, and here differed markedly from the policy of the Nationalists.

The new coloured policy stated that the Party would resist any proposal to change the existing franchise, it recognised that social separation was 'in accordance with the desire of both Coloureds and Europeans', and it stood for the development of separate self-governing residential areas.

Hofmeyr's judgement of the new statement was, 'Negative but not unsatisfactory.' Those four words summed up the whole dilemma of himself and his Party. His curious ambivalence towards the Party persisted. On one day he was inclined to let it stew in its own juice, on another he was relatively optimistic about its future. On his first Sunday in Pretoria, a day spent quietly at home after he returned from worship at the Presbyterian Church, he wrote:

'I am glad to be home again. The Session has been interesting, and has gone reasonably well for myself—and for the United Party. I think it will have helped to make the public realise the magnitude of the issues at stake. The real fight of course lies ahead—and it will be a difficult one. It may however well be that the Government's position will be weakened on the economic and financial side. There are increasing signs of declining confidence, and if that continues our financial difficulties, already in evidence for the skilled observer, will increase and ultimately be brought home to the public as a whole.'

He was feeling better than he had felt for many years. And of course there was the quiet life, the writing, the cats, the radio, the patience, and the neglected garden that his mother was bringing back to order. Political activities were few; he spoke at a big meeting in Johannesburg to protest against the threat to the franchise, and at a few minor Party meetings, but he no longer needed to go daily to an office. He lunched with William Addison, editor of the *Star*, and agreed to write a series of articles for him. Addison told him that his information was that 'Havenga was very unhappy in his present position'. There were continuous rumours about the possibility of Havenga's going over to Smuts. James Gray, editor of the London journal *South Africa*, after an extensive tour of the country, reported to Hofmeyr that English-speaking South Africans had been bitten deep by the Havenga bug, and were willing to turn away from Smuts. Hofmeyr asked himself the question, 'Is it not perhaps an evidence of a tendency towards cynicism about politics which is characteristic of the more or less decently educated English South African?'

Ten days later he recorded it as his own opinion that the political situation generally was still far from satisfactory, and that the Havenga bug had bitten deep. He put on record both his fear and his hope: 'At the moment it is difficult to discern any turning of the tide. Probably the breach will come either as a result of the Government getting into economic difficulties or quarelling among themselves.' Yet simultaneously he continued to view these things with great dispassionateness.

His first article in the *Star* was given deferential treatment. To use his own words, the *Star* did him proud. The article had more bite than the *Cape Times* articles, no doubt because Hofmeyr had sat through a session of Parliament. He sounded a grave warning to the public, declaring that when Havenga called the revolution 'a bloodless revolution', he had good reason.

About Strijdom, who seemed destined to succeed Malan, he wrote: '. . . he not only declares that, despite the entrenchment clause, it would in his opinion be lawful to make all these changes by a simple Parliamentary majority, but he is reported in *Die Transvaler* to have said: "But even if it's not lawful, shall we allow the white race to go under? The continued existence of white South Africa demands it and therefore we must." '

Hofmeyr concluded with prophetic words:

'The constitutional rights of one section of the people are threatened today. The rights of the rest of us may be threatened tomorrow. A breach is contemplated in the moral fortifications of our nationhood. Such a breach may lead to complete disintegration and decay. The cynical disregard of moral obligations and the pledged word which is fore-shadowed cannot but weaken South Africa's position in the eyes of the world. We may yet become a reproach and a byword among the nations.'

Although he was feeling better, he was far from robustly well. A flight to Port Elizabeth, with three speeches and an unveiling in one day, quite exhausted him, and he was glad to return home.

He and his mother now seldom visited the Smuts home. His relationship with Smuts remained difficult to understand. During the session at Cape Town he had had André Siegfried, the French political scientist, to lunch, with Smuts and Marquard. Conversation between Smuts and Siegfried was lively and wide-ranging, and after lunch Hofmeyr said proudly to Marquard, almost as though he were personally responsible, 'The old man was in form, wasn't he?'

In turn Smuts paid a fine compliment to Hofmeyr, after he had been unanimously elected chairman at the annual congress of the Transvaal United Party, held in Johannesburg. Hofmeyr's election was received with acclamation, and when the applause had died away, Smuts spoke.

'Hold fast to what we have. We have in Mr Hofmeyr a man of vision and thoroughness. I regard character as one of the greatest values in life. Ability, yes, but one could almost say that you buy that. But character is something different. If you look at the standard Mr Hofmeyr has kept in public life, I say it would be most ungrateful to listen to the calls of our opponents. These are devilish calls, and I am therefore pleased that you have given your answer today to all that poisonous venomous propaganda that has been directed against us.'

Hofmeyr recorded nothing of Smuts's remarks, not even the gist of them. He wrote merely, 'My re-election (unanimous) seems to mark the end of the witch-hunt.'

Down in Durban at the annual congress of the Natal United Party, a resolution was put forward asking for the immediate appointment of a national deputy leader, 'acceptable to all sections of the Party'. A ticklish debate was avoided when an amendment was carried to refer the question to the Union Congress at Bloemfontein later in the month. Strauss was right when he said that, from the point of view of the Party, Hofmeyr was too heavy to carry, too brilliant to drop.

Hofmeyr found the Congress successful but wearying, yet there was no sign of tiredness when on the day after it ended, he attended the jubilee at St John's College, Johannesburg, his last school function. Never during his long public life was he more brilliant. He began with an old joke, that one could not decline a headmaster's invitation, because it was always couched in the categorical imperative. He told his audience, and he was clearly proud of it, that he had received this invitation after the events of 26 May 1948; he was in fact saying that he had been invited because of the things he stood for, not because of any high office.

After these introductory words, he took advantage of the head-master's omission to address the boys, and said that he would speak to the most important part of the audience, so far not even mentioned, namely the boys; for this he was given thunderous applause. He said that he knew, and he hinted that he knew it on the highest authority, that they were contented and excellently fed, and these remarks were received with decorous hooting from the boys and laughter from the others, even from the headmaster, who appeared quite overcome, though as a rule he was not given to joking about such matters. It was not so much the jokes as the manner of their making. When Hofmeyr spoke about the excellent feeding, he was able to convey the subtle intimation that he and the boys knew something that on such an occasion could only be hinted at. By this time he had them all in his power, headmaster, staff, parents, boys, and he proceeded to the more serious part of his address, again directed pri-marily to the boys, on man's duty and privilege to serve his community and his neighbours.

It was the kind of address that boys would remember, if not the words, then the splendour of them. And parents too. Many of them would be grateful that their growing sons, about to go out into the world of chance and compromise, should hear the great verities ex-pounded by a man so eloquent and noble. Some of them would wait around for a chance to thank him, or if they were not bold enough, for a chance to see him. For tens of thousands of people he was still the living embodiment of what was good and right. While he lived, they had hopes for the future, that men would experience the 'change of heart' and turn again and live; they would go forward in faith, not fear.

Shortly thereafter at a United Party meeting a Nationalist ques-tioner asked him whether the United Party would restore the Indian franchise if it returned to power, and according to press reports, Hofmeyr said it would. Hofmeyr's reported reply caused consternation in Natal. The United Party head office in Johannesburg denied the report, and reported Hofmeyr as declaring that he would never arrogate to himself the power to say what the Party would do or would not do if it returned to power. The questioner had indeed asked the question and Hofmeyr had replied that the United Party had already declared its policy before the election, namely that it stood by the Act of 1946. The questioner then asked whether the United Party would re-enact Chapter Two, which the Nationalists had repealed, and Hofmeyr had replied that he could not answer that question, but that his own opinion was that the Party should act in terms of its own statement of Policy and stand by the Act.

No wonder the United Party in Natal was full of consternation. It had given up the Act of 1946 as hopeless, and had at its own congress of a week before evolved a new compromise, namely that Indians would be represented by white persons in both Assembly and Senate. The *Natal Mercury* with an extraordinarily fine choice of language declared, 'Natal is in no mood to accept discriminatory legislation,' meaning of course legislation that forced Natal to have Indian representatives on the Provincial Council while the Transvaal need not. The paper declared that Hofmeyr, and those who thought like him, would be foolish to overlook the fact.

It was the old Nationalist game, of course, to ask Hofmeyr a question that would embarrass the Party; and it was an old United Party game for the right wing to hold up the Party to ransom, with the threat that if they were not listened to, more voters would go over to the Nationalists. It was this that led people to say that the United Party was no different from the Nationalists; this was not true, but it was true enough to be painful.

When Hofmeyr returned he spoke to the general council of the United Party on the Witwatersrand and was well received. He was making good progress with his writing when on 19 November the dreaded kidney trouble came back, and he wrote in his diary, 'Hope it will clear up,' and these unornamented words seemed to contain, to this reader at least, a note of anxiety. It did clear up, for on the 20th he spent a delightful day on the cricket field at Government House. The next day the trouble returned; after a busy Sunday in Johannesburg he had a bad night, and on the Monday it was a struggle to write his next article for the *Star*.

It was called 'Christian Trusteeship as the Only Satisfactory Native Policy'. He considered Hoernlé's dictum, framed late in his life, that total separation into distinct 'areas of liberty' must be considered a general liberal ideal, but he rejected the ideal as impracticable, partly because white South Africa would never pay the price for it, partly because its realisation would require the use of such force that it would cease to be a genuine liberal ideal. Following his 1936 line of thought, he rejected the idea of human and racial equality, and reiterated his belief in equality of opportunity. He clung to his idea that under Christian trusteeship the ward would grow up, but said that this did not mean social equality and race-mixture. He reproached those who refused to face the question, what happens when the ward grows up?, but he himself did not answer the question, does equality of opportunity include opportunity to become equal?

Yet, however confused his thought may appear to some of those who came later, he saw clearly that complete apartheid was a myth and partial apartheid an injustice. Although he could not see clearly how to go forward, it was forward he wanted to go. He condemned white domination, but he could not see what to go forward to except white leadership, based on merits and deserts. This journey forward must be made in faith because it could not be made in fear. He wrote:

'The only real alternative to a policy of Christian trusteeship is a policy of repression—a policy of maintaining the white man's domination at all costs, including the surrender of justice and Christian principles.

'Such a policy, the world being what it is today, will surely as night follows day, lead to disaster for the white man in South Africa. The alternative policy, which stands firmly by Christian principles, has a far better chance of ultimate success.'

The next day, 24 November, was the day of the Union congress of the United Party in Bloemfontein. He was feeling wretched, and the little colour in his face had as usual drained away. But to him it was unthinkable that he should not be there. After the disaster of May he had fought his way back, through the executives and the committees and the congresses, and how could he not be there at the most important of all?

What did his mother think? In writing of such a thing the writer treads not only on dangerous ground, but on the most intimate. There is no evidence as to what she thought. In the area of his work and his duty he was supreme, but his health had been her responsibility since the day when he was born. The writer believes that she said he was not to go, or that she wished him not to go, and that he replied that he must go. When he left for the airport, he knew that he was going against her will.

Smuts opened the congress on the evening of 23 November. His speech went off well, but when he had finished there was a spontaneous demand for Hofmeyr, and great warmth and applause for him. This reception heartened him, and filled him with humble pride.

The congress revealed a considerable change in the attitude of the Party towards Havenga. They still wanted him, but they no longer wanted him at the expense of Hofmeyr. There were what Hofmeyr called 'evidences of growing impatience' in the ranks of Havenga's Afrikaner Party, of dissatisfaction with Nationalist attitudes, and of a desire to come to terms with the United Party.

'Some of our people got together and subsequently spoke to me. They felt that some approach should be made to Havenga but were very emphatic that no arrangement should be come to at my expense. I advised against any public approach, indicating that the furthest we could go would be to get someone to take soundings as to Havenga's attitude. It was agreed that I should speak to Smuts on these lines.'

Something had happened to change his attitude to Havenga, and one can only suppose that it was the assurance that no arrangement would be made at his expense. Hofmeyr may not have been bursting to succeed Smuts, but the idea that Havenga might do so affronted him. Perhaps the 'renewed favour' of the Party was inclining him again to consider the possibility of leading it. He was blamed in later years for allowing personal considerations to prevent the coming together of Smuts and Havenga, and for turning down the last chance to topple the Nationalist Government. Yet it seems clear that in November 1948 he was willing to recommend a coalition to Smuts.

Back in Johannesburg, Addison of the *Star* told him that he had heard that the Government would not attempt to abolish the Natives' Representatives in 1949. He had also heard that Havenga had said that he would not agree to by-pass the entrenched clause, and that he expected to be out of the Government by April. Hofmeyr and Addison discussed the meaning of these two pieces of information, and their possible inter-relation. Was Malan going to hold back his Bill because he dare not lose Havenga? And did Malan believe the rumours which he must have heard that Havenga might go to Smuts?

Late in the afternoon Ockie Oosthuizen came to see Hofmeyr in Pretoria to report on further discussion in Bloemfontein.

'It appeared that Havenga's friends there who had been in touch with us had sent an emissary (Edeling) to see Havenga on his farm, that H. had confirmed his intention to break with the Nats, but that he wanted to know what our attitude would be. He had also indicated his desire to co-operate with us and wanted to know what out attitudes would be. He had said that he would not insist on any conditions for co-operation. O. and I went out to see Smuts, who after discussion instructed O. to let it be known to H's friends that he S. was willing to see H.—and the sooner the better.'

Barlow must have had some sort of reconciliation with Hofmeyr. He wrote in his memoirs that 'some of us' asked Hofmeyr to see Smuts and try to arrange a liaison with Havenga. Was Barlow one of those who assured Hofmeyr that no arrangement would be made at his expense? Did Barlow, after his away-with-Hofmeyr campaign, contemplate a party led by Hofmeyr assisted by Havenga? Whatever the truth, he wrote that 'nothing came of it', and again, 'nothing seemed to happen'.

Was a great opportunity lost? Would Havenga have joined Smuts, and brought about the fall of Malan? Would Smuts have abolished the 15 per cent overloading and underloading? Would that have halted the growth of an Afrikaner Nationalism detemined to share nothing of its power? why did nothing come of it? Is it possible that Havenga went to Malan, or that Malan sent for Havenga and told him to stay where he was, to use his influence to moderate the excesses of the Strijdoms and the Verwoerds, and to take over the Party when Malan retired? Will History be able to answer these questions, to explain how Smuts and Hofmeyr and Oosthuizen thought that Havenga wanted to leave Malan, while Malan thought Havenga's loyalty to be beyond all question?

Whatever negotiations there were, Hofmeyr played no part in them.

At some time during the night or in the early morning he suffered a heart attack. It is possible that he did not know how serious was his condition. He was due to play cricket that day on the YMCA's new ground at Bedfordview, and to declare the ground open. This appointment he was determined to keep, in spite of his mother's strong opposition. On the back of an envelope he wrote notes for the speech that he would make. His handwriting, never good, was almost undecipherable, and appeared to have been written, either in great pain, or in some equally wretched condition. One of his old jokes was there, that in his tour of the Eastern Province he had made more speeches than runs; also his old story of receiving the ceremonious first ball from the mayor of a Reef town, who bowled so wide of the wicket that Hofmeyr, overcome with giggling no doubt, had to rush out into the field to try to get at the ball.

His mother did not wish him to go, but his mind was made up. He left for Johannesburg in the shadow of her displeasure. Some time later he picked up Bill Horak in Cilliers Street. Hofmeyr arrived late, for the first time Horak had ever known. His appearance, the darkness of his face, the evidence of a man almost at the end of his strength, made Horak say to him, 'Mr Hofmeyr, what's the matter with you?' Hofmeyr's only reply to that was to say, 'Mr Horak, would you drive?' Horak took over the wheel in deep distress, and if it had not been for his veneration, he would have driven Hofmeyr back to William Street instead of to Johannesburg. They did not talk, Horak did not dare to, Hofmeyr did not want to. They stopped at the Tower Garage outside Johannesburg, and there Hofmeyr had to go through the ordeal of greeting and shaking hands with the YMCA dignitaries who had come out to receive him, while Horak went to look for water and aspirin. There would usually have been talking or joking, Hofmeyr being formal with those he did not know well, and giving his little digs to those he knew better. Now when his friends and co-workers saw his condition, they were unable to speak.

When they arrived at the ground, René de Villiers said urgently to Horak, 'Good God, what's happened?' It was clear that Hofmeyr would not be able to play, but he was still determined to receive the first ceremonial ball, and to make his little speech. He went to the dressing-room, and de Villiers, counting on their long association, urged him not to do either, but Hofmeyr would not listen to him. John Martin, chairman of the Corner House, at whose word many trembled, came to the dressing-room and tried to persuade Hofmeyr to go home, but to no avail. Helped by de Villiers, Hofmeyr put on his batsman's pads, and began to walk to the wicket. As he went on to the ground, the subdued fieldsmen crowded round him to shake his hand. The spectacle was terrible, of a great man foolishly risking his life for a trivial duty, surrounded by other men, of character and substance, who stood in such awe of him that they could only watch and do nothing. Hofmeyr now realised that he could go no further, and he left the field and sat down on a bench. He now agreed to Martin's repeated request that he should go home, but first remembered to ask Horak to take charge of his car. Martin took him to his own home, because Hofmeyr wanted to telephone his mother, and prepare her for his return. He merely told her that he had decided to come home.

He was still in shocking condition, and Martin wanted to get a doctor then and there, and to take him to a nursing home, but Hofmeyr insisted on going back to Pretoria. Mrs Martin offered him tea, but he asked for brandy. He stayed longer than they expected, and Mrs Martin wanted to ring Pretoria again to say he was leaving, but he would not allow her to do so in case it further alarmed his mother. Although Martin was far from well, and had only gone to the cricket because Hofmeyr was to be there, he decided that he should go to Pretoria. He and his wife wanted Hofmeyr to sit in front with the chauffeur, but he refused. He distressed Martin by sitting at the back, and talking about the new budget and other financial matters, including the latest news of Havenga.

When they were near 191 William Street, Hofmeyr made them stop a short way from the house as he did not want to be seen arriving in a strange car. He got out with difficulty and the chauffeur followed him, and was there to catch him when he swayed going up the steps. Mrs Hofmeyr came out to see Martin and the chauffeur helping to carry her son into the house; he was unconscious. Mrs Hofmeyr was alone, and Martin, unable to get Loveday, found his junior partner, who, when he had seen Hofmeyr, went at once to look for Loveday. By this time Hofmeyr had come round and wanted to listen to the broadcast of the game between the M.C.C. and Natal. When Loveday arrived, he diagnosed a coronary thrombosis. Most people recover from it, but Hofmeyr had a blood pressure that had on occasions reached a count of between 230 and 240; he had also a chronic disturbance of the kidney, and passed small stones from time to time. Loveday took the most serious view of the incident, and ordered complete quiet.

Mrs Hofmeyr asked Horak to stay in the house that Saturday night, and made up a bed for him in her son's room. He slept there on the Sunday night also, but woke to find Hofmeyr in great distress. He switched on the light and was shocked again by Hofmeyr's appearance. He said, 'Mr Hofmeyr, what's wrong?', and Hofmeyr asked for one of the pills Loveday had prescribed for him. Horak asked, 'Shan't I get the doctor?', but Hofmeyr said, 'You must sleep, turn off the light, you have work to do.'

Horak saw Loveday on the Monday and urged him to engage nurses. Everyone knew the problem, which was that Mrs Hofmeyr did not like to have women in the house. But she consented, and two sisters came, one for the day and one for the night. When Hofmeyr was able to, he would laugh and joke with them. His mind would not, could not, rest. Horak had to send telegrams and messages to all those whose relatively trivial affairs were being put out of joint by his desperate illness. On the Tuesday, 30 November, he was worse again, but he was able to whisper to Horak, 'How much do I owe you for the telegrams?'

His mother lived through these days silently and darkly. She had reconciled herself to his death and said to Loveday, 'He can't recover from this.' She and her son were not given to demonstrations and endearments. He was dangerously ill, but his illness was partly his own doing, in that he had ignored her advice and wishes. That this threw a shadow over these last days, the writer does not doubt. There is evidence that something in her—some self-willedness which she may have wished she could control—was affronted by her son's disregard of her wishes. There was in her what can only be described as a fatal quality, so that even if the world had been falling to pieces, amidst floods and pestilence and conflagrations, she would not have been able to forget an affront to her self-will. She was one of those who could destroy what she loved. Indeed there were many who said that she had destroyed it long before, half a century before, under the mountain of that southern city.

It was not widely known that he was so ill. Smuts inquired after him, and Loveday admitted his anxiety. Whether because of Smuts's inquiry or not, on Wednesday, 1 December, Loveday called in Dr Roseman of Pretoria for a confirmatory opinion. On that day and the day following, when Horak paid his daily visit, Hofmeyr lay and looked at him without moving or speaking. Very few were allowed to visit him; his brother A. B. and his wife Bertha came over daily to Pretoria, to say a word or two to him, and to be with Mrs Hofmeyr. Although Hofmeyr could barely speak, he was able to say to Mrs R., who had been at Botha House for that unforgettable holiday in 1946, 'How is Peter? how are his exams going?' A little later he was able to say to her, 'Wish him luck for me.'

That Thursday was the day of the great cricket match at Government House, the Governor-General's eleven to be captained by the Rt. Hon. J. H. Hofmeyr, stay and strength of the Commonwealth, against the famous MCC. That evening Farquharson brought him a souvenir card, signed for him by all the players, which present pleased him.

On Friday, 3 December, Loveday knew the situation was grave. He visited the house twice, and after the second visit asked Guy Elliott, Professor of Medicine at the University of the Witwatersrand, to come over urgently to Pretoria. Elliott brought over his cardiological team and took several cardiographs. His opinion was that there was nothing to be done. Nevertheless in the afternoon Loveday thought the position had improved a little, for Hofmeyr seemed brighter and more cheerful. He had a light evening meal, and then the nurse left him and joined the others. After a short while she returned to look at him, and was horrified by his appearance. A. B. stayed with his brother while the nurse tried to get hold of Loveday. Hofmeyr whispered to his brother, 'Tell my friends to carry on.' Soon after saying these words he died, shortly after eight-thirty.

Next morning Ockie Oosthuizen and Horak helped A. B. to make the necessary arrangements. Horak said there was a tragic, almost macabre, atmosphere in the house, not so much of grief as of recrimination, especially against Smuts. He said to the writer, 'I felt they had all been living in his reflection, and now were bereft.'

So a great light went out in the land, making men more conscious of its darkness. It was a light of a man not radiant by nature but by character. There were those who put his faults on the scales, and thought they outweighed his virtues, but they had lost for this reason or for that their sense of value. On the morning of 4 December tens of thousands of hearts were filled with unspeakable grief, not only because they had loved him, but because he was the man who had been to them 'as a hiding place from the wind, and a covert from the tempest; as rivers of water in a dry place, as the shadow of a great rock in a weary land'.

For many men will always have courage so long as the man who leads them has courage. When a great man dies, we weep not so much for what he was, as for what we thought him to be, and are therefore all the more deeply bereft.

Not again would some foolish man rise in the House to taunt him, and to ask him, 'Where is your courage?' If he had any virtue at all, it was his courage. Many of his ideas have long since gone out of currency. Many of the categories of his thought have no validity, not even meaning, in modern Africa. But there was one thing for which men and women loved him, and admired him, and followed him, that he was ready to go forward, not in fear, but in faith. And now they were desolated. For one day, two days, perhaps many days, they would wake every morning with the thought, 'Hofmeyr is dead,' and think it again and again, many times in the day.

One of these wrote words for him.

Toll iron bell toll extolling bell
The toll is taken from the brave and the broken
Consoling bell toll
But toll the brave soul
Where no brave words are spoken

Strike iron bell strike ironic bell
Strike the bright name
From the dark scrolls
Of the blind nation
Strike sorrow strike shame
Into the blind souls

Clap iron bell clap iron clapper
Clap your iron hands together
Clap the loud applause
That life denied him
Clap the dead man
And if you can
The dead man's cause
Clap in beside him

Strike iron bell
Strike iron hammer
Strike deaf man's ears
Lest man's earth hears
Heaven's clanging and clamour

Clap iron bell clap iron clapper
And drown the clapping of the million million
Who clap the great batsman returning
To his Captain's pavilion

The bits about the bells and the clappers he might have thought a bit far-fetched but 'interesting'. His face might have twitched when he read the piece about the great batsman returning to his Captain's pavilion. The idea would not have been strange to him, for he would have known well the sentence, 'And the trumpets sounded for him on the other side'; but he would not quite have liked the idea of being made—publicly—the central actor in a cosmic drama, a sort of universal Test Match between Good and Evil.

In any case he already had Newbolt to put the whole thing more clearly and simply.

> And it's not for the sake of a ribboned coat,
>   Or the selfish hope of a season's fame,
> But his Captain's hand on his shoulder smote—
>   'Play up! play up! and play the game!'

And what did that mean but the lesson, learned gaily in youth and soberly in age, that righteousness must be its own reward?

EDITORIAL NOTE

The course of South African politics since the dramatic overthrow of the United Party of Smuts and Hofmeyr and the death of the latter in 1948 is a short tale which may be summed up in a phrase—the absolute increase in the power of Afrikanerdom.

At the outset, however, a secure majority was to be had by the Nationalists only with the nine votes of N. C. Havenga's Afrikaner Party. Then in 1950 in the first elections in South West Africa the Nationalists secured all six seats, and in the following year the Afrikaner Party was absorbed by the Nationalists. Since then its parliamentary majority has been unchallenged.

The following table of the seats won in the successive general elections reflects clearly the increase in the political strength and domination of the Nationalists.

	1948	1953	1958	1961
National	70	94	103	105
Afrikaner	9			
United	65	57	53	49
Labour	6	5		
Progressive				1
National Union				1

In 1954 Dr Daniel François Malan, who had led the Nationalists to victory in 1948, resigned as Premier. The choice of the party caucus as his successor was Johannes Gerhardus Strijdom, the apostle of *baasskap*. He died in 1958 and was succeeded by Dr Hendrik Frensch Verwoerd, who is regarded as the supreme architect of the policies of apartheid. On May 31, 1961, following a close vote in a referendum in the preceding fall, South Africa was proclaimed a Republic, whereupon it ceased to be a member of the Commonwealth of Nations.

The United Party constitutes the official opposition. However, its ambivalent attitude towards the problems of race and colour has rendered impossible the square presentation of any clear issue as regards the extensive legislation that has been enacted by the Nationalists in the implementation of its apartheid policy. This role has been supplied by the Liberal Party with its program of universal suffrage, and by the Progressive Party with its programme of qualified franchise. The Liberal Party, which was formed after the 1953 elections, has yet to secure a single seat in parliament, and the Progressive Party, a dissident offshot from the United Party, secured one seat in the 1961 election.

A question suggests itself—what percentage of the electorate does this parliamentary majority represent? A catagorical answer is impossible because of the difficulty in a parliamentary system of allotting the votes in the case of uncontested seats. However, a painstaking analysis of the returns in the 1953 election convinced a competent impartial observer that "on no calculation could the Nationalists be said to have polled even 50 percent of the votes" (*The Politics of Inequality—South Africa since 1948*. Gwendolen M. Carter, N.Y., 1958, at page 158). An illuminating sidelight on the split in the South African electorate is furnished by the vote in the referendum in the fall of 1960 on the establishment of the Republic. The turn-out was large—90.7 percent. The vote was 850,458 for and 775,878 against. If this revealed proportion can be applied to the parliamentary situation, it will be seen that the Nationalists, with a bare popular majority, if that, control two thirds of the seats in parliament.

The paradoxical conclusion is that the inner strength of Afrikaner Nationalism is thereby revealed. It derives from a variety of factors. The virile strains in the religion, education and culture of the Afrikaners, aided by the solidarity of their press, interweave and interlock to strengthen the traditional mores and homogeneity of their community. Basically it is this that enables an astute, powerful, and ably organized political leadership, relying upon the traditional strength of the Afrikaner in the *platteland* and more recently in the cities in consequence of the trek to them, and likewise in reliance upon the under, and overloading of the votes, to deliver in election after election, the right vote in the right place. Thus do they maintain and strengthen their parliamentary majority. A rough analogy to this is to be seen in the operation of the American electoral system, as was exemplified in the election of 1860 when Lincoln with less than a majority of the popular votes received a majority of the votes of the Electors.

Change, peaceful change, can only be envisioned as a consequence of a reorientation of heart and mind within this Afrikaner community.

Writing in another connection in 1959 and speaking of the early Voortrekker, Pieter Retief, the author of this biography has written:

"Here was Pieter Retief, an upright and respected man, obviously one of substance and integrity, and not lacking in determination and courage. But to him the liberal idea of a common society to which both white and black might belong was unthinkable; what was more, it would remain unthinkable. For him, as for his sister, there were natural distinctions of race and colour. It might be said that for him race was an immutable category. *Apartheid* was therefore for him a morality, a religion, a philosophy, and a politics all in one. It is necessary to understand this if we are to understand present-day South Africa." (*Hope for South Africa*, Alan Paton, N.Y., 1959, p. 27).

Dudley C. Lunt

INDEX

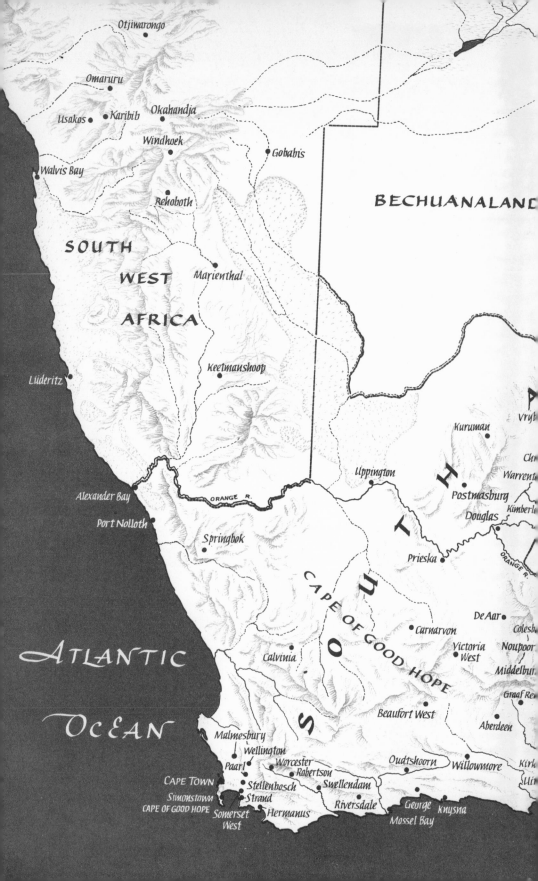